RED RUBBER, BLEEDING TREES

RED RUBBER,

BLEEDING

TREES

Violence, Slavery, and Empire in

Northwest Amazonia, 1850–1933

Michael Edward Stanfield

University of New Mexico Press Albuquerque

FIRST EDITION

Library of Congress Cataloging-in-Publication Data
Stanfield, Michael Edward, 1957–
Red rubber, bleeding trees : violence, slavery, and
empire in northwest Amazonia, 1850–1933 /
Michael Edward Stanfield.
p.   cm.
Includes bibliographical references and index.
ISBN 0-8263-1986-6 (cloth). —
ISBN 0-8263-1987-4 (pbk.)
1. Rubber industry and trade — Putumayo River
Valley — History.   2. Indians, Treatment of —
Putumayo River Valley — History.   3. Putumayo
River Valley — History.   I. Title.
HD9161.P882S7   1998
338.4'76782'0986163 — dc21   98-2508
                                                 CIP

CONTENTS

TABLES

ACKNOWLEDGMENTS

Numerous individuals and organizations throughout the Americas assisted in the research, writing, and completion of this project. In Bogotá, Colombia, María Mercedes Ladrón de Guevara, Augusto Gómez, Angelina Araujo, and Alberto Pérez Triana welcomed me to the Archivo Nacional de Colombia and enlivened many a cold, damp afternoon while teaching me about life in their beautiful but troubled country. The staff of the Archivo del Congreso also facilitated a fruitful scan of pertinent documents.

In the lush colonial setting of Popayán, Hedwig Hartmann Garcés introduced me to the Centro de Investigación Histórica of the Universidad de Cauca and wisely suggested that I enlist the assistance of Jaime Eduardo Mejía and José Ignacio Ruíz in tackling the daunting but rich "archivo muerto" of the republican period. Farther south, in the dignified Andean city of Pasto, the staff at the newly opened Archivo Histórico patiently responded to my many requests.

During my field research in the Putumayo in 1994, the lively health workers at the Hospital de San Rafael clued me in on some social and environmental skills necessary for non-Amazonians new to the rain forest. Deep thanks to cacique Touera Buinama of La Chorrera for sharing with me some Huitoto oral histories concerning life before, during, and after the rubber boom. Finally, without the wisdom and perspective of Capuchin missionary and menche Father Miguel Dels Sants Junyent i Rafart of San Rafael, Amazonas, Colombia, I would not have understood much concerning the Putumayo and its history.

South of the border in Ecuador, Juan Fraile G. and Jorge Jarrín Valdivieso of the Archivo Nacional de Historia in Quito graciously facilitated my inquiries focused on the Oriente, Ecuador's Amazonian province. Enrique Ayala Mora and Father Lorenzo García both took time away from their busy schedules to share their expertise on Ecuadorian historiography. At the Archivo y Biblioteca de la Función Legislativa, Cecilia Durán, Alexandra Martínez, and Soledad Córdova guided me through that archive's complex cataloging system. Finally, sra. Aida Najas gracefully responded to my requests at the Biblioteca General del Ministerio de Relaciones Exteriores.

In Lima, Peru, Roberto Matos, Nora Gomero, and César Durand at the Archivo General de la Nación made my stay in the "City of the Kings" most profitable and enlightening. Miguel and Pilár Mansilla opened their home to me, offering a peaceful haven from the occasionally tense street life of Lima. Alejandro Juan de la Flor Fernández generously shared with me his fine thesis on rubber exportation from the Peruvian Amazon.

In bucolic and sultry Iquitos, Alberto Chirif of the Centro de Estudios Teológicos de la Amazonía briefed me on his city's extensive if scattered historical documents. Pedro Salazar Angulo and María Teresa Angulo Castro generously made space for me in the offices of El Oriente to peruse bound copies of that important newspaper published during the last stage of the rubber boom. At the "archive" of the Palacio de Justicia, Luis Ramírez Pérez, Honorio Arce Alvarez, and Carlos Falconi Robles led me to the ultimate dream/nightmare of a historian: a huge, unlit, damp, forgotten basement full of spiders, cockroaches, and mountains of uncataloged and unworked primary documents. I hope this important collection will someday find a more suitable home.

North of the Rio Bravo/Grande, I owe a profound debt to Professors Thomas M. Davies, Jr., Brian Loveman, and Paul Vanderwood of San Diego State University, who taught me how to look at Latin America from comparative and critical angles. At the University of New Mexico, Professors Linda B. Hall, Peter Bakewell, Karen Remmer, Robert Kern, and Bob Himmerich y Valencia demonstrated yeoman dedication to earlier drafts of this work. Finally, Jane Rausch, Paul Gootenburg, Charles Bergquist, Catherine LeGrand, Barbara Weinstein, and J. León Helguera all kindly offered their expertise and suggestions concerning sources and contacts in Colombia, Ecuador, and Peru.

Grants from the Tinker and Mellon Foundations, from the Student Research Allocations Committee and the Vice President's Research Fund of the University of New Mexico, the James R. Scobie Prize from the Conference on Latin American History (CLAH), and Faculty Development Funds from the University of San Francisco made this research both possible and pleasant. In particularly lean times, my mother, Marilyn Gae Stanfield, covered travel expenses. I thank one and all.

Finally, I am indebted to Thomas M. Davies, Jr., Larry Durwood Ball, Jr., Paul Bruce, Susan Stanfield, and Michael Harrison — all real or fictive kin — for laboring over my lengthy dissertation and making this a shorter, better book.

I respectfully dedicate this book to the people of New Mexico.

INTRODUCTION

L egends, myths, and ghosts often provide research topics for historians and for Latin Americanists. Historians endeavor, not always
successfully, to separate fact from fiction, myth from history. Latin
Americanists frequently confront the legacies and chaos of the past during
their studies and travels: pre-Columbian and colonial monuments sharing
space and time with an unpredictable modernity; indigenous languages and
cultures sustaining ongoing encounters with Western and European arti-
facts; the dead residing among the living; myth informing history; cycles
rather than lines promising progress. Colonial themes rekindle and trespass
neat chronological periodization, reminders of the complex legacies of contact, conflict, and confusion in multiethnic and diverse societies.

This book focuses on the complex and often contradictory issues and
transformations introduced to northwestern Amazonia by the rubber industry from 1850 to 1933.[1] As a regional history of northwestern Amazonia, roughly described by the Caquetá River in the north, the Putumayo
River in the center, and the Napo River in the south, it's important to
reconstruct the indigenous environment prior to its rapid and violent incorporation into larger economic, social, and political networks (see map 1).
People's lives changed dramatically during the rubber boom, but not in
uniform, "modern" directions. The larger world, indeed, altered the region
and its peoples, yet the region's environment and social structures also affected national and global systems.

As a crossroads of conflicting border claims between Colombia, Ecuador,
Peru, and Brazil, the Putumayo experienced intense violence and laborious

diplomatic negotiations before borders were tentatively set in the 1920s. An area rich in rubber trees and full of potential Indian laborers, the Putumayo attracted international trade and investment during an era of a seemingly insatiable global appetite for rubber. In short, this book will chronicle and analyze the history of the Putumayo from regional, national, and international perspectives.

A diverse group of anthropologists and historians assumed the task of writing the history of the non-Brazilian Amazon — the huge crescent of rain forest running through Colombia, Ecuador, Peru, and Bolivia. Hybrid anthropologist-historians in Colombia, such as Augusto Gómez, Camilo Domínguez, and Roberto Pineda Camacho, have illuminated the patterns of slavery, violence, and extractive industry in the Caquetá and Putumayo.[2] From the Peruvian side, the *indigenismo* of the reformist military government of Gen. Velasco Alvarado from 1968 to 1975 unleashed a generation of activist/scholars into the Peruvian countryside. Indicative of this wave of SINAMOS organizers — a Peruvian government development agency — is Alberto Chirif, who for decades not only has researched the patterns of European/Amazonian interactions but also has struggled to protect remaining indigenous cultures.[3] Other important works by Peruvians treating western Amazonia and the rubber boom include the early efforts of Jesús Víctor San Román and José A. Flores Marín.[4] Guido Pennano, Peruvian president Alberto Fujimori's first minister of labor, recently completed an economic history of rubber in Peru.[5] All of these authors probed the question, Why did such a rich and complex environment become underdeveloped rather than prosperous?

In comparison to the growth of Colombian and Peruvian research and publication about northwestern Amazonia, Ecuadorian scholarship has not demonstrated equal dynamism. Ecuadorians still feel ambiguous and even defensive about their Amazonian lowlands, called the *Oriente*, a region of both national pride and shame. Nonetheless, ecclesiastical histories by Lorenzo García, O.C.D., and José Jouanen touch on the Putumayo, while the active presses of Abya-Yala and Mundo Shuar frequently publish serious contemporary ethnologies of the northwest Amazon.[6]

One of the major goals of this work is to approach the region's history from various ethnographic perspectives — an approach possible only because of the significant work of anthropologists. Along with their South American colleagues mentioned above, European and North American anthropologists deserve high praise for their research contributions. Anthropologists began to work in the Putumayo early this century,[7] but an unusual effervescence in scholarship developed over the last generation. Jürg Gasché, Nivia Cristina Garzón, and Mireille Guyot, for example, made careers studying Huitoto,

Bora, and Ocaina culture.[8] Michael Taussig wrote a brilliant but occasionally impenetrable study of Putumayan culture during the rubber boom, describing it as a "culture of terror, space of death."[9] Indeed, the terrorist regime built on forced labor and violence associated with the infamous "Putumayo scandal" continues to attract new research and interpretation.

The Putumayo scandal began in 1907 in the northwestern Amazonian boomtown Iquitos with the publication of shocking articles in a muckraking newspaper, *La Sanción*. Editor Benjamín Saldaña Rocca alleged that the leading rubber company in the Putumayo, the Casa Arana, employed a system of terror and torture against its mostly indigenous work force. That very year, Arana registered his company in Britain as the Peruvian Amazon Rubber Company (subsequently renamed the Peruvian Amazon Company), thereby linking the world's leading nineteenth-century antislavery nation, Great Britain, to a company enslaving Indians in the twentieth century. American adventurer and engineer Walter E. Hardenburg carried the scandalous Putumayo allegations to London in 1909. Eighteen months earlier, Hardenburg had wound up on the wrong side of a gun battle between Colombian and Peruvian rubber traders, or *caucheros*, and subsequently suffered mistreatment, imprisonment, and property loss. After his misfortune in the Putumayo, Hardenburg tarried in Iquitos, teaching English, earning money for his return passage, and collecting allegations against the Casa Arana and the Peruvian Amazon Company.

Upon arrival in London, Hardenburg contacted Rev. John H. Harris, secretary of the Anti-Slavery and Aborigines Protection Society, a Quaker organization formed in the 1830s. Harris suggested that Hardenburg take his dossier to G. S. Paternoster, assistant editor of the muckraking periodical *Truth*. In his subsequent book on the Putumayo, Hardenburg reprinted the sensational allegations listed in *Truth*: pacific Indians worked day and night, kept in nakedness, not given food, bought and sold at market; Indians beaten, mutilated, tortured, or murdered as punishment or for the amusement of sadistic caucheros; women and girls raped, children's brains dashed against trees, old folks killed when they could no longer work. These charges, reported in the same sober voice used by Bartolomé de Las Casas some 370 years earlier when he decried the excesses of Spanish colonialism in the Americas, provoked both public outrage and official inquiries.[10]

Public pressure and intense lobbying of the British foreign office and the Peruvian Amazon Company by the Anti-Slavery and Aborigines Protection Society resulted in the naming of a mixed commission to investigate the Putumayo allegations. In a subsequent report to Parliament, foreign office representative Roger Casement sustained the worst allegations: the systematic starvation, whipping, torture, and murder of thirty thousand Indian victims in a decade's time.[11]

The scandal raised a storm of hyperbole, recriminations, and indignation. While the British and the Peruvians sought to avoid responsibility for the crimes, Colombia and Ecuador used the scandal to draw attention to their respective territorial claims in the Putumayo and to underscore the brutality of the rapacious Peruvians. The British government tried to shift some of the Putumayo cleanup to the Brazilian and North American governments, a task that policymakers in Rio de Janeiro and Washington, D.C., wisely ducked. For seven years, until the guns of August 1914 introduced Europe to new and unimaginable atrocities, the remote Putumayo region captured global attention and became synonymous with death, savagery, and greed.

The Putumayo scandal of 1907 to 1914 contained various sources of conflict (personal, cultural, economic, political, diplomatic), which taken together explain why the scandal developed and flourished, forcing powerful individuals, organizations, and governments to respond to the allegations and investigations it provoked. The charges, recriminations, and scandal politics are interesting in themselves, and they illuminate cultural prejudices and ideological viewpoints of important participants. Yet, as is true with most scandals, the compression of the time/space continuum—the convex lens through which the Putumayo was perceived—tends to obscure and distort the realities of the region. One of the major objectives of this study is to place the scandal into the context of the region's history.

The scandal is compelling enough reason to select the Putumayo for a regional study, but other magnets attracted me as well. First, this project had to be approached from a comparative and international perspective, for the Putumayo frontier reached into the histories and archives of three fascinating South American nations: Colombia, Ecuador, and Peru. It is my hope that the inclusive parameters presented in this study will serve as bridges rather than barriers for peoples of different nations and of diverse cultures.

Second, with the quincentenary of European colonization of the Americas, the general issue of cultural contact and conflict again commands center stage for scholars of the Americas. The cultural diversity of indigenous Putumayo and the rapid changes introduced by "whites" provides a classic case study of colonial processes treading into the twentieth century.[12] As a "living museum," a magical reality defying linear stoic development, Amazonia provides us with seemingly timeless cycles of experience.

Finally, I plan to reintroduce humanity to the study of the Putumayo. The veneer of the scandal covers all characters with a farcical patina: vicious, depraved "black legend" Hispanics, those who enjoyed colonial violence, killing meek and weak noble savages; upright British reformers ending the excesses of greasy Latin brutes, the scene happily closing with a spectacular British sunset. To achieve a holistic perspective, I will place the scandal into the larger historical context of the Putumayo, stripping away the nationalism and hyperbole that have clouded the region, to illuminate how life evolved during and after the rubber boom.

Incorporation, violence, slavery, and adaptation are the four overarching themes of this work. Each will be addressed from comparative angles to explore the complexities of a multiethnic and international region undergoing great change. Incorporation involved ethnic, economic, and political aspects for both white and Indian societies. Violence predated white contact, with the Indians already slaughtering one another over real or perceived wrongs, but violence intensified and assumed new forms and meanings with the rubber boom. Slavery, practiced in Amazonia for centuries and but one of the manifestations of an unfree labor tradition, survived past the rubber boom, revealing both great continuities and changes in the history of the Putumayo. That great human trait, adaptation — to new cultures, labor demands, trading opportunities, and politics — allowed some people to prosper and others to simply survive in an unstable environment. Nonetheless, incorporation, violence, slavery, and adaptation took a huge toll on thousands of individuals, people caught by the destructive side of colonialism, capitalism, and nationalism.

What follows is a mosaic of fact, myth, emotion, analysis, politics, and ethics. It is my contention that history and life can only be comprehended from various, usually conflictive perspectives. This is especially true for the Putumayo, a region heretofore known for its infamy, its darkness, and its politics of colonialism and nationalism. By studying how the rubber industry changed life in the Putumayo from 1850 to 1933 — while remaining mindful of the interactions of culture, society, economics, and politics at regional, national, and international levels — we can appreciate the complexity and abundance of history. It seems that without inclusive parameters, any study advocates more than it informs.

RED RUBBER, BLEEDING TREES

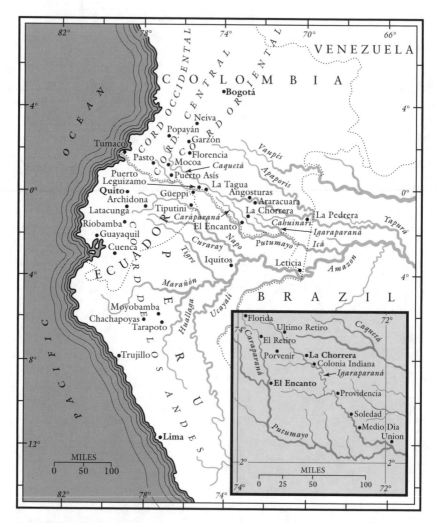

NORTHWEST AMAZONIA

ONE

THE SETTING

T he Amazon River basin drains close to half of the South American continent, an area larger than the continental United States. The great "River Sea" drains waters from the Guiana and Brazilian shields and from the eastern slope of the imposing Andes Mountains, collecting from more than five hundred major tributaries on its eastward journey through Brazil and into the Atlantic Ocean. This huge basin contains the planet's greatest biodiversity and its largest rain forest, one absorbing carbon dioxide and providing Earth with much of its oxygen. Although often described as a "paradise" of scantily clad natives in primordial forests or, conversely, as a "green hell" of voracious insects, tropical fevers, and man-eating predators, Amazonia has long served as a challenging yet fragile home for human beings.[1]

Two tributaries in northwestern Amazonia, the Putumayo and Caquetá Rivers, establish the geographic center of this study. Born in the jagged and lush Cordillera Oriental of southern Colombia, these thousand-mile-long rivers flow along roughly parallel southeasterly routes and join the Amazon River in Brazil. Much of this study focuses on the middle reaches of both rivers and their respective tributaries: the Igaraparaná and Caraparaná of the Putumayo, and the Cahuinari of the Caquetá. This "notorious region" of the Putumayo allegations and Casa Arana hegemony lies between the equator and three degrees south latitude and seventy and seventy-five degrees west longitude.[2]

The Upper Putumayo and Caquetá, northwest of the notorious zone, are included in this regional study, especially when tracking the Colombian trade and colonization links between the Andean foothills and lowland Amazonia. Iquitos, another important site for the Putumayo, and the central trading center for *caucheros* all over northwestern Amazonia, also falls into the purview of this study (see map 1). And, of course, when discussing the Putumayo's integration into national and international systems, and the Putumayo's import to the larger world, the strict parameters of an isolated region will indeed be stretched.

Amazonia is not a homogenous realm of undifferentiated, flat tropical forest; elevation, rainfall, soil composition, temperature, humidity, and fauna and flora vary greatly by region and ecosystem. In the Putumayo, for example, elevation differs from 100 to 300 to meters (330 to 1,000 feet); annual rainfall totals between 2,500 and 3,500 millimeters (98 to 138 inches); and temperature differs depending on altitude, but averages about 25 degrees centigrade (75 degrees Fahrenheit). Steep hills, direct sunlight, and streams swollen by downpours make overland travel arduous. The days are comfortable if one stays under the shade of the forest canopy, but nights, particularly in June and July, can be quite cold. The *várzea,* the sediment-rich floodplains of the Lower Putumayo and Caquetá harbor the richest agricultural lands, while upland terra firma farmers must contend with poor and leached soil. A plethora of plant and tree species grace the area, and insect, animal, and fish species add to the exceptional biodiversity of northwestern Amazonia.[3]

"White Rivers" born in the Andean piedmont, such as the Caquetá and Putumayo, are rich in nutrients and attract a wide range of vegetable, aquatic, and animal species. Conversely, "Black Rivers" or "Rivers of Hunger" rising from the ancient soils of lowland interior regions such as Vaupés in eastern Colombia carry far fewer food sources. Wildlife resources and soil fertility set the carrying capacity of land throughout Amazonia, so the "White Rivers" of western Amazonia could, and did, support a relatively greater concentration of human inhabitants; however, competition for control and access to the best hunting, gathering, and agricultural lands did set off violent clashes between clans and tribes. Those peoples who could not protect their lands along the rich rivers were pushed into forests with poorer soils and less game.[4] But even the victors of such struggles in a delicate ecosystem could not settle permanently in one area; protein sources and crop yields declined after a few years, requiring migrations to new lands.[5]

Unlike other regions of Amazonia, the Putumayo and Caquetá lack a true dry season, which hampers terrestrial transport over muddy or flooded paths. Riverine transport also can be subject to interruption for lack of sufficient water depth, especially on the upper reaches of the Putumayo between Puerto Asís and Leguizamo. Nonetheless, during the rubber boom steamboats drawing twelve feet ascended far up the Putumayo and about midway up the Igara-paraná and Caraparaná.[6] Although modern technology made the remote and geographically complex Putumayo accessible to regional and world markets, falls and rapids, notably at Araracuara on the Caquetá and at La Chorrera on the Igaraparaná, impeded river traffic and presented natural barriers to river commerce and communication. They also lent native peoples some degree of insulation from white contact prior to the rubber boom.[7]

Rubber, border squabbles, and scandal brought to world attention the Putumayo and Caquetá, a region bound together by similar cultural and physical geography, by paths and tributaries linking the two great rivers, and by persistent boundary disputes. A border region coveted by four South American nations, the Putumayo attracted more than its share of geopolitical intrigue. It was also a frontier—a place neither uniform, deserted, nor linear, but one defined by cultural contact, social change, and political conflict. It was a place of many cultures, not just two; Portuguese and Brazilian, Spanish American, Caribbean, European, and North American cultures mingled and clashed with the abundant native Putumayan cultures. More than two nations met there, indicated by the fact that Colombia, Ecuador, Peru, and Brazil fought for and now share pieces of the Putumayo. In short, when we study the Putumayo, the traditional dualism of frontier definitions (civilization/barbarism, European/indigenous, linear/procedural) must be expanded to incorporate plural European and plural indigenous cultures and experiences expressed within a spherical, not a linear, frontier.[8]

Yagua oral tradition provides a glimpse of an indigenous perspective on central and peripheral experiences. For these people, residing south of the Putumayo near the Amazon River, tribal grounds served as the center of human creation. The Yagua called themselves "nihamwo" or "the people"; others with whom they did not share language comprehension, customs, beliefs, or goods received the label "mununu," or "savages." But all peoples—Yagua, Cocama, Ticuna, Bora, Matsés, white, black—began life at the Yagua center. The non-Yagua peoples, however, had emigrated away from the chosen land: the whites or "viracochas" moving west toward the Andes; the blacks, downstream toward Brazil. Yagua myth and oral tradition noted that these migrations resulted from fighting, with the Yagua finally driving these challengers away from the creation source.

During the rubber boom, the Yagua say that whites returned angry from their displacement to the far side of the world and were intent on reconquering the central lands of the creators. As such, myth allowed the Yagua to accept white presence, and even violence, as the reclamation of their former status and place in the world. Yagua recognition of their own centrality, the relegation of non-Yaguas to remote frontiers, and their eventual return illuminate another distinctive indigenous perspective on the frontier. The acceptance and inclusion of these immigrants allowed the Yagua to perceive white presence as a natural process, albeit highly disruptive, and not as a cataclysmic conquest by alien beings.[9]

Numerous distinct peoples inhabited the Putumayo during the last five centuries. The Huitoto (Witoto), also referred to as the Murui or Muiname, were and still are the largest ethnic group in the Putumayo. Their traditional enemies, the strong and powerful Bora (Miraña), occasionally raided Huitoto villages for booty and captives. The Huitoto-speaking Ocaina (Okaina), the Andoke (Andoque), and the fierce Carib-speaking Carijona (Karijona) also occupied areas of the Putumayo during the rubber boom. Most adults stood about five feet tall, their uncovered bodies revealing muscle and painted designs. Body and facial hair were often plucked to enhance an individual's beauty. Depending on the area and local customs, noses might be perforated with decorative feathers or sticks, or the earlobes might be distended by a wooden disk.[10]

Each people, or tribe, was subdivided into small and often warring clans. Clan members lived in a large communal house, or *maloca,* which served as the symbolic and physical center of existence. Clans drew their respective names and identity from plants, animals, or mythical progenitors. Between fifty and two hundred people lived in a maloca, reflecting the limits of a delicate environment and the carrying capacity of the land.[11]

A clear hierarchy existed in these patrilineal clans. A person's family, ritual and political function, age, and gender established relative status. For instance, high-status families slung their hammocks close to the chief near the center of the maloca, while those of less importance resided on the edges of the building; older siblings demonstrated power over less privileged siblings by excluding them from ritual preparations. At the bottom of the status hierarchy one might find *jaïenikis,* or orphans, beings separated from their original clan or family. Warfare, disease, migration, and social decomposition created many of these orphans, individuals thought to have lost their culture and therefore their connection to humanity. Orphans lived in the maloca, and if allowed, learned the culture and secrets of the new clan, thereby regaining a legitimate identity and humanity.[12]

Hunting, gathering, fishing, and slash-and-burn agriculture provided foodstuffs. The major Amazonian staple, yuca (or manioc), has been cultivated for at least three thousand years. Yuca is a hearty root crop, high in carbohydrates and easy on soils for it draws away little nitrogen. It is often made into a flour or served as a fermented but nutritious drink. Other cultivated plants and trees surrounding the maloca included corn, beans, palms, pineapple, banana, papaya, mango, coca, and tobacco . Hunting and fishing provided the necessary animal proteins.[13]

Marriage customs encouraged individuals to select a mate from a distant but friendly clan. Mothers encouraged sons to live with another appropriate clan to begin the search for a suitable wife. After learning the language of his girlfriend's clan, and working for and presenting gifts to her father's family, the couple received parental blessing only if the arrangement seemed mutually beneficial. Marriage legitimacy did not depend on a ceremony but on affinal relations, birth of children, and material or labor exchanges between family and kin. Exogamous marriage, then, acted as an important centripetal force that bonded potentially rival tribes and clans, encouraging crucial communication and trust in the often insecure and hostile Putumayo environment.[14]

By 1870 most indigenous dwellers of the Lower Putumayo and Caquetá carried a single name. Some adopted clan names as a surname, and a few acquired Spanish last names. Children started to work for their family and clan at an early age. Male babies outnumbered female ones three to one, suggesting the practice of female infanticide. Most people in these communities were under twenty-one years of age, married according to local customs, and died before the age of fifty. Both in indigenous malocas and in towns of the upper reaches of both rivers, female artisans — spinners, weavers, seamstresses, potters — contributed significantly to the local economy.[15]

Census data and written reports teach us much about northwestern Amazonia, but so, too, do myths and oral histories. Amazonia is a region of rich and living mythology, especially in its northwestern corner. The Huitoto tell a great many myths reflecting the creation and evolution of themselves and their world. For Putumayans, no clear line divides the spiritual and physical worlds; myth and history blend in tales sensitive to both tangible and magical causation. Myth defines, teaches, and preserves culture and historical consciousness.[16]

In the mythic past, the Huitoto say, the Son of Cold Nothingness, troubled by his solitude, began the process of creation. The first creation, however, did not meet God's liking and was destroyed by fire, thereby creating carbon. The fire also consumed God's body, and on that spot sprang forth sacred coca and tobacco. Man was created during the second creation; the Sun opened a breach in Mother Earth's womb, from which men and women emerged. Those creatures leaving the womb at night had their tails cut off by a huge spider and became human; those leaving by day kept their tails and became monkeys.[17]

In the upper world, a man/serpent tempted a young beautiful woman with fruit. Her mother interceded and killed the man/serpent. In exile, the young woman bore a son whom she planted in the ground, and who flowered into the first fruit tree. Soon many people came to gather fruit and seeds from this original food source. When jealous rivals cut the tree down, water flowed from its trunk, creating the Amazon and its tributaries. A great flood followed water's creation, and only the refuge of a tall hill near La Chorrera enabled a few young men to escape drowning.[18]

Although tribes shared common Putumayan myths, each tribe and clan practiced their own rituals to maintain cultural and physical life. The most important ceremony recalled the memory and teachings of their original ancestor, or *yurupari*, the personage responsible for their existence. To re-create and remember "the knowing word" of their progenitor, select men gathered at the center of the maloca and ingested tobacco juice, coca, or yagé, a powerful psychotropic drug derived from a native tree. During these ceremonies, the men returned to the timeless existence of their ancestors and sought the route of enlightenment and empowerment through the creator's knowledge and that of the "Wisdom Basket."[19]

Responsibility for guaranteeing the future and maintaining ritual and musical instruments fell upon a captain, or chief. The captain shaped the history of the clan; he provided happiness, well-being, and prosperity, while guarding against disease, ritual contamination, and death. His power derived from timeless knowledge of ritual secrets, and the spirit world communicated through his "good word." The captain's responsibilities were great indeed, and he enjoyed high status, oversaw important rituals, and expected lower-status persons to serve and work for him.[20]

Try as they might, captains could not always ensure peace and prosperity for their people. Although some writers romanticize Amazonian life prior to European contact, Putumayans never enjoyed the lives of so-called noble savages: peaceful, relaxed, and egalitarian.[21] Raids and warfare erupted frequently, yet served many purposes. First, fighting over choice lands and hunting grounds reflected the basic struggle for resources, while tensions tended to maintain the necessary ecological distance between clans. A defeated tribe or clan had to relocate to less desirable, less fertile lands. Second, warfare gave warriors the opportunity to test their mettle and to shame their enemies in battle. Third, Putumayans viewed death and disease as spiritually induced conditions caused by rival captains or shamans. Therefore, raids against those presumed responsible evened the score and removed the shaman's spell. Fourth, warriors often plundered their rivals seeking material and spiritual advantage, and often kidnapped women and children. Captive warriors were usually ritualistically slain, whereas women and children became low-status "orphans" and served as a demographic and cultural reserve for the victors.[22]

Captains and shamans found it difficult spiritually to manage whites and their exotic goods. One Indian leader, or cacique, complained that whites were impervious to Indian spells because "they ate a lot of garlic." The cacique recalled that white goods were "too hot" and that they introduced envy and greed to indigenous societies. These goods therefore had to be "cooled" spiritually in the interest of social balance.[23]

Ethnocentrism, a remarkably pervasive cultural trait around the globe, also divided Putumayans; each tribe, even each clan, believed itself superior to all others. Traditional antipathies inherited from the past, distrust of strangers, and hostile physical or spiritual acts kept people vigilant and put them to fighting. A Bora woman stated that the Muiname, Andoke, and Bora remained friendly, but that the Bora warred with the Huitoto and especially with the Ocaina. The fearsome Carijona attacked the same two tribes and traded their war captives for European goods.[24]

Regardless of thousands of years of human history, many people continue to think of Amazonia as a remote and even untouched rain forest. But one must remember that even Europeans explored and sporadically settled in Amazonia for almost half a millennium. Beginning in the 1530s, Spanish conquistadores persistently probed the fringes of northwestern Amazonia in the stubborn search for glory, honor, and the riches of El Dorado. In 1541, Francisco de Orellana began his perilous but ultimately successful descent of the Amazon River. Hernán Pérez de Quesada completed a bloody military sweep of the Upper Putumayo the following year. Subsequent Spanish efforts to concentrate and Christianize Indians in supervised villages (*reducciones*) set off frequent and effective Indian rebellions.[25]

During the seventeenth and eighteenth centuries, Jesuits and Franciscans were diligent in their evangelical and missionizing efforts. Although clerics had joined various sixteenth-century *entradas,* missionary activity did not begin to increase until after 1630. By 1693, Franciscans had established twenty-eight missions or towns in the Upper Putumayo. The padres used a mixed strategy of offering material inducements, most commonly metal tools, with a strong dose of compulsion and violence to congregate and control Indians. Once they were able to get the Indians to the missions, they relied on the power and prestige of indigenous captains to cajole or convince their people to stay and work in their new but alien setting. The Franciscans, however, encountered persistent problems. Indians of various clans and tribes often fought in their now integrated setting, and they tended to melt back into the forest after receiving tools and gifts, fleeing the disease and discipline of the *reducciones*. Of the twenty-eight towns created sixty years earlier, only seven remained by 1750. A generation and a half later, the Franciscans completely abandoned the Upper Putumayo.[26]

Gold dust, forest products, and a large number of potential laborers had attracted conquistador and missionary alike, but the Putumayo proved a difficult region to dominate and settle permanently.

The Portuguese, of course, also actively expanded up into Amazonia from the east as early as the sixteenth century. The famous Brazilian *bandeirantes* explored the hinterland in search of riches and Indian slaves. Portuguese westward expansion, complete with mythical pioneer heroes similar to those of the western United States, gained momentum in the seventeenth and eighteenth centuries. Pará, located at the mouth of the Amazon, was founded in 1616, followed by Manaus fifty years later.[27]

Both Iberian colonial powers used ecclesiastics as instruments of territorial and administrative operations. Early in the eighteenth century, the extraordinary Jesuit missionary Samuel Fritz attempted to claim northwestern Amazonia between the Napo and Negro Rivers for Spain. These efforts met stiff resistance from the Portuguese crown and its surrogates, officials in Pará and the Carmelite missionaries. Subsequent migrations of Spanish and Portuguese colonists exacerbated geopolitical tensions and placed severe demographic pressure on existing tribes. The 1750 Treaty of Madrid, drawn up to settle numerous competing Iberian territorial claims in Latin America, essentially recognized Portuguese control of much of central Amazonia.[28]

Treaties, however, proved ineffectual in defining clear and respected boundaries in northwestern Amazonia. In 1754, Spanish Franciscans established San Joaquín at the confluence of the Putumayo and Amazon Rivers. Subsequently attacked by Portuguese and Brazilian expeditions, the Franciscans abandoned their outpost twelve years later.[29] The world's first modern world war, the Seven Years' War (1756–63), also spilled into the Putumayo as both Iberian kingdoms attempted to enlist the support of Indian allies to fight for their respective geopolitical ends. The 1770s brought no relief from intercolonial warfare, with the Portuguese pushing ever west, enticing some Indians to relocate downriver while enslaving the recalcitrant. The 1777 Treaty of San Ildefonso stipulated that a binational commission establish boundaries in northwestern Amazonia, touching off yet another round of violence. In 1782, the commissioners found the Caquetá devastated by malaria and warfare.[30]

Indigenous peoples paid the costs of European contact, conquest, and conflict, and many tribes disappeared from disease, social decomposition, or violence. Others were enslaved through the colonial practices of "just war" against rebellious infidels or *rescate,* the putative rescue of Indians purported to be captives of hostile, slave-trading, or even cannibalistic Indians. Once "rescued," the Indians became the lifelong property of their new owners.

Nonetheless, some Indian tribes prospered through their participation in European trade. The Carijonas, for example, became powerful merchants in northern and western Amazonia by exchanging slaves for European goods with both white and Indian customers. By the end of the colonial period, the Carijona enjoyed greater military power and commercial influence than they did prior to European arrival.[31] The Bora, or Miraña, also benefited from the thriving trade of European goods for Indian slaves during the early nineteenth century. Luso-Brazilians and even an Italian businessman, Ricardo Zany, dealt with a prosperous Bora chief who specialized in trading slaves for goods.[32] Clearly, not all Indians became immediate victims or pawns of the Europeans; some indeed prospered under new and revolutionary circumstances.

The independence of Brazil and Spanish South America after 1822 marked a radical alteration in political structure and authority but left intact many social and economic patterns inherited from the colonial period. Economic activity declined in the Putumayo, suggesting an interruption in imports and a weakening demand for Indian labor. In fact, some writers suggest that the early nineteenth century marked an era of indigenous renaissance and autonomy. But Indians along the major rivers continued to be held by colonial mechanisms such as patron-client and debt-peonage relationships. By the 1830s, Indians and mestizos manufactured simple goods like woven mats, turtle butter, salted fish, and hammocks. By mid-century, alcohol had become an important trade good throughout Amazonia.[33]

Although government policies had little direct effect in Amazonia during the early years of independence, they do reveal the mind-set and goals of policymakers. The Peruvian government actively encouraged European immigration to its claimed Amazonian territory as early as the 1830s. Behind this policy lurked the notion that "whitening" the Amazon would lead to a secure and prosperous future, and that the Amazonian lowlands were deserted, an implicit denial of the existence and value of indigenous societies.[34] From the east, the independent Brazilian empire mirrored the colonial Portuguese policy flip-flops of exploiting and protecting Indians. Indian legislation adopted in 1845 prohibited traders from enslaving or forcing Indians to work, but it stipulated that Indians be acculturated and forced to work for the state.[35] Gran Colombia, of which Ecuador was still a part, used the Putumayo as a dumping ground for criminals (and, one would presume, political enemies) early in the century. Very few exiles managed to extricate themselves from the tangled and remote Putumayo.[36] Gran Colombia did, however, make early administrative appointments to the region. In 1829 the governor of Cauca, responsible for a huge department covering much of western and southern Colombia, named a prefect for Caquetá based in Mocoa. By the 1850s, Caquetá prefect Salvador Quintero was naming *corregidores,* or local magistrates, to Indian villages throughout the Putumayo and Caquetá. These officials oversaw the collection and exportation of cacao, wax, sarsaparilla, drugs, and gold. These products, and at times some Indians, then made the long voyage to market in Pará, Brazil.[37]

World demand in temperate climes for tropical and semitropical agricultural products stimulated frontier expansion in many areas of nineteenth-century Latin America. In Colombia, a tobacco boom in the 1850s gave way to a cotton boom during the U.S. Civil War of the 1860s, with indigo joining the export list late in the decade.[38] In Ecuador, cacao was king not only along the Pacific Coast but also in the Amazonian forests of the Oriente. Peruvian exports by mid-century mirrored the colonial mineral tradition, with guano production supplying cheap fertilizer for increasingly large and efficient European farms.

By the 1860s, a new tropical forest product touched off exploration, colonization, and conquest in northwestern Amazonia. Chincona tree bark, or *quina,* yielded quinine, which proved effective as a remedy and prophylactic against malarial fevers. Malaria, a major world disease, affected not only tropical continents but also extensive reaches of the United States, southern Europe, and the Middle East. The promise of relief or protection from malaria found a huge global market, especially as the quina boom coincided with European colonization of much of tropical Africa and Asia. The major supply of chincona trees stood in South American tropical forests.[39]

One of the most important families to build its economic and political power during the quina boom carried the regal name "Reyes." Following the death of his father, Elías Reyes moved part of his family to Popayán, a beautiful colonial town on the southern edge of the Cauca Valley. In 1868 this aggressive entrepreneur journeyed to Europe and the United States to acquire import/export connections, subsequently entering into commercial competition with the only retailer of imported goods in Popayán.[40] Elías built his quina company using both provincial and cosmopolitan business techniques, bringing together a group of respected and wealthy businessmen and some trusted relatives to share the risk and labor of quina exploration. After locating rich stands of trees, Elías Reyes Hermanos petitioned for legal land title and set about organizing and training laborers. Once collected, the quina was shipped to foreign consumers in England, France, Germany, and the United States. On the return journey, the Reyes brothers packed their ships with much-desired and expensive imported goods. Among other partners and employees recruited by Elías were in-laws José María and Florentino Calderón. Salvador Quintero, the prefect of Caquetá who had years earlier established trade relations with Amazonian Indians, joined the new company, as did Elías's brothers Enrique, Nestor, and Rafael.[41]

Quick-tempered, energetic, and ambitious, Rafael Reyes started his adult career by helping make a fortune for the family business. By the mid-1880s, he had distinguished himself as a Conservative Party general during one of Colombia's frequent and bloody civil wars. He capped his public career as president of Colombia from 1904 to 1909, when he fashioned a bipartisan government following yet another civil war. Here was a leader who made his fortune and steeled his will in the jungles of the Putumayo, and who later went on to become a famous national and international figure.[42]

Rafael Reyes's initial quina explorations led him to upland areas between Popayán and the southern border town Ipiales, and along the western Andean slopes adjacent to the Pacific Ocean. From 1870 to 1872, the mountains around Santa Rosa, Patía, Tasajeras, and Aponte yielded a total of four million gold pesos worth of quina exports for the Reyes firm. With money in his pocket and carrying his deep belief in virtuous capitalism, the twenty-two-year-old Rafael set off for his first business and pleasure trip to the United States and Europe.[43]

After a perilous passage via Buenaventura and Panama, Reyes arrived in New York City. Then a city of one million inhabitants, New York impressed the young Colombian with its tall buildings, affluence, and commercial activity. Here Reyes met with Colombian Conservative Party expatriates who had fled the country after the 1860 civil war. Reyes sealed a deal with his compatriot partisans for future quina transactions and then undertook a tour of the East Coast. After a month, Reyes returned to New York and bought a passage to Europe.

In Paris, Reyes once again sealed personal and business deals with Colombian expatriates, negotiating deals for future import/export business and for much-needed credit. Ironically, the Reyes family's access to foreign markets and credit was brokered, and even supplied, by Colombians exiled from their homeland because of political violence. After completing the grand tour of Europe, the English- and French-speaking Reyes returned to Colombia at the end of 1872.[44]

During the next year, Reyes worked in the family business, courted his future wife, Sofía, and received permission from Elías to explore for quina in the Putumayo rain forests. The Reyes brothers had heard of a mulatto tradesman who annually descended the Putumayo and then cut up the Amazon and

Huallaga Rivers to trade salt for sarsaparilla.⁴⁵ Rafael and his dozen carriers and bushwhackers followed the lead of these earlier explorers and merchants, starting the long and difficult trek for the Putumayo in February 1874.

In canoes on the wide milky river, the party experienced the splendor of life in the Putumayo: acrobatic monkeys, vibrant and noisy birds, and schools of fish clustered along the river's edge, attracted by overhanging fruit trees. The river rolled and turned through dense emerald forests, its course punctuated by sandbars, massive ceiba trees, and spectacular sunsets. Occasionally, darker, clearer waters from tributaries flowed into the milk-chocolate Putumayo, disparate waters woven together by surfacing freshwater dolphins. Halfway down the river, where the current slowed, Reyes encountered a tribe of Orejones, a Huitoto clan.⁴⁶ About a month earlier, the Orejones had suffered an attack by neighboring Boras, losing many killed and captured. According to Reyes, the Orejones proposed that they form an alliance, thereby strengthening themselves against the Bora.⁴⁷ After the Orejones agreed to collect quina in exchange for more of Reyes's *brujerías,* or magical goods, Reyes proceeded downriver.

Deeper into the Putumayo, Reyes and company encountered the feared and presumably bellicose Bora. After a tense initial face-off, the short, skinny, and almost nude Rafael befriended the great Bora chief Chúa. Chúa boasted of his victory against the Orejones and claimed to be the most feared and respected Indian chief in the Middle Putumayo and Caquetá. Rafael, always the pragmatist, cemented both a social and economic relationship with the Bora, much like his earlier agreement with the Orejones.⁴⁸

Jungle exploration presented many dangers and discomforts. Rapids and whirlpools capsized canoes; intense sun, sustained downpours, and changeable weather took their toll on health and spirit; and tropical fevers attacked most members of the Reyes group, adding to the discomfort and demise of poorly fed and exhausted men. Mosquitos and other biting insects, in swarms as thick as smoke, devoured exposed skin and flew into eyes, ears, and mouths. For relief and to sleep, Reyes retired to the river's edge, exposing only his face to air and to insects. But once asleep, the currents carried him far downriver, requiring a long, early-morning swim back to camp. The others in the exploration party preferred to bury themselves in the sand, leaving only their nostrils uncovered, but to Rafael this technique of burying one's nude body in a sandy grave to escape the relentless plague of biting insects was, at least initially, repulsive.⁴⁹

While Rafael was dealing with native peoples and biting insects, upriver the Reyes family was facing other nuisances, such as economic competitors and regulation from the small bureaucracy in the Caquetá. In July 1874, W. Ruiz

Salgar, the Caquetá prefect, requested an armed guard after one of his prisoners was sprung from jail by an armed mob that included José María Calderón, a friend and employee of Elías Reyes. The mob had taunted and threatened Ruiz, who subsequently complained that the quineros were a wild, woolly, and drunken lot who committed crimes without fear of reprisal. Aware of other famous frontiers, Ruiz noted that soon "the Caquetá will be like California where each person defends his own life and interests."[50] Ruiz warned the large number of armed men in the vicinity, some working for Reyes, to avoid violence with rival quineros and not to steal food and goods from Indians.[51] Ruiz's regulation of the Reyes quina operation, and Enrique Reyes's insistence on confronting the competition, cost Ruiz his job. In November 1874, Enrique carried an official letter from Popayán naming Reyes Brothers employee Pedro F. Urrutia the new prefect of Caquetá.[52]

With Enrique attending to the politics of business, Rafael spearheaded efforts of the newly formed Compañía del Caquetá in Amazonia. Rafael planned to open an Amazonian trade route, one potentially easier and more profitable than the trans-Andean Pacific route. In 1875 he made his first trip to Pará at the mouth of the Amazon. There he met an important rubber broker, Manuel Pinheiro, and told him of his mercantile and financial connections in Europe and the United States. Pinheiro subsequently agreed to serve as Reyes's business agent in Pará. That deal cut, Rafael next went to secure permission from the imperial Brazilian government to navigate and carry goods on the Amazon and Putumayo Rivers.

In Rio de Janeiro, the scrawny and bedraggled Rafael (who weighed 50 kilos, or about 110 pounds), was granted a one-hour audience with Emperor Dom Pedro II. Dom Pedro, who had an interest in science and exploration, was impressed with Reyes and his plan to open the Putumayo to steamship service. In September 1875 Reyes secured the desired permission to open the Amazon and the Putumayo to both Colombian and Brazilian shipping.[53]

Rafael returned to Pará and told Pinheiro of his Rio success. The Brazilian government agreed to lend Reyes a small steamboat and crew for the ascension of the Putumayo, and Rafael rented another boat and filled it with goods. Before departing, Reyes met twenty-five-year-old British explorer Alfred Simson and granted Simson's wish to command the Brazilian launch in exchange for preparing firewood for his craft. Rafael then proceeded to Iquitos, where he purchased a seventy-foot-long, four-year-old English steamboat that he named the *Tundama*. Simson and Reyes rendezvoused on the Putumayo in February 1876. The crews on board the three boats reflected the increasingly cosmopolitan and complex Amazon: mulatto and black sailors shared duties with black slaves and Indians, and nationalities included Brazilian, Portuguese, Spanish, Argentine, Peruvian, English, and Colombian. The ship's cargo contained boxes of crackers, cans of sugar, sacks of sea salt, and bundles of Indian trade goods.[54]

Rafael accomplished much for the Compañía del Caquetá in two years: he had contacted Indian tribes who would collect quina; he had found an important import/export partner in Pinheiro; he had negotiated an agreement with the Brazilian government (although he was not a representative of his government); and he had acquired steamboats for the company and commenced importing and exporting on a grand scale. Reyes was thus hailed the "Amazonian hero," responsible for opening the Putumayo to progress.[55]

The quina boom and Amazonian territory did not escape the notice of the Peruvian government, nor that of Ecuadorian merchants. Although Reyes claimed to be the first to open the Putumayo to steamships, this was not the case. As early as 1873, Peruvian and Brazilian warships plied the river's waters, presumably part of a joint border-marking expedition. By early the next year, the Peruvians and Brazilians had divided the Lower Putumayo between themselves.[56] By December 1875, the Peruvian government ordered the naval commander of the department of Loreto, Peru's huge and poorly mapped northeastern territory, to name military, maritime, and police officials to the Putumayo. Officials in Lima worried that the Reyes concession would open the way for Bogotá to stretch its territorial control over the Putumayo, and they also correctly suspected that Brazil would try to play the Colombians and the Peruvians off one another. Brazil had just completed a territorial agreement with Peru and then opened the Putumayo to Reyes and Colombia.[57] Reyes learned of this Peruvian decree soon thereafter and personally delivered correspondence from the Colombian consul general in Yurimaguas, J. N. Montero, to the Caquetá prefect. Montero urged, presumably with Reyes's blessing, that the prefect counter the Peruvian move by naming political and civil authorities to all Indian villages in the Putumayo. This move would sew up Colombian access to Indian labor and bolster Bogotá's claim to the region.[58] The Peruvians needed more time to gather personnel and money for their expedition, giving Reyes the opportunity to best the Peruvian political and military challenge of 1876.

Economic competitors, brandishing both market hunger and armed muscle, did exist, however. In the eastern reaches of the Tungurahua and Chimborazo provinces of Ecuador, the Cañadas Peña Company carved out monopoly control of the quina forests south of the Reyes operation. It was rumored that this company employed a fearsome armed band of thugs to repulse any challenge to their territory, and to control their estimated one thousand Indian laborers.[59] The Amazonian route to prosperity during the quina boom and the subsequent rubber boom was indeed fraught with geopolitical, economic and physical risks. But the real or perceived profits beckoned an increasing number of determined fortune seekers.

The Compañía del Caquetá and the Reyes brothers did quite well in the late 1870s. Older brother Elías focused some of his attention on building a road from the montaña down to a port on the Caquetá. Predictably, Elías and the road contractor fell into legal battles over the schedule, route, and cost of the road.[60] Meanwhile, Rafael was busy in the Amazonian lowlands. He made $100,000 in New York from the first shipment of quina transported on the *Tundama,* but not all his time was so profitable or glamorous.

Much of Rafael's time was spent drafting laborers for quina collection and transport. Some laborers were *enganchados:* hooked by an advance and then required to pay off the debt. *Enganches* came from all corners of Colombia: Nariño, Cauca, and Tolima in the south; the Reyes family home department, Boyacá; even as far away as the Caribbean coastal provinces.[61] Indicative of the labor contracts was one he made with a Laguna Indian chief near the southern Colombian town of Pasto. Reyes needed five hundred Indians to carry quina down to Mocoa for shipment, and the chief agreed to deliver the workers in exchange for a specified commission per worker. After agreeing to broker the labor deal and receiving his advance, the chief got completely drunk, and Reyes feared that all was lost. But the chief honored the deal, and Reyes got his carriers.[62]

Over the next few years, the Compañía del Caquetá capitalized on the Amazonian trade route and exported most of the quina and imported most of the goods in and out of the Putumayo. The increasing volume of trade made necessary the building of a large warehouse in the Upper Putumayo by the late 1870s. A custom's house was added in 1881 after the Colombian government started to collect revenues and to regulate commerce.[63]

The steamboats plying the Putumayo created an ever greater demand for firewood to stoke their engines. Rafael depended on Indians to prepare this wood, often giving them metal axe heads, chickens, or fruit and vegetable seeds. He would then return two or three months later to repeat the exchange. In 1876 he made such an arrangement with the Cosacuntí Indians during his first steam-powered ascent of the Putumayo. The healthy and robust Cosacuntí numbered about five hundred and lived atop a pretty hill overlooking the river. They agreed to cut wood, and Reyes bid them a fond farewell, promising to return in three moons.

Upon arrival three months later, Reyes blew the boat's steam whistle, but no Cosacuntí came down to the riverside to greet him. In fact, the hill looked overgrown and eerily quiet. Reyes and a couple of sailors hiked up the hill to the village, knowing something was desperately wrong. A hundred meters away from the village, they were hit with a noxious odor and covered their noses and mouths with bandannas. As they walked closer, the stench became so thick that they could hardly breathe. Upon entering the chief's maloca, they found a Dantean scene of death: thirty or so decomposing bodies littered the ground. They found only two survivors, an emaciated mother with a baby clinging to her breast. Reyes believed that most of the Cosacuntí had died from "galloping consumption" (tuberculosis). Horrified, Reyes and his men carried the two survivors from the maloca and then burned all the structures with the bodies inside. Even if an adventurer or trader treated Indians well, as Reyes claimed he did, contagious and lethal diseases could, and did, annihilate entire tribes.[64]

The quina boom of the 1870s and early 1880s stimulated exploration, fostered Indian/white contact and exchange, and opened a remote corner of Amazonia to world commerce and modern transportation. Roads and paths connected the montaña to lowland river ports, and local officials oversaw growing administrations. The governments of Brazil, Colombia, Ecuador, and Peru awoke to the fiscal and geopolitical advantages of the Putumayo, foreshadowing inevitable international conflicts.

Quina prices dropped precipitously in the mid-1880s when British plantations in Asia offered tons of cheap quina on world markets. Clements Markham had managed some years earlier to collect chincona seed in Amazonia and shipped them to Kew Gardens for germination and later transplantation in Asia.[65] By 1884 Elías had fallen ill to heart disease in Cali, Rafael had married and fathered five children, and quina prices had collapsed, leading Rafael to pull out of his Putumayo operations.[66] Another civil war was brewing, and in this one Rafael would play a major role. Although the quina era was over, another was just beginning to bloom. The Reyes Brothers started exporting rubber in 1877 when international demand and prices seemed promising. Brother Enrique stayed on in the Putumayo, as did Benjamín Larraniaga, a worker who had accompanied Rafael on his initial exploration of the Putumayo. Rafael might be away, but the Reyes/Putumayo connection remained strong.[67] Now rubber offered opportunity and promise as the new tropical forest product, one which changed both the Putumayo and the world.

RUBBER

R emote regions and natural products emerged as essential compo-
nents in the new international economy of the late nineteenth and
early twentieth centuries as industrialization, modernization, and
urbanization changed life in much of the world. Scientific discoveries, technological breakthroughs, and backyard tinkerers added new and wondrous
machines to the industrial and consumer-oriented societies of Europe and
North America. Steam, electric, and internal-combustion engines revolutionized travel on land, water, and air. People could now travel great distances more economically and with greater ease, allowing intrepid explorers to "discover" the world's resources and then have them funneled to the
burgeoning centers of "progress." Rubber became one of the vital raw materials collected in tropical climes and shipped to the developing centers of
industry and capital.

Rubber in the Americas came to the attention of European explorers and
conquerors soon after their arrival in the 1490s. On his second voyage to
the Indies (1493–96), Christopher Columbus reported that the inhabitants
of western Santo Domingo (Haiti) played a game with a rubber ball that
amazingly bounced high into the air after it was thrown to the ground. After
the conquest of the Aztecs in the 1520s, murals revealed that the rulers of
central Mexico collected rubber as tribute from subject peoples and used
it in religious ceremonies. Subsequent European writers commented that
Indians used a flexible but durable substance on the soles of footwear and
on their hats and cloaks to protect them from soaking rains.

During the next three centuries, Europeans tinkered with rubber, using to good advantage its elastic and impermeable qualities to fashion waterproof footwear and clothing.[1] But rubber presented some problems, too. Its texture and elasticity changed with temperature: it became hard and brittle in the cold, and soft and tacky in the heat. During the first half of the nineteenth century, Europeans and Americans intensified their efforts to stabilize or "improve" rubber. Building on the earlier work of English, Scottish, and compatriot American inventors, Charles Goodyear in 1839 heated a solution of rubber, lead, and sulfur, stabilizing (or "vulcanizing") the rubber to retain its elasticity, strength, and utility. Ironically, although Goodyear helped open the way for thousands of new uses for rubber, and gained a U.S. patent for "Vulcanized Rubber" in 1844, he lived, worked, and died a poor man.[2]

The temperature-resistant, waterproof, elastic, and durable qualities of vulcanized rubber made it useful in numerous industrial and consumer goods. The "Iron Horse" railroad used rubber for car bumpers, for coach interiors, and for engine gaskets, hoses, and belts. Terrestrial and marine telegraph and telephone cables received a protective layer of rubber insulation after 1850. In the new factories, one found rubber on assembly lines and on floors, providing a safe, nonslick, and electrically insulated surface. Underground, rubber hoses pumped air, water, or gas in or out of mines to facilitate operations. For the average consumer, rubber on buggy and coach wheels softened the ride and protected rims; rubber boots and rain slickers screened fisherman, hunter, and pedestrian alike from the discomfort of rain, mud, and slime; at the growing number of spectator sports around the world, something made of rubber could be found among basketball, baseball, football, soccer, tennis, golf, and hot-air balloon enthusiasts and fans; among the burgeoning urban office staffs, women wore undergarments made with rubber and reached for rubber bands, erasers, and gloves; and, finally, for family planners, cheap and fairly reliable rubber condoms became available by mid-century.[3]

In addition to these other uses, tires and tubes for bicycles and automobiles dramatically catapulted both world rubber demand and its collection in Amazonia to new heights. Scottish tinkerers built a big-wheel bicycle in the 1830s, and five decades later, British inventors developed a chain-driven model with wheels of equal size. Durable but hard rubber tires covered their wheels until Samuel Dunlop "reinvented" the pneumatic tire in 1888, a design originally patented by the Scotsman R. W. Thompson in 1845.[4] With the modern bicycle astride softer tires with inflatable tubes, the 1890s experienced the first of many bicycle crazes. Consumers around the world sought the fun, freedom, and convenience of two-wheel drive, a trend that significantly increased world demand for rubber.[5] Cyclists successfully lobbied governments in Europe and the United States to improve their respective road systems, actions directly contributing to the next rubber-dependent transportation breakthrough, the automobile.

Some of the bicycle mechanics of the 1880s began to build carriages powered by steam, electric, or gasoline engines. By the mid-1890s, American tinkerers such as Charles and Frank Duryea and Ransom E. Olds built gas-powered cars, some rolling on pneumatic tires; within a decade, Olds was cranking out thousands of vehicles a year and became a millionaire. Beginning in 1908, Henry Ford's motor company started producing its inexpensive but dependable Model-T, a concept making the automobile available to millions of new consumers.[6] The automobile industry became one of the world's most complex enterprises, and rubber was a strategic product in its success. With the mass market for automobiles, trucks, and buses, tire and tube manufacturers consumed between 60 and 75 percent of all rubber produced.[7] Keeping with the spirit and trend of big business and industrial concentration of the era, five major tire and rubber companies emerged in the thirty years after 1870.[8]

North American rubber imports increased dramatically throughout the nineteenth century. Imports more than doubled during most decades after 1840: imports jumped from 260 to 615 tons between 1840 and 1850; by 1860 they reached 1,675 tons and climbed to 3,500 by 1870; imports ballooned to 8,109 tons in 1880 before reaching 15,336 by 1890. From 1875 to 1900, the U.S. market consumed about half of all rubber produced in the world.[9] The Amazonian rubber boom responded symbiotically to this robust market fueled by industrial growth in the United States during the late 1800s.

The scientific improvement and the industrial and consumer uses of rubber led to the "discovery" that Amazonian forests nurtured the greatest quantity and variety of wild rubber trees on the planet.[10] Once again, Amazonia's "strange vocation" for extractive industry — be it for gold, vegetable, ivory, forest dyes, drugs, lumber, slaves, quina, rubber, or petroleum — responded to world market demands.[11] The tonnage of Amazonian rubber exports reflected the importance of rubber to the industrializing world. Exports increased by a factor of 160 from 1830 to 1900 (from 156 to 25,000 metric tons): metric ton rubber exports quadrupled each decade between 1840 and 1900.[12]

Large-scale rubber collection began in eastern Amazonia near the Brazilian port city of Pará and then expanded west. Rubber collection and Amazonia's integration into the world economy profoundly changed the basin: hundreds of thousands of migrants poured in from impoverished northeastern Brazil after a horrible drought in 1877; other immigrants from around the world helped push the basin's estimated non-Indian population from 250,000 in

1853, to 380,000 in 1890, to about a million by 1910; markets distorted or supplanted subsistence economies, while new technologies and products opened regions and native peoples to other worlds, often to their detriment.[13]

The rubber industry did introduce fundamental social, economic, and cultural transformations into Amazonia, but not in a uniform, rational, or capitalist fashion.[14] For example, Manaus, the upriver boom city par excellence at the confluence of the Amazon and Negro Rivers, remained a small, undignified town as late as 1866. Elizabeth Cabot Carey Agassiz, accompanying her famous husband, Louis, on a scientific expedition, noted Manaus's humble environment but foresaw its future as a center of commerce and navigation.[15] Indeed, Mrs. Agassiz had a prescient eye; within thirty years Manaus boasted heavy commercial traffic, one of the most expensive costs of living on the planet, some of the best public services in all of Brazil, and a world-famous, two-million-dollar opera house.[16]

Transportation revolutions and new technologies not only created unprecedented demand for rubber, but also proved crucial in opening the Amazon to international trade. Steam-powered launches revolutionized travel and commerce throughout much of Amazonia. Prior to machine-driven propulsion, travelers and merchants relied on the wind and their muscle, setting sails, paddling canoes, or poling rafts to move themselves and their goods along the riverbanks. Now, on board steamboats, more people and more goods ascended and descended hundreds of Amazonian rivers in less time and at a cheaper rate.

A rich Brazilian businessman established the first Amazonian steamship company. In 1853, the Barão de Mauá began operations of his Navegação e Comércio do Amazonas with eight steamships serving six different lines, one going as far west as the Peruvian border. In the 1860s, two other Brazilian shipping lines entered into competition with the Barão's company, each of them exporting forest products such as quina and rubber, and returning with tons of imported goods.[17]

Foreign governments and businessmen noted the importance of steamship service and the rubber trade and began to lobby Imperial Brazil to open the Amazon to international shipping. By 1866, pressure from the United States, France, and Britain elicited the desired action from Rio de Janeiro. Within a very few years, British steamship companies dominated transport services on the Amazon.[18] A British firm entered into competition with the three existing Brazilian lines in 1872, and a scant two years later incorporated them into the British-owned Amazon Steam Company. This company dominated trans-Atlantic shipping of rubber for the next forty years and became a highly visible symbol of foreign penetration into Amazonia.[19]

By 1876, the ocean-going *SS Amazonas* steamed directly from London to Manaus, and on its return trip it literally carried the seeds of the future downfall of the Amazonian rubber boom. On board the *Amazonas*, Henry Wickham transported thousands of rubber tree seeds that became the germ of the huge Asian rubber plantations developed over the next decades.[20] The dialectic of transportation and technological revolutions alternately creating and then destroying a boom economy in Amazonia would not be fully understood for some time. In the meanwhile, more steamships plied Amazonian waters. By 1882, the Amazon Steam Company offered direct service of a one-thousand-ton ship between New York and Manaus, a sweetheart deal subsidized by the Brazilian government and one that helped shift the center of the rubber industry westward.[21] Smaller boats and launches, many of them based in Iquitos, steamed through the shallower headwaters of northwestern Amazonia.

A number of different rubber-bearing trees grew throughout the Putumayo. Various species of *Sapium* flourished in the temperate climes of the Upper Putumayo and yielded a latex called *caucho blanco*. Two *Castilloa* (*Castilla*) species, *Castilloa ulei* and *Castilloa elastica*, grew alongside *Sapium* but also adapted well to hotter regions of the Middle and Lower Putumayo; the plentiful *Castilloa* produced a rubber called *caucho negro*. *Hevea brasiliensis*, which produced the finest rubber in all Amazonia, called *jebe fino* or *siringa fina*, existed in great quantity in Brazil but was confined to the far southeastern corner of the Putumayo. Its relative *Hevea guianensis*, however, could be found in the Middle and Lower Putumayo and relinquished a lower-grade jebe, called "jebe débil."[22]

Caucho and jebe were the two most important varieties of Amazonian rubber exports, but they were often found in different soils, and their latex was extracted in distinctive manners. *Hevea* and *Castilloa* trees could be found close to one another, but it was unusual to find *Castilloas* in low-lying flooded areas, conditions *Heveas* could stand. Therefore, *Castilloas* could be exploited almost all year, for they grew above flooded areas; on the other hand, *Heveas* could only be tapped about six months of the year because the rainy season and flooding disrupted operations. Another crucial difference between them centered on extraction methods: jebe latex flowed down a series of shallow incisions cut into the *Hevea* bark, and a tapper collected this rubber over a period of years without severely damaging the tree; conversely, caucho latex could not be tapped because the *Castilloas* yielded little latex, and incisions often invited lethal fungi, so the tree was drained of all its latex at one time. Deep cuts in the trunk, branches, and roots of the *Castilloas* exposed a great quantity of rubber, but also killed the tree in the process.[23]

These different extraction methods dictated radically different work regimens. The *Hevea* tapper established a sedentary operation, cutting a path, or *estrada,* through the rain forest to the two hundred or so trees along his route. Once established, the tapper built a simple hut, cleared land for a garden, and tended half of his rubber trees each day. The tapper might live alone or, if he were lucky, with family members who helped with chores and provided welcome company. The life of the *seringuero* was not an easy one; diseases, harsh weather, poor diet, and insect pests dogged seringueros, as did poverty, for most of the tappers owed debts to *aviadores,* the middleman traders who exchanged essential goods (food, tools, clothing) for the seringuero's rubber. Although the *Hevea* tappers usually experienced hardships, their lives were contained and defined by the estradas they worked.

Whereas the seringuero was likened to a simple conservative farmer, the *caucheros* reminded contemporary observers of courageous and footloose miners. Like the seringueros, the caucheros entered the thick jungle to find rubber trees, but the necessity of bleeding the *Castilloa* trees dry meant that the caucheros' search for more rubber required them to lead a seminomadic life. The sedentary regime of the rubber-tapping seringuero was impossible for the cauchero. If he were lucky, the cauchero might find an area relatively thick with *Castilloas,* allowing him to stay put for awhile before moving on once the area was fully exploited. The mobility necessary for caucho collection resulted in a less stable lifestyle, one that proved highly disruptive for the caucheros, the environment, and Amerindians alike.[24]

The quality of the jebe and caucho latex, and the process by which it was cured, decided its market value in Amazonian ports such as Iquitos, Manaus, and Pará, and in international rubber markets. In general, good-quality latex, the finest being jebe fino drawn from *Hevea brasiliensis,* coagulated and cured by a smoking process and free of most impurities brought the highest prices. Less-valued species, such as *Hevea guianensis,* or latex only partially cured and holding high amounts of moisture or impurities (jebe débil) brought a lower price. Caucho generally was cheaper than jebe, but a well-smoked caucho ball sold for a higher price than did dirty or adulterated jebe. A final category for both caucho and jebe carried the name, *sernambí.* Coagulating naturally on the trunk of the tree, it was only washed or soaped clean and therefore, lacked the inevitable impurities — sticks, sand, nonrubber latexes — found in cured rubber. Consequently, it fetched a relatively high price.[25]

Peripatetic Colombian caucheros began focusing their energies on the Putumayo's *Castilloa* trees in the 1870s. Whereas a tapped *Hevea* yielded 5 to 7 pounds (3 kilos) of dry rubber annually, a large, one-hundred-foot-tall *Cas-*

tilloa might grant 200 pounds (90 kilos) of caucho in just two days. A seringuero could collect about 1,000 pounds (450 kilos) from his estrada annually; two caucheros could collect the same amount of caucho in one month.[26] True, jebe demanded a better price in Iquitos, the primary market for Putumayan rubber, but caucheros could collect an enormous quantity of caucho, which encouraged a "bonanza" mentality among men who dreamed of enriching themselves. Caucheros in the Putumayo only shifted their focus to *Hevea* tapping in the 1890s, after they had exhausted most of the *Castilloas*.[27]

The collection of caucho, like that of quina, followed the quintessential and durable Amazonian extractive pattern: plunder the rain forest as quickly as possible regardless of resource destruction. As early as 1874, the U.S. consul in Buenaventura reported that rubber and quina exports had declined along the Colombian Pacific Coast because extraction of these products involved killing the trees.[28] By the mid-1880s, Colombian officials in Caquetá, Popayán, and Bogotá all expressed concern about the destruction of rubber trees. Officials recommended that the state oversee the industry, introduce missionaries to improve the social and moral atmosphere, and commence a program to plant rubber trees and replenish depleted forests.[29] By 1894, the Ecuadorian Senate also discussed a law to regulate caucho and quina collection in its national forests to prohibit the felling of immature trees and to teach and enforce proper tapping methods. The Senate tabled the proposal, however, because Ecuador shared a problem with its northern neighbor: neither country had the fiscal resources or the manpower to rationalize and manage rubber extraction.[30]

The Putumayo's plentiful rubber trees offered only one strong attraction to ambitious caucheros during the late nineteenth century. The region's potential labor force, drawn from the large indigenous population, had brought *conquistadores,* slave raiders, merchants, and missionaries for centuries. Prior to Rafael Reyes's much-vaunted descent and exploration of the Putumayo in the 1870s, public officials and private individuals had profited from Indian labor and trade. Tomás Jaramillo, for example, had contacted, congregated, and traded with Boras for twenty years prior to his 1868 request of the Cauca governor for three hundred metal axes to introduce other Bora clans to "civilization and commerce." Jaramillo had managed to attract the Bora to the banks of the Caquetá and needed the axes to keep them there. Caquetá prefect Pedro F. Urrutia forwarded Jaramillo's request to Popayán, but Tomás died a few months later, and the Boras dispersed.[31] Less than a year later, Urrutia reported that another Colombian had contacted a Huitoto tribe between the Putumayo and Caquetá Rivers, the Jurama, a people numbering eight hundred individuals. Urrutia claimed that the Jurama, like the Bora, were a peaceful Stone Age tribe, and he repeated his pitch to the Colombian state and national governments to send goods, presumably metal axes, to assist in introducing the Jurama to a stable and productive life.[32]

North and South Americans alike were trading with Amazonians on the eve of the rubber boom in the late 1860s. On the southern edge of the Putumayo region, James Orton reported that Huitotos carried on a thriving trade in jungle potions and poisons, hammocks, and provisions. He noted that commerce could be dangerous for whites and disruptive for Indians — "Anguteros" or "Putumayos" had killed several trespassing sarsaparilla collectors — and that he saw only twenty-five people along a lengthy stretch of the Napo River, suggesting that the Indians had fled from the riverine highway.[33] About the same time, Orton's American compatriot John Howxuell (Howell) imported a bundle of surplus U.S. Civil War cavalry lances for future exchanges with Napo tribes. The Peruvian government took a dim view of Howell's enterprise, citing "the danger of supplying savages with weapons," and ordered the lances reexported at Howell's expense.[34]

Rafael Reyes, Benjamín Larraniaga, Crisóstomo Hernández, and Julio César Arana emerged as the central quaternary of Putumayo conquerors at the turn of the twentieth century. By 1877, Reyes, credited with introducing steamships on the river, had various tribes collecting rubber and cutting firewood to help fuel the family fortune.[35] Reyes's bushwacker and ex-employee Benjamín Larraniaga stayed in the Putumayo after his boss's exit and became an important and rich cauchero by 1900. Huitoto oral history recalls that Larraniaga and Arana brought "things of necessity" — including axes, hammocks, and matches — which the Huitoto acquired either by collecting rubber or by trading women.[36] Arana absorbed his Colombian partner Larraniaga during the first decade of the new century and made the Putumayo his personal and infamous domain. Perhaps most interesting, however, is the story of Crisóstomo Hernández, a Colombian mulatto who became a murky and controversial figure, living for several years among Indian tribes of the Middle Putumayo.

Information about Crisóstomo is sketchy at best. Roger Casement, who conducted the British investigation of the Putumayo scandals, was told that Crisóstomo conquered areas of the Putumayo in the early 1880s. Casement, bothered by the connotation of "conquistadores," assumed that Hernández was just another abusive filibuster injuring innocent Indians and reasoned accordingly: "That these wild Indians welcomed the coming into their country of Hernández, Larrañaga, and other Colombians who succeeded the earliest of these modern 'conquistadores,' it would be absurd to assert."[37] The Irishman Casement had clearly learned his "black legend" lessons — that the Spanish and their Spanish-American descendants were particularly adept and cruel at exploiting and slaughtering Indians — and Crisóstomo fit nicely into Casement's colonial ideology.

A much different interpretation of Crisóstomo and his relations with Putumayans emerges from the oral history told by Aquileo Tobar. Tobar's mother was a Huitoto, his father a white employee of the Casa Arana. He grew up in the 1920s in El Encanto, speaking both Spanish and a Huitoto dialect, Bué. Aquileo's father told his son a myth-history of Crisóstomo, one cleansed of violence, pain, even disease, but one probably no more skewed than Casement's.[38]

Aquileo was told that Crisóstomo worked as a cauchero near Florencia in southern Colombia, where he killed a fellow worker during a drunken dispute and then fled to avoid imprisonment. After floating down the Caquetá on a simple raft, he saw above the forest canopy the thatched roofs of a village. Driven by hunger, he trekked towards the village but was confronted by four Carijonas, who froze with fright at seeing him. After a few minutes, he was taken to an elder who decided that Crisóstomo was a refugee from his people, an orphan without a home, a harmless visitor. Over a period of time he learned the language and customs of the Carijona, and he was honored with a wife. Unfortunately, Crisóstomo took a fancy to another unavailable woman, and the illicit couple fled the village.[39]

Crisóstomo continued his journey with his Carijona partner, and following six long and hot days of travel, the couple came upon a Huitoto village. This meeting, like the one with the Carijona, created initial tensions and questions: Was this black creature a person? Were the Huitoto savage cannibals? Who were the victims? the aggressors? the humans? the spirits? After studying Crisóstomo's behavior and admiring his iron axe, machete, and shotgun, a Huitoto cacique stated:

Our history says that on the edges of the world exist inhabitants of white color and of black color. These people have come and arrived among us and therefore they are identical to us. Don't you see? His face, hands, legs, nose, eyes and mouth, teeth, his gait are the same as ours. They are our brothers from other worlds. God made many peoples on the other side of the sea; therefore, we don't have to abhor or hate him, but serve him in every way. We have to take him to our houses and care for him well. None of you will be rude with the white man. Only his color is black, but he is of the white world.[40]

Troubled by guilt, suspicion, and nightmares, Crisóstomo again decided to move along, but this time two hundred Huitotos accompanied him on his march into the jungle. Upon arrival at a large village, Crisóstomo met the town

elders, who were preparing for a large fiesta. The Huitotos included Crisóstomo in their process of renewing myth, history, and culture. Becoming a Huitoto in this new physical and ritual environment, he was no longer a wanderer,
an outcast, an orphan. The Huitoto gave him some land, another wife, and a
house, while Crisóstomo began to fish, hunt, and clear land for a garden.[41]

After a four-year residence, Crisóstomo told the Huitoto chief Iferenanvique that he was restless and wanted to visit his friends in the white world. He
mentioned that he could not return empty-handed, and so the accommodating
chief asked him what he wanted. Crisóstomo raised his arm above his head
and marked out a space three meters long to be filled with rubber. In three
months, Iferenanvique oversaw the operation of collecting the rubber, building canoes, and drafting men to paddle the heavily laden dugouts upstream
toward Florencia. Crisóstomo promised that he would return with gifts in
exchange for the rubber.

As promised, Crisóstomo returned to the Huitoto with a mountain of magical gifts: clothes and cloth; metal axes, knives, machetes, and shotguns just like
his own; mirrors, needles, beads, pots, combs, salt, and cane liquor. Initially,
Iferenanvique feared the magic and power of the new goods and would not acknowledge Crisóstomo. Mindful of etiquette and hierarchy, Crisóstomo told
the chief that the goods were his to distribute, but the cautious Iferenanvique
shared some of the responsibility of distributing the goods with Crisóstomo
and said, "In this case you are our chief; please open the packages for us, for
now you will make the work orders and I will order my people to carry them
out."[42] This was a remarkable statement. The Huitoto, like the Carijona, had
included and acculturated this Colombian mulatto and his magical goods into
their society. The strong-willed and powerful Crisóstomo found an honored
place in this society and increased his power and prestige within it by introducing revolutionary goods on the eve of the rubber boom. Crisóstomo's relationship with the Huitoto, according to Aquileo Tobar, found expression through
material and cultural exchange rather than through a physical or military
conquest.[43]

Most of Aquileo's oral account reads like a "white legend" diametrically
opposed to Casement's or Hardenburg's "black legend" packaging of white/
Indian relations. His myth/history closes with a pacific scene: a few whites
peacefully and justly lived among the Indians; those people who so desired
collected rubber; babies didn't die, sickness didn't prevail, and young bronze-
skinned couples enjoyed their nude innocence in the luxuriant forest.[44]

Other Huitoto, Bora, Nonuya, and Andoke oral histories relate the multiple
consequences associated with white commerce. The Andokes recall a time last
century when whites steamed up the Caquetá in a launch loaded with food

and merchandise. The Andokes boarded the vessel after the whites tempted them with delicious fruit. But once on board, they recognized their mistake; the creatures on the vessel weren't white men, but fearful and deadly *bufeos,* or fresh-water dolphins. To their horror, the launch dipped below the water, and the Andokes lost their lives. The bufeos, adept sexual seducers of both men and women, as well as being messengers of disease, took many Andoke victims.[45] The Andokes learned and remembered that white trade could also bring death.

White goods not only revolutionized the material culture of Putumayans but altered their spiritual world as well. The metal axe represented much more than a tool: it was many entities with many faces. It could be a nurturing life source for those who could control its power; it could also become the dark and threatening "Tiger Axe" or the "Merchandise Jaguar" or the "Fearful Axe" to those fearful or aware that they would be traded or enslaved in exchange for this metal spirit. All goods, including the axe, held the potential for both creation and destruction.

The white traders, moreover, possessed the consuming powers of hungry tigers or jaguars, or even the spirit of a cannibalistic shaman, craving not only riches but also Indian flesh and blood. They could take on many forms and could overpower indigenous leaders. Decades later the Bora sang the lyrics to a song as they danced and remembered the hungry spirit who came upriver:

Today it's the same thing
Always from the East
The spirit of the jaguars comes eating
And it scared the peoples of the tribes
But here no more, here no more
Because our people ate
The spirit of the jaguars.[46]

The Bora and some other caciques could deal with the white traders by turning themselves into jaguars in order to treat with whites on equal terms. Others, however, could not control the "Spirit of the Axe" and either avoided trade or resigned themselves to poverty and failure, which allowed new Indian leaders to broker the material and spiritual terms of white trade.[47]

Huitoto oral tradition recounts the dangers that a leader faced by trading with whites. The Carpintero clan remembers Brazilians being the first whites to trade up the Caquetá. As a leader of "tradition, origin, and culture," Maka-paamine allowed the Brazilians to live alongside his maloca, and the Carpin-teros began to collect forest products in exchange for axes and other goods.

Indian captains from surrounding villages came to inspect the whites and their goods, but then things turned bad. Some Brazilians began to abuse the Indians, stealing goods and raping women. Makapaamine attempted to establish rules of comportment for the whites, but the other captains questioned whether he had the authority to do so. Makapaamine noted the "bad violence" brought by the Brazilians and ordered that they be attacked and driven away, and that their goods be seized. According to one Huitoto analyst, the problem centered on a lack of communication and comprehension: "Because neither of the two peoples understood the other's language, the solution was death."[48]

More violence followed. The other captains claimed that Makapaamine was responsible for the bad turn of events. They wanted trade reopened with the Brazilians, for they saw them as their sons. Jealous of Makapaamine's power, and angry at the interruption in trade, the captains resolved that Makapaamine must die. But killing the powerful man would be no easy task. He was a leader of great power and prestige, and he possessed red and blue crystals through which he could foresee the future. The challengers stole his crystals to deprive him of his spiritual eyes, and blinded through their deceit, Makapaamine was assassinated by his carbine-wielding bodyguard. Thereafter, the captains reopened trade with the whites and decentralized political power. Now, no captain could ignore the maloca counsel and "do just what he wanted," even if he were a leader of "tradition, origin, and culture." In this case, trade offered opportunities to new leaders who made the maloca more representative.[49] But Makapaamine paid with his life, having failed to foresee the troubles and consequences of white trade.

The rubber industry and international trade altered indigenous societies while restructuring the political economy of northwestern Amazonia. The development of Iquitos, the largest port in the region, illustrates how steamships and the rubber industry fundamentally altered social, political, and economic realities.

In 1840, Iquitos Indians and their white *patrón* resettled Iquitos near the confluence of the Nanay and Amazon Rivers, a site initially founded a century earlier by Jesuits. One year later, survivors of a Huambisa attack on Borja fled to the small village.[50] By the 1850s, the three hundred or so residents of Iquitos received political and military authorities for the province of Loreto, but the capital of this sprawling territory was in Moyobamba, not Iquitos. Indians and poor mestizos comprised 80 percent of the village's population, one dominated by a white elite. Cane and mud-walled houses covered with thatched roofs fronted the grassy streets of this village, one reputed to have an unusually healthy climate. Commenting on the moral climate, however, one Victorian

Table 1. Commercial Traffic in Loreto, 1854–70
(in Peruvian soles)

Year	Imports	Exports	Total
1854	350	74,907	75,257
1856	21,000	180,848	201,838
1858	49,350	246,775	295,775
1860	150,000	159,889	309,889
1862	100,000	120,388	270,088
1864	126,922	274,754	401,676
1866	303,292	238,394	541,687
1868	190,726	276,747	467,473
1870	617,065	508,106	1,120,171

Source: "Estado commercial de la región peruana del Amazonas el año 1872 por don José Fermín Herrera," in Larrabure i Correa, Colección de leyes, 16:137–38.

observer noted that, "Sodom would shine alongside of Iquitos in point of morality and temperance."[51]

Steamboats, steam-powered machine shops, and a naval factory brought rapid growth to Iquitos starting in 1864. English steamboats arrived that year to replace two American vessels lost in the 1850s. The Peruvian navy and a British company established the naval shipyard, floating docks, and a manufacturing center, one boasting an ironworks, a brickyard, a steam-powered sawmill, and machine, metal, and wood shops. Thirty British workers won the contracts from the Peruvian government to construct this impressive port and industrial center, and to initiate their operations. Over the next fifteen years, these new facilities stimulated construction of both boats and housing for the navy and local entrepreneurs. Little Iquitos was becoming a town, but one still subject to setbacks: in 1865, Independence Day fireworks started a blaze that destroyed most of the town, and another one roared through town in 1872.[52]

Commerce and trade in Iquitos and in the department of Loreto in general increased dramatically after the arrival of steamboats. Loreto had long exported forest products downriver to Brazil, but by the mid-1860s, ships steamed upriver to introduce an unprecedented amount of imports. Food, spirits, wine, beer, cloth, shoes, guns, and tools flooded in and occasionally surpassed the value of Loreto's exports (see table 1). Backwater Iquitos now played an active role in international trade.

Prior to the 1870s, hand-woven straw hats comprised the biggest export earner for Loreto. This cottage industry employed almost one-third of the economically active population and annually produced about 100,000 high-quality "Panama" hats for markets in both the southern and northern Atlantic. Surprisingly, Loreto had the largest percentage of artisans (31 percent) in all of Peru according to the 1876 census, far outdistancing Cuzco (10.5 percent), Lambayeque (16.2 percent), and Piura (24.4 percent).[53] Unfortunately, machines and mass markets in distant lands undercut Loreto's hatmakers, which included many women. When cheaper machine-produced felt hats became the fashion rage in Europe and the United States in the 1870s, the price of a dozen straw hats dropped from forty to fifteen dollars.[54]

The seventies marked a decade of transition for the economy of Loreto and Iquitos. As early as 1872, a local writer noted the decline of hat exports and the rise of rubber. Loreto's rubber exports totaled only 2,088 kilos in 1862 but jumped to 58,584 kilos by 1870.[55] The optimism surrounding the future of rubber, however, confronted the realities of economic hard times during the decade. The world financial panic of the 1870s coincided with a drop in Peru's export receipts as the guano industry declined. The Peruvian government could no longer afford to subsidize Loreto's political and economic growth, nor even guarantee payment for Loreto's administrative expenses.[56] By 1877, the economic crisis was so deep that the Peruvian government sold the ships, docks, and riverfront shops in Iquitos to a group of private businessmen.[57] It seemed that Peru's economy and Loreto's administration were disintegrating just when rubber offered such promise.

Indeed, Peru did disintegrate between 1879 and 1883, fighting a disastrous war with Chile. In the War of the Pacific, Peru and Bolivia battled Chile for control of the rich nitrate fields of the coastal Atacama Desert.[58] Initially, a group of Loretano volunteers rallied in Moyobamba and readied themselves for the arduous trans-Andean march to Lima, via Chachapoyas, Cajamarca, and Trujillo. By July 1879, this 125-man force received financial compensation from Lima for its long trek en route to fight the Chileans.[59] Although these so-called Volunteers of Loreto demonstrated an impressive dedication to the nation, Loreto's connection to the central government dissolved once Chilean forces fought their way up the coast into Lima and took control of key areas of the Peruvian Andes. In a very real sense, an independent Loreto rode out the war and most of the 1880s on a wave of rubber exports.[60]

Two years after the war began, Loretanos took control of local affairs. With the coast engulfed in the war, many highland dwellers looked east to Amazonia for economic opportunities. Deserters from both the Peruvian and Chilean armies found safe haven in the tropical lowlands and freelanced as bandits or became caucheros.[61] Cut off from Lima by the war, yet tightly connected to world commerce, several Loretanos simultaneously took charge of the department's administrative vacuum in the midst of an export and import boom.

Table 2. Peruvian Rubber Exports, 1880–90
(metric tons)

1880	84	1886	1,228
1881	95	1887	828
1882	151	1888	2,045
1883	155	1889	1,177
1884	541	1890	1,164
1885	1,041		

Source: Thorp and Bertram, *Peru, 1890–1977: Growth and Policy in an Open Economy,* 330.

From 1881 to 1887, various unauthorized custom houses popped up around the department, each with its own colonel, commander general, or prefect. Appointed and self-declared officials in Moyobamba, Iquitos, and San Antonio collected export tariffs on rubber, with each official insisting that he was the rightful authority in the department. Some of them could justify these claims, having been appointed by one of the various presidential pretenders in Peru at the time. Indeed, the war had a strong centrifugal force on Loreto and on the country; revolts, disorder, discord, and sedition became the norm in the early 1880s.[62]

In 1883, competing prefects Tadeo Terry in Iquitos and David Arévalo Villacis in Moyobamba squared off against one another, each naming his respective supporters to lesser posts and threatening civil war. Terry pledged to use customs money to buy arms and ammunition and to impose his will on all of Loreto, a threat that Arévalo swiftly called to Lima's attention. Both men allegedly exceeded their authority, did what they wished, and personally profited from their control of their respective custom houses.[63] The war certainly disrupted Loreto's administrative structure, as well as communications with Lima, yet rubber exports furnished new financial and political opportunities. Rubber collection boomed in the 1880s (see table 2), and each administrator reaped a bounty of money and men by charging unauthorized export duties.

The residents of Iquitos did not stand idly by as Prefect Terry dictated rules, set export duties, and attempted to consolidate his political power. Around Christmas 1883, these *vecinos* took exception to Terry's decrees and declared his customs house illegal. They complained that the town had no cemetery, church, jail, municipal buildings, or schools, and that parents had to send their children abroad for even a primary education. Where then, except into the pockets of Terry and his cronies, was the customs money going? The vecinos tacitly accepted the customs house but declared that all duties were "voluntary" and that the money collected should be spent on developing vital municipal services. Following an ancient Spanish tradition, the vecinos, presumably including merchants and rubber traders, took charge of their own local government. They even established a 7.5 percent ad valorem tax on imports, a measure suggesting that Iquitos enjoyed heavy commercial traffic.[64]

Loreto's administrative difficulties dragged on until at least 1886. Two to three prefects still competed for power, dipped their hands into customs revenues, trafficked in rubber and imported goods, and perpetuated the general sense of insecurity and illegitimacy. An inspector sent to Loreto from Lima, Timoteo Smith, commented on this administrative uncertainty and the anarchy engendered by the war with Chile. Smith noted that at least two thousand families had emigrated from the vicinity of Moyobamba to seek subsistence jobs downriver on the Amazon, thus highlighting the misery and prostration affecting Loreto.[65] Smith correctly reported on the pain, poverty, and abuse of authority notable around Moyobamba, but he missed something very important: downriver near Iquitos, rubber collection offered both real and perceived opportunities for families and individual caucheros. The regional economy boomed and attracted laborers from far afield. The political economy supported not one, but three departmental governments, suggesting that rubber exports offered tangible rewards for some Loretanos at a time of general crisis in much of the rest of Peru.

Cane liquor producers and salesmen, for example, did quite well in the 1880s, as thousands of thirsty caucheros crowded into the lower Huallaga Valley. A Tarapoto city official, Pedro Estrella, reported that thirteen distilleries operated in the area, producing *aguardiente* for four soles a jug, and selling it for three times as much. Estrella noted that local caucheros loyally consumed a healthy amount of spirits and stimulated local liquor manufacturing. But he did complain that they resisted paying the duty on liquor, part of a larger popular tax revolt originally sparked when Iquiteño officials began charging export duties on rubber. Estrella needed the liquor tax to pay for municipal expenses, and he blamed Iquitos for prompting the local tax resistance.[66] Meanwhile, in Iquitos, liquor also played an important part in the rubber economy. Traders bartered liquor for rubber with both caucheros and Indians. The aguardiente clouded judgment, however, permitting these traders, or *regatones,* to cheat or to steal rubber from clients.[67]

Liquor, rubber, imports, exports, taxes, and politics all seemed to revolve around Iquitos after 1880. Geography helped make Iquitos the premier commercial center of northwestern Amazonia: ocean-going steamboats could call at Iquitos and collect rubber flowing out of the Caquetá, Putumayo, Napo,

Huallaga, and Ucayali river systems. The department capital in Moyobamba, located on a luxuriant plain 2,700 feet above sea level, was better situated for Andean commercial exchanges at a time when the rubber industry shifted the focus of the economy to the Amazonian lowlands and eastward toward Brazil and the Atlantic. By the mid-1880s, Iquitos supplied all the department's legal revenues and handled most of the registered regional and international trade. In 1883, the naval shipyards and docks reverted to government control, and nearly forty steamers called at Iquitos by 1884.[68] Thirteen commercial houses carried most of this trade, nine of them foreign owned. British, French, and American imports filled store shelves and helped contribute to the city's municipal growth.[69]

The increasing commercial and fiscal importance of Iquitos naturally added to the city's political clout. By 1893, Loreto prefect Alejandro Rivera suggested that the department's capital be moved from Moyobamba to Iquitos. Rivera spent most of his time overseeing the customs house in Iquitos, while the other members of the governing committee, the *junta departamental*, resided and met in Moyobamba. The junta could meet in Rivera's absence but could make no controversial or firm decisions without him.[70] From a village of two hundred in 1850, to a town of two thousand in 1880, to a city of fourteen thousand only twenty years later, Iquitos gained the size and power to warrant being named the capital. More proposals surfaced throughout the 1890s similar to Rivera's, and in 1898 Iquitos became the capital of Loreto.[71]

The career of the first president of the Iquitos junta departamental, Julio César Arana, is emblematic of the major social, economic, and political changes introduced into northwestern Amazonia by the rubber boom after the War of the Pacific. Little Julio started life in Rioja, a town in the Peruvian montaña neighboring Moyobamba. As did most of Rioja's middle-class families, Julio's father, Martín, supported his clan in the hat trade. From his home on the town square, the serious and reserved Julio began to learn the family business at age nine. Five years later, he was already trading and selling fine Panamas up the mountain in Chachapoyas and Cajamarca.[72] With the outbreak of the war with Chile in 1879, Julio tried to enlist in the army, but Martín withheld permission and instead sent his son to Cajamarca to work as a secretary. There he learned business administration and bookkeeping. As an adolescent and adult, Julio impressed people with his relentless drive to work, achieve, and prosper.[73]

In 1881, Arana began his career as an Amazonian tradesman, hawking hats and other goods to the burgeoning number of caucheros. The seventeen-year-old businessman usually bartered his goods for rubber with both white and Indian customers. His adventures during the early 1880s to faraway Brazilian rivers — including the Juruá, Yavari, Purús, and even the Acre — involved great hardship but also netted profits of up to 400 percent.[74] Julio initially established a trading post in Yurimaguas, and then in 1888 he opened a new one with his brother-in-law, Pablo Zumaeta, in Tarapoto. It seems that Julio was also pursuing a romantic interest, for he married his sweetheart, Eleonora, in Tarapoto the same year.[75]

Arana and Zumaeta expanded their mercantile pursuits and established a rubber-collecting business the following year. They bought some rubber estradas near Yurimaguas and then traveled thousands of miles to recruit twenty *peones* in the desperately poor state of Ceará in northeast Brazil. Far from home, these Brazilians amassed a large debt from the passage and goods supplied to them by their new patrons. Like many other indebted caucheros, they never seemed able to erase the red ink in Arana's account books. With these peons hard at work, Julio then moved his business headquarters to boomtown Iquitos.[76] Iquiteños took note of their new neighbor and recalled when he went off to the Yavari River on the Peruvian/Brazilian border: Arana left Iquitos one night, and two or three years later he reappeared "with a sunburned face and calloused hands but with a fat pocketbook."[77] This tireless and audacious worker, this Amazonian Horatio Alger, was earning his place in the folklore and business structure of the rubber industry.

Arana's next big move, one which Rafael Reyes had initiated twenty years earlier, involved a partnership with a powerful foreigner. The Frenchman Charles Mourraille had been a member of the private consortium that owned the boats and port facilities of Iquitos from 1877 to 1883. By 1892, Mourraille held positions as the president of the Chamber of Commerce, a merchant banker, and a prosperous importer of goods from Brazil and Europe. Arana, along with his Colombian partner Juan B. Vega, collected vast amounts of rubber from peons along the Río Yavari and then sold it to Mourraille. Arana was such a shrewd rubber collector, trader, and speculator that he bought out his French partner Mourraille within four years. The thirty-two-year-old Julio moved his family into a ten-room Iquitos house in 1896. This former hat hawker now oversaw businesses in rubber collecting and exporting, in importing, and in banking. He could call on a forty thousand pound sterling credit line from large foreign firms in Iquitos. His new firm, J. C. Arana y Hermanos, was the only one operating in various regions, and it could tap into commercial connections in Manaus, Lisbon, London, and New York.[78]

The great expansion of world rubber demand created by the scientific, transportation, industrial, and consumer breakthroughs of the nineteenth century directly changed life in northwestern Amazonia. Steamboats plied many rivers, bringing with them tons of new imports. The changing material culture and economy altered the cultural, religious, and political structures of many Indian peoples, some groups adapting better than others, while simultaneously they attracted thousands of non-Amazonian migrants from the Andes and from Brazil. Loreto weathered the crisis of the War of the Pacific on the unprecedented opportunities — mainly financial and political — offered by the rubber industry. Iquitos became the commercial center of the region and the home to ambitious men like Julio César Arana. But obstacles remained for entrepreneurs and assorted scoundrels hoping to make a fortune: rubber trees abounded and many regions had access to markets, but the scarcity of labor thwarted many get-rich-quick schemes. Arana ventured all the way to Ceará for twenty peons in 1889. Other systems needed development to cope with the labor problem. In the Putumayo, Indian labor became the indispensable component to ground the region to the international economy.

THREE

LABOR

In both history and myth, the Putumayo scandal is part of the unholy triangle of colonial exploitation of Amazonia. The criminal exploits of Lope de Aguirre, the rampaging expeditions of the Brazilian bandeirantes, and the infamous Putumayo scandal combine to represent the destruction wrought on Amazonia from the outside world. In comparative terms, one modern author argued that the horrors in the Putumayo eclipsed the "half-hearted and piecemeal" depredations of the bandeirantes and set new but terribly inhumane standards for white exploitation of Amazonians.[1] Strangely, it seems that history regresses and progress destroys in South America's vast rain forest. Abusive gold miners obliterate Yanomani culture; cholera spreads down the Andes and threatens the Ticuna; ranchers attack and murder rubber gatherers in the Acre — and not just in past epochs, centuries, or decades, but today in the 1990s.

What explains this persistent exploitation of Amazonian resources and its people? Part of the answer revolves around cultural patterns brought to America by Europeans. Throughout the hemisphere, the myths of golden El Dorado and cinnamon-rich La Canela, of beautiful and able female Amazon warriors and the fountain of youth, lured conquerors and explorers to remote places.[2] Amazonia conjured images of riches, of paradise, a land of succulent fruit and gold-bearing streams beckoning to audacious and fearless men. It offered millions of acres of seemingly fertile soil, which when cleared of the dense and fearsome forests would make way for farms, ranches, progress. But the place was full of "pagan" and "slothful" natives, whom the Europeans asserted must be taught industry, discipline, morality, and Christianity to become civilized and saved. The Portuguese and Spanish crowns allowed various religious orders to "reduce" and convert Indians, processes which often involved as much force as prayer. Spanish institutions such as the *encomienda* and the *repartimiento* allowed some individuals the right to draft Indian labor and to collect compulsory tribute and taxes. Thus part of the persistent exploitation in Amazonia was, and is, tied to a cultural and institutional "colonial hangover," one uncured by time. Even in the late twentieth century, many people still believe that Amazonia is largely deserted, full of easily exploitable resources, and populated by a few lazy or backward Indians in need of civilization, Christianity, and the discipline of work to help them along the road to progress.[3]

Paradoxes and dichotomies abound in the byzantine history of Indian labor in Amazonia. Indians served as essential teachers, guides, and allies to whites. As pioneers, environmental experts, and stealthful warriors, Amazonians assisted European exploration and conquests. On the other hand, whites always exploited Indian labor. In an area economically unsuited to African slavery, cajoled or coerced Indian labor served as a cheap and plentiful, if uninspired, workforce.[4] The lines separating allies, servants, and slaves often shifted and blurred with circumstances in this colonial setting where outsiders needed and wanted so much.

One of the biggest preoccupations during the Amazon rubber boom was the scarcity of labor. During the last half of the nineteenth century, when worldwide demand inflated prices for rubber, Amazonia had the largest number of wild rubber trees in the world, but the fixed number of collectors limited output and profits. Why, if demand for labor was high and its supply limited, didn't labor command better compensation?[5] Even a partial answer to this question contains many facets. Economically, most of Amazonia operated on a barter economy. Cash was always scarce because it was exported to buy goods or was invested in developing capitalist markets in Europe and the United States. Without cash and an internal market, wage labor was impossible.

Isolation and divisions also precluded the improvement of conditions for rubber collectors. Collectors often toiled alone or in small groups in remote areas of the jungle. A tapper's union with a collective-bargaining strategy proved impractical. Although the scope of rubber collection was impressive, its simple methods and lack of organization tended to reinforce traditions rather than encourage innovation. Even for the northeastern Brazilian and Andean migrants, the reality of debt-peonage clouded dreams of prosperity. In addition, debt obligations tied native peoples to a patrón, but the relationship was not simply economic. For example, what was a metal axe worth to an

Andoke, Bora, or Huitoto who had neither seen nor owned one? Was this cauchero who requested blood from the trees a man, god, spirit, or devil? Given these technological and cosmological issues, what one person called exploitation, another might experience as opportunity.

The traditions of treating Indians as legal children, as moral, religious, and cultural savages, as natural slaves outside the realm of civilization, rode comfortably into the nineteenth century. Yet even though whites relegated Indians to an inferior status, they still wanted forest products — and Indians to collect them. Colonial language and institutions informed the vocabulary and mindset of quineros and caucheros looking for labor in the Putumayo; Huitotos were *conquistados* (conquered), *reducidos* (reduced), and *repartidos* (split-up) by *"esos héroes colombianos"* (these heroic Colombians) who followed the path of Rafael Reyes after 1876. Whites forced goods on Indians, the old *repartimiento de bienes* practiced by Spanish colonial *corregidores.*[6] In societies where slavery was legal until mid-century and in Brazil until 1888, the practice of forcing Amazonians to work in exchange for cheap goods seemed reasonable. A Brazilian governor defended this tradition late in the nineteenth century by arguing that Indians forced to paddle canoes would become better citizens as they learned "love of work, love of family, and of order."[7] After reviewing the history of Colombian and Brazilian abuse and enslavement of Indians in the Putumayo, Camilo Domínguez and Augusto Gómez concluded, "Colombians and Brazilians simply exploited *their* territory and *their* Indians, following the old Ibero-American colonial custom of considering resources and natives as masterless property that one appropriated without any consideration."[8] Jesús San Román found a similar seigniorial attitude among Peruvian caucheros who took possession of some territory and called it "their property," expanded their "extractive authority" over it, and imposed "their law" over both.[9]

Perceiving Amazonian economics as a "mode of extraction" rather than a "mode of production" explains why poverty, resource destruction, and abuse of labor have continued. Stephen Bunker argues that Amazonian economies functioned over the last 350 years by extracting value, energy, and resources rather than producing value by labor.[10] Likewise, resources extracted from Amazonia increased value and energy flows to industrial centers. Bunker reasons that unfree labor systems and the extraction of value from nature sustained development and production in centers of finance and industry, while leaving the environment and the social system of Amazonia in a poor and stunted state.[11]

As an integral part of forest extractive enterprises throughout Amazonian history, how did Indians respond to labor demands, slavery, and violence from whites?[12] It is essential that we know more about Indian societies: How did cultural contact and conflict with whites change them? And how did whites and Indians interact?[13] Human beings must be perceived as such, and not as archetypical "noble savages," as saintly or martyred victims, or, in Roger Casement's words, as "docile and obedient . . . grown-up children," whose "weakness of character and docility of temperament are no match for the dominating ability of those with European blood in their veins."[14] Putumayan Indians at times acted brutally against one another, some made informed choices, and some even adapted to white presence. In 1850, Henry Bates found domestic servants in Tefé, an Amazonian town near the mouth of the Japurá (Caquetá), who had been brought downriver and apparently had no desire to return to their ancestral tribes.[15] Why did some Putumayans make contact with whites and volunteer to work for them? And why did Andokes, Boras, Huitotos, and Carijonas capture and trade unfortunate individuals for European goods?[16]

Hierarchy, exploitation, and violence, usually attributed to the insidious influence of brutal white colonials, internally defined and shaped indigenous societies. Within Andoke clans, for example, hierarchies permeated almost every aspect of life. The captain (jefe or cacique) exercised much power within the maloca. Usually the eldest son of the previous captain or one who traced his lineage to the primordial ancestor, a captain of "tradition and lineage" used his technical, mythological, and ceremonial wisdom to bring good to his clan. He needed to be a man of prestige and generosity, a peacemaker, a protector — someone able to maintain harmony and balance in spiritually and environmentally delicate worlds. For his talent and services, the captain claimed perquisites and authority: he took many wives and controlled, coordinated, and directed the production of goods for his family and for ceremonies; he instigated *mingas*, tasks involving collective labor, and had lesser chiefs oversee them; and he had the power to redistribute goods throughout the maloca, a crucial practice in subsistence economies. Although he held a high position, the captain could be challenged verbally by elders or militarily by another captain seeking preeminence over a number of clans. But one did not treat the captain lightly. The Andokes reported that those who rebelled against him could be "sacrificed." A Huitoto testified that an undesirable person could be expelled from the clan and then "eaten" by a spirit, creature, or rival group.[17]

Individuals and families who claimed lineage with the "captain's people" outranked "ordinary people." High-status Boras resided on the right of the maloca close to the captain, while those of less esteem were relegated to the left toward the maloca's opening. Elites tended to settle with mates of the same rank to preserve their social, political, and ceremonial status. Older children — or the "pretty, good, those of the right" — dominated their younger siblings — "the ugly ones, those of the left." This dialectic within families created tensions; ritually, low-status individuals assumed conflictive and provocative roles, ones challenging the established hierarchical order.[18]

Relations between clans and tribes also exhibited great tension. Competition for resources, real and perceived injury, demographic and cultural considerations, and a well-developed cult of the warrior often drove men to attack neighboring malocas. They would loot rival villages, kill or capture rival warriors, and kidnap women and children. The fierce Carijona developed a specialty using European weapons to attack and subdue Huitotos and Tukanos, whom they traded for more European goods. In an oft-cited example from 1879, Jules Crévaux met a Carijona chief with a war chest of ten rifles, cutlasses, and four boxes of goods received from Brazilian traders in exchange for Indians.[19]

One reason Indian headmen approved such attacks involved control over women. As the reproductive potential of any society largely depends on its number of fertile women, the tussle to control "female resources" set clans and tribes to fighting. The future survival of a people often depended on its women and the children they bore. As European diseases swept through the Putumayo, the violence involved in stealing women and children became imperative. For headmen, who could take several wives, female captives also offered economic advantages. Multiple wives and children gathered and provided more goods, which headmen then redistributed to clients to improve their political and social status. Clients, on the other hand, demonstrated their political subordination or paid tribute to a superior by presenting him with a woman.[20]

The hierarchies within native societies, war captives, and social dislocations provided a pool of low-status and exploitable individuals. Adult male captives met a harsh fate: they were either ritualistically killed or exported out of the village and traded for some desirable good. Women and children might also be traded, or they might find a home within the new clan. New arrivals were labeled "orphans," creatures cut off from culture and lineage, floating in a society highly aware of place and status. Orphans often became the charges of headmen and labored for them. The orphans could only regain their humanity if the headman chose to teach them the necessary mythical, ritual, and cultural secrets. These adoptees then found a place in a family. The Huitotos, for instance, adopted orphans of all ages, but they only incorporated the young into their culture.[21]

The decision to incorporate or trade an orphan involved complex choices. If threatened by a demographic crisis, the clan imported orphans to insure its cultural survival. If, however, the clan had plenty of people and desired some particular product, exporting or trading orphans seemed logical. Indeed, the powerful allure of a metal axe actually sparked a new mythology and ideology to justify trading orphans for axes. The Huitoto created the myth of "The Axe from the East" as the source of abundance, fertility, and multiplication. To possess its power insured survival. This mythology helped quiet discontent among the orphans and low-status individuals within the clan slated for barter. Trading lowly orphans then became a necessary collective sacrifice, one which brought life and prosperity to the Huitoto.

The ideology surrounding survival, hierarchy, warfare, and sacrifice created an exploitative and servile system within Putumayan societies, one that symbiotically responded to the introduction of European goods and labor demands. Captives, orphans, and subordinate members of the clan formed a ready pool of slaves or merchandise. Interestingly, these individuals were not thought to be equal or even human — notions common to other slave-holding societies — and therefore became expendable. One could, however, obtain slaves without recourse to violence. The Carijonas, for example, simply traded European goods with other tribes to tap into this existing pool. Colombian anthropologist Roberto Pineda Camacho posited the possibility that low-status families might have been obligated to surrender one of their younger children to this pool in order to have access to metal tools.[22]

A Nonuya oral account illustrates the attraction of these goods and the predicaments they created. A Huitoto chief asked his Nonuya peer about the power and origin of his first metal axe. The Nonuya responded vaguely and rejected the Huitoto's offer of fine thread, nets, and coca leaves in exchange for the axe. But then the Nonuya chief said that he would trade the axe for the Huitoto's daughter. The Huitoto chief agonized some time but then decided that the magical powers of the axe were too great to pass up. Instead of sacrificing his own daughter, however, the Huitoto shrewdly prepared two beautiful and plump orphan girls for the swap.[23]

Traditional exploitation and hierarchy in both European and indigenous societies established the structural basis for caucheros to demand labor from Indians. Observers at the eve of the rubber boom were already noting the injurious effects of such demands. In September 1865, Elizabeth Agassiz found disheartened Indians working either for "good will" or for liquor. She mentioned that they cared little for money and suffered from frequent sickness. Concerning the unintended biological disaster linked with contact, she wrote,

"They are very subject to intermittent fevers, and one often sees Indians worn to mere skin and bone by this terrible scourge."[24] She was also shocked that Brazilians stole children from Indian villages. Defenders of this practice argued that "children are taken from an utterly savaged and degraded condition, and it is better they should be civilized by main force than not civilized at all." The plucky and eloquent Mrs. Agassiz commented, "It may be doubted, however, whether any providence but the providence of God is so wise and so loving that it may safely exercise a compulsory charity."[25] Her professor husband likewise discovered that the Brazilian armed forces impressed Indians along the Middle Amazon into service to fight the tough Paraguayans during the brutal War of the Triple Alliance (1865–70). Five years later, Henry Wickham, collecting rubber seeds, found the Rio Negro deserted, most of the Indian males having been rounded up and impressed during the Paraguayan war.[26]

Certainly, a cauchero could resort to intimidation, threats, violence, and slavery to force Indians to work for him, especially if he felt he had the power or the right to do so. But it was also true that some caucheros, especially those who formed the first wave of explorers, or those integrated into clans, used more subtle means of influence. These commercial and cultural pioneers carried their most powerful inducements with them in their canoes — new and revolutionary goods assumed by Indians to possess great spiritual powers. Socially, the caucheros imported two durable and crucial institutions found throughout Latin America: patrón-client relationships and fictive kinship ties, or *compadrazgo*. The cauchero assumed the paternalistic role of the patrón — one inestimably potent if his Indian clients perceived him as a supernatural being — bestowing life-giving gifts to his workers. The Indian clients cared and labored for their patrón, supplying him with food, company, and rubber. The patrón-client relationship might be cemented through a ceremonial exchange of compadrazco, one involving obligations for both parties. As a result of this asymmetrical but reciprocal exchange, the patrón assumed more seigniorial power, while the client raised his social status and gained a certain sense of security.[27] These types of social relationships helped close cultural gaps and tempered some of the more extreme labor demands of caucheros.

Along with Indian workers, northeastern Brazilians comprised another major labor source for rubber collection. The institutional decline of Brazilian slavery after 1850, coupled with a major drought in the northeast from 1877 to 1879, pushed thousands of former slaves upstream. Estimates of the number of such migrants who fled poverty and sought prosperity in Amazonia from 1870 to 1920 range from 60,000 to 300,000. Many of these workers, shut out by Italian immigrants from São Paulo's coffee plantations after 1888, heard the stories of work and riches in Amazonia and had their passage subsidized or paid for by a patrón and went to work as rubber tappers. Once there, however, the northeasterner faced the danger, isolation, and indebtedness of the seringuero. Their unannounced arrival close to Indian villages often led to competition for forest resources, cultural conflict, and violence.[28]

Most rubber collectors never escaped indebtedness to their patróns, who advanced them goods. In a noncash economy in which control of credit and debt, rather than control of the means of production, defined social and economic relations, a closed, vertically integrated chain of creditors and debtors determined the exchange system. At the apex of this Amazonian hierarchy of trade, called the *aviamiento* system, stood the big import/export houses of Pará, Manaus, and Iquitos. These houses, in direct contact with international markets, established base prices for both rubber exports and imports. Within Amazonia, each big import/export house forwarded goods to important aviadores (seringueiros in Brazil, caucheros in Spanish America) who traded rubber in exchange. Aviadores traded directly with rubber collectors, or they improved their rank and profits by establishing a network of petty aviadores who worked on their behalf. At the bottom of this pecking order toiled the collectors. They might be Indians, mestizos, northeasterners, or Colombians, Ecuadorians, Peruvians, or Bolivians contracted in the montaña or the sierra. Patróns held collectors in debt, who in turn owed rubber to an aviador, who likewise ran a bill with a big import/export house. The system functioned on debt relations, credit access, and control of products.[29]

The degree of power a patrón exercised over his peons depended on several conditions. In remote regions dominated by a single patrón or company, clients were discouraged from raising crops, thereby becoming dependent on the supplier for food and other essential trade goods. In such situations, suppliers set low prices for rubber and high prices for food and goods. Rubber areas close to an urban or agricultural market offered more economic opportunities and were worked by various aviadores, allowing rubber collectors to bargain for better terms of exchange or to simply ignore the more obnoxious demands of patróns. Aviadores tended to "steal" workers from one another in such situations, competition that often sparked violence between them but also offered better conditions for workers.[30]

In regions as remote as the Putumayo, separated by thousands of miles from the main import/export centers in Pará and Manaus, the terms of trade never favored workers. Patróns at the end of the trading chain demanded high prices for their goods and set low values for the caucho collected in the area. Along with greed, the aviamento system and high transport costs increased the

Table 3. Cost of Goods to Indian Workers in Various Putumayo Sections, 1911 (prices in kilos of rubber)

Goods	Highest	Lowest	El Encanto/La Chorrera Cost
Hammock	60	25	12.6–15
Gun, single-barrel	100	30	29
Gun, double-barrel	120	40	50
Trousers, shirt, hat, and belt	60	15	36
Machete	20	7	3–4.5
Axe	25	9	4
Blanket	30	12	12.6

Source: GBFO, *Report and Special Report from the Select Committee on Putumayo*, 609.

prices of imports moved down the chain, and of rubber exported up the line. Table 3 demonstrates the range of prices for goods available to workers in the Putumayo.

Cultural factors, along with geography and market access, also influenced exchange terms. Contemporary observers believed that Indians could easily be cheated in a trade because they often lacked knowledge of market values. Yet a patrón might forward goods to Indian workers before receiving any rubber and then have to wait months for reimbursement. Although it was believed easier to cheat an Indian than an acculturated mestizo or mulatto, called *caboclos* in Amazonia, it could be difficult to control or understand Indians. With different norms, values, cultures, cosmologies, and visions, Indians became very unpredictable rubber collectors. They might work a while and then stop, being content with the material and spiritual goods in hand. They might accept advances from a cauchero, then melt back into the rain forest, having never collected any rubber, leaving the patrón with more debt of his own. Alternately, they might violently resist any cauchero incursion in an effort to keep them, their diseases, and their spirits out of the region. In such an environment, terms of exchange and the exploitation of Indian labor depended not only on a system but on individual circumstances worked out in particular locales.

Documentation abounds on the abuses of the debt-peonage system practiced throughout Amazonia and the Putumayo. Wealth flowed to the top of the aviamento chain, leaving many workers impoverished, ill-nourished, and exploited. The patrón threatened violence, at times resorting to beating and whipping to enforce labor demands and to demonstrate his dominance. Debt servitude, the last link in the aviamiento system, held entire families in its grip for generations because the debt of a missing or dead peon was passed along to the next closest living relative.[31] Patróns also sold or traded Indian debtors like chattel, essentially exchanging their past debt and future labor. The ability to buy and sell Indian workers and to inherit debt obligations over generations amounted to slavery.[32]

Although patróns could be brutal, thoughtless thugs when interacting with Indians, one can comprehend, if not accept, their behavior. In debt himself to a merchant or a primary aviador, yet still dreaming of power and position, the cauchero inevitably met frustrations. His workers never delivered as much rubber or respect as he wished, and they might run away into the jungle. Moreover, the cauchero risked his own hide in collecting rubber and trading goods, for disease, accidents, thieves, and violence could touch anyone. If rubber prices dropped in London or New York, he had to trade more of his devalued rubber for the more expensive imported goods controlled by his own merchant patrón. On his return upriver, he had to demand more rubber from his Indian workers in compensation for the more expensive goods he carried.[33] The system lacked justice or stability. Profits accumulated at the top and were exported to foreign markets. Those who worked hardest earned the least. Nevertheless, Amazonian caucheros and peons supplied the world with most of its rubber until 1914.

Throughout the last half of the nineteenth century, government officials addressed the thorny issues raised by the great demand for workers in Amazonia and the persistence of obnoxious colonial and even pre-Columbian labor practices. As early as 1854, a local Ecuadorian official in Napo complained that Indians in his jurisdiction were required to pay an inflated annual tribute of "one gold castellano" worth one peso. Lerda ordered that whites and Indians recognize that a gold castellano was worth two pesos, thereby lightening the tribute exactions on Indians.[34] Tribute—a system to extract money, goods, and labor from the indigenous population—continued in various guises for the rest of the century.

Laws and rules concerning tribute and labor obligations for Indians changed with circumstances. In 1845, the Peruvian government excused Indians of Loreto from paying the "contribución de indígenas" (the Indian contribution) for a period of twenty years, a ruling extended for another twenty years in 1865. Although the dictator General Canseco attempted to annul the 1865 decision one year later, municipalities could not legally collect the "Indian contribution" until 1885, so they began to raise revenues by taxing local urban property.[35] About the same time, the prefect of Caquetá ruled differently across the hazy border north of Loreto. Maximiliano Díaz Erazo decided that his house and the Mocoa jail needed repairs, so he ordered all resident men eighteen to fifty years old to muster for a *"trabajo personal"* (a corvée labor draft, or *mita*) to complete the necessary repairs.[36]

Some years later, and across another vague territorial boundary, the Ecuadorian governor of Oriente province, Francisco Andrade Marín, reached yet another administrative decision concerning Indian labor drafts. Andrade Marín noted in 1885 that the Indians of Papallacta had consistently offered important services to a fledgling agricultural settlement in the area and exempted themselves from the local labor draft, the *"trabajo subsidiario."*[37] Perhaps the governor felt genuine gratitude to the natives of Papallacta. It is also likely that Andrade Marín wished to retain an important workforce for the agricultural colony. Even given the changing political and administrative circumstances in all three countries, one could not ignore the fact that Indians furnished the bulk of the labor force for both public projects and private enterprise.

The Ecuadorian and Peruvian governments continued their attempts to regulate Indian labor relations throughout the 1880s and 1890s. The presence of caucheros and colonists from the Ecuadorian highlands underscored the need to construct roads and roadside rest stations, or *tambos,* in the Oriente. As always, roads presumably brought with them civilization and progress, but Amazonian Indians had to construct them. Indians were either compelled to labor or compensated with trinkets, tools, or occasionally cash. For example, in 1884, Isidro Caguatijo earned twenty-four sucres for supplying fifty-four peons to bear goods for arriving colonists. The peons each earned about two sucres, and of the fifty-four, thirteen carried the surname Caguatijo.[38] Isidro apparently used his position as a headman to earn some cash for himself and for clan members.

Women and children formed crucial sectors of the local workforce. Along with their daily agricultural and domestic chores, they collected rubber and carried heavy loads over jungle paths. Oriente governor Andrade Marín reported another important pursuit of theirs along the Napo River: panning for gold. While the Indian men hunted and drank, Andrade claimed that their women and children sifted the river's sediments for gold. The governor hoped that more women would take up this task in order to increase the Oriente's public revenues. But he could not rely on his small army squad, composed of men from Quito hooked (*enganchados*) into the service, to help him attract more women to gold panning. Andrade complained that his own guard perpetrated most of the crime, disorder, and violence in the area, fighting amongst themselves and extorting goods from the local Indians.[39]

By the early 1890s, Ecuadorian governors were renewing their efforts to protect Indians from abuse. In July 1891, Juan Mosquera prohibited patróns from paying Indian workers with glass beads and ordered that Indians only be offered goods they wanted. He also asked the Ecuadorian consul in Iquitos to seek safe-passage guarantees from Peruvian officials for a group of Indians voyaging to the salt deposits in the Huallaga, men contracted to deliver this precious compound to the residents of Archidona. The following year, the Ecuadorian president, Luís Cordero, took a bold if ineffectual step to halt forced labor in the Oriente. Cordero focused on the section of the "Ley de Oriente" that prohibited forced sales of goods to Indians, the advancement of goods to hold workers in bondage, and the insistence by patróns that all such debts be honored. This presidential action challenged the basis of the avia-mento system and legally allowed Indians to ignore the seigniorial demands of patróns who had broken the law.[40]

Whereas President Cordero's idealistic action ignored the realities of the Amazonian economy and the centuries of Indian exploitation, pragmatic laws passed in Peru attempted to regulate rather than prohibit demands on Indian laborers. In August 1888, Loreto's prefect, José G. Basagoitia, decreed a new labor code for the department. Basagoitia argued that firm labor guidelines for forest collectors, agricultural workers, and domestic servants would end the irregularities and abuses committed by some patróns. He harbored special concern for some "deserted regions" where caucheros had enslaved and then exported Indians to work in rubber zones in foreign lands (presumably in Colombia, Ecuador, Brazil, or Bolivia). To avoid this labor drain, Basagoitia decreed that all future labor contracts had to be written, registered, and wit-nessed by authorities. If a cauchero wanted workers, the subprefect would arrange labor recruitment. Patróns could not take workers outside the depart-ment, and they needed a passport from the authorities even to move workers to a different site within Loreto. Moreover, patróns could not steal or seduce workers away from other employers, and if they took workers upstream to-wards Madre de Dios or downstream towards Iquitos, they had to leave a deposit of two hundred soles for each one. Peons, on the other hand, had to register with the same officials to receive an obligatory work permit that bore information concerning their labor contracts, which was checked monthly by employers. Of course, with all this regulation and brokerage of labor con-tracts, officials expected a fee or commission for their services.

The teeth of this decree, however, favored employers. Various articles stipu-lated that peons could not break the terms of their contracts or leave employ-ment while they were indebted to a patrón. If they did, the political authorities would assist the patrón in capturing and punishing runaways.[41] Such a labor code authorized the exploitation of Indians but attempted to institutionalize it by protecting the local labor pool from extreme abuse or exportation by employers. The code also sought to lessen conflicts between competing patróns and their workers.

Another law passed in 1897 and pushed through Congress by Peru's first vice-president and future president, Guillermo E. Billinghurst, mirrored the bureaucratic, protective, and exploitative characteristics of Basagoitia's nine-year-old decree. Again, those wishing to exploit Amazonian forests had to register themselves and their workers before submitting their business proposal to local subprefects. Employers had to protect peons from the weather, infectious diseases, sexual temptation, and the evils of alcohol. Female employees had Sunday off and could not be forced to do heavy or dangerous tasks; legally, they were entitled to two and a half months maternity leave. Children under twelve could not work except as domestic servants; those under fifteen could only legally work a six-hour day with Sunday off; and those under eighteen could not consume alcoholic beverages.

But here again the progressive spirit of reform only lightly masked the codification of Indian exploitation. Three cities in the central Peruvian Andes — Tarmac, Huancavelica, and Ayacucho — opened labor-recruitment centers (oficinas de enganche) to broker and register deals to send highlanders down the mountain and into the service of caucheros. Patróns paid three soles for each worker recruited through these offices, while the officials earned a commission on each worker they hooked. Patróns, moreover, could require that officials compel workers to fulfill their contracts. Similar to the 1888 Loreto decree, workers needed a work book listing their labor contract and the name of their patrón. Persons without such documentation, and those who had not worked for a patrón during the past six months, were labeled "vagos" (wanderers or idlers) and could be forced into employment.

Other articles of this 1897 law attempted to reinforce the position of patróns over workers. Peons who could not prove that they had honored previous contracts would not be recommended to a new employer. Although article 49 stated that cash should be paid to workers, article 56 unequivocally bolstered debt-peonage: "No workman may leave employment without first paying with work or money any outstanding debit balance."[42] Whereas the 1892 Ecuadorian law quixotically lanced at the centuries-old tradition of forced labor in Amazonia, the 1897 Peruvian law accepted and used this tradition as the foundation for labor relations in Peru's rubber zones.

True, debt-peonage and the resulting extra-economic exploitation could be found throughout Amazonia, the Andean region, and in Latin America in general.[43] Yet peonage differed given economic, geographic, social, and political conditions, and it tended to be more oppressive if the workers were Indians laboring in a remote region controlled by a single trader. An event in 1895 near the Andean town of Pasto in southern Colombia illustrates the treatment Indians encountered even close to cities. The local government of Funes arrested a group of Indians, charged them with rioting and with participating in a political rebellion, and then shipped them off to Panama to serve in the army. The wives of these deported Indians petitioned department officials for their husbands' return. Luckily, a military officer in Panama released them and put them on their way for the six-hundred-mile journey back to a judge awaiting their arrival in Pasto.[44] If these highland Indians from Funes received such treatment, what could those in the Putumayo expect?

To justify the enslavement, abuse, and conquest of Putumayans, many caucheros, explorers, and authors charged that the Indians were hostile, barbaric cannibals. As with so many other issues concerning the Putumayo, the evidence supporting this charge is ambiguous and incomplete. It is not unusual to read in a single paragraph from a contemporary source an equivocal statement on the nature of Putumayan Indians. For example, a 1913 British report asserted that the Indians are "a simple people, of naturally friendly disposition, whose confidence and affection it would be difficult not to gain," but, "cannibals they undoubtedly were and in outlying parts still may be."[45] Reflecting the pro-Indian British bias stemming from the Putumayo scandal, Richard Collier described the Bora as "a mild, inoffensive tribe, clad in beaten-bark loincloths, who treat their womenfolk with rare respect."[46] Antithetically, a Peruvian employee of the Casa Arana, Carlos Rey de Castro, asserted that the Bora were "undoubtedly cannibals."[47] Upon reviewing these statements, it appears that politics rather than evidence often determined an author's opinions about cannibalism and its practice in the Putumayo.

Traveler's accounts abound with references to the cannibalistic Putumayans. Rafael Reyes recalled an incident during his initial descent down the Putumayo River in 1874 when he feared the "cannibalistic" Indians in his midst, but the skinny Reyes took some solace in his belief that the cannibals would prefer to sink their teeth into the stocky, well-muscled meat of his assistant rather than gnawing on his sinewy flesh.[48] While Reyes managed his stress with humor, North American adventurers preferred to revel in the barbarism, savagery, and darkness of the frontier to spice their sensational accounts and to bolster their titles as "intrepid explorers." Consider, for example, the account of recent college graduate and fraternity member F. W. Up de Graff, remembering his trek down the Napo and Amazon Rivers: "In that primeval maze of forest, swamp, and river, peopled by men as wild and free as the animals which shared their gloomy home, untrodden by civilized man since the beginning of time, were locked a thousand secrets! Would that I share them all." While Up de Graff and his companion Jack Rouse (a Western buffalo hunter, Klondike gold miner, Nevada stagecoach driver, and outlaw "sioux-venir collector") cut a swath of violence and murder of their own, they never in seven years saw any "infieles," unconquered Indians, but assumed them to be primitive, naked, and savage.[49]

Another New Yorker came closer to a "firsthand" account of cannibal rites. In the introduction to his book, Algot Lange also employed the theme of the white hero in a dark frontier to entertain his increasingly urban and naturally alienated readers. Lange wrote that a Mangeroma (Mayoruna?) chief "convinced me that, even at this late period of the world's history, our Earth has not been reduced to a dead level of drab and commonplace existence, and that somewhere in the remote parts of the world are still to be found people who have never seen or heard of white men."[50] It seemed that any intrepid explorer worth his salt had to encounter savage cannibals just to prove that he had indeed left the safety of civilization and entered a forbidden and wild place.

Lange spent about nine months along the Yavari (Javari) River, southeast of the Putumayo, and noted the hatred the Mangeroma felt for raiding Peruvian caucheros. He described various booby traps the Mangeromas prepared along access paths to their malocas: covered and camouflaged pits dug deep into the earth, poisoned stingray barbs laid along the ground, and blowguns loaded with poisoned darts, triggered by saplings sprung by intruders. Lange also purportedly witnessed and participated in a Mangeroma attack on twenty Peruvians. The dozen Indians laid an ambush and exercised a coordinated pincer action to dispatch all twenty caucheros. According to Lange, the Mangeroma suffered only four dead but killed all the intruders to avoid a future retaliatory raid.[51] Clearly, whites had plenty to fear from these fierce and able warriors.

As for the charge of cannibalism, prominently displayed in his subtitle, Lange hedged. In a four-hundred-page book, the author's "firsthand" witnessing of a cannibalistic feast covers barely two pages. He reported that two Peruvian mestizos fell into one of the Mangeroma's deep pits and were quickly killed by warriors. The Indians carried the corpses back to the village where their hands and feet were cut off, probably to deprive their spirits the means to walk and strike in revenge. The Mangeroma prepared for a feast, a cannibalistic one Lange presumed, so he retired to his hammock to avoid participation in the ritual. He reportedly saw the skin of the hands and feet fried in tapir lard, but he never witnessed anyone eating human flesh. Although Lange worried that he might also be made into a meal, the chief assured him that he was safe.

This New Yorker's conclusion about his Indians hosts was conventionally ambiguous: "It is true that the Mangeroma are cannibals, but at the same time their habits and morals are otherwise remarkably clean."[52]

Anthropological writings display a similar dubious quality. In the reputable *Handbook of South American Indians,* Alfred Métraux reported the following in a section entitled "Warfare, Cannibalism, and Human Trophies":

> Cannibalism was rampant among the tribes of the Putumayo River, espe-
> cially among the Witoto, the Andoke, and the Resigero. Prisoners were
> executed during a drinking bout which lasted eight days. The head and
> limbs were eaten, but the brains and entrails were not. The male genital
> organs were presented to the wife of the chief, the only woman who
> shared in the feast. Each man boiled his share in a large pot, retrieving the
> flesh with a string.[53]

Julian H. Steward authored a chapter on "The Witotoan Tribes" in which he repeated that "cannibalism of war victims is attributed to the Muenane, Witoto, and Bora."[54] Even the esteemed Colombian anthropologist Roberto Pineda Camacho cited questionable evidence concerning cannibalism in the region.[55]

The mistake all of the above anthropologists committed was to cite as evidence the highly unreliable travel account of Thomas Whiffen. Whiffen was a part-time British army officer — one prone to debt and an unhealthy attraction to alcohol — who traveled through the Putumayo in 1908 and 1909. Whiffen played an important part in the Putumayo scandal investigations, so one must question the political motivations behind his book. Whiffen opened his preface with the stock adventurer's salvo, "In the remoter parts of these districts the tribes of nomad Indians are frankly cannibal on occasion, and provide us with evidence of a condition of savagery that can hardly be found elsewhere in the world of the twentieth century."[56]

Plodding on to support his work's subtitle (*Notes on Some Months Spent Among the Cannibal Tribes*), Whiffen wrote that the Boro (Bora), Andoke, and Resigero were "indisputably cannibals," and he described for his Victorian audience the details cited by Métraux. But then, to his great credit, Whiffen admitted in a footnote, "I was never present at a cannibal feast. This informa-tion is based on Robuchon's account, checked by cross-questioning the Indians with whom I came in contact."[57] So, while Métraux, Steward, and Pineda Camacho cited Whiffen as the authoritative source, Whiffen relied on the 1907 publication presumably written by the Frenchman Eugenio Robuchon.

This "authoritative source" also contains major flaws. Robuchon was an experienced Amazonian explorer, having spent eight years in this vocation. He married an Indian woman in Madre de Dios before the Peruvian government and the Casa Arana solicited a study of the Putumayo in 1904. Robuchon accepted the job and trekked into the Putumayo in 1905 without his wife—reportedly because he feared attack from the Huitoto—but accompanied by his trusty Great Dane, Othello.[58] Fear of cannibalistic Indians permeates Robuchon's account. He especially mistrusted his hosts when they recited chants and oaths during ceremonies, for he wondered if he might soon be the main course.[59] Here again we have the same fear of Indians reflected in the works of Reyes, Up de Graff, and Lange, yet no direct and incontrovertible evidence of cannibalism. To complicate matters for this seminal source, Robuchon probably did not even write most of the book that bears his name.

In February 1906, the fever-stricken and weakened Robuchon sent his Indian carriers out to search for food. About a month later, they returned to find only some of the baggage and notes of their missing employer. Subsequent search parties found more of his belongings, but the explorer's body never appeared; supposedly, the fearsome Huitoto had made themselves a tasty French dinner. Left without an author or a complete manuscript, the task of editing the weathered and partially legible notes fell upon the business manager of the Casa Arana branch office in Manaus, Carlos Rey de Castro.

Rey de Castro had glaringly obvious political, economic, and social motivations for writing that fifty thousand mostly cannibalistic Indians were impeding progress and the rubber industry in the Putumayo. But never fear, the Casa Arana had assumed the noble task of converting them to civilization and good work habits. Coincidentally, the Casa Arana was offering public stock in London for its new company, the Peruvian Amazon Company (PAC), during the same year that Robuchon's book was published, 1907. Here, then, was the perfect public relations vehicle to sell PAC stock, to quell disquieting rumors of abuse of Indian workers in the region, and to justify the conquest and reduction of "cannibalistic Indians."[60] Indeed, the legality of conquering and enslaving bellicose or cannibalistic natives, explicit in the concept of "just war," had been revived and implicitly invoked by Carlos Rey de Castro in the "authoritative" text on cannibalism in the Putumayo supposedly penned by Eugenio Robuchon.

It is possible that clans or tribes practiced some form of ritualistic cannibalism, but it is also clear that we lack the evidence to prove they did.[61] We certainly know that some tribes kept trophy heads; the Jívaro of Ecuador, for example, removed the skull and brains to reduce the remaining skin into the infamous "shrunken heads." These fetishes became so popular in world markets that the Ecuadorian Senate tried in the 1890s to prohibit their production and sale.[62] But skull trophies and head shrinking do not constitute proof of cannibalistic practices.

Perhaps if we ponder the symbolic, rather than the physical, definition of cannibalism from an indigenous perspective, we might better comprehend it. Among the Piaroa of Venezuela, Joanna Overing Kaplan probed the symbolic meaning of death, violence, and cannibalism. She found that the Piaroa believe that killing, disease, and domination are all forms of cannibalism for they involve the process of consumption. Although they are physically pacific, the Piaroa inhabit a spiritually dangerous and tense realm. If a shaman sends the powerful boa to eat the entrails of an enemy, seen as a direct act of cannibalism, he will face dire consequences and retaliation.[63] In a world of negative reciprocity, one in which animals and spirits feel jealousy that Piaroas have culture and eat food, one can easily become the spiritual feast of another. But if a cauchero during the rubber boom saw human skulls displayed around malocas, witnessed or heard of strange ceremonies and dances, or imaged Indians as "cannibals," none of this would make sense and he would probably assume the worst. What is at issue here is not the reality of cannibalism, but how whites perceived Indians and ascribed to them traits of their own creation. Nonetheless, imaginary or real cannibalism could give a cauchero a moral and traditional justification for conquering and enslaving Indians.

In addition to the politics of cannibalism, both world markets and local realities established the social and economic conditions in which Indians became commodities. The desire for imported goods led many Indian headmen to offer orphans in exchange, or to order clan members to collect rubber. For the caucheros bent on quick profits, slave raids, or *correrías*, yielded a relatively large labor force in a short time. But here the line between conquest and slavery was unclear; disease, flight, warfare, and anger quickly thinned the number of potential captives. But since slaves were cheap—costing the effort and time of a raid or the equivalent of a common tool—one could abuse Indian laborers and quickly replace the dead and missing.[64]

The recruitment and control of labor introduced various types of violence. After enticing or coercing Indians to collect rubber, jealous caucheros protected "their" Indians from all other patróns. But raids on Indian workers continued in this labor-scarce market. For example, the Colombian corregidor of Mesaya, José Antonio Ordoñez, discovered in 1861 that Brazilians were collecting forest products and Indian slaves around Araracuara on the Caquetá River. Ordoñez descended the Caquetá to investigate the matter and found in Tefé sixty shackled Huitotos bound for market in Manaus. Ordoñez was not troubled by the moral or humanitarian issues at hand, but he did register a strong protest with the Brazilians for carrying off "his Indians."[65]

A short excerpt of a letter sent by Lizzie Hessell to her parents grimly illustrates the spectrum of violence one could encounter during the rubber boom. In September 1897, Lizzie, a Victorian lady traveling up the Amazon to Bolivia with her rubber-prospecting husband, wrote:

> Some of the Indians who have been away rubber cutting arrived here yesterday saying they had been attacked in the forest by the savages. They brought two wounded back with them, one woman shot with an arrow through the two breasts and a man shot in the leg. They managed to kill two of the savages.
>
> Five canoes of them were up here for provisions last week. They were going up one of the rivers to attack smaller tribes, then they capture all the children and sell them as slaves. Three of the slaves of this house, two girls and a boy, ran away a few weeks ago, but they hunted them down and brought them back. They were then chained up that night and the next day beaten until they were so exhausted they did not cry any more, Mrs. Fitzcarrald looking on the whole time. She is a brute, I was so sick I had to get away from the house. She now chains them every night to her bed. She beats all her servants about once a week herself.[66]

Women and children comprised a notable portion of the slaves and workforce of northwestern Amazonia. Of course, the orphans and war captives traded from Indian villages tended to be females and youths, so more of them found their way to white patróns. Some became domestic servants in places like Iquitos or Manaus. Some of the children, who might have lost their parents to disease or dislocation, became acculturated rubber collectors over time. The trafficking of women and children did not escape the notice of Santiago Santacruz, a priest touring the Caquetá and Putumayo in 1874. Santacruz alerted the Caquetá prefect that Peruvians were seizing children in the area and killing their mothers if they tried to stop them.[67] Isabel, a Bora Indian, related another episode of a mother trying to protect her child. When Isabel's grandmother saw a cauchero tying her daughter's hands and leading her away, she interceded and hit the cauchero, who responded by shooting her.[68]

The presence of thousands of male caucheros created demand for the assistance, labor, and sexual favors of women and girls. Nude or partially clad females certainly inflamed the passions and desires of lonely men. Caucheros might claim a woman by trading goods, by receiving her as a gift or as part of a political deal, or through mutual attraction and courtship. Predictably, violence against women occurred frequently, and rape was common. Caucheros particularly prized the women of the Caquetá for their beauty and figures, so some of these females became part of the flourishing traffic of Indian women throughout Amazonia.[69]

Colombian, Peruvian, and Ecuadorian officials all knew that caucheros mistreated, killed, and enslaved Indians in northwestern Amazonia in the 1880s and 1890s. One Peruvian official, Lorenzo Malasén, wrote from Leticia in January 1890 that merchants and caucheros frequently committed crimes and atrocities with impunity, including savage whipping and murder. Malasén stated that slavery and violence robbed Indians of their freedom and of their rights as Peruvian citizens when they became "vile commodities." He also complained that rubber dealers "traded people like they were things." The military commander of Loreto forwarded Malasén's report to a bureaucrat in Lima, who filed it, noting that the Peruvian government could do nothing without the names of the perpetrators and the exact dates of all the alleged crimes.[70]

Rogerio María Becerra reported other problems from the Colombian Putu-mayo in 1896. Becerra found a great many Peruvians introducing Brazilian and Peruvian goods as they explored for caucho and Indians. He also charged that an Ecuadorian cauchero, David Andrade, had stirred up warfare between rival Indian tribes to gain captives; as a result, the Orejones (Huitotos) had almost obliterated the Angoteros. Becerra argued that all caucheros, regard-less of nationality, "should be occupying jail cells . . . in this region without justice, where Indians fall prey to peons who hunt and kill them, and to patróns who enslave them." He concluded; "In my opinion, the caucheros don't colonize . . . they destroy, leaving behind desolation and immorality."[71]

Like his colleagues Malasén and Becerra, the Ecuadorian provincial gover-nor, Antonio Llori, was aware of widespread abuses against Indian laborers but could do little to stop them. Llori complained that he lacked the men, money, and canoes to investigate crimes committed in remote areas, some requiring eighty days of travel round-trip. But closer to home, along the Rio Napo, he knew that five hundred caucheros of various nationalities committed many abuses against Indians. What could he do about crimes of such scale and scope without even a small police squad?[72] When a police force was finally furnished six years later, another official reported that its members received no pay, so they ran up debts with merchants and stole food from Indians.[73]

On the other hand, local officials and policemen could become targets of indigenous rage. An episode in Chazuta, on the bank of the Huallaga between Tarapoto and Yurimaguas, illustrates the danger that public officials encoun-tered if they angered the local populace. The indomitable and thousand-strong Chazutanos operated a thriving riverine trade between their village and the steamboat terminus at Yurimaguas. For more than twenty years, they refused to maintain a road linking Chazuta to Tarapoto, stating that this terrestrial toil was below them. Without this land link, trade between Yurimaguas and Tarapoto — in part controlled by the Chazuta Indians — was limited. Noting this situation, the new and ambitious subprefect of the district, José Abel Bello, resolved that he would pressure the Chazutanos to perform their obligatory road work.

In early July 1893, Bello managed to draft 160 men from the village, but trouble soon began. The Indians refused to work unless they immediately received machetes and axes in compensation. When some tools and gifts were delivered, the workers failed to wait for the headmen to distribute them, and simply took what they wanted, including two large jugs of cane liquor. The next day, Bello had no workers, so again he resolutely pressed the matter and went to round them up. Although he was accompanied by two local representatives and four armed policemen, Bello confronted a threatening and uproarious mob, not a work crew. After some initial pushing, punching, and stone throwing, the violence turned to machete slashing. The fury escalated when the rebellious Indians seized a policeman and tried to drown him in a nearby creek. An officer discharged his rifle into the air, and then another fired into the crowd and killed an Indian headman. The villagers then closed for the kill. Emilio Sandoval, an Ecuadorian and the resident governor for twenty-four years, was knocked to the ground and awaited death until some local women and his family came to his defense. The nearly drowned soldier suffered a worse fate; beheaded and flayed, his mutilated body was paraded around the town plaza and then deposited on the steps of the church. Bello and his remaining guards managed to shoot their way out of Chazuta but were captured and killed on the river.[74] Bello clearly miscalculated. He was dealing with an independent, proud, and economically important Indian people, and he had treated them like servants.

Although violence against Indians and workers was frequent, it was less common for an official and his guard to suffer the same treatment. Loreto's prefect, Alejandro Rivera, felt he must punish the guilty or risk losing all influence with the Indians living near Chazuta. He ordered a contingent of forty men to occupy the town and to arrest those persons responsible for the killings. But this posse, reinforced with volunteers from Tarapoto, found Chazuta abandoned, for all the inhabitants had fled into the forest to avoid reprisals.[75]

The very week of the occupation of Chazuta, Prefect Rivera faced another bloody episode up the Napo. Although cauchero and Napo police inspector José María G. Mourón had directed Indian collectors in the region for five years, one night two of Mourón's "civilized Indian workers" led an attack that killed nine of Mourón's peons. They also managed to capture José's brother,

Julio, and five other peons, all subsequently killed. Lacking the manpower to send out another armed unit, Rivera opined that "these events will continue as long as the audacious caucheros continue to press into regions inhabited by ferocious savages, who take advantage of the caucheros' confidence to pick a good opportunity to kill them."[76]

The institutionalization of forced labor mixed with myriad forms of violence during the rubber boom to sustain slavery in northwestern Amazonia well into the twentieth century. Comparative studies of the psychological, social, and physical foundations of slavery assist in understanding this emotionally wrenching but historically pervasive institution. Social biologists such as Anatol Rapoport interpret slavery as "human parasitism," the function of unequal terms of exchange displayed when one party gives more than he takes, producing an unstable social situation.[77] Orlando Patterson chose to explore the relations of domination inherent in slavery. Patterson delineated the social, psychological, and cultural facets of power relations allowing masters to intimidate subordinate slaves. In a frontier colonial society brimming with explorers, conquerors, and natives, these facets merged through both white and indigenous lenses to image a slave society. Masters derived personal power and social honor by dishonoring or controlling subservient instruments, a practice notable among both Indian caciques and vulgar caucheros.[78]

Patterson's most intriguing notion hinged on the social/psychological marginalization of slaves through "social death" and natal alienation. Although masters saved slaves from certain death, in the process the slaves became uprooted and socially "dead." Symbolically and ideologically, marginalization and natal alienation acquired either an intrusive or an extrusive representation of social death:

> We may summarize the two modes of representing social death that was slavery by saying that in the intrusive mode the slave was conceived of as someone who did not belong because he was an outsider, while in the extrusive mode the slave became an outsider because he did not (or no longer) belonged. In the former the slave was an external exile, an intruder; in the latter he was an internal exile, one who had been deprived of all claims of community. The one fell because he was the enemy, the other became the enemy because he had fallen.[79]

These notions of natal alienation and social death have some interesting applications for indigenous "orphans" and other individuals cut off from their lineage, clan, culture, and humanity. Whether their social death was defined intrusively or extrusively would depend on where the marginal or orphaned person became a slave.

Patterson's list of the various ways that free persons became slaves also applies to the Putumayo: captive in warfare and kidnapping; tribute and tax payments; debt and punishment for crimes; abandonment and sale of children; self-enslavement and birth.[80] But Patterson would probably term slavery in the Putumayo "unsuccessful" because masters found it almost impossible to alienate slaves natally and to institutionalize their power and position. In reviewing various cases of in-situ enslavement in the Americas, Patterson found that masters, rather than slaves, were the social intruders. Therefore, caucheros in the Putumayo could never completely dominate indigenous societies culturally, socially, or psychologically. They might wield such power over individuals or clans, but not over the larger community. Moreover, individuals could easily flee or find refuge in their own homeland.[81] In short, in-situ slavery placed masters in a less powerful institutional position than the one filled by masters dominating slaves separated from their geographic, cultural, and psychological roots.

This lack of power concerned caucheros. If their honor, status, and livelihood depended on forced Indian labor, and they could not control it, they experienced frustration and anger. Fear, too, tugged at their darker emotions, for they were outsiders, the minority, surrounded by independent and fearsome Indians. They feared the environment, its wild animals, poisonous plants, and powerful spirits; they feared Indian attacks and uncontrolled savagery along trails where they could see only five meters into the thick foliage. They used violence themselves to compensate for this lack of control and confidence, and to display their position. Patterson noted that masters could murder their slaves with impunity in most societies, but Alistair Hennessy provides us with a plausible explanation for the violence perpetrated by caucheros within in-situ slave societies. Hennessy focused his remarks on colonial Brazilian society, but they strike home in the Putumayo: "The savagery of the slaveholding system was displayed at its most brutal in the punishments meted out to captured runaways — branding, public castration, dismemberment, roasting over slow fires, all the civilizing devices of frightened societies which sensed on what slender bases their legitimacy rested."[82]

Exploitation, opportunity, conflict, warfare, hierarchy, culture — all of these elements combined to create complex and even contradictory labor systems in northwestern Amazonia. Many times the allure of trade goods prompted Indians to deal with or work for caucheros. Occasionally these interactions benefited both parties, at least in the short term. Over time, however, the obligations, regulations, and debts of the peonage system imposed more demands on workers, leading in some cases to outright slavery. Both indigenous and white societies provided the historic, mythic, and cultural foundations for this era of dynamic exchange, conflict, and exploitation. The Amazonian tradition of forced labor and slavery persisted because it was economically, culturally, and politically familiar to both whites and Amerindians. Much of the blame for the intense violence and lawlessness in remote regions fell upon economic and international competition for resources and labor unregulated by governmental authorities.[83] But as we shall see, governmental and ecclesiastic authorities also played crucial roles in promoting administrative, economic, and social violence in northwest Amazonia.

FOUR

REGIONAL ADMINISTRATIONS, 1850–1895

The "colonial hangover" in the Putumayo not only dragged the region and its inhabitants through the muck in terms of making the area a "living museum" of extractive industry and forced labor, for it also had lingering effects on political issues.[1] Aggressive westward expansion by Brazil, mixed with the nebulous colonial boundaries of the viceroyalties of Nueva Granada and Peru, established the eventual four-way struggle for the Putumayo. Colombia and Peru claimed the Putumayo, as did Ecuador, a small breakaway country forced to carve out its Amazonian niche after 1830 in a nonexistent neutral zone between its larger northern and southern neighbors. Meanwhile, Brazilians loitered stage right, pressing their political and economic agenda up the reaches of the Amazon. Inevitably, political conflicts reached the boiling point during the last half of the nineteenth century. Competing national interests clashed in a realm of vague jurisdictions; governments cited different colonial precedents to support their respective territorial claims. The rubber boom brought all these issues to a head, sending governmental officials in Bogotá, Quito, Lima, and Rio de Janeiro scurrying to find allies, documents, or just a reliable map to bolster their respective claims.[2]

The region offered both liabilities and opportunities for Colombia, Ecuador, and Peru. Each country faced the possibility of a three-pronged invasion from neighboring states along its Putumayan border. Each confronted the problem of supporting its representatives in that remote region over the Andes Mountains. Without some sort of presence, each country risked losing potentially valuable territory to its neighbors or to separatists unhappy with their own government's weak or nonexistent policies. On the other hand, the commerce brought by the rubber boom heightened not only the strategic importance of the Putumayo but also its economic value. The collection of head, property, and business taxes along with import and export duties enhanced the potential of the Putumayo filling, rather than draining, national treasuries.[3]

The relations between regional and national interests exhibited dynamism. Penurious and centralist governments looked askance at the needs of remote regions and hoped to maintain or gain as much as possible at the least expense. Colombian and Ecuadorian regional officials ensconced along the montaña often found their respective central governments less than generous in paying for the men and material necessary for their duties. Downriver in Iquitos, Loretanos also experienced administrative and fiscal crises, but their favorable location at the heart of the northwestern mercantile economy allowed them easier, if unauthorized, access to money, men, and materials.

National authorities occasionally did regulate and overturn the actions of regional officials, especially in cases where the latter overstepped their bounds. But governments used caucheros and local functionaries to further territorial ambitions, and, symbiotically, caucheros cloaked their economic motives in the guise of nationalism. Much of the violence in the Putumayo then was not the result of a lack of government regulation — for Colombia, Ecuador, and Peru maintained Amazonian administrations after 1850 — but rather of governments consciously employing violence as a mechanism for territorial aggrandizement and economic gain.

PERUVIAN ADMINISTRATION, 1850–95

The 1850s and 1860s marked the formative decades for the Amazonian administrations of all three countries, but Peru took the early lead in the region (see map). Peru initiated its efforts in Loreto with a militaristic approach stimulated by both internal and external sources. Internally, Gen. Ramón Castilla consolidated power in the 1840s and 1850s, thereby slowing the destructive cycle of civil war. Castilla deftly mixed military and political tactics to take control of the government, while he and Peru rode the economic wave of the stinky but profitable guano deposits. Externally, Brazilian westward expansion and Brazil's organization of the province of Amazonas in 1850 pushed Castilla to respond to the pressures from his eastern neighbor. Three years later, Peru created the military and political government of Loreto.[4]

In 1864, the establishment of docks and the naval shipyard in Iquitos and the importation of six steamboats helped Peru establish a viable presence in the area.[5]

Lima maintained a strong connection to the administrative, territorial, and martial development of Loreto in the remaining years of the 1860s. The Loreto bureaucracy maintained a monthly correspondence with Lima, some of it carried on steamboats plying the department's many rivers. In January 1867, the secretary of war ordered the commandant general of Loreto to erect a fortress at the Brazilian border near Tabatinga.[6] The twenty-five-man unit built posts defensible against attacks from both Brazilians and Indians, and they purportedly protected the latter from Brazilian kidnappers. Furthermore, the minister of government directed the unit commander to dispatch accurate and detailed reconnaissance reports of the region and to keep his men out of private business dealings.[7] Of course, such a campaign required money, and, surprisingly, Lima was quite generous. Throughout 1868, the department's budget included a monthly allocation of 20,000 soles for this unit's explorations and labors. This expenditure absorbed more than two-thirds of the total budget and predictably raised internal squabbles over its control. In March 1868, the commandant general complained to the prefect that his unit had not received its pay in January. He warned that the blame for any resulting damage to the nation would fall on the prefect's desk.[8]

In the 1870s, Peruvians continued developing a viable administration based on a growing economy. With 30,000 soles of Brazilian goods imported monthly, seventeen merchants from Iquitos petitioned the prefect to form a board of trade to regulate prices and quality, and to arbitrate commercial differences. Although Lima took four years to approve this petition, this new business organization seemed to be operating by early 1870.[9] About the same time, Prefect Lino Olario named twenty-four "men of property and knowledge" to report to him about any lands in Loreto possessed in violation of the rights of the nation, of municipalities, or of Indian communities.[10] The Peruvians were rapidly moving to regulate commerce and to define property rights.

But they also needed money for the developing bureaucracy, always a problem in a remote region short of cash. In the late 1860s, a prominent merchant in Iquitos bought the contract to tax farms and to pay the salaries of Loretano officials. This arrangement worked well until May 1869, when the military unit out exploring the Peruvian-Brazilian border piled up unexpectedly high expenses. Caught with a large deficit at a moment when the nation was trying to extend its eastern frontier, the Peruvian minister of finance ordered Peruvian financial agents in London and the United States to release funds and to pay the expenses of the commandant general in Iquitos.[11] Once again, the Peruvian government ably responded to a pressing need in far off Loreto. Diplomatically, Lima also demonstrated a dynamic effort to establish border treaties with Brazil. From 1869 to 1873, Peru signed a series of formal agreements with Imperial Brazil setting borders on the Putumayo, Caquetá, Apaporis, and Yavari Rivers.[12]

Although the Peruvian administration in Amazonia and the support it received from its national government outshined those of Colombia and Ecuador, problems invariably arose. For example, in early 1872, the department's treasurer fled with close to 100,000 soles, supposedly with the assistance of the prefect. This theft caused great consternation and shocked many Loretanos, largely because of the amount stolen.[13] While some officials took advantage of their positions, others found it dangerous imposing order and enforcing the law. In May 1873, Lt. Cayetano Rivadeneya received orders to escort seventeen prisoners from Tabalosos (Tabalosas) to Moyobamba. The only problem for the lieutenant and his squad — besides the heat, bugs, and mud — was that the residents of Tabalosos planned to ambush them before they got to town. Loreto's prefect sent ten extra men to reinforce Cayetano for his eventual confrontation with these rowdy locals.[14]

Military matters also presented persistent difficulties. Insurrection and revolutions from the coast spilled into the department as the guano bonanza fizzled and the Civilista Party contested for national power. In 1872, officials seized shotguns imported into the department but then released them once Lima determined that the owners presented no military threat.[15] But two years later, a countrywide revolution engulfed Loreto and set off factional fighting that took the life of an ex-prefect. In late 1874 and early 1875, units of the Guardia Civil (Peru's national police) and the regular army from Chachapoyas participated in actions to repress rebellion and disorder.[16] Although Peru faced serious internal economic and political crises in the 1870s, a decline capped after 1879 with the Chilean victory over Peru in the War of the Pacific, Loreto hung on because the rubber economy provided it with world trade and vital income.

Because of Loreto's integration into the international economy, Peru emerged with the best position in northwestern Amazonia, even after its humiliating defeat and occupation by Chilean forces. Peruvian losses to Chile in the south underscored the importance of settling boundary squabbles with Ecuador and Colombia to the north.[17] New military bases in Loreto such as Tacna and Arica, named after two of the Chilean-occupied southern departments, reminded Peruvians of past losses but also foreshadowed a future wave of Peruvian expansion into the Putumayo.[18] Geopolitical losses in the southwest certainly propelled national expansion toward the northeast. In Loreto, the rubber industry buffered the department from a severe economic crisis gripping much of Peru and supplied the administrative and political opportunities to support two, if not three, competing governments.[19]

The career of Manuel Pinedo illustrates the twists and turns one's life could take as a public servant in Loreto. The nineteen-year-old Manuel took his first position in 1864 as a secretary to the perfect in Moyobamba. He slowly made his way up the ranks, working as an assistant to the prefect. He did, however, spend about fifteen months on board a steamboat, serving as a purser from 1866 to 1868. By 1876, after almost ten years of service in Loreto and two years in Lima, the thirty-year-old bachelor became Loreto's treasurer.[20]

The War of the Pacific (1879–83) and the subsequent chaos undoubtedly disrupted Pinedo's public career. From 1881 to 1884, he labored alone in Moyobamba after the rest of the office staff quit. In January 1882, thieves broke into the treasury office and stole not only money and receipts but also Pinedo's desk and chair. By 1884, he faced unauthorized competition after one of many self-declared prefects named his own treasury officials in Iquitos. Pinedo also claimed that the legitimate prefect in Moyobamba was ripping off the public treasury by, for example, paying salaries to nonexistent soldiers.[21] Things got so bad by 1886 that Pinedo left his position and went down the Amazon to try his luck at rubber collection.[22]

But he was back soon. Like many other Loretano officials, he found Iquitos a more promising site to advance his career. In 1887 and 1888, Pinedo worked as a treasurer in the active customs house in Iquitos, one annually collecting close to 100,000 soles from import and export duties. By 1891, he had taken the important and lucrative position of custom's director in Iquitos. But for Lima to recognize his position, Pinedo needed to post a large bond to "guard the public interest." He faced the classic bind: how could one afford to secure a new position without working awhile and perhaps skimming some of the receipts to raise the necessary cash for the bond? Throughout 1891, Pinedo ignored the bond requirement and hoped that Lima would take care of the matter. Lima did act, but not the way Pinedo preferred; in February 1892, he was sacked and charged with malfeasance.[23] Manuel subsequently returned to public service, but his career from the 1860s through the early 1890s reflects both the liabilities and opportunities in Loreto's dynamic bureaucracy.

The task of rebuilding a stable administration in Loreto began in 1887 and was one shared by national and local officials, yet efforts to impose order and standardization met resistance. Lima wanted to cut Loreto's payroll and have the department assume more responsibility for the salaries of the gendarme.[24] On other economic issues, Lima set import and export tax rates in Loreto and stipulated that the department allocate 10,000 soles annually for schools in

Moyobamba. Lima continued the program of distributing up to 120 hectares of free land to anyone who solicited it.[25] Finally, the prefect joined the act of reordering Loreto's social and economic relations by distributing several thousand soles to various military expeditions and by promulgating a decree institutionalizing the debt-peonage system.[26]

Loreto's administration was back on its feet. Duties on English, French, and American imports brought in much of the department's income. With more money, the administration created new positions and oversaw more of the thriving commercial traffic in Iquitos.[27] But even burgeoning revenues caused friction. For instance, in May 1889 the subprefect in Moyobamba assured the two new congressmen from Loreto that the customs house in Iquitos would gladly supply them with the necessary funds for their long journey to Lima. But the prefect in Iquitos was not amused that his subordinate had usurped his authority by promising the deputies money. Neither was he happy when three congressmen, not two, arrived in town, each requesting a thousand soles for travel expenses. The prefect decided to give them something just to get them out of town.[28] Nonetheless, having weathered the chaotic 1880s, one could not help but notice that Loreto's administration was growing in size and sophistication.

Loreto moved out of the eighties and into the nineties led by an exceptionally active prefect, Samuel Palacios. The Young Turk Palacios rejected his predecessor's programs and laid out his own agenda. He determined a road project from Lima to Iquitos impractical — today there still is no road down to Iquitos — and focused his attention on borders and river patrols. He proposed that each district have its own police unit and that the borders be protected by able forces. He admitted that crimes and cruelty would continue in places like the Ucayali, Tigre, and Yavari, but he believed that more police and more steamships, the latter outfitted for war, would help impose order. He did see a need for some roads to facilitate colonization, and he capped his objectives by suggesting the "use of intelligence and force to pull savage tribes into the national community and civilized work."[29] Loreto had an energetic and aggressive new prefect.

Palacios kept very busy during his one-year tenure. In October 1889, he dispatched ten men to Barranca to put down an attack by Huambisas and therefore could not spare ten more men requested by leaders in Moyobamba. He reasoned that he must keep some of his force in Iquitos to guarantee the interests of foreigners and merchants. That same month he asked Lima to shift an 8,000 soles subsidy to the British-owned Amazon Steam Company from a line up the Huallaga to another up the rubber-rich Ucayali. Lima approved this request and also okayed an annual subsidy of 12,000 soles for a line linking Liverpool and Iquitos.[30]

The following month, Palacios confronted the sticky problem of customs fraud and commercial problems with Brazil. He knew that corruption and smuggling permeated Amazonian trade, but he wanted to clean it up a tad, starting with the Peruvian customs agent in Pará. Palacios claimed that said official routinely accepted bribes from merchants in exchange for underreporting the value of imports destined for Iquitos. The director of customs in Iquitos chided Palacios for questioning the honesty of his colleague in Pará, and mentioned that imports were not purposely undervalued but just marked up four to five times before they made it to Iquitos.[31] The other problem downriver occurred when Brazilian officials halted ships destined for Iquitos under suspicion of smuggling. As usual, Palacios squarely faced this issue and requested permission to travel to Manaus and Pará to meet personally with Brazilian customs directors and to study their regulations. Essentially, Palacios would serve as Peru's trade representative in Brazil. Although it is not clear whether he made the trip, Lima had enough faith in their Loreto prefect to approve his plan and to send him instructions.[32]

Palacios also adopted a strong defense of his jurisdiction over contested frontiers. In December 1889, he received word of Ecuadorian and Colombian administrators ceding lands along the Napo River to caucheros in the name of their governments. Palacios ordered the Peruvian military commander for the Ecuadorian frontier to take a steamboat up the Napo as far as Aguarico and check out the situation. Palacios gave the commander authority to arrest or displace any foreign leaders he found. If he encountered any Colombian or Ecuadorian officials, he could take their credentials and send them down to Iquitos for closer inspection. He could then arrest these officials found without credentials and transport them as prisoners to Iquitos. In essence, the Peruvian commander had the authority to clear the Middle Napo up to the present-day Ecuadorian border of all non-Peruvian personnel.

As he expanded his jurisdiction to the west, Palacios did the same to the east. In March 1890, he appointed a customs inspector to Leticia near the Brazilian border.[33] That same month, rheumatism struck Palacios, and by November he resigned his post.[34] Peru had lost an able and energetic prefect, but Palacios's myriad actions clearly signalled a renaissance of the country's power in northwestern Amazonia.

Subsequent prefects followed Palacios's lead in augmenting police forces, establishing customs houses, and regulating commerce in outlying districts and in booming Iquitos.[35] Nonetheless, corruption, fraud, and smuggling remained inescapable realities, for Loreto simply had too many business opportunities to keep public servants honest. Almost two-thirds of the rubber extracted and exported from Loreto managed to escape the notice and taxation of departmental officials. Moreover, small-time customs agents out in remote regions often collected duties for six to seven months, rolled up 6,000 to 8,000 soles in the process, then deserted their posts and went into business for themselves as aviadores or tradesmen.[36] Nonetheless, by the mid-1890s, Loreto maintained a system of customs houses, police and border forces, and naval and military personnel overseen by an array of appointed officials, whom Lima usually supported. In fact, the rubber industry and the Iquitos customs added enough coin to public coffers that by 1894, Loreto subsidized schools in the distant Andean town Chachapoyas to the tune of 10,000 soles a year.[37]

Over the previous forty-five years, a combination of factors favored the development of the Peruvian administration in Loreto. First, as early as the 1850s, the national government in Lima had adopted an aggressive policy in Loreto of sending army and navy units to Iquitos, followed in the 1860s with the purchase of technologically advanced steamboats that gave Peruvians great advantages over the Colombians and Ecuadorians in later decades. Moreover, Lima, more so than Bogotá or Quito, consistently supported its departmental officials based in Moyobamba and Iquitos. In part, Peru had a distinct advantage by controlling Iquitos, a vital port and commercial hub for northwestern Amazonia.

The second factor favoring the Peruvians centered on the economic growth of the rubber industry in Loreto. While much of the rest of the country floundered during the upset caused by the War of the Pacific, Loreto, connected to world trade through the Amazonian trade system, experienced unprecedented economic growth and opportunity. Political leadership at the regional level displayed dynamism as well. The two to three prefects ruling simultaneously during the confused but profitable 1880s gave way to the stable and focused direction of Samuel Palacios. His aggressive policies — which his successors pursued in subsequent decades — encouraged Peruvian commerce and bolstered the nation's control over disputed border regions. By 1895, Peru enjoyed a strong economic, political, and military position in northwestern Amazonia. The situation for Colombia was less certain.

COLOMBIAN ADMINISTRATION, 1850–95

National disintegration, a chronically weak state, and civil wars posed serious crises for Colombian efforts to administrate its beautiful but rugged territory in the latter half of the nineteenth century (see map). Simón Bolívar's dream of Gran Colombia shattered with the secession of Venezuela and Ecuador after 1830. Bogotá officials worried that frontier regions such as the eastern llanos, skinny Panama, and the Putumayo would also split away from Nueva Granada.[38] For a country torn by eight major civil wars and fourteen local civil wars just in the nineteenth century, it is remarkable that Colombia maintained as much territory as it did.

In the 1830s and 1840s, Nueva Granada used the Putumayo as a dumping ground for political exiles and criminals, but by the 1850s, Caquetá had a prefect naming corregidores to Indian villages throughout the Upper Putumayo and Caquetá, as far south as Aguarico.[39] But the bloody Federal War of 1860 to 1863 disrupted this early administrative effort by cutting off trade routes to Nueva Granada. Throughout these years, Brazilian slavers raided into the Caquetá and forcibly reoriented the region's economic focus toward Amazonia.[40]

After the Federal War, the quina boom of the 1860s offered economic and political opportunities for Colombians such as the Reyes family and stimulated a new administrative effort in the Caquetá and Putumayo. In early 1868, Reyes Brothers partner and Caquetá prefect Pedro F. Urrutia reappointed corregidores for posts stretching up and down the two rivers.[41] Urrutia selected experienced and tough individuals for these unpaid positions, men familiar with Indian tribes through their roles as patróns overseeing quina, caucho, and other forest-product collection. The following year, Urrutia unveiled plans for colonization and recommended an administrative reorganization. He hoped that a change of white-Indian ratios from 1:200 to 1:10 would have a salubrious "civilizing effect" and that salaried corregidores would no longer steal or extort goods from Indians. He also requested twenty-five soldiers and some missionaries to bolster efforts at both physical and cultural conquest, in part responding to the Peruvian initiative at Tabatinga.[42]

In September 1869, Urrutia confronted a dangerous situation in the Upper Putumayo. The Santiagueño Indians staged a nocturnal raid on their neighbors, the Putumayos, and managed to take more than twenty prisoners, including the Putumayo governor. The Santiagueños placed their captives in stocks and whipped them thirty to forty times, while boasting that the Putumayos "deserved such treatment." Urrutia decided to punish the kidnappers and managed to capture the governor of Santiago, but then he and his four armed guards had to release him when townspeople surrounded them all. These two Indian towns had engaged in a long-standing land dispute, sometimes punctuated with violence, and their inhabitants usually ignored Urrutia's orders. The prefect decided that forty well-armed men would be needed to reduce Santiago and impose order.[43] Clearly, Indians living and acting independently of local white officials presented a danger to Urrutia's reorganization plans and to effective Colombian administration.

During much of the 1870s, the Colombian administration muddled through as the quina boom began. Indians continued to migrate at will, frequently across borders drawn or imagined by governmental officials.[44] For the geopolitical ambitions of national authorities and the economic fortunes of local officials, such freedom foiled the best-drawn plans. Local officials also moved about erratically, often abandoning their posts, presumably for greener pastures downriver.[45] Foreign raiders further added to the climate of flux. By 1874, Peruvians entered Aguarico and seized children for future sale, trade, or labor. Simultaneously, Brazilians tested Colombian jurisdiction along the Putumayo. Both these thrusts compromised Colombian interests between the Putumayo and Napo Rivers.[46] Two years later, Peru readied a small steam-powered gunboat for the ascension of the Putumayo in a bid to take control of the territory. To fend them off, the Colombian consul in Yurimaguas urged the Caquetá prefect to name political and civil authorities to all the villages along the Putumayo to demonstrate Colombian sovereignty.[47]

By the late 1870s, following another civil war from 1876 to 1877, the Colombian administration in the Caquetá rebounded, riding the quina boom and the commercial bonanza carried by the steamboats owned or rented by the Reyes Brothers. The prefect rebuilt the local administration as he sent out exploratory teams to find riverine links between Cauca and the Caquetá and across the Putumayo to the Napo.[48] He oversaw the creation of the corregimiento of Putumayo, centered around the new village of Cantinera and its fifty-meter-long warehouse. The corregidores in such spots received monthly salaries and enjoyed regular mail service, real luxuries in such peripheral posts.[49]

Through the early 1880s, both the Caquetá and Putumayo boasted a mail service and salaried corregidores and procurators. Although the Mocoa customs house could not collect enough duties to pay for its operation, the one at La Sofía on the Putumayo River provided income. Brazilian steamships could not reach Mocoa, but they could call at La Sofía (near Puerto Asís, and named for Rafael Reyes's wife), and thereby they helped shift commercial activity away from the Caquetá foothills and toward the Putumayo lowlands.[50] Quina and caucho exports and the imports handled by the Reyes brothers essentially supported the customs officials in both areas.[51]

Things were going so well in 1882 that the Colombian government felt strong enough to protest the presence of Peruvian troops at Tutapisco, on the Lower Napo, a scant fifty miles overland from Iquitos. To block future Peruvian incursions and Brazilian slave raids to collect Indians for market downriver — there had been three since 1878 — Secretary of Foreign Affairs L. W. Quijano suggested that the Caquetá prefect make a detailed study of the region, and that the Sovereign State of Cauca send troops down to the disputed zone. In the meantime, Quijano ordered that Indian tribes appearing along the Aguarico River be reduced, presumably to beat the Peruvians to the punch.[52]

Following the disruptions caused by the civil war of 1884 and 1885, the regional bureaucracy grew larger in 1888 and 1889. The province needed circuit judges, absent for some years, not to protect Indians from abuses by caucheros but to guarantee the property rights of merchants. Prefect Urrutia (a former Reyes Brothers employee) complained that merchants suffered the disrespect and taunts of debtors who refused to fulfill their obligations. Urrutia recommended that district and circuit judges, aided by salaried secretaries, be appointed soon. To facilitate effective administration, Caquetá was divided into four municipal districts — Mocoa, Upper Caquetá, Aguarico, and Lower Caquetá. By 1889, police forces patrolled the gold-mining districts of Upper Caquetá, overseeing production and keeping an eye on delinquents, presumably Liberals.[53]

Various unpleasant incidents greeted Colombian officials responsible for the Caquetá and the Putumayo in the early nineties. In May 1891, the governor of Cauca alerted Bogotá that an unknown tribe had assassinated about forty whites, "among whom, some are from notable Colombian families." The governor suggested that a stronger military and missionary presence would "prevent future Indian attacks and the slaughter of peoples of the white race."[54] Conflicts between rival rubber companies over lands, commercial routes, and workers also caught the attention of regional, departmental, and national authorities.[55] But the killing of a resident Englishman became the most delicate matter of the year.

John Parker lived for many years near the confluence of the Napo and Aguarico Rivers, one of the hot spots for Ecuadorian, Colombian, and Peruvian collisions. One day in late May or early June 1891, an angry and drunk local official, Juan Higinio Díaz confronted, insulted, and then shot Parker in the leg. Parker limped to the hut of a friend, but Díaz broke in and attacked him with an axe. After being disarmed, Díaz ordered two subordinates to finish Parker off. One discharged his shotgun but the pellets only caught Parker in the ear. The other fatally wounded Parker in the back, and then the three finished their ugly deed by dumping the corpse in the river.[56]

This murder caused considerable diplomatic fallout in London, Bogotá, and Popayán, but surprisingly, Ecuador took the lead in pursuing and capturing the murderers. Oriente governor Juan Mosquera raised an expedition to collect on-site evidence, arrested the suspects by May 1892, and requested reimbursement from Quito for his expenses.[57] In essence, Ecuador used John Parker's murder to demonstrate its judicial purview over a contested territory.

Although the Caquetá administration could not rival that of Loreto in size or sophistication, it did function relatively well, especially in the upper reaches of the territory. Taxes on caucho, liquor, and public events such as town dances brought in revenue, as did user fees on bridges and roads. Local political and police bosses, or *comisarios,* oversaw Indians in their districts. Labor drafts still supplied most of the workforce for public works projects. The Mocoa town council even suggested that Caquetá, Pasto, Barbacoas, Tuquerres, and Obando form their own department, foreshadowing the future creation of Nariño in the deep south of Colombia.[58]

Colonization and open land focused attention on the Upper Caquetá. Colonists from Caldas — in central Colombia — established the town of Santa Rosa on the Caquetá in 1874. Twenty years later, their farms and ranches had so crowded the south side of the river that they requested more land along the northern bank. Other colonists and land speculators laid their claims to federal lands, or *baldíos,* in the mid-nineties. Of course, white colonists and competition for land increased pressures and conflicts with Indians. By June 1894, the classic colonial scenario of white-owned cattle eating or trampling Indian crops brought antagonisms to a head. The extant colonial "Two Republics" system of separating white and Indian societies, another legacy of centuries past, provoked whites in Sibundoy to request permission to integrate with Indians to "civilize them," and to claim ownership of lands that Indians did not cultivate. The colonists wanted direct access to the Indians, and hoped to get more acreage for themselves.[59]

Whereas Peruvians used the rubber industry, steamboats, and their concomitant revenues to fan out across Loreto, Colombian colonists progressively pushed down the Caquetá and Putumayo to incorporate territory into the national system. This colonization movement became the cornerstone of Colombian efforts to control the two regions. Looking toward the future then, Colombia had to colonize the upper reaches of the Putumayo and Caquetá and, from those bases, hope to counter Peruvian power downriver. Ecuador took a different path.

ECUADORIAN ADMINISTRATION, 1850–95

Peru's military and commercial activities combined with Colombia's colonization policy in northwestern Amazonia provoked a reaction from Ecuador (see map). Building on the colonial jurisdiction of the Audiencia de Quito and the Pedemonte/Mosquera Protocol of 1830, Ecuadorian territorial claims stretched deep into lands claimed by Colombia, Brazil, and Peru — north to the Caquetá, east beyond Tabatinga, and south below Yurimaguas. Ecuador therefore inevitably clashed with her neighbors. In 1853, Ecuador protested the Peruvian formation of the political and military government in Loreto, perceiving it as a usurpation of Ecuadorian sovereignty. The same year, Ecuador declared the free navigation of the Putumayo and Napo Rivers, among others, and hatched plans to colonize the Oriente.[60] Four years later, Ecuador tried to cancel part of its foreign debt by ceding a large chunk of her Amazonian claim to English creditors. Peru responded to this last scheme by breaking diplomatic relations with its northern neighbor.[61]

Regionalism, factionalism, and civil war — real problems for many Latin American countries at the time — plagued both Colombia and Ecuador throughout the nineteenth century. With Quito and Cuenca the foci of sierran political and economic interests, and Guayaquil that of the coast, the enormous but unknown Oriente drew small notice from the government. Civil war wracked the country from 1854 to 1861 and gave the Peruvian general and president Ramón Castilla the opportunity to occupy Guayaquil and to force Ecuador to acknowledge Peruvian possession of all the navigable reaches of the rivers emptying into the Marañón and Amazon.[62]

Nonetheless, a provincial government did persist throughout these years of civil and foreign wars. Operating from small towns and villages such as Tena, Napo, Archidona, and Santa Rosa, governors occasionally toured the surrounding areas to arrest criminals and to patrol their jurisdictions. But as early as 1857, Ecuadorian local officials faced challenges to their authority from both Peruvian and Colombian raiders. In June, Joaquín Panduro entered the villages of Aguano and Napotóa and forced many families to migrate down the Marañon into Peruvian territory. Two months later, the Ecuadorian president, Francisco Robles, ordered an investigation into Panduro's crimes. The provincial governor of the Oriente investigated the matter but admitted that distance and poor communications would make the investigation a slow one.[63]

After whites from various countries enticed or forced Indians to move around or out of the Oriente, the governor had to act, but he was unsure about many crucial points. Where was his jurisdiction, and how could he police it without an armed squad and a reliable launch? Had the migrating Indians been impressed, or had they moved freely?[64] The governor's questions highlighted an inescapable reality of Ecuador's tenuous administrative presence in the Oriente; it was centered in the central reaches of the province in towns relatively close to the Andes. The northern rivers, including the Coca, Aguarico, and Putumayo, were beyond the reach of effective Ecuadorian jurisdiction.[65]

Table 4. Selected Ecuadorian Exports by Percent of Value, 1855–1900

Year	Cacao	Coffee	Panama Hats	Tagua	Rubber
1855	27.6	.4	50.1	–	.8
1864	58.5	1.8	17.8	–	4.9
1879	53.5	.9	.2	5.1	1.0
1884	63.4	2.8	4.7	1.4	4.1
1889	74.7	6.5	–	6.7	3.3
1893	73.7	7.8	–	6.4	1.4
1897	66.2	7.5	3.5	6.8	9.6
1900	70.7	5.4	2.1	10.4	7.0

Source: Rodríguez, *The Search for Public Policy,* 179, 181.

Communication and transportation between highland Quito and coastal Guayaquil, let alone the Oriente, imposed great hardships. A railroad project to link these two major Ecuadorian cities, begun under President Gabriel García Moreno in 1872, promised to link the sierra and coast and further the political and economic integration of the country. However, steep mountains, frequent washouts, and political wrangling delayed completion of this line until 1908.[66] In the meantime, rain closed or flooded the dirt road from Guayaquíl up to Chimborazo from January to May. In many months of the year, Indian carriers strapped mail pouches to their backs when they forded raging streams.[67] Regardless of these difficulties, the country needed a transportation link between the sierra and the coast. This was especially true because of the coastal focus of Ecuador's export economy. Grown on lowland Pacific plantations, cacao oriented the country's economy to the west, away from the Oriente, as the rubber boom hit stride (see table 4). Perhaps, if Amazonian rubber had had more economic clout among Ecuador's exports, Quito might have directed more attention and resources to meet the territorial and administrative challenges in the Oriente.

Over and down the eastern slope of the Andes, Ecuadorian governors tried to fulfill their tasks in the Oriente but faced shortages of funds, men, and supplies. Based in the pleasant montaña town of Archidona, two thousand feet above the jungle floor, they could at least count on a healthy climate.[68] But even Archidona lacked a decent road to Quito. It often required two months for a governor's correspondence to reach the capital.[69] Isolation, penury, and frustration usually defined a governor's term.

Periodically, national political turmoil, such as the 1875 assassination of the Conservative caudillo and president García Moreno, upset regional administration as it spilled into the Oriente. In January 1878, Gen. Ignacio Veintimilla appointed a new governor to the region, but the standing governor refused to relinquish his post until he was formally dismissed.[70]

Nonetheless, two weeks later, the new appointee, José de la Guerra, sent off his first report on the state of the territory. De la Guerra stressed the immediate need for reforms: a road link to the capital and monthly mail service, the reduction of "barbarous and savage Indians" into towns to encourage a "civilizing effect," and the need for the ex-governor's appointees to stop the forced sales of goods to Indians. Furthermore, he complained that he lacked a decent canoe, let alone a steamboat, in a land of riverine travel.[71]

Over the next two years, de la Guerra had the tall order of "liberating the Indians and restoring peace and order," yet he had no guard, support, or supplies. His political enemies constantly attacked his actions but it appears that the governor performed ably under difficult circumstances. A disciplined bureaucrat who went through channels and wrote timely reports, de la Guerra received the honorable title "Proprietary Governor of Oriente Province" in February 1879.[72] But the bureaucratic relationship between de la Guerra and Quito had definite drawbacks. In April, for example, the governor had to petition the central government just for authorization to pay the salaries of his new eight-man squad for another three months. Over the next two months, moreover, he sent three prisoners under guard all the way back to Quito, yet he could afford neither to pay the civilian escort nor spare any member of his personal guard.[73] Even with great ability and energy, de la Guerra never achieved his goals because of the real and imposed limitations on his office.

Ecuador started the 1880s on a sour note. With both the Liberal and Conservative parties internally divided, the corrupt and brutal dictator Gen. Ignacio Veintimilla ran an inept and opportunistic regime, one punctuated by harsh repression, jail, whippings, and firing squads for political opponents. The government missed an opportunity to prosper economically and politically during the War of the Pacific as Peru weakened and as world demand strengthened markets for the country's exports. After the general skimmed off close to two million pesos from public coffers, Liberal and Conservative armies ran the dictator out of the country in 1883. For good measure, or out of spite, Veintimilla sacked two banks in Guayaquil in the last moments prior to his ignoble exile.[74]

As might be expected, the Oriente received little attention in the first half of the decade. It lay outside the political, economic, and social core of the country. By mid-decade, of 1.3 million Ecuadorians, only 15,850 people were counted in the Oriente, while close to a million lived in the highlands.[75] The Oriente received no money or coherent direction from the national government during this period, understandable given the political chaos and civil war of the era. The responsibility of formulating a de facto policy fell upon local and regional officials — those working for the military, the state, or the church. Each institution brought its own agendas, prejudices, attitudes, and cultures, ones often casting Indians as dangerous uncivilized savages, or *aucas*.[76]

In such a situation, Oriente governor Francisco Andrade Marín assumed a tough post in 1884. Before he left Quito, Andrade Marín managed to sign up 96 prospective colonists, supported by 14 carriers, to accompany him to the lowlands. But by marching time, only 40 of the 110 signatories showed up. An amusing list of excuses covered the absences of the remainder: fathers disliked the plan, and some mothers objected to it as well; wives prohibited their husbands from leaving; some colonists got sick, others went to the coast, and many just backed out. By October 1884, the governor counted only 25 colonists and carriers in his new colony along the Napo River. Ironically, Congress pointed to the great success of Andrade's efforts as evidence that the Oriente needed no further governmental assistance.[77]

In the mid-1880s, caucheros of various nationalities busily exported their precious goods duty free through Iquitos. Ecuador, unlike Colombia and Peru, neglected to establish a system of customs houses, and therefore the boom industry failed to fatten national or regional coffers. Although Ecuadorian citizens from Quito, Cuenca, and Pelileo worked the eastern forests, their efforts did not stimulate state action to plant the Ecuadorian tricolor behind them. Although Andrade Marín alerted the government of the export value of caucho, tobacco, and coca (a cocaine craze was on), bureaucrats in Quito ignored his recommendations and directed their attention elsewhere.[78] Subsequent warnings from an Ecuadorian cauchero concerning the activities of Peruvians, Colombians, and Chinese in the Oriente were similarly filed away and forgotten.[79] While Oriente governors traveled by canoe, their colleagues in Iquitos steamed in heavily armed launches. Technologically, economically, and administratively, the Ecuadorians literally and figuratively missed the boat.[80]

The Oriente administration recovered remarkably from the previous decade in the first half of the 1890s. Although governors still had to cope with harsh living and working conditions, isolation, foreign incursions, and little or no support from Quito, the regional government functioned adequately. Like Colombians, Ecuadorians dreamed of a bright future in the Amazonian lowlands. For example, in 1890 a group of artisans in Quito hatched a scheme to colonize the Oriente with the assistance of a government subsidy. Such aid seemed vital for agricultural colonists to survive through the first few lean years.[81] Meanwhile, work continued on a road from Quito to Archidona, a link which hopefully would encourage future colonization and the integration of the sierra and the selva. Short of tools and building materials, however,

Governor Mosquera requested that Quito send him supplies, and incredibly, only two weeks later, President Antonio Flores Jijón ordered the necessary goods dispatched to Mosquera.[82] Occasionally, Quito could and did act quickly to attend to the needs of the Oriente, although one could question the wisdom of having the president involved in a decision about tools for a road. But another decision did demonstrate wisdom: Quito appointed Gen. Rafael Reyes, former quinero and cauchero, as Ecuador's consul general in Colombia. Quito astutely selected a man with great political clout, excellent international business connections, and an intimate knowledge of northwestern Amazonia.[83]

Unfortunately for the native peoples, the government did almost nothing to halt the true scourge of white presence: disease. In 1889, measles spread among villagers and forest residents, followed the next year by a smallpox epidemic. Such diseases created panic among the local population, driving many of them to seek refuge in the jungle. Individuals who remained in towns ran a great risk of infection; in Archidona the smallpox epidemic took a high toll on afflicted adults, killing twenty-eight of thirty-five during the first six months of 1890. Officials requested food and medicine, but little or none arrived by June, when the governor and missionaries declared the epidemic over and began the difficult task of recongregating the Indians into towns and missions, and ordering parents to send their children back to school.[84]

Along with disease and a tiny budget, the mercantile and national interests of foreigners placed stress on Oriente governors. In July 1890, a Peruvian steamship under orders of the prefect in Iquitos called at Tiputini (Tiputino) near the existing Peruvian/Ecuadorian border on the Napo River. The Peruvian commander refused to acknowledge Ecuadorian jurisdiction and named his own local officials on the Upper and Lower Curaray River. The Ecuadorians lacked the men, transportation, and weapons to turn back these challengers, and depended on the vague patriotism of foreign missionaries, enterprising caucheros, and Indians to stop them. By late 1890, the Peruvians had planted their flag and were exploiting Indian workers, capturing women, searching for caucho, and settling in along the Napo.[85]

Both residents and Oriente officials alerted Quito of the danger that Peruvians, Colombians, and Brazilians posed to "the land of Ecuador's future." They believed that a border treaty, starting with Peru, would end much of the confusion and conflict on the fringes of the territory. Ecuadorian caucheros also lobbied Quito to establish a trade agreement with Lima, one to facilitate commercial traffic up and down the Amazon. Without such an agreement, Peruvian customs officials in Iquitos seized caucho and imports carried to or from Ecuador. But here, too, it appears that national officials shirked their responsibilities. By early 1892, the exasperated Oriente governor, Juan Mosquera, had written to both an Ecuadorian minister in Quito as well as to the Peruvian prefect in Iquitos complaining of extortions perpetuated by a Peruvian in the Oriente.[86] If Mosquera could not get any action from his own government, why not try another?

Throughout 1891 and 1892, Governor Mosquera attempted to incorporate more of the Oriente into the national domain. He persisted in efforts to complete the Quito-Archidona road, requesting from Quito cloth, trinkets, and metal tools to compensate Indian laborers. He also tried to build up his tiny civil bureaucracy, made up of only three officials: two in Archidona and one in Tiputini. But in doing so, Mosquera raised the bureaucratic fences of ministers in Quito — men uncomfortable with the governor's independence, and seemingly determined to guard and centralize authority no matter the consequence.[87]

Such a penurious and feeble administration lacked the power to demand acknowledgment and obedience from whites and Indians alike. Although caucheros often abused, killed, and enslaved Indians, occasionally Indians turned the tables on the rubber men. Early in 1891, for example, Angoteros ambushed and killed a Colombian cauchero, his Peruvian wife, four Christian Indians, and three Zaparos along the banks of the Middle Napo. In such cases, if the governor maintained good relations with the missionaries, he could expect their support in rounding up fugitives. Nonetheless, local inhabitants often ignored the provincial government's dictates. For example, when Governor Mosquera needed exotic animals collected for Ecuador's exhibit at the 1893 Columbian Exposition in Chicago, Indians demanded high prices for any animal they trapped. Some Indians also carried firearms, usually shotguns or rifles acquired from traders. Local officials expressed concern about "putting arms into the hands of barbarous people who have no inkling of right."[88] They knew too that an armed Indian majority could never be controlled by a small administrative staff.

A large-scale rebellion during the last few months of 1892 illustrates Ecuador's tenuous hold on the Oriente. A change of administrations signaled the moment for a revolt against the standing civil and religious authorities. Rebels appealed to Indians to leave the missions and to ignore their forced duties — like the ongoing road building and repairing — imposed by the governor. Although it appears that few people died in the rebellion, it was nonetheless widespread.[89] Unfortunately, Quito seemed happy simply to mete out punishment to the unruly rather than attempt the more difficult task of reforming and improving the provincial administration.

Ecuadorian ignorance of the Oriente again caused serious problems in

1893. Criminals operated with impunity, dispensing liquor to Indians, intercepting and stealing mail, and killing at random. If the few government employees did not receive their monthly salary (a common event), they tapped the local Indians for goods and food.[90] Some rogue Ecuadorians murdered whites at will, enslaved Indians, and carried out a profitable rubber business on the Lower Napo beyond the reach of both Peruvian and Ecuadorian authorities. Although Lima sent a letter to Quito protesting such deeds, Loretanos went about expanding their zones of operation into contested frontiers. Their control over the export/import markets through Iquitos, and their superior access to goods and cash, proved to be effective mechanisms for attracting Ecuadorian loyalties to Peru. For instance, in September 1893, an Ecuadorian colonist and cauchero planted the Peruvian flag on his plantation near Tiputini. Whether he did this freely or out of fear is unknown. The local political boss sent to seize the flag and replace it with the Ecuadorian tricolor instead accepted a bribe of 130 soles to leave the Peruvians and their banner unmolested. Moreover, all the inhabitants of Suno and thirty families from another village moved from Ecuadorian to Peruvian territory, either forced to do so or attracted downriver by Peruvian goods.[91]

Peru kept up the pressure on Ecuador's vast and unprotected eastern flank the following year. Portuguese by birth but now the Peruvian inspector on the Napo, José María Mourón steamed up the Napo to test Ecuadorian defenses at Tiputini, and on the way seized the peons and property of several Ecuadorian caucheros. Governor Pío Terán only sent about a dozen men to face Mourón and his crew. While Mourón's men had dependable rifles and supplies on board their steamboat, Pío Terán sent his men ill-equipped and balanced in canoes. Pío knew he could not simply impress Indians to paddle and guide the canoes. Too many had already left in disgust and gone downriver, where they received the Peruvians and their goods with anticipated delight.[92]

Although national politicians in Quito and Guayaquil pointed with pride to Ecuador's huge Amazonian claim, they did little to attend to the problems of the Oriente province. Quito furnished a minimum amount of material, personnel, and money to the province. Economically and geographically, the country faced west toward the cacao plantations of the Pacific lowlands, not east toward the rubber-rich Amazon basin. Moreover, regional partisan divisions and civil wars kept Ecuadorians divided and preoccupied with concerns other than that of their eastern frontier. In the Oriente, the provincial capital at Archidona also faced west and up the mountain to Quito rather than downriver toward the Amazon basin. Governors depended on appropriations from Quito and failed at the regional level to establish a network of customs houses to collect revenues from the rubber trade. Lacking the necessary men and supplies, Ecuadorians neglected the Oriente's far-flung borders. When the governor sent out a patrol, his few men traveled in canoes, not in steamboats. Moreover, Ecuadorian dependence on Iquitos — like that of Colombians — for trade and transportation links into the Amazon basin reinforced the Peruvian position, while it further undermined that of Ecuador in northwestern Amazonia.

MISSIONARIES AND REGIONAL ADMINISTRATION

Another reason why Ecuadorian secular officials had such trouble gaining money and support from the national government is that Quito subsidized a relatively large ecclesiastical administration in the Oriente. More so than Peru or Colombia, Ecuador relied on missionaries during most of the thirty-five years after 1860 to "civilize," Christianize, and congregate Indians and, at the same time, solidify the country's rule in the region. Conservative President García Moreno deserves most of the credit for fashioning an intimate relationship between the Catholic Church and the state. In 1862, he invited the Jesuits back into Ecuador after a ten-year exile as part of his resolve to reinvigorate missionary activity in the Oriente. By 1869, García Moreno had supplied the guiding hand behind a constitution centralizing power in a state wedded to the church. That same year, church and state funds flowed to Jesuit and secular priests, who resolutely pressed their efforts to reestablish the presence of the Catholic government of Ecuador in the Oriente.[93]

In little time, the missionaries found themselves in the middle of territorial disputes. In 1870, the Colombian corregidor of Mocoa ordered a census of the town of Coca, but the Jesuits and secular priests sent from Quito claimed the area for Ecuador. The Jesuit Ambrosio Fonseca, himself Colombian by birth, claimed to hold civil and religious authority in the region and pressed his claim to Coca by late 1870. Fonseca petitioned for permission to exercise priestly functions in Coca, but the prefect of Caquetá rejected Fonseca's request because he was a Jesuit, and thus barred from Colombian soil by the Liberal government in Bogotá.[94]

Ecuadorian missionary efforts provoked similar efforts by Colombia. In 1872, the active Santacruz brothers, one a corregidor and the other a priest, reconnoitered the Upper Napo to select future mission sites. Although this initiative seemed to produce few results, Father Santiago Santacruz baptized 120 Indians, married forty couples, and forced two Indian caciques to choose one of their two wives before he would baptize or marry them.[95] Instead of relying on missionaries, however, Colombian fortunes in the Putumayo and the Napo ascended with the commercial activities of the Reyes Brothers. Indeed, by 1878, Father Santiago, the only priest in the area, "preferred to occupy himself in the extraction of quina and caucho for the Caquetá Company" and ignored his priestly duties because "there aren't people here who want to give him pesetas to get souls out of purgatory nor anyone who will grant him a modest subsistence."[96]

As one might expect, relations between church and state took a decidedly partisan path in the Colombian Putumayo. In mid-1878, Liberal partisans claimed that Father Manuel Guerrero prohibited Indians from joining the Liberal Party, and that Guerrero was undermining "blessed liberty and the delicious environment of liberalism." It appears that these partisans, likely more interested in access to Indian labor than in the protection of liberty, denounced Guerrero in a forged document purportedly penned by the *cabildos* (councils) of several Indian towns in the Upper Putumayo. In response, these cabildos issued a statement in support of Father Manuel and urged prosecution of the Liberal forgers.[97] Partisan politics trickled into the Putumayo, placing Indians in the midst of a struggle defined more by profit than ideology.

In Ecuador, President García Moreno's autocratic and theological government established the groundwork for a violent reaction from moderate Catholics, Conservatives, and Liberals. García Moreno exiled political opponents to the Napo as he advanced his support for the Jesuits; such practices led to his assassination. In 1875, after he had named a Colombian, Faustino Lemus Rayo, to be the next governor of the Oriente, the Jesuits lobbied against his appointment, and it was rescinded. On August 6, a disgruntled Lemus, among others, attacked García Moreno with a machete and killed him. Political chaos ensued during the next year, when provisional Liberal governments ordered the free exploitation of the eastern forests, thereby challenging the ecclesiastical hold on the Oriente. Although Jesuits fled both Quito and Guayaquil during this secular backlash, it seems that their operations in Amazonia suffered few serious reverses.[98]

The political disruptions in Ecuador associated with the Veintimilla dictatorship of the early eighties certainly interrupted correspondence with the Oriente, but they seemed to do little permanent damage to the missions. Five Jesuit priests supported by a like number of lay assistants labored around the Napo and continued to share governmental duties with the governor. By 1884, the Ecuadorian Congress assumed from the executive branch the legal responsibility for the Oriente missions, a change that stimulated new and ambitious plans to augment the ecclesiastic presence in the region.[99]

The archbishop of Quito lost little time before lobbying Congress to pass pro-mission legislation. In 1885, Archbishop José Ignacio asserted that Indians unprotected by the church quickly suffered violence, fraud, and the debilitating effects of alcohol. He recommended that Congress prohibit all forced sales of goods and the distillation of alcohol, allow for the expulsion of all persons abusing Indians, and establish two new vicariates in the Oriente. The Ecuadorian Senate included most of these recommendations in a decree issued soon thereafter, and it also stipulated that the missionaries assist the governor in creating Indian reductions, choosing Indians leaders, and regulating commerce.[100]

Dominican missionaries partook in the spirit of religious salvation, guiding Ecuadorian policy in the late eighties. In 1887 and 1888 the French Dominican François Pierre explored the northern and central Oriente in search of suitable sites for missions. Pierre warned Ecuadorians that they had better develop commerce in the region, for if they did not, others would. He mentioned that Brazilians, Peruvians, North Americans, and Europeans were aggressively exploiting jungle resources downriver toward Iquitos. But Pierre's personal mission was to save the jungle Indians from the grasp of the devil by bringing the cross and the gospel to them. Congress must have taken notice of Pierre's deeds and words; in 1888, it passed a joint resolution to contract with Dominicans in Europe to establish schools for both sexes in the province.[101]

That same year, the Ecuadorian Congress and President Jijón requested that the Vatican establish two new apostolic vicariates as additions to those run by the Jesuits in the Napo, and the Dominicans in Macas. Each district received, at least officially, an annual subsidy of three to six thousand sucres to pay for operations. Congress justified such expenses, amounts that dwarfed the annual budget of the civil administration, stating "that it fills one of the principal duties of a civilized government of sending the light of religious and literary instruction to that unhappy people sunk in barbarism and savagery. This will be an advancement on the true path to progress."[102] But even this great duty confronted fiscal reality. A religious commission reported in 1890 that none of the vicariates had received their annual funds, monies collected from various taxes and tithes levied by church and state. But by year's end, a national tax on gunpowder provided a steady income for the four ecclesiastical districts.[103]

Both the religious and civil administrations grew in the 1890s, but both found it difficult to control affairs in a vast region undergoing an economic boom, cultural contact and conflict, and repeated foreign incursions. The missionaries occasionally drew the ire of the governor, setting off a bureaucratic showdown between the two estates. In 1890, Governor Antonio Estupiñán blasted the Jesuits for their restrictive hold over Indians and asserted that they were abusing their custodial powers by inhibiting the governor from drafting Indians for public works. Estupiñán further complained that the Jesuits routinely whipped and chained recalcitrant Indians, practices the governor and other civil servants could not legally employ. The energetic and firm-willed Jesuit vicar, Gaspar Tovía, fired off his own charges at the governor, pointing out the legal and moral basis for the protection missionaries gave Indians. Each disputant aired his case in Quito, but Estupiñán subsequently lost his post and was replaced with a more tractable and pro-church candidate.[104]

Vicar Tovía, from Sardinia, was arguably the most powerful individual in the Oriente. Both he and his Jesuit brethren, along with the Dominicans and the Mothers of the Good Shepherd, busied themselves building missions and schools, and contacting and congregating Indians. They insulated their neophytes from the debilitating contact with secular whites, because the prescriptions of a separate "Indian Republic" found in Spanish colonial law were still in force in the Oriente. Whites could not legally own any land within a ten- to fifteen-kilometer radius of any mission town. In seclusion, the Jesuits used tools, fine silks, and Gothic altars to conquer the savage mind. Of course, many Indians died of disease, regardless of good intentions, but the padres found solace in knowing that the dead had been baptized before leaving their jungle world. With the dislocations imposed by disease, violence, and a changing economy, orphans began to trickle into missions and schools. These children had lost their parents or their clan identity and were either forcibly or voluntarily incorporated into the new cultural home of the mission.[105] It is highly probable that the missionaries tapped into the marginal orphan class within Indian societies, as did caucheros and slavers, to recruit converts and laborers for their expanding operations.

Tovía and his colleagues maintained active schedules. If they were not out touring the farthest reaches of the Oriente, they were teaching school, building roads, or congregating Indians in "convenient" places. They also routinely lobbied Quito, as when Tovía urged the government not to send troops from the highlands to bolster the defense of Tiputini. Tovía argued that the Indian peons under the orders of the local political lieutenant offered enough Ecuadorian presence, and that stationing troops there would be impractical and expensive. Tovía's opinion, one not shared by the governor, backfired a few months later when Peruvians sent more men to Tiputini, and the big Indian rebellion of 1892 left many missionaries the unprotected targets of cauchero and indigenous wrath.[106]

One reason Tovía might have opposed a stronger military presence in the Oriente, besides protecting missionary clout in the region, was his concern that armed and undisciplined soldiers would certainly abuse Indians. Although amusing in retrospect, Tovía took a dim view of the local police squad sneaking down to the riverbank to spy on the female charges of the Mothers of the Good Shepherd as they bathed. If the missionaries complained long and often enough, an undesirable person could be exiled from the province. But besides morality and purity, Tovía and others had to contend with a growing number of Andean migrants squatting on Indian and mission lands, a threat to missionary and acolyte alike.[107]

The Jesuits also had to contend with the aggressive actions of Peruvian administrators and caucheros. In November 1891, Tovía decried the Peruvian practice exporting caucho duty free from the Oriente, while charging Ecuadorians a tax for all goods imported or exported through Iquitos. Eight months later, Tovía warned Quito of the worsening situation. He claimed that Peruvians committed violence and atrocities against Ecuadorian Indians, captured many of them, and sold some downriver for as little as twenty soles each. He highlighted the tenuous state of the Indians with these words:

Today their situation is extremely desperate. Whatever their condition, be they aggressive or peaceful, they must always be dead or slaves. If they are aggressive and try to defend their territory against the Peruvian caucheros, they are killed without mercy because what kind of resistance can they put up with palm lances against the Peruvians armed with Winchesters and other precise weapons? If they are meek and offer no resistance they are grabbed, put in canoes, and transported to be sold. In both cases, their farms pass into Peruvian hands who keep them until they are used up.[108]

Tovía urged Congress to halt such attacks, but usually Quito felt content to send a diplomatic letter of protest from the minster of foreign affairs to his counterpart in Lima. Even the Peruvian prefect in Moyobamba praised the humane work of the missionaries in Ecuador as he criticized the rapacious caucheros of his own country. But he did, nonetheless, claim that the energetic missionaries had inflamed border and diplomatic tensions between the two republics.[109]

The fortunes of the Jesuit missions in the Napo reflected those of Father Tovía. By 1893, the vicar encountered increasing resistance from both local and national governments. His consistent and strident exposés had earned him many enemies. In one remarkable case, he somehow managed to insult both the president and the minister of interior in a single correspondence. In this climate, the central government decreased its financial support of the Jesuits, and the aging priest traveled to Europe to raise needed monies. Upon his return in 1894, he denounced various schemes by the governor, land speculators, and colonists to settle upon or steal Indian lands. And then Governor Pío Terán lowered the boom on the Jesuits and tried to close down their gold-washing operation along the Napo. Tovía countered Pío's action by arguing that Indians had washed gold for generations and depended upon it for their livelihoods, and that shutting it down would only weaken Ecuadorian presence in light of persistent Peruvian pressure. Tovía had lost none of his fire after almost twenty years in the Oriente's jungles, but he had lost influence in Quito and so retired in 1895.[110]

It was fitting that Tovía's retirement coincided with the decline of yet another wave of Jesuit efforts in Amazonia. As in the 1760s and the 1850s, the Jesuits were about to face a resurgent secular backlash, one attacking the order's power and autonomy. As Tovía settled into the splendor of La Compañía, the magnificent Jesuit church in Quito, radical Liberal general Eloy Alfaro took control of the government and disposed of Ecuador's Conservative policies in the Oriente.

FIVE

PERUVIAN CONSOLIDATION, 1895–1905

The quinquennia on either side of 1900 held within it the beginning of the twentieth century and the germ of Peruvian predominance in the Putumayo. While Liberal administrations in Ecuador busied themselves with partisan and factional political battles, the Colombian polity experienced yet another severe fracture through civil war. Meanwhile, opportunistic Peruvian caucheros and bureaucrats took advantage of their neighbors' ills to solidify Peruvian economic, political, military, and diplomatic positions in the disputed border zones of northwestern Amazonia. In short, Ecuadorian inattention plus Colombian self-destruction opened the rivers and forests of the region to Peru.

In Ecuador, relations between church and state defined many of the factional and partisan political conflicts affecting both the Oriente and country at large. Father Tovía's retirement to Quito created a political vacuum in the Oriente for other ambitious men to fill.[1] In May 1895, a group of Liberal rebels from Napo, calling themselves "The Political Transformers," attacked both missions and civil offices in and around Archidona. Jesuit missionaries and state officials organized a counterattack in the Napo and killed the Colombian leader of the rebels and captured other ringleaders. The missionaries bankrolled and supplied this campaign to regain order because, as usual, Quito did not supply the necessary men or money to handle the job.[2]

Quito could not respond because the capital and other areas of the country were experiencing political instability of their own. From April to June 1895, Ecuador had three presidents as the Conservative Party lost its grip on national power to the resurgent Liberals in August, led by fifty-three-year-old Eloy Alfaro. Alfaro's credentials included having been a guerrilla leader in the 1860s, a Liberal partisan in Central American wars and a supporter of Cuban independence from Spain. As a Liberal, Alfaro stood for the separation of church and state, freedom of religion, and increased personal liberties, all ideas antithetical to the Conservative Garciano regimes.[3] Inevitably, Alfaro faced numerous church- and Conservative-backed revolts, for neither the institution nor the party readily ceded power. Quito's archbishop, Pedro Rafael González y Calisto, preached that the Conservative cause was a holy one as he exhorted the faithful to resist the Liberals: "Take up arms then and have good spirit. With us without a doubt is the most holy Virgin Mary, who is the queen of victories. . . . With us is God, and if God is with us, who would dare resist us?"[4] Moreover, Alfaro and the Liberals experienced revolt and disorder within their own ranks as various *caudillos* (political bosses) jockeyed to succeed Alfaro in 1900.[5]

While Alfaro battled challengers and continued the railroad project down to the Pacific coast, the cacao plantations kept the country's economy focused west. Once again, the Oriente assumed the role of the lost region. What attention Alfaro did direct its way proved destructive in the long run. In June 1895, the nuns of the Mothers of the Good Shepherd, fearing for their security under a Liberal government, left the Oriente for Quito. The following year, Oriente governor Alejandro Sandoval, one of the Liberal leaders of the April 1895 attack on Archidona, carried out orders to expel the Jesuits as "foreigners" and prohibited Indians from giving them any future assistance.[6] In essence, the government's expulsion of the Jesuits gutted the best organized and financed Ecuadorian administration in the Oriente, leaving the region open to foreign incursions.

The task of rebuilding the administration of the Oriente fell to Sandoval, a Napo gold-washing operator and now governor. Sandoval had had numerous quarrels with the Jesuits in past years, but surprisingly he expressed little joy upon being elevated to the top spot in Archidona. He called his new home "forsaken," but drafted Indians for the annual road maintenance nonetheless. Unfortunately, smallpox again ripped through the territory just when Sandoval needed the most labor. The governor also complained bitterly when Congress promulgated a Special Law of the Oriente on 8 August 1895, restricting the sale, production, and distribution of alcohol and regulating other commercial pursuits in which Sandoval had interests.[7]

Because of those complaints, Sandoval lost his job to Enrique Hurtado in 1896. As usual, penury dogged Hurtado's attempts to increase the size and scope of the Oriente's administration over the next two years. Although he congratulated the national government for restoring some semblance of order by 1898, he still found fault with its lax attention to his province. He tried to build up the police force, but Quito sent neither salaries nor weapons. Without such support, Hurtado saw some of his guard drift away to more promising occupations. When Quito did fulfill its obligation and sent money, it could easily be misappropriated or stolen. One police comisario, Germán Quirola, arbitrarily spent his men's wages, leaving them in want and in low spirits; two months later, he abandoned his post and started a business down in Iquitos.[8] In a final irony, Hurtado noted the complete absence of any priests, foreign or native, to administer the appropriate rites for birth, death, communion, and confession.[9]

In the realm of labor, the church's absence allowed Hurtado and caucheros to enjoy an era of ecclesiastically unrestrained access to Indian labor. In February 1898, Hurtado reported that Indians from Archidona, attracted by white commerce, had freely moved down to Tiputini. Perhaps they had ventured downriver on their own, but increased and unregulated contact between white merchants and Indians led to trouble. In June, a group of caucheros seized the Indian governor of Baeza, Fermín Inga, and tried to replace him with their own leader. In November, a group of unconquered Indians killed a number of Indian peons in the employ of Ecuadorian cauchero Elías Andrade. The peons had allegedly planned to contact the hidden tribe, trade with it, and to steal children if possible.[10]

Many of the problems plaguing the Oriente — lack of aid from the central government, salary shortages, tense relations with Indians — assumed dangerous proportions when foreigners capitalized on the province's weak administration. In a single report to the interior ministry, Governor Hurtado listed these and other outstanding difficulties. He opened with a plea for Congress to recognize that the Oriente was indeed Ecuadorian territory. He stated that Colombian caucheros routinely attacked Indians and coerced them to work, using forced sales of goods, debt-peonage, and violence as mechanisms of conquest. He added that both Colombian and Ecuadorian merchants instructed Indians to ignore the directives of governmental authorities — as they had earlier told them to ignore the missionaries — and were thereby hindering public works and official duties. Finally, Hurtado complained of his inability to halt such practices, lacking both the men and the money to impose justice in such a vast domain.[11]

Peruvians also lurked along the river banks, periodically pressing west into the Oriente. Along with the usual Peruvian cauchero explorations, Hurtado contended with invasions by Peruvian troops aboard armed steamboats. In May 1898, Loreto's prefect named a Peruvian governing commissioner for the Napo River, and in July, the commissioner arrived in the company of several soldiers to assume his new post. Peru claimed all territory in the region up to the points where rivers such as the Napo were no longer navigable. In reply, the Ecuadorian government granted land to caucheros around Tiputini, their border of effective control, but lands claimed by Peru. The Peruvian commissioner decided to return to Iquitos to sort out this boundary question, but he did manage to bolster Peru's influence in the disputed zone. He received some logistical assistance from Ecuadorian cauchero Elías Andrade, a man like many others up the Napo who did business in Iquitos and with Peruvian officials. Andrade's assistance thus promoted Peruvian expansion upriver and improved his own business future.[12]

Peruvian administration in Loreto continued to grow and prosper during the last few years of the nineteenth century. Iquitos solidified its privileged commercial and political position over much of northwestern Amazonia as the focus of the Amazonian rubber industry shifted westward. Peruvian exports of rubber—most of it shipped from Iquitos—rode the boom of the 1880s into the following two decades. The value of rubber exports averaged between 13 and 18 percent of Peruvian exports, percentages that kept rubber in a tight second-place race with copper and silver, sugar being the biggest export earner of the era.[13]

Rubber exports and the concomitant flood of imports placed little Iquitos on the world commercial map. By the mid-1890s, for instance, Wesche and Company, one of many European trading companies operating in Iquitos, regularly transacted business and financial deals with firms in New York City to the tune of U.S. $10,000. Winchester rifles and the appropriate cartridges composed two important Wesche and Company imports, and shipments of up to four hundred rifles a voyage were common. Such massive importation of firearms did attract the wary eye of Limeño bureaucrats, who worried that such modern hardware could be used during a future rebellion or civil war. But a special commissioner in Iquitos vouched for the company's good intentions, arguing that the weapons were necessary to caucheros, for they "determined the efficacy of work in these mountains full of infidels and not a few savages."[14]

Even though business was booming (or because it was), Loreto's prefect, Emilio Viscarra, suggested that the government needed a bigger cut of the profits. He believed that Loreto only collected about one-half of the import and export duties it deserved. He suggested a 10 percent hike in import duties, up to 25 percent ad valorem, and export duties of about one-half the Brazilian rate. He did the latter hoping that both Brazilian and Peruvian caucheros would register their rubber exports at the Peruvian customs ports along the Yavari River, rather than at the more costly Brazilian posts, thereby stimulating commercial traffic and augmenting departmental revenues along the Peruvian side of the border.[15]

The boom in a commercial and extractive industry also created headaches. In October 1896, for example, the Guanvices Indians attacked towns near Barranca, southwest of Iquitos on the Marañón River, taking with them five captives and leaving twenty dead and five wounded. Subsequent parties searched the forest around Barranca to "rescue" the captives, but failing that, they lynched a group of Indians whom they believed had led the attack.[16]

That same year a large-scale separatist revolt rocked Iquitos. The separatists managed to attract important followers from both military and commercial circles, men presumably worried about the threat of higher taxes and tired of the reformist directives from the Piérola government in Lima. These rebels hoped that an independent Loreto could carry them into more prestigious and lucrative positions. Lima, however, acted swiftly to put down this movement, dispatching an expedition to march overland and a naval force through the Straits of Magellan and up the Amazon. The rebellion fizzled out before the troops arrived, but Lima nonetheless served notice that it would not allow Loreto to go its own way. The government spent more than half a million soles on these military expeditions, signaling Peru's relative fiscal health.[17]

Although Col. Juan Ibarra arrived too late to squelch the uprising, he did stay on awhile in Iquitos to make sure a loyal government was reestablished. He also participated in a scene foreshadowing the future trend in the rubber business: the rise of great rubber barons, men who commanded commercial and political control over territories measuring thousands of square miles. In December 1896, two such famous men, Isaiah Fermín Fitzcarrald and Bolivian kingpin Nicolás Suárez, hammered out a deal with Ibarra allowing the two barons exclusive navigation and commercial rights over the Urubamba, Manú, and Madre de Dios Rivers. Essentially, in this five-year contract, Fitzcarrald and Suárez owned much of the central and southern Peruvian Amazon. In exchange for this monopoly, the two *ricos* had only to establish a regular steamship service on the three rivers, carry the mail, fly the Peruvian flag, and obey the laws of the land. This attempt at trust building dissolved the following year when Fitzcarrald drowned in a river accident, but it marked the way for other ambitious men, such as Julio César Arana, to carve out their fiefs in rubber-rich western Amazonia.[18]

The administration of Loreto stabilized quickly following the revolt of 1896. Experienced bureaucrat Manuel Pinedo returned to civil service, taking an interim position as the customs director in Iquitos. After a thirty-year career in Loreto's burgeoning bureaucracy, Pinedo certainly had the experience for the job. Yet in September 1897, Pinedo reported to Rafael Quirós, a special commissioner appointed by Lima, that the department was running a large annual deficit. Quirós looked into the matter and realized that the purchase of new steamships and warships, along with an expanding payroll, had put Loreto almost 50,000 soles in the red. He also noted a decline in rubber export duties, for the extraction zones were now far from the customs house because of the destruction and exhaustion of rubber trees around Iquitos. Quirós increased export duties on rubber — rates still only about 40 percent of those in Brazil — to raise more revenue and to cancel the debt. Surprisingly, Lima rejected the special commissioner's decree, perhaps worried about another rebellion from merchants and caucheros, or annoyed that the independent Quirós had exceeded his authority.[19]

Blocked on this front, Quirós augmented revenues coming from existing customs posts rather than increasing export duties on rubber. After grappling with the usual smuggling, corruption, and political intrigue, Quirós felt optimistic about the future. Noting that customs receipts had more than doubled over the last five years, he predicted that in 1898, Loreto could collect about 600,000 soles in revenues, cover all its obligations, and remit 200,000 soles to Lima.[20]

As part of his busy schedule, Quirós also ended the governing schism between the official capital in Moyobamba and the de facto center of operations in Iquitos. In November 1897, he ordered both the governing council (*junta departamental*) and its fiscal agent to move to Iquitos. This shift of governance effectively recognized the preeminence of Iquitos in economic and political affairs. Julio César Arana, the up-and-coming cauchero, merchant, and banker, was named president of the body during its first meeting in town. To support its first project, that of building a primary school network in Iquitos, Arana and the other council members had to raise money. They decided to impose an annual fee for the various business organizations and guilds in the city — wholesale and retail merchants, druggists, brick makers, carpenters, tailors, lawyers and doctors, silversmiths, barbers, photographers, mechanics, restaurant and bar owners — and they also initiated a quasi-sin tax on tobacco and coffee to collect more monies for schools. In this instance, the man who later became the infamous pariah allegedly responsible for a brutal system of terror, torture, and murder in the Putumayo was playing the role of the mild-mannered but determined school superintendent.[21]

Both Quirós and Lima focused a watchful eye on the incorporation and administration of border zones along Loreto's vast territory. In early 1898,

Loreto and the national governments sponsored a "scientific commission" to explore the Juruá, a river hundreds of miles to the east of Iquitos in present-day Brazil. Not only did this commission reflect the positivist spirit of the day, but also an optimism on the rubber-bearing potential of this distant region. Indeed, by year's end, the Juruá generated about twelve million soles worth of commercial traffic. The Chamber of Commerce in Iquitos recognized this golden goose and suggested the building of a road between the Upper Ucayali and the Juruá in order to increase the plaza's revenues. Brazilian officials, however, thwarted such efforts by cracking down on Peruvian traffic in the Juruá, Purús, Madeira, and the Lower Putumayo Rivers.[22] Indeed, as the Peruvians and Brazilians well knew, the flag followed the audacious caucheros most readily.

Brazilians routinely hindered Peruvian commerce up the Putumayo in an effort to protect Brazilian interests. Col. Juan Ibarra, one of the commanders sent from Lima to put down the 1896 revolt, complained that only Brazilian intransigence stunted commercial growth along the river. In contrast to the Napo, where Peruvian caucheros and steamboats controlled most markets, the Putumayo drained into Brazilian territory and jurisdiction. Ibarra reported that Peruvians had built a trail network from the Putumayo down to the Napo, whose mouth entered the Amazon near Iquitos, to avoid Brazilian red tape and customs duties. But regardless of the harassment from the Brazilians, Ibarra proudly noted that Putumayan Indians were now familiar with the Peruvian flag, but not with those of Ecuador or Colombia.[23]

Yet Alejandro Quintero, Colombia's prefect in the Caquetá, would certainly have challenged Ibarra's statement, especially for the Colombian-controlled Upper Putumayo. Throughout 1895 and 1896, Colombians continued filtering down the Caquetá and Putumayo Rivers, clearing and settling land, searching for rubber, and entering into trade relations with Indians. This colonization process generated the usual difficulties. In Santiago and Sibundoy, two Indian towns in the Upper Putumayo, inhabitants refused to take part in compulsory labor drafts and blocked whites from living in their towns and taking part in their ceremonies. Colombian officials complained that the Indians had forgotten many of "their ancient customs and the respect with which they used to obey the commands of authorities," and that they had succumbed to moral decay evidenced by the four hundred "suicides" in the Sibundoy cemetery. Accordingly, Quintero and others pushed through a provision — over the complaints of the indigenous inhabitants — to create a 150-acre area in Sibundoy for white habitation in hopes of spreading civilization and Christianity to the Indians. Subsequently, the town council of Mocoa named police inspectors (*comisarios*) to Indian villages along the Upper and Middle Caquetá and Putumayo Rivers; these comisarios received no salary but could legally draft labor from Indians to secure some remuneration.[24]

Colombia also had to contend with foreign incursions into the rubber-rich Putumayo. While partisan battles occasionally erupted there, the bigger problem involved Ecuadorian, Peruvian, and Brazilian caucheros sweeping through the region in search of rubber and Indian laborers. For example, several hundred Brazilians and Peruvians exported rubber duty free, and captured or bought Indian women and children and then sold them downriver. Both the Colombian vice-consul and the Caquetá prefect warned Bogotá of the impending disappearance of the Indians from the Middle Putumayo, and of the real threat that Colombia would soon lose control of the entire area. An oft-related suggestion to halt these attacks from "savage and ferocious" foreigners centered on establishing legitimate borders, first with Brazil and then with Peru.[25]

As pressures mounted along Colombia's Putumayan border, the country again experienced a major civil war. The War of a Thousand Days (1899–1902) marked a turning point for the country and for the Putumayo. The economic crises of the 1890s, declining coffee prices, and the emotional appeals of the "war Liberals"—young Turks like Rafael Uribe Uribe, who favored war over polite politics—pushed some Liberal leaders and their clients into a full-scale rebellion. Along with devastating much of the country and killing an estimated 100,000 Colombians, the war disrupted trade routes from Florencia, Pasto, and Mocoa down to the Putumayo. Liberal insurgents threatened Mocoa in 1901, and the town experienced a smallpox epidemic that year. Caucheros no longer could count on commercial or governmental links with Colombia and therefore looked to Peruvian Iquitos for markets and supplies. Subsequently, Colombian caucheros became dependent on Peruvian tradesmen, including Julio César Arana, who began to refer to the Putumayo as "my river." Conversely, an unknown number of Colombians fled the violence of the war and sought refuge in the rain forests of the Putumayo and Caquetá, placing them in intimate and often deadly contact with indigenes.[26] During the three-year-long war, Colombian documentation on the Caquetá and Putumayo almost disappeared.

This was certainly not the case on the Peruvian side. As the Colombians once again took to slaughtering one another on a mass scale, Loreto built on an impressive economic base to expand its effective control over contested border zones. True, Iquitos was not immune to political and military conflict, evinced by the 1899 rebellion led by none other than ex-prefect and now colonel Emilio Viscarra. Viscarra and his unit of fifty men took over Iquitos in May and apprehended the acting special commissioner, Rafael Quirós, the

Table 5. External Trade in Iquitos, 1897–1907
(prices in Peruvian pounds)

Year	Imports	Rubber Exports	Total Exports
1897	178,497	198,710	—
1899	249,523	288,939	289,644
1901	145,459	283,392	283,392
1903	298,284	438,909	438,909
1905	558,637	905,923	914,278
1907	715,797	818,825	818,825

Source: De la Flor Fernández, "Economía de exportación," 109.
  Note: Ten soles equal one Peruvian pound.

man sent from Lima to settle matters after the 1896 separatist movement. Quirós condemned Viscarra for his "criminal and brutal conduct," but it is noteworthy that this rebellion attracted much support in the departmental bureaucracy and was strong for almost six months in both Iquitos and Moyobamba. The merchant-dominated junta departamental, headed by President Julio César Arana, wisely chose to refuse recognition of the rebel government and remained officially loyal. Government forces enabled Quirós — who managed to flee to Chachapoyas — to regain control of the department's administration by November. Yet even the following year, "pacification campaigns" continued in various corners of Loreto.[27]

Even throughout the political disturbances of 1899, business boomed, and both rubber exports and foreign imports swelled to record levels with the turn of the century. Near Christmas 1899, the *Huáscar* steamed toward Iquitos with more than 14,000 bundles of goods, yet all the warehouses were already full; the thriving port needed three new warehouses just to keep up with the carrying trade.[28] Rubber provided the catalyst for this business bonanza (see table 5).

Public revenues swelled along with commerce. The junta departamental of Iquitos annually collected 100,000 soles in urban and rural business and property taxes, which at least on paper was spent on jails, schools, a hospital, doctors, roads, and a church.[29] Loreto's prefect noted the growth of population and wealth in Iquitos, stating that foreign and Peruvian businessmen were becoming quite affluent. He complained, however, that distance, transport costs, and the resulting inflation pushed the cost of living in Iquitos up six to eight times that of other Peruvian cities. Therefore, he asked the national government for another 400 soles to preserve order and to keep "the bad boys of Peru" under control. But a Lima official nixed this decree, noting that the prefect received a whopping 1,000 soles monthly, more than enough, he reasoned, for the prefect to cover all his expenses.[30]

In these favorable commercial and fiscal conditions, and as Colombians continued to butcher one another, Peru began an aggressive move up the disputed Putumayo River. In early 1900, customs agents and a military unit arrived in the Putumayo, and work continued on a trail linking the Putumayo and Amazon Rivers near the Brazilian border. By using this trail, Peruvians could avoid hassles with Brazilian customs. By November, the gunboat *Cahuapanas* steamed up the Putumayo, commanded by its salaried sergeant major carrying instructions to "ratify Peruvian dominance over the Putumayo River." Once again, the opportunistic administrations in Iquitos and Lima used favorable timing and their relative strength to push Peruvian borders outward at the expense of their neighbors. Such expansion did, however, bring difficulties. For one, Peruvian caucheros continued to carry peons outside the country to exploit rich, untapped stands of rubber trees. To slow this flow, Iquitos increased the peon deposit—a sum theoretically guaranteeing the return of each peon to Loreto—from 200 soles in 1899 to 500 soles in 1900.[31]

While the Peruvian position seemed strong in northwestern Amazonia, world-market fluctuations and problems with the Brazilians tempered any premature euphoria. Brazilian customs continued to badger Peruvian merchant ships by charging duties on goods exempt from such exactions and by forcing Peruvian citizens to renounce their citizenship after entering Brazilian waters. Moreover, a glut of rubber on European markets sparked a commercial crisis in Pará and Manaus that damaged the economy of Iquitos during late 1900. While no person or country deserved blame for these capricious economic fluctuations—which forced salary reductions and school closings at the local level—some Iquiteños blamed Brazil for their troubles. The recession continued on through 1901. Fewer ships called at Iquitos, rebellion was in the air, and the department closed its customs house up the Putumayo, ostensibly to save money.[32]

The economic downturn of 1901 brought inflation and suffering for the working class of Iquitos. Essential items such as salt, distributed through a state monopoly, became expensive and out of reach of the lower class. Moreover, a great amount of devalued foreign currency from Ecuador, Chile, Venezuela, and Bolivia flooded into Iquitos, and Peruvian soles could hardly be found. This scarcity of national currency raised the value of foreign coin, but when it was paid as wages to workers, it was discounted 33 to 50 percent. So as prices rose, real wages dropped. Although employers found such conditions favorable, ninety-three workers petitioned the prefect for relief. Luckily for the laborers, an able and understanding prefect sided with them. Prefect Pedro

Portillo, a man with administrative experience in the dry and poverty-stricken department of Ayacucho, opened salt to free trade, thereby increasing the supply and leading to a drop in its price. Next, he asked Lima to send him 20,000 soles, coin to be exchanged for a like sum of devalued Chilean currency. Portillo sided with the underdogs on both issues and preserved urban peace.[33]

Portillo acted with similar resolve to incorporate disputed river territories into his purview. Like his predecessor of a decade earlier, Samuel Palacios, Portillo consistently sent out expeditions to remote regions during his three-year tenure in office. He personally commanded forays up the Pastaza, Morona, Santiago, and Napo Rivers (all claimed by Ecuador), and he commissioned others up the Putumayo, Purús, and Juruá Rivers. This steely-eyed prefect never backed away from the adventure, glory, and territory offered in a fight.[34]

Portillo maintained a very intimate and, at times, stormy relationship with the Peruvian foreign ministry. He carried with him instructions from Minister Felipe de Osma y Pardo to support Peruvian commerce and administration in the disputed territories claimed by Ecuador, Colombia, and Brazil. Given this policy from Lima, Portillo believed "that it was of the utmost importance to sustain and defend our sovereignty on the Putumayo River, as well as on the Napo, Yuruá, and Purús."[35] With such a firm mission, Portillo occasionally created diplomatic problems for the Lima government as it negotiated international border treaties with its neighbors. But even with its frequent admonitions and orders for Portillo to slow his adventurous activities, Lima certainly had in Portillo more of an asset than a liability.[36]

While the foreign ministry publicly warned Portillo to avoid clashes with foreigners, it privately funded several incursions into disputed territories, thereby provoking bloody clashes that it publicly repudiated. From September to December 1902, for instance, the foreign ministry paid 1,800 soles for supplies and expenses needed for incursions up the Napo. The machetes, axes, oil, kerosene, salt, shotguns, and ammunition suggested that Portillo and his naval escort planned to engage in some commercial exchanges with Indians, but that they were also prepared for any type of hostility. The following year, Lima paid for more arms and ammunition to bolster the Peruvian arsenal up the Napo, and at the same time it authorized the appointments of more minor officials far up the Upper Marañón, Napo, Putumayo, Juruá, and Purús Rivers. Pedro Portillo led these charges, but Lima paid the bills.[37]

Such actions inevitably led to violence. In July 1903, Indian soldiers fighting under Ecuadorian and Peruvian commanders clashed at Angostera (Angoteros) on the Napo about a hundred miles downstream from the mouth of the Aguarico. This rather minor firefight — involving only about thirty men, with two killed—set the stage for a larger, bloodier affair the following year. This time, seventy soldiers under Ecuadorian command attacked a Peruvian outpost at Torres Causano on the Napo near the Ecuadorian/Peruvian border. Both sides now had better weaponry, including small cannons and Winchester, Mannlicher, and Cropachel rifles. After a two-hour battle, more than twenty Ecuadorians lay slain, along with two Peruvians. Prior to the fighting, the Ecuadorian commander tried to convince his Peruvian peer to withdraw and to recognize the diplomatic status quo established jointly by their respective foreign ministries. The Peruvian commander replied that he was ignorant of the diplomatic arrangements made by the two governments but trusted that Prefect Portillo was aware of them and would do the right thing. Leaving no doubt about his position on this matter, Portillo dispatched more men up the Napo carrying a machine gun to bolster Peruvian firepower.[38]

Ecuador was in a weak position to block such incursions effectively. Even after Eloy Alfaro stepped down from the presidency in 1901, transferring power to his handpicked successor, Leonidas Plaza Gutiérrez, the country continued to live under the impending cloud of war. President Plaza faced ongoing Conservative and Catholic plots to undermine his government, while he also worried that the Colombian civil war would spill into Ecuador. Moreover, he had to contend with a wily and power-hungry Eloy, who attempted to regain the presidency just as Plaza took office. In such a politically charged and unstable environment, the country lacked the will, focus, and resources to govern Oriente province properly. Nor could the Plaza government build a coherent and consistent diplomatic position from which to confront Peruvian challenges and claims to the disputed Amazonian borders.[39]

The Oriente subsequently suffered through yet another period of neglect. The provincial administration consisted of a handful of officials, most serving in montaña towns close to the eastern base of the Andes, joined by a few poorly paid (twenty sucres a month) political lieutenants serving downriver. Economically, Iquitos served as the center of lowland commerce. Goods were imported and exported through the Oriente unhindered by any Ecuadorian customs collector. Lacking a viable economic, political, and fiscal infrastructure, Ecuador lost out to Peru. In fact, Ecuador even lost one of its few caucheros, David Elías Andrade, to the other side. Andrade owned a steamship and plied the Napo, exporting caucho and importing goods from Iquitos. He had served as an Ecuadorian official in Tiputini, but then in 1900, as a naturalized Peruvian, Andrade became Peru's commissar in the Napo.[40]

Upriver in Archidona, Governor Enrique Trajano Hurtado seemed more intent on making money than defending remote provincial borders. Trajano allegedly monopolized the sale of butter, chickens, and eggs in Archidona and used the police to coerce Indians to work for him. He appointed his absent wife head of the local school system, found sinecures for other relatives, and operated a liquor still in the municipal building.[41] Like many of his colleagues in Amazonia, Trajano recognized the commercial benefits offered by his public position. Trajano's successor, Governor Alomía, discovered the same thing and began charging a 4 percent fee on the transfer of Indian debts from one patron to another. With some Indians indebted as much as five hundred to a thousand sucres, Alomía had indeed found himself a good business.[42]

While Trajano and Alomía made money in Archidona, Prefect Portillo sponsored yet another thrust into disputed territory, this one up the Putumayo. In late 1901, he sent Sgt. Maj. Ildefonso Fonseca to reconnoiter the Putumayo and its major tributaries. Fonseca found a region rich in rubber, teaming with nude "savages," and offering bountiful food and great potential profits. Fonseca was in the employ of Julio César Arana, the future owner of much of the region, who accompanied the expedition. Fonseca's mission, then, served a dual purpose: to expand Peruvian territorial control upriver and to advance his boss's commercial fortunes. Fonseca met numerous Colombian caucheros, joined by a few Peruvians and Brazilians, and he engaged in trade with various Indian tribes. In his travels, he settled numerous commercial disputes between caucheros, in favor of Peruvians and Arana. His visit spawned an official report that stressed the geopolitical and economic promise of the Putumayo for Peru. It also highlighted the military advantage in building a series of trails linking the Amazon and the Putumayo to facilitate troop movements during international crises.[43]

In addition to offering civil, commercial, and military assistance, Portillo tapped ecclesiastical resources to expand Peruvian jurisdiction. Augustinian missionaries arrived in 1901, charged with evangelizing and civilizing Indians along the northern border reaches of Loreto. Father Paulino Díaz complained, however, that Colombian and Ecuadorian forces impeded the work of the missionaries, and he urged Peru to take control of the contested areas. To do so, Díaz suggested that paths and telephone lines be constructed to link the Putumayo to Iquitos. He had no patience for impediments to his work, like the proud Aguarunas who resisted evangelization, nor would he countenance his poorly paid priests leaving their duties for more lucrative commercial pursuits.[44]

Portillo accomplished much during his three-year tenure ending in 1904. Excursions up the Napo, Putumayo, and Juruá increased de facto Peruvian control over much disputed land. Although he had engaged in some very acerbic public disputes with officials in both Lima and Iquitos — he derisively called them "unpatriotic" — the Peruvian government used its resolute prefect to good measure. Iquitos and Peru now dominated much of northwestern Amazonia. The city was now linked to Manaus and the outside world by both trade and a new telegraph line.[45] It was the business of Ecuador and Colombia to catch up.

The Ecuadorian interior ministry and Congress responded to Peruvian expansion up the Napo and Putumayo by drafting an elaborate but hopeless plan to annex vast reaches of the Putumayo, Caquetá, and Amazon Rivers. The interior ministry called for the enlargement of the Napo province across all of the Putumayo and Caquetá. The plan provided for the reduction of Indians into towns, and allowed for the legal coercion of Indian labor, although it banned forced sales of goods and whipping. Congress got so carried away with the spirit of the plan that it decreed the formation of the Amazon province with its capital in Iquitos! Although these plans proved politically popular — the one from Congress was dedicated to the incoming president — and set the stage for some stirring speeches, they rang hollow, for the government did not, and could not, implement them.[46]

Colombia, on the other hand, faced the daunting task of patching together the country after the murderous War of a Thousand Days. Especially in the southern sections of the country where the fighting was fiercest, partisan hatreds and conflicts remained explosive. In the Upper Putumayo town of Sibundoy, for example, government troops forced Liberals to return Indian lands seized during the war. The troops remained to guard the town from future rebellions and to protect the arriving Capuchin missionaries from a secular backlash.[47]

At war's end, companies and individuals scrambled to protect their territories and to regain control of the regional administration. In 1902, one of the Calderón brothers, José Gregorio, and another cauchero both requested grants to operate the customs house on the Putumayo. But along with the customs question — clearly an important one, for the cauchero who ran the house could harass his competitors — these men knew that they would have to deal with Peruvian incursions downriver. Calderón promised in his request that Peruvians and Brazilians would be required to recognize Colombian laws and commercial rights. This was not enough for another interested group of thirty enthusiastic residents of Nariño, who in 1904 requested from Rafael Reyes, now president of Colombia, the honor of reconquering the eastern lands and of carrying the "conquest of civilization" to the Indians. They did, however, want a subsidy: 50 percent of the customs receipts from the Pacific port of Tumaco to pay for the construction of roads down to the Putumayo.[48]

Another Colombian cauchero adopted a more pragmatic approach to Peruvian presence and the disruptions caused by the war. Benjamín Larraniaga, employed by Rafael Reyes in the 1870s, and a tough man with more than thirty years experience in the Putumayo, used his knowledge of the region and the interruption of the upland trade to tap into the booming market in Iquitos, where he exchanged rubber for imported goods. But opportunity had its costs. Over time, Peruvian officials and merchants made him dependent on them. Larraniaga, for instance, had three men from Huila arrested and shipped to jail in Iquitos, presumably because they refused to pay or work off their debts. He also allegedly captured a great many Indians and sent them down to Iquitos as merchandise.[49]

Although Larraniaga accepted Peruvian assistance in building his business, relations were often less than cordial. When Ildefonso Fonseca led Peruvian forces up the Putumayo in 1901, he had various acerbic exchanges with Larraniaga when he tried to get him to settle some outstanding disputes with other caucheros. The following year, the crafty prefect, Pedro Portillo, sent Peruvian soldiers up the Igaraparaná River after Indians revolted against the cruelty of some of Larraniaga's employees. Portillo's opportunistic assistance allowed him to claim Peruvian jurisdiction over not only the rubber-rich Igaraparaná but also upriver over the parallel Caraparaná.[50]

Another misfortune for Larraniaga transpired the following year. A group of Indians killed two of his employees, and he opted to avenge their deaths. He and his son, Rafael, allegedly attracted a large group of Ocainas and Huitotos to La Chorrera by offering them goods. But once they arrived, Rafael's men captured twenty-five leaders, who were then whipped, tortured, and shot during a drunken orgy. Word of this brutal revenge killing and Larraniaga's dependence on Peruvian merchants led to his downfall. Peruvian officials summoned Benjamín to Iquitos for questioning, and once there, they forced him to sign an agreement turning over his property and Indians to his Peruvian creditor, Julio César Arana.[51] Perhaps Arana did use a little extra-legal muscle to get Larraniaga to sell—he reportedly took son Rafael hostage—but Arana already had great leverage over Benjamín, supplying the goods, credit, and steamboats that he needed. For Benjamín, a man of unquestioned grit, a cruel fate awaited; en route from New York to Iquitos, he and his wife drowned in an accident.[52] Larraniaga's passing marked the end of an era, while Arana's ascension opened another.

A man of great intelligence, drive, and ambition, Julio César Arana's interest in the Putumayo had begun to grow in 1899, the initial year of the civil war in Colombia. He already counted on excellent business networks downriver in Brazil and across the Atlantic to Europe and the United States. From Iquitos, he and his managers oversaw growing businesses in regional and international trade and shipping, and in banking. In the Putumayo, Arana bought rubber from caucheros and supplied them with goods and credit. In little time, the normal working of this aviamiento system — bartering goods and credit for forest products — and Arana's aggressive practices placed many of the caucheros in the Putumayo in debt to him.[53]

Julio César visited the Putumayo three times from 1901 to 1905 to settle accounts with debtors and to inspect operations. He also had his first chance to observe the Indians of the Caraparaná and Igaraparaná — women, children, and men who in the next few years became his workers. Arana expressed a classic colonial attitude about Indians, saying, "It was then that I heard for the first time that the Indians in the Igaraparaná and Caraparaná had resisted the establishment of civilization in their regions. They had resisted effectively for many years, practicing cannibalism and, once in awhile, murdering white colonizers. But from 1900 onward, the Indians became more tractable, and a system of exchanging rubber extracted by the Indians for European goods developed between them and the referred trading posts. From then on, my business in the Putumayo grew gradually but slowly."[54]

Perhaps the Indians were tractable as Arana poured desirable goods into the region, but he misrepresented the growth of his Putumayo concerns. This man with the best library in the area did few things slowly. He kept his hands in politics in Iquitos to protect his business interests while he imported tons of goods, including many firearms, for the "civilizing work" in the Putumayo. He also opened a branch office of J. C. Arana and Brothers in Manaus in 1903 to undercut middlemen in that important Amazonian boomtown.[55] And in the Putumayo, he did remarkably well. From 1904 to 1907, he consolidated his hold over the region by absorbing the debts and properties of most of the caucheros operating in the Middle Putumayo and Caquetá. He claimed that it cost him 150,000 pounds sterling to release men like Larraniaga and the Calderón brothers from their debts, and he also asserted that he spent three million soles to rid the Putumayo of "rowdy and morally dubious elements." Within four years, Arana owned more than twelve thousand square miles of lands full of wild rubber trees and Indian laborers.[56]

Arana put his brother-in-law, Pablo Zumaeta, in charge of operating the business in the Putumayo. From his office in Iquitos, Zumaeta designated managers to the two supply and shipping centers, La Chorrera in the Igaraparaná, and El Encanto in the Caraparaná. These two managers supervised the caucheros who organized rubber collection and the distribution of goods in over forty different sections. These section bosses enjoyed a great deal of autonomy in running affairs in their respective areas. Each boss negotiated with the company a commission percentage on each kilo of rubber produced

Table 6. Rubber Exports by Julio César Arana and Company from the Putumayo, 1900–1906

Year	Kilos	Arana Exports as % of Iquitos Rubber Exports	% Increase from Previous Year
1900	15,863	1.85	—
1901	54,180	4.40	242
1902	123,210	7.31	127
1903	201,656	11.61	63
1904	343,493	15.70	70
1905	470,592	18.88	37
1906	644,897	29.96	37

Source: Kilo exports from Larrabure i Correa, Colección de leyes, 18:129–30; percentage figures and kilos cited in De la Flor Fernández, "Economía de exportación," 50.

in his section. In 1906, for example, section chiefs earned an average 17 percent commission on the rubber exported. The Casa Arana — which monopolized the supply, credit, and transportation systems to and from the Putumayo — cleared 82 percent, while Indian workers received only the equivalent of .85 percent of the market value of the rubber. Obviously, the commission system and the autonomy of the section bosses encouraged abuse and exploitation of the native workers, but the system worked well for Arana and for some of his employees. By 1906, Arana had about 13,600 Indians working for the company.[57] Rubber exports boomed during Arana's first six years in the Putumayo (see table 6).

Arana received vital state assistance in building his empire in the Putumayo, including help from the Peruvian army and navy when faced with challenges from competing caucheros or rebellious Indians. It was common for an Arana rubber station to also house an army unit. When Prefect Portillo sent expeditions and warships up the Putumayo, Arana counted on their support. If prisoners were taken after a conflict, they might end up in the "Arana Company annex," the Iquitos jail. Moreover, many public employees in the growing Putumayo bureaucracy worked for Arana and eventually sought full-time employment in his company, lured by the prospect of earning more money.[58]

Along with his excellent relationships with local officials, Arana also had influence at national levels. In 1907, his personal lawyer and another business associate landed positions as the two senators from Loreto serving in Lima. At the presidential level, Civilista Party presidents José Pardo (1904–8) and Augusto Leguía (1908–12) supported Arana's expansion up the Putumayo.[59] This intimate partnership between public and private interests was, and still is, normal in much of Amazonia. In areas of geopolitical tensions and of real or perceived riches, governments routinely support extractive enterprises and allow companies to exploit the poorly organized work force.[60]

Lima not only gained de facto control over the Putumayo by backing Arana, but it also reaped bountiful revenues from the burgeoning commerce in and out of Iquitos. Rubber exports from Iquitos increased from 15 percent of total exports to 97 to 99 percent of total exports in the decade after 1895.[61] On the national level, little Iquitos handled about 12 percent of total Peruvian foreign trade from 1900 to 1912, and from 1905 to 1912, Iquitos furnished Lima with 16 percent of all customs receipts.[62] Both Arana and the Peruvian state were making big money.

Peruvian support of Arana's operations in the Putumayo sparked violent conflicts with Colombian caucheros. While some authors blame Arana and his insatiable appetite for riches for much of the bloodshed after 1903, one cannot ignore that both sides were locked into a battle for the same resources, namely rubber trees, native labor, and port facilities. Arana emerged the clear winner in this contest, in part because he received consistent assistance from his government, while the Colombians often had to fend for themselves.[63] But the Putumayo was by no means the only scene of such discord. Lizzie Hessell, the Victorian lady who followed her husband to the rain forest of Bolivia, wrote to her parents in 1898 about how business transpired near her new home:

> I must tell you how they do business here. This house and another house wanted to buy a large rubber plantation a few days off. The man was here, the other house took possession of him, made him drunk and locked him up here for two weeks and he signed papers selling his business to us. In the meantime the other people went off armed and took possession of his estate, so a few days ago a lot of our people with Indians all armed and with the owner of the estate went off to turn them out. They say it will come to fighting; that's the way they manage things here. The estate is a valuable one and the law counts for nothing in these parts, everyone looks after himself.[64]

And once Arana took over most of the rubber stations in the Putumayo, the violence did not stop. Arana's operations depended on Indian laborers, and the salaries and profits of the supervising section chiefs depended on the output of their workers. While some section chiefs made agreements with Indian caciques to broker the exchange of rubber for European goods, others resorted to brutal methods of labor coercion. If Indians fled, collected little rubber, refused to work, or revolted, the whip and the stocks became the primary instruments of discipline. All the elements enhancing the abuse of Indians presented themselves: a social, economic, cultural, and political setting that made whites masters over Indians; a tradition of unfree labor coupled with a boom industry; and a monopoly company claiming the labor of Indians in its jurisdiction backed up by its government.[65] Moreover, some of Arana's men insisted that Indians adopt a new moral code, one defined by the section chiefs but one alien to Indian culture.[66]

Some Indians violently opposed the presence of the many outsiders and their obnoxious demands. In 1903, Boras attacked the Cahuinari rubber stations located between the Putumayo and Caquetá Rivers and forced caucheros to abandon many of the besieged sites. At Atenas, the section chiefs placed all their buildings on stilts, pulled up ladders at night, and maintained guards until morning.[67] In another case, a Bora woman recalled that her uncle burned down an Indian maloca to deprive caucheros of the site and sustenance from which to search for Indians hiding in the forest. The whites had to leave soon, finding little shelter or food and few Indians.[68]

But it was measles, smallpox, tuberculosis, yellow fever, whooping cough, influenza, and malaria that inflicted more violence on natives than did the whip or the Winchester rifle. As they had for centuries in Amazonia, epidemics ripped through regions and left many dead in their wake. At times, only 25 percent of a maloca's population survived a particularly virulent scourge.[69] While whites died of the same maladies, they recognized that Indians were more susceptible, but they didn't know why. Indians, on the other hand, saw death and disease as unnatural acts, the work of an enemy shaman's sorcery or that of an offended spirit, and they therefore sought revenge.[70] Ironically, Indians attacked other clans and tribes during periods of greatest biological and demographical risk; following an attack, more people died from warfare or contracted disease through the unpleasant contact of battle. On occasion, Indians blamed caucheros for the disease and misfortune among them and drove them away. But this action involved great risk as well: the caucheros might well return with a punitive raid and take Indian captives as slaves; or the trade, its effects, and its interruption might provoke political uprisings among younger leaders of the tribe, men who blamed the cacique for the troubles in their midst or who wanted to recover the life-giving powers of European goods. And the disease problem could be just as bad in Iquitos as it was in the jungle. In late 1903, 70 to 80 percent of newborns died during a whooping-cough outbreak.[71]

Officials in Iquitos knew prior to the Putumayo scandal that the combined effect of the rubber industry, colonization, geopolitical conflicts, and disease had serious and often fatal consequences for Amazonian peoples. The new prefect of Loreto, Dr. Hildebrando Fuentes, sounded the alarm in 1905. Along with his duties of exploring frontier regions, delineating de facto borders, and tending to the growing bureaucracy, Fuentes took time to investigate allegations that caucheros bought and sold Indians like any other merchandise in northwestern Amazonia.[72] He sadly admitted that caucheros indeed bought and sold Indian debts — and therefore their persons — and exported their human property to rubber-rich areas in Brazil. Fuentes alleged that twenty-six thousand "Peruvian Indians" worked along the Brazilian Javari, Purús, and Juruá Rivers, a labor force that enriched their owners and the Brazilian bureaucracy. However, Prefect Fuentes noted that Peruvian caucheros failed to deposit the required five hundred soles when exporting a peon outside Loreto, and that this labor drain left many areas deserted of all inhabitants.[73]

Also in 1905, Jorge M. Von Hassell hurriedly completed an anthropological report on the critical state of northwestern Amazonian Indians, fearful that his subjects might soon vanish forever. Von Hassell stressed many crucial features leading to indigene deculturation and extinction: cultural and biological mestizaje with whites and blacks; the ravages of disease and alcohol; warfare, slavery, and high infant mortality; and the demands of the rubber industry, which displaced many and placed others in swampy and unhealthy environments. He warned his readers that their generation would earn the opprobrium of future generations if the Indians completely succumbed to "civilization." He therefore urged the governments of South America to draft viable plans to protect the surviving Indians from total annihilation.[74]

But the concern for making money overshadowed efforts to conserve native cultures. Midway through the first decade of the twentieth century, international firms such as Wesche and Company, Kahn and Polack, Luís Morey and Company, and, of course, Julio César Arana and Brothers, made thousands of soles monthly in trade, finance, and transport ventures. Iquitos served as the business hub, handling, in 1905, 267,670 Peruvian pounds worth of rubber from outlying rivers and sending in return supplies worth 185,785 Peruvian pounds. The Putumayo figured prominently among these rivers, exporting the second highest total of rubber by value to Iquitos but placing a lowly sixth of the nine regions in the amount of goods received.[75] In the booming port, Indians and partially acculturated cholos formed the working class, Chinese merchants and restaurateurs figured prominently among the petty retailers, while European merchants controlled most of the lucrative wholesale trade. Along the muddy streets, one could see — along with the harried Indian porters and the pigs routing through garbage — newcomers from Germany, Brazil, Spain, Italy, France, England, China, Portugal, Morocco, Colombia, Ecuador, as well as a few from North America and Russia.[76] With the bars and the restaurants full, and times good, why worry about the plight of some distant jungle Indians?

Colombia had plenty to worry about, however, especially once Arana absorbed lands and Indians belonging to Colombian caucheros, and Peruvians took over administration of much of the Middle Putumayo. Yet the country now had Rafael Reyes in the presidency, a man with intimate knowledge of the region and its problems. As part of his territorial reorganization, Reyes oversaw the establishment of the intendancies of the Upper Caquetá and the Putumayo. Colombia needed to build roads and bridges down into the upper reaches of both regions and then establish a riverine transport system in order to retake control of their middle reaches. Once completed, Colombian planners hoped that these routes would carry more colonists and cattle downriver and, in turn, strengthen commercial ties between the Amazon lowlands and the montaña. Of course, all these plans made in 1905 required more money and a larger bureaucracy, but the Reyes administration — often with Rafael pushing things — initially took up the task with gusto. In 1905, for example, the federal government covered 75 percent of the expenses of the Putumayo intendancy.[77]

Along with assigning prefects, secretaries, and police inspectors to the Putumayo, Reyes also found room for some political appointments. In early 1905, Gen. Eloy Caicedo began opening roads in the Upper Caquetá to facilitate the extraction of forest products. Although one of Caicedo's critics admitted that the general possessed a noble character and proven military skill, he concluded that he lacked the experience and the constitution to work well in the lowlands. For one thing, Caicedo was from cold and cloudy Bogotá, and he found it difficult to summon energy in a hot tropical climate. He also ran up high costs by overpaying workers. Finally, the critic alleged that the general took "much morphine." As it turned out, Caicedo did not stay on the job very long, but Reyes found him a post as governor of Cauca the following year.[78] Reyes also took care of Gen. Rafael Uribe Uribe, the "war Liberal" who helped launch the disastrous War of a Thousand Days. In 1905, Uribe Uribe busied himself working out a commercial treaty with Ecuador, and the following year he served with the Colombian legation in Rio de Janeiro.[79] Reyes knew how to care for potentially dangerous Colombian generals.

For the truly dangerous or the less tractable opponents, Reyes ordered the creation of a new penal colony in the Middle Putumayo. This variation on internal exile had two benefits: first, it disposed of various political prisoners; and second, it bolstered Colombian claims to contested lands. Among the political prisoners slated for the penal colony were Santiago Rozo, a future Colombian consul in Iquitos. But, as usual, problems emerged. Many of the prisoners contracted malaria and became too sick to travel. In addition, moving, guarding, and feeding the prisoners cost a tidy sum. Nonetheless, some prisoners were shipped downriver.[80]

Indicative of the president's hands-on approach to the Putumayo, Reyes strongly suggested that the capital of the new intendance be at La Sofía, his old quina operation headquarters, named after his wife. Aware of this sentimental favorite, intendant Rogerio Becerra did what he could to please the president. Within his office, Becerra surveyed the worn sofa and chairs, the portraits of Bolívar, Santander, and Reyes, the intendance's rather large and well organized archive, and wondered how all of it could be safely moved. The problem for Becerra — besides Mocoa being the legal capital of the Putumayo — was that La Sofía hardly existed. To build a town, Becerra suggested that the Indians of four surrounding villages be congregated in La Sofía. He reasoned that the Indians would benefit from contact with whites, especially the children who would "lose their antipathy for the white race and after a few years, the races would mix, the only way to civilize the bad Indian."[81] But the president's will and Becerra's efforts proved insufficient; Mocoa, geographically closer to the governor's office in Pasto, remained the legal capital of the intendancy.[82]

Public land grants formed another program of the Reyes administration to colonize and control the Putumayo. The administration decreed that the government pay the moving expenses for all colonists interested in settling in the Caquetá and Putumayo, but then canceled the program in 1906. Although colonists did respond to the allure of free public land, it was more the land speculators, both Colombian and foreign, who tussled for the really big grants.[83] Many of the land battles raging in 1905 focused on the routes from Garzón and Florencia down to the Caquetá.

While companies and colonists battled upriver, the focus of activity in the region shifted downriver toward the Igaraparaná and Caraparaná, two tributaries of the Putumayo and the center of Arana's rubber operations. A couple of factors contributed to this southeastern shift. First, most of the rubber trees in the upper reaches of the rivers had been exhausted. Second, President Reyes wanted to reassert Colombian claims to his old stomping grounds, to plant a customs office downriver, and to begin collecting revenues from the booming commercial traffic.[84] In June 1905, President Reyes and his cabinet issued orders to organize two administrative districts (*corregimientos*) — one in the Igaraparaná and the other in the Caraparaná — a customs house, and a police force. Putumayo intendant Rogerio Becerra confidently reported to President Reyes that thirty thousand Indians and millions of rubber trees would soon be in Colombian hands.

The first group went downriver under the command of a Colombian general, while Becerra led a subsequent unit. Liberal general Rafael Uribe Uribe was dispatched to Rio de Janeiro to secure from the Brazilian government important navigation rights on the Putumayo and Amazon Rivers. For the aging president, all of this must have rekindled memories of his exploits during the quina boom thirty-odd years earlier. But during the later rubber boom, Colombian fortunes rested almost solely on the Putumayo because the Caquetá was not navigable above Araracuara, and the Napo was firmly in Peruvian hands. The Peruvians, however, were in a much stronger position to contest its control. Mindful of this situation, Becerra alerted President Reyes that the expedition needed a credible armed force to achieve its objectives. For his part, Reyes directed his cabinet members to dispatch the necessary men, money, and material needed by the expedition.[85]

To guard against abuses of the local population, the Upper Caquetá intendant general, Benigno Velasco, issued strict military orders for the men he led to the Putumayo. Velasco prohibited the abuse of alcohol, contact with women, and the abuse of the rights of Indians and foreigners. Many of the men under his command were prisoners, men slated to build rafts and transport supplies to the expedition, or to be parceled out as peons to hacendados. Indicative of the authoritarian character of Velasco's mission, Reyes gave the general permission to halt all river traffic down the Caquetá until the expedition reached its destination. Apparently, Reyes hoped to slip Colombians quietly into the Middle Putumayo without alerting Arana and the Peruvians.[86] To further assist Velasco and the intendance, the Colombian government bought axes, knives, machetes, firearms, and other supplies, items useful to colonists and penal laborers, and as trade goods with Indians.[87] In essence, Reyes and his government were again in the business of finding and then exploiting the resources of the Putumayo.

All the plans seemed in place, but implementing them and making them work proved tricky. Supply problems dogged the expedition because the government could not, or did not, furnish enough money for transporting material downriver. Although Intendant Becerra kept Reyes's dream of La Sofía alive, he admitted that a similar policy of congregating Indians would not work in the Middle Putumayo. Although Becerra himself favored a forced acculturation policy, he decried some troubling abuses of Indians. He claimed that missionaries still publicly whipped Indians, in one case so severely that an Indian woman whipped in front of her husband and children died the following day. He also reported seeing gallows in some rubber stations, and the use of "horrible tortures" to enforce labor discipline among Indians. In reprisal, Becerra said the Indians invented their own tortures, crucifying whites, cutting their bodies into pieces, roasting the chunks, and then trying to eat them.[88] Besides these disturbing reports, Becerra alluded to the biggest problem facing the Colombian expedition in the Middle Putumayo; it depended on upriver trade links because Arana controlled those downriver. He estimated, for example, that Colombians transported about 5,750 kilos of rubber upriver and over the mountains to Pasto, but during the same period floated downriver more than 50,000 kilos.[89] Caquetá intendant Velasco elaborated on the stranglehold Arana had on the Middle and Lower Putumayo in a letter to President Reyes. Velasco highlighted the tense relations with the Peruvians and the need for Colombians to exercise great caution when dealing with the Casa Arana. But General Velasco remained optimistic; he thought that a modus vivendi hammered out between Reyes and the Peruvian government would settle matters.[90]

The 1905 modus vivendi, signed by representatives of both countries in Bogotá on 12 September, might have settled things had it been implemented. President Reyes had pushed for some type of formal agreement to protect both the interests of Colombian caucheros and those of Arana, one he hoped would make the Putumayo "safe for our interests and those of civilization."[91] On paper, he got that and more. The agreement opened the Putumayo to both countries and gave each a sphere of influence — Colombia provisionally controlled the north bank of the river, Peru the south — and established a mixed customs house at Cotuhé near the Brazilian border. Nonetheless, conflict flared. Colombians ran into Peruvian resistance when they moved down river, especially near the Igaraparaná and Caraparaná. Moreover, Arana had plenty of reasons to rid himself of the mixed customs house: formerly, Arana had paid no export duties on rubber extracted from a contested frontier zone. The Cotuhé customs, ostensibly manned by both Colombians and Peruvians, rubbed Don Julio the wrong way.[92]

The ensuing "dangerous and difficult conflicts in the region" led to the revision of the 1905 agreement the following year, when Colombia and Peru signed a 1906 modus vivendi on 6 July. This agreement called for the withdrawal from the Putumayo of "all garrisons, and all civil, military, and customs authorities" from both countries. But this stopgap measure designed to cool tensions did just the opposite. The Colombian minister of foreign relations interpreted this agreement to allow Colombia to place officials in the Caraparaná and Igaraparaná, the heart of Arana's territory and the site of much violence.[93] Naturally, misunderstandings and competition for the same resources precipitated more difficulties. President Reyes apparently tried to clarify and calm the situation by sending a telegram to Brazilian, Colombian, and Peruvian rubber companies. Reyes allegedly guaranteed the property of all companies in the region, even if a future boundary settlement favored Colombia. Rafael Uribe Uribe argued that this telegram only disheartened

Colombian caucheros, for it guaranteed the property of the Casa Arana and caused Colombians to lose faith in the future and to sell out to Arana. Uribe Uribe predictably favored a more bellicose approach toward the Peruvians, wanting to build a road down to Aguarico from which to threaten the Peruvian western flank.[94] Regardless of the wishes of Reyes and Uribe Uribe, Colombians lost more ground to Arana in 1906 as violence intensified. Colombia rescinded the second modus vivendi in October 1907, provoking both sides to augment their forces and leading to a series of violent clashes over the next few months.[95]

These temporary measures to defuse conflict in the Putumayo invariably failed because neither caucheros nor their governments could agree on the borders between their respective territories. Diplomatic machinations bouncing around the four countries interested in the Putumayo only complicated matters further. For example, while Colombia and Peru hammered out their 1905 and 1906 modus vivendi, both countries separately but simultaneously carried out border negotiations with Ecuador. All three countries tried to hatch independent deals with Brazil to secure their respective claims to the eastern edge of the Putumayo. Each country tended to push its maximum conditions for settlement, to quote different and contradictory diplomatic precedents and documents, and to accuse its neighbors of aggression and dishonor.[96]

While diplomatic representatives argued over paper and law, the real limits of effective administration had solidified at the local level in the ten years after 1895. Peru built on the strategic and economic importance of Iquitos to expand its hold over border regions. In contrast to Bogotá and Quito, Lima consistently backed its able prefects in Loreto with money, material, and men. Once Arana set his sights on the Putumayo, he counted on assistance not only from his national political allies but also from that of the Peruvian army and navy. Ecuador, in comparison, lacked a coherent policy in the Oriente and allowed it to slip away to foreign competitors. The Liberal uprising of 1895 and the subsequent expulsion of the Jesuits gutted the Oriente of its best regional administration to date. Mired in penury and oriented economically toward the Pacific coast, Ecuador ignored the threat to its eastern flank. Colombia, perhaps even more so than Ecuador, experienced a severe political fracture in the War of a Thousand Days, which disrupted Colombian commercial and political attention to the Putumayo. Peruvians filled this vacuum and subsequently fought to expand their hold upriver. The Reyes government reacted to this challenge but could never dislodge the Peruvians because it lacked the necessary technology, supply routes, material, and will.

Julio César Arana was in London in late 1907 when relations with Colombia deteriorated, and Peruvian and Casa Arana forces began bracing for an eventual attack. With the diplomatic situation unsettled, but his business in the Putumayo booming, Arana was in England looking for some insurance. He hoped to register his company in London, attract foreign investors, and thus protect his commercial and territorial claims over the Middle Putumayo. Arana's proposed stock offer and the registration of the Peruvian Amazon Rubber Company opened a new stage for the history of the region. These international connections, however, predated Arana and the boundary problems of 1907, for, indeed, the Putumayo had long been integrated into the larger world system.

INTERNATIONAL CONNECTIONS

The international economy radically altered life in northwestern Amazonia. World demand for quina in the 1870s and for rubber in subsequent decades provided the engine for profound economic, social, cultural, technological, and political change. Omit the international exigencies of industrial and capitalist demand for raw materials, and northwestern Amazonia — and much of the world for that matter — would not have experienced such intense assaults on traditional culture and local autonomy. One can argue about the relative importance of the world system or of local conditions in shaping the resulting human and social relations in the affected regions, but one cannot ignore that the international economy served as an important, if not omnipotent, catalyst for changing life around the globe from 1870 to 1920.[1]

The industrial nations of northern and western Europe comprised an important market for Amazonian rubber prior to the First World War (see table 7), but even as early as 1875, the United States consumed close to half of all rubber produced in the world. U.S. consumption averaged between 40 and 50 percent of world output, but during the Great War, U.S. consumption jumped to 58 percent in 1915 and then swelled to a whopping 73 percent in the early 1920s. With German U-boats in the Atlantic and the cataclysm of the world war in Europe, U.S. imports increased relative to Europe because of America's growing appetite for rubber, thanks to Henry Ford, mass production, and the American love affair with the automobile. U.S. automobile production and the concomitant demand for rubber went through the headlining and right out the roof from 1900 to 1920. In 1900,

Table 7. World Net Imports of Rubber, 1900–1922
(tons)

Year	USA	UK	Germany	Russia	France
1900	20,308	10,983	8,515	4,225	2,480
1904	26,089	9,884	12,635	5,832	3,562
1908	32,403	10,827	10,446	7,448	4,041
1912	55,937	18,725	15,396	9,197	5,577
1914	62,265	18,570	8,439	11,646	4,377
1916	117,611	26,760	n.a.	11,182	12,784
1918	143,382	30,044	n.a.	n.a.	14,213
1920	249,521	56,969	11,890	n.a.	13,885
1922	296,394	11,724	27,546	2,493	24,352

Source: Drabble, *Rubber in Malaya, 1876–1922*, 222.

the United States manufactured 4,000 automobiles, increasing to 25,000 five years later and jumping to 187,000 in 1910. In 1915, 970,000 cars and trucks preceded the 2,227,000 shiny new units that rolled off the lines in 1920 on their way to American and foreign buyers.[2]

Prices for rubber, however, fluctuated widely in world markets. Booming demand, high-level speculation, and irregular shipments of rubber from the Amazon basin, Mexico, Africa, and Asia all influenced price. Prices in New York remained fairly level from 1890 to 1900, but then rose and fell precipitously with the advent of the automobile. During the first decade of the twentieth century, prices in London showed a similar dynamic: in 1908, the price range for fine rubber fluctuated from U.S. $1.39 a pound to $.72 a pound; in 1909, from $2.22 to $1.26; and in 1910, from $3.06 a pound to $1.34.[3]

While rubber flowed out of northwestern Amazonia in record amounts from 1890 to 1910, imported goods flowed in at a comparable rate. Ships full of food products, drinks, tools, clothing, luxuries, rifles, and a dizzying array of other items sailed from Liverpool, The Hague, Hamburg, Lisbon, and ports in the United States. English goods seemed to dominate many store shelves, but one could easily find German beer, French cognac, or Portuguese wines. Canned and imported foods replaced native comestibles, especially among the middle class and elite in Iquitos, and the availability of imported goods stunted the boomtown's development of manufacturing and food processing.[4] Up the Yavari River in 1910, an American traveler, Algot Lange, found an impressive variety of American goods available to workers, but all at steep prices: Pabst beer ($4.60 a bottle), crackers and cookies from the National Biscuit Company, Swift and Armour canned beef, Heinz's sweet pickles, canned California pears, Horlick's malted milk, and Henessey cognac ($14 a bottle).[5] All of these goods had been shipped via Iquitos to middlemen (*aviadores*) who used them as trade goods with caucheros and Indians. Given the price of these goods, it is understandable how workers amassed large debts to aviadores and patrones.

The rubber boom and the accompanying flood of imports introduced new and revolutionary technology. Simple goods such as steel axes and machetes fundamentally altered cultural, economic, social, and political relations within Indian clans. More advanced manufactured goods—shoes, clothing, canned food, alcoholic beverages, engines, and firearms—altered Indian and white life alike. Modern transportation and communication systems tied the Putumayo into the world economy. Steamships, telegraph lines, and an urban electrical system in Iquitos—all constructed or controlled by foreigners—provided a veneer of "progress" and the mechanisms to exploit the resources of the Amazonian rain forest. English companies controlled much of the steamship system within Amazonia, and all of it connecting the Amazon basin to Europe and North America.[6]

Railroad projects also attracted great interest from Latin American countries and foreign companies. Ecuador was no exception. The most important line, linking Guayaquíl and Quito, suffered many delays and interruptions and took forty-three years to complete.[7] But between 1893 and 1906, British and North American engineers optimistically envisioned a series of lines running from the coast up over the Andes Mountains and then down to the Oriente. The rubber boom stimulated this interest, for these lines could carry imported goods and rubber, thus avoiding the complex aviamento trade system in Brazil. Whether the plan called for a line down to the Napo, Curaray, or Santiago Rivers, all remained dreams rather than realities; they were too expensive, and the unstable and troubled Ecuadorian government could not underwrite their construction.[8]

Foreigners took more overt control of technology, finance, and property in Peru. With Peruvian finances in disorder following the chaotic early years of independence, the bust of the guano boom, and the Chilean occupation of Peru during the early 1880s, general and president Andrés Avelino Cáceres reached an accord with impatient British creditors in 1889. In the famous Grace contract, Peru ceded control of its railroads to British bondholders for sixty-five years. British creditors assumed that Peruvian debts could be collected given control of these lines. The bondholders organized the Peruvian Corporation to consolidate the debt and to offer stocks. Overnight it became the biggest corporation in Peru and a conduit for increased British investment and trade in the country.[9]

Along with foreign ventures in markets, technology, and finance, campaigns to introduce white colonists to Amazonia abounded in the nineteenth century. Most of these schemes revealed strong racist, social Darwinist, and positivist overtones. Both Latin Americans and foreigners perceived Amazonia as a "desert," one debauched by "lower races." Ironically, Professor Louis Agassiz adopted a social Darwinist perspective inspired by the followers of his nemesis, Charles Darwin, on commenting on the biological and social absorption of the "higher race" Portuguese by Indian savages. Agassiz concluded that the mixing of races produced an inferior product, one promoting savage institutions such as slavery. After the Civil War and the resultant violent end of slavery in the United States, Agassiz bizarrely concluded that "a better class of emigrants would suppress many of these evils [slavery and debt-peonage]. Americans and Englishmen might be sordid in their transactions with the natives . . . but they would not degrade themselves to the social level of the Indians as the Portuguese do."[10] Agassiz focused his comments on Brazil, but they would have gained nods of agreement upriver in Colombia, Ecuador, and Peru.

While the notion circulated that Europeans and Americans would raise the level of cultural and social life in Amazonia, and that their machines and scientific initiative would begin the inexorable march to progress, it proved difficult to attract enough emigrants to the wilds of northwestern Amazonia to put a dent in "savage" nature.[11] Colombia tried to attract foreign colonists to its remote frontiers, but the lands were too far from markets and supply centers to attract either foreign or national settlers.[12] Peru made numerous appeals to European emigrants, but an 1888 report by Samuel Palacios highlighted the grave difficulties facing any and all prospective takers. Palacios recognized that Loreto was backward and needed "whitening," but then he provided a long list of reasons why the department scared away outsiders. Along with the endemic and epidemic diseases — beriberi, measles, yellow fever, hepatitis, flu — Palacios listed several nasty insects and wild animals that could make life short and unpleasant.[13]

Ecuador also tried to lure whites to the Oriente from the mid-nineteenth into the twentieth century. The government hoped, as it did in Colombia, that foreigners settled along contested borders would bolster national claims. In the 1850s, German settlers came upriver to the Oriente to claim lands granted by the government, and fifty years later, an Italian doctor, Federico Mariani, gained a contract to introduce five thousand Europeans or North Americans — no blacks or Asians permitted — to the Oriente in exchange for favorable land and commercial concessions. In 1906, the government signed another contract ceding 500,000 hectares of the Oriente to Oscar Alexander and Company, which promised to settle five thousand Dutch and German families on the grant.[14] All of these ventures failed to meet expectations, and even while Ecuadorian officials deluded themselves into thinking that foreigners provided a solution for their geopolitical and administrative weakness in their eastern province, the Oriente proved too alien and inhospitable an environment for Europeans and North Americans.

For the foreigner unwilling to risk life and limb in Amazonia, armchair travel accounts provided vicarious hair-raising adventure. Two New Yorkers shared their exploits with a public still hungry for frontier tales, and Algot Lange's 1910 travel account related the dangers, struggle, and conflict of the rubber-boom years along the Yavari River.[15] F. W. Up de Graff's *Head Hunters of the Amazon* was written in a darker, psychotic tone. The author and his rugged and brutal sidekick, Jack Rouse, consistently expressed their hopes of gaining untold riches, but also their paranoid fears of savage, infidel Indians. But the fraternity kid Up de Graff and the erstwhile "sioux-venir collector" Rouse went beyond hopes and fears and allegedly cut their own swath of violence through the Amazon basin, murdering Indians and whites they suspected of treachery, and then stealing what rubber or goods they happened upon. Their "code of the West," transplanted to Amazonia — canoe thieves equaled horse thieves, an axe mark in a rubber tree recalled a rancher's brand, violence alternately defined savagery, individual bravery, and justice — imparted a familiar and rugged morality on a strange but largely unknown environment.[16]

Other foreigners came to northwestern Amazonia, not as colonists or adventurers, but as laborers and businessmen. Iquitos attracted the majority of these enterprising souls, men and women who generally toiled in the wholesale, retail, or service sectors. Some tried their luck at rubber collection, hoping to strike it rich. But most failed, including Fred and Lizzie Hessell. In 1896, Fred was named manager of the British- and French-financed Orton Rubber Company in the Beni, Bolivia. Lizzie accompanied her husband on the long and eventful journey from London to the remote Beni, which was thick with rubber trees, and the Hessells optimistically expected that money would flow freely from the trunks. In a letter to her parents, Lizzie mentioned the opportunities, but also the hardships, found in her new jungle home: "I am afraid we take life so easily in these countries. We must make our fortunes before we settle down in London again, so that we can take it easy there too. The mosquitos here are dreadful, I have to wear two pairs of stockings."[17]

While Lizzie dreamed of a life of leisure, the ninety-six degree Fahrenheit heat, the high humidity, and the mosquitos took their toll on her, as did the environment of race relations in Amazonia. Lizzie came to contradictory conclusions about Indians, depending on her social setting. Out in the jungle,

Lizzie commented that "the Indians are very clever and practical people, it seems a shame to interfere and try to civilize them, they are happy as they are." But in Iquitos, she criticized her future house servants, saying, "The servants are Indians and can only be made to work by the whip. To be kind is no good, they only laugh at you. They are lazy people, but I think they are faithful. The climate makes everyone lazy, I cannot work at all, I stare out the window, sleep and eat, but work I cannot."[18] Lizzie lived barely twenty-one months in the Beni before a tropical fever ended her life in December 1899. Five months later, Fred, in poor health and grieving for his wife, left the Beni for La Paz, Bolivia, a broken man.[19] Like many others, the Hessells had paid dearly for their dreams of striking it rich in Amazonia.

Other British subjects of a different class and caste than the Hessells ventured to Amazonia: black migrant workers from the Caribbean. Declining economic conditions coupled with a growing population had pushed many Caribbean residents to seek work on the American mainland. Many went to Panama to labor on the canal, while others traveled to the banana plantations along the eastern coast of Central America. An undetermined number signed contracts to work in Amazonia during the rubber boom,[20] but approximately two hundred West Indians went to work in the Putumayo between 1904 and 1906. Most were young men (eighteen to thirty) from Barbados, so they were generically called "Barbadians," but a few hailed from Dominica, Jamaica, Antigua, and Montserrat. At least five Barbadian women also worked in the Putumayo in late 1904.[21]

These workers signed two-year contracts with the Casa Arana for what in Caribbean standards were high wages. Those with a particular skill worked in Iquitos or on Arana's fleet of steamboats. Most, however, oversaw Indian rubber collectors from stations in the Putumayo. Many had to struggle simply to survive in a new environment. The company paid them relatively low wages for the Putumayo and furnished them with insufficient food. With little or no currency circulating in the region, the Barbadians had to barter for or steal food and other goods from Indians. As expected, many Barbadians also amassed debts to the company, debts that could vanish or multiply over card games. Some of the men gambled their debts and company IOUs, with the winner presenting these chits to the company bookkeeper. Although Roger Casement highlighted the abuses imposed on the Barbadians by the Casa Arana, some did reasonably well. Of twenty-four men who went to Matanzas in 1904, twelve fulfilled their contracts and returned to Barbados, seven stayed on with the company in the Putumayo or Iquitos, and five died by 1910. One man at La Chorrera told Casement in 1910 that he wished to amass fifty or sixty pounds sterling before he headed home.[22]

Conflict and violence punctuated life in the Putumayo, a reality that the Barbadians did not escape. In their dealings with the company, they might be harshly disciplined by their Latino supervisors for insubordination or unsatisfactory behavior. Barbadian males ran into grave difficulties with both whites and Indians if they pursued an unavailable female. They could also experience trouble for simply bartering with Indians, because some section chiefs insisted on monopolizing trade with "their Indians." On the other hand, section chiefs encouraged and forced Barbadians to whip, beat, and even kill Indian rubber collectors. They also took part in organized military raids on Indian villages in order to capture or slaughter Indians.

Yet in this paranoid colonial society, such behavior seemed normal. Clearly some Barbadians did suffer severe company exploitation and abuse, but many became themselves a part of the organized system exploiting Indians. Like relations between other peoples, however, social relations between Barbadians, Indians, and Latinos displayed characteristics of cultural exchange as well as cultural conflict. Barbadians learned Spanish, and some mastered Indian languages after some years in the Putumayo. Many took Indian wives and became integrated into their spouse's clan. In many ways, the Barbadians — who were both servants and masters, working closely with both Hispanic bosses and Indian workers — became cultural brokers between whites and Indians.[23]

The turn of the century not only marked the arrival of the Barbadians to the Putumayo but also the proliferation of foreign-owned rubber companies in Amazonia. Foreigners began investing in land in the 1890s after already gaining control of the markets and transportation systems servicing Amazonia. These companies hoped to intensify rubber collection, and to rationalize labor and exchange relations, dispensing with the costly aviamiento system by paying cash directly to the collector for his rubber. With the demand for rubber increasing, and Amazonian output stuck at about thirty-five thousand long tons a year, such plans seemed to make sense. Most of these ventures failed miserably, however, for collectors needed goods and food supplied by aviadores to survive in a harsh environment, while vast distances from markets made cash of little value.[24]

Governments and caucheros in South America recognized the opportunities presented by intense foreign interest in owning a chunk of Amazonia. The Calderón brothers of Colombia, for example, tried to sell a large tract of ill-gotten land in the Caquetá to a French company, and David Serrano and Julio César Arana selected foreign partners to strengthen their territorial claims to contested properties. The Peruvian government had the same thing in mind when in 1900 it ceded 102,500 hectares of lands in the Napo, claimed by

Ecuador, to Lionel Rupert Stuart Weatkerly, allowing him to introduce English colonists into the region to collect rubber.[25] The Bolivian government
followed a similar tack, offering in 1900 a huge chunk of the Acre (75,000
square miles) to U.S. and English companies in order to stunt Brazilian territorial ambitions there.[26]

But greed, too, propelled foreign investors and speculators to dump money
into risky Amazonian operations. The shady Peru Pará Rubber Company, for
example, advertised 75 percent annual returns for investors in the newspapers
of Chicago in 1905. During the spectacular jump of rubber prices in 1907,
seventy-seven rubber companies with assets of six million pounds sterling
were organized in London just between July and November.[27]

In this dynamic business environment, Julio César Arana traveled to London
to secure a loan of sixty thousand pounds sterling and to register his company.
He had prepared himself well for this transaction, and an English accountant
had already come to Iquitos to vouch for the financial strength of the Casa
Arana. Arana had emerged as the biggest rubber exporter in Iquitos (see table
8), he employed British subjects in his operations, and he enjoyed excellent
business contacts in England and on the continent.[28] In 1907, Carlos Rey de
Castro, Peruvian consul and Casa Arana manager in Manaus, finished editing
Eugenio Robuchon's fragmented and damaged papers, and the company published his book. Although the contracted French geographer Robuchon had
mysteriously disappeared in the Putumayo in 1906, Rey de Castro packaged
his work and wrote a glowing account of the Casa Arana's activities in the
book's introduction. Rey de Castro reported the Putumayo rich in rubber and
"populated by 50,000 mostly cannibalistic Indians" whom the Arana company was putting on the road to civilization. In this public relations piece, Rey
de Castro listed the business structure and assets of J. C. Arana y Hermanos in
the book's appendix.[29]

All of this worked to good result. In September 1907, Arana organized the
Peruvian Amazon Rubber Company, capitalized at one million pounds sterling. Arana kept firm financial and administrative control of the new company,
however, offering 300,000 stocks at one pound each, but reserving 700,000
shares for himself, his brother Lizardo, and his two brothers-in-law, Pablo
Zumaeta and Abel Alarco.[30]

There were several reasons why Arana formed the Peruvian Amazon Company (PAC). Perhaps Arana was motivated by purely economic motives, hoping that the PAC would allow him to rejoin his family and the good life in
Europe. But by 1904, with his family living in Biarritz, his children receiving
instruction from French and English tutors, and Arana already a rich man,

Table 8. Rubber Export Houses in Iquitos, 1902, 1907

	1902			1907	
Firm	*Kilos*	*% of Total*	*Firm*	*Kilos*	*% of Total*
Kahn & Polack	140,012	8.3	J. C. Arana	540,869	18.6
Wesche Co.	138,367	8.2	Marius/Levy	323,420	11.1
J. C. Arana	135,604	8.0	Kahn Co.	247,518	9.0
Kahn Co.	132,481	7.8	Wesche Co.	228,119	8.0
L. F. Morey	123,951	7.3	Iquitos Co.	225,402	8.0
A. Morey	85,471	5.0	Kahn/Polack	174,738	6.0

Source: De la Flor Fernández, "Economía de exportación," 136.

other motivations must have entered his mind.[31] For one, Arana foresaw the decline of Amazonian wild rubber collection, aware that Asian plantation rubber would soon outstrip it in quality and quantity. He therefore used the PAC as financial insulation against the inevitable bust.[32] Second, Arana hoped that the PAC would protect his territorial claim—if not that of Peru—in the Putumayo, especially against Colombian challenges. Arana feared that the two governments might reach an international accord on borders prejudicial to his operations. Third, he wanted to ship rubber directly from Iquitos to England and to avoid the expense and delays involved in off-loading and paying taxes on it in Pará. Although Arana already owned part of a U.S. registered shipping company, Arana and Bergman Company, it only ran steamboats on the Amazon and had no Atlantic service. By forming the PAC and a concomitant deal with a British shipping company, he could dispense with these transportation and customs problems. Finally, Arana knew that other foreign companies had designs on the Putumayo. A rumor was floating around that American railroad builder Percival Farquhar had reached an agreement with the Colombian government to build a line down to the Putumayo. If completed, this line would integrate the region into Colombian economic and political spheres, and would allow Colombian caucheros to shed their dependence on Arana and Iquitos for supplies and markets.[33]

Further complicating matters for Arana was the formation in April 1907 of the Amazon Colombian Rubber and Trading Company in New York. So, in fact, Colombian rubber speculators beat Arana by five months in offering public stocks for an international company, with nominal capital of seven million dollars, but competing for some of the same lands claimed by the Casa Arana.[34] As usual, Arana understood the business and political situation and in mid-1907 registered the PAC in England both to protect and improve his economic and political position.

To gauge the complex impact of the international political economy on Amazonia, many authors have focused their analyses on the macrohistorical forces of imperialism, colonialism, dependency, and capitalism as the causal agents that changed and wrecked regions like the Putumayo. True, markets, merchants, colonists, technology, and capital all helped transform economic, social, and political relations there. An extractive and dependent economy in northwestern Amazonia did, indeed, reorient production toward distant poles. Local production of food, that most basic substance, lagged at low levels, with the result that many urban and rural people depended on expensive imported food. And although the regional economy grew, it did not develop. Exploitative labor systems held many workers in servitude, if not slavery, while Indian rights to life, liberty, and culture were often trampled or ignored.[35]

By viewing the region from international, national, and regional levels, the complexity of its history emerges into the light. Clearly international trade became the catalyst for profound change in the Putumayo. The demographic, political, economic, social, and cultural situation in the region changed significantly. At times, negative consequences haunted these alterations at the local level; it appears that extractive industry drained, rather than filled, local ecosystems, economies, and societies. But at the national level, the political economy of the world-system (whether labeled capitalist or imperialist) enabled local elites — like Rafael Reyes in Colombia and Julio César Arana of Peru — to form international relationships that promoted the expansion of Colombian and Peruvian territorial claims to the Putumayo. Ecuador, although it tried, failed to fashion such an alliance and lost ground at international, national, and regional levels.

Looking from the jungle floor rather than from the clouds, however, evidence suggests that the local society — both indigenous and white — helped shape the changes introduced from outside. Particularly in the realm of labor, one must consider both native and European perspectives on labor and trade to comprehend how things worked in northwestern Amazonia. Although their motivations in pursuing trade often differed because of culture, both Indian and white elites employed their power in a hierarchical and exploitative environment to justify the practices of forced labor, debt-peonage, and slavery. Moreover, the local environment — defined in social, cultural, economic, political, and biological terms — placed restraints on the depth, if not the breadth, of changes associated with external forces. In short, international systems, local realities, and national policies collectively shaped life and change in northwestern Amazonia during the rubber boom, leaving in their wake victims and actors of various hues and tongues.

Long before future analysts weighed the historical impact of capitalism (and

Arana) on the Putumayo, a crusading newspaper editor launched an emotional and sensational campaign against them both. Benjamín Saldaña Rocca, residing at 238 Prospero Street in Iquitos, filed a criminal complaint in August 1907 against Arana, Vega and Company, J. C. Arana y Hermanos, and their section bosses in the Putumayo. Saldaña swore that malice did not motivate his action, and he claimed that humanitarian sentiments and a desire to "serve the poor and helpless Indian settlers of the Putumayo River" inspired his campaign. He listed shocking allegations: that Victor Macedo, the manager at La Chorrera, had taken part in the drunken slaughter of Ocaina Indians ordered by Benjamín Larraniaga during Carnaval in 1903; that section chiefs José Inocente Fonseca and Armando Normand, along with Arana's brother-in-law Bartolomé Zumaeta, had raped, whipped, or killed Indian women; that Abelardo Agüero had used Indians for rifle target practice, switched to children for more of a challenge, and then butchered their bodies with a machete and burned the pieces; that Barbadian overseers whipped Indians and killed others under orders from their drunken Latino bosses; and that all over the Putumayo, Indians suffered the crack and tear of a tapir whip, terrible tortures, and death if they refused to work, ran away, or collected too little rubber. Moreover, Saldaña claimed that Arana and other top bosses knew of these crimes and did nothing to stop them, a charge that a dozen witnesses could corroborate. He ended his criminal complaint with a plea for a court to order the arrest of all section heads in the Putumayo and to bring them to justice in Iquitos.[36]

Two weeks later, Saldaña introduced his muckraking newspaper *La Sanción* (The Sanction) to the reading public of Iquitos. The masthead claimed that *La Sanción* "Defends the Interests of the People," and the editor pledged to protect the interests of the proletariat against injustice, abuse, and crimes. The first page of the first edition included an ode to socialism, the doctrine of justice, equality, and happiness. After this unashamed salvo of political faith, Saldaña included on pages two and three a hodgepodge of straight news, reports of massacres by whites and Indians in the Caquetá, and verbal attacks on the personnel and management of the Casa Arana. He also reprinted a letter from Julio F. Murriedas, an ex-employee of the Casa Arana, who corroborated some of the charges filed with the court.[37]

One must at least question the political and personal motivations behind Saldaña's campaign against Arana. Ideologically, the editor staked out a position critical of capitalism and the exploitation of the working class. As a journalist, Saldaña competed with the pro-Arana paper, *Loreto Comercial*, and raised the rhetorical stakes to attract more readers to *La Sanción*. As for the timing, Benjamín waited to file his criminal complaint and to begin the paper until Arana was in London raising money and registering his company as the Peruvian Amazon Rubber Company. What better time to create or air a scandal? Finally, Arana and Carlos Rey de Castro charged that both Murriedas and Saldaña tried to extort money from the company in exchange for scotching the story.[38]

Over the next four months, Saldaña kept up his pressure on the criminal court, the Casa Arana, and *Loreto Comercial,* reprinting letters listing explicit crimes. Ex-Casa Arana employee Juan Castaños chronicled his problems with supervisors José Inocente Fonseca and Victor Macedo. Castaños stated that Fonseca irrationally insisted on absolute allegiance from Castaños, going so far as to order him to witness and participate in the murder of an Indian woman. In effect, Castaños decried Fonseca's machismo, an aggressive and violent masculinity leading to severe abuses against both men and women. When Castaños complained to Macedo, the manager at La Chorrera, Macedo allegedly said, "You did not respect your boss and you didn't obey his orders; here killing is necessary; no employee is exempt from carrying out orders given him." Castaños replied, "I didn't want to kill people unjustly," but Macedo insisted that he "obey orders and nothing more."[39] Besides complaining about Fonseca's brutalities and Macedo's authoritarian orders, Castaños also claimed that the Casa Arana owed him money.

Saldaña kept up his crusade, even in the face of court inaction, the Casa Arana supposedly buying silence from prospective witnesses, and a boycott aimed at *La Sanción.* In print, he linked the words "assassin, torturer, and thief" to the leadership of the Casa Arana. When shipments of rubber arrived from the Putumayo, Saldaña rhetorically asked his readers how many lashes, mutilations, tortures, tears, and murders the rubber had cost the Indian workers. He claimed that the court in Iquitos did nothing because Arana either controlled or intimidated it. By December, the editor had renamed his paper *La Felpa* (The Reprimand), as his campaign lost momentum at the local level.[40]

To air his allegations before a wider audience, Saldaña needed a foreign courier, and he found one in a twenty-one-year-old American adventurer and engineer, W. E. Hardenburg. Hardenburg and his sidekick, W. B. Perkins, had worked on the Cauca Railway in Colombia, but in October 1907 the two young men headed for excitement and opportunities in Amazonia. They had originally hoped to find employment on Percival Farquhar's ill-fated Madeira-Mamoré rail line, but along the way from Pasto to Sibundoy and then down to Mocoa, the two Americans acted like petty *aviadores,* trading a wide variety of goods with the Indians they encountered. Hardenburg found the Indians, in this case Cionis, to be shrewd traders, and he did not make as much as he had hoped.[41] He therefore often ran short of money and wrote home to Pennsylvania for loans from his parents, in the meantime keeping his eyes open for money-making ventures in the rubber business.

Hardenburg had been fascinated by the Spanish conquistadores and the Amazon basin as a child, and as a young man, his journey into the rain forest took on an epic quality. After their Indian paddlers refused to go deeper into unknown territory, Hardenburg and Perkins floated down the river and hunted and gathered along its rich banks. At one point, their canoe became stranded on a sandbar overnight, and they could not push the heavily laden craft to the river's edge. After long hours in the hot sun, they saw a group of Indians passing in a canoe, and they yelled for help, but the Indians just smiled and laughed at the Americans' misfortune. Hardenburg lost his temper and was tempted to direct a rifle shot across their bow but decided not to after seeing that the Indians were well armed themselves. Still fuming, Hardenburg killed a tapir to cool his blood.

With malarial fevers dogging Perkins, and the sun, rain, and gnats taking their toll on body and spirit, progress was slow, and Hardenburg tarried frequently with Colombian caucheros and political exiles.[42] In early January 1908, Hardenburg met David Serrano at La Reserva, a rubber-collection station on the Caraparaná, one of only three stations not yet owned by the Casa Arana. Reinforcing what Hardenburg had heard before, Serrano told him of the brutal tactics used by the Casa Arana to absorb all Colombian competitors. As did the other independent caucheros, Serrano traded with Arana and inevitably fell into debt to him. But in Hardenburg he saw an asset: the American might secure his property and Indians from future assaults by Arana's men, and so he offered Hardenburg half-ownership of the business.

Hardenburg was elated. He needed money, and Serrano's land contained much wild rubber and several thousand cultivated rubber trees. But then the region's problems became Hardenburg's problems. On January 11, he was detained at a Peruvian Amazon Company post at Argelia but then was released. The very next day, the Peruvian gunboat *Iquitos,* accompanied by the PAC *Liberal,* steamed up to La Reserva, and Peruvians raided the establishment. In the ensuing chaos, Hardenburg was kicked, cursed, beaten, and shamed by men he derisively called "coffee-colored brutes." He also lost his canoe, supplies, and his dream of riches at La Reserva. After this rude introduction to the geopolitical and economic realties of the Putumayo, Hardenburg was unceremoniously deposited in Iquitos on February 1, 1908.[43]

While in the Putumayo, the roughed-up Hardenburg heard about many more crimes than he actually witnessed. He did, however, see a woman raped aboard the *Iquitos* by Capt. Arce Benavides. At El Encanto he saw many sick and dying Indians, which he attributed to a poor diet and overwork.[44] Along with these Indians suffering from various diseases, he also saw Indian girls aged nine to fifteen kept as concubines, presumably against their will. However, the sight that most troubled him at El Encanto was "la marca de Arana," the scars from the whip, which many Indians carried on their buttocks and backs.[45] What Hardenburg witnessed, although unfortunate and even brutal, was not out of the ordinary for Amazonia.

Hardenburg lingered awhile in Iquitos, and in fifteen months, he designed a hospital for the city, taught English to make ends meet, met with Arana to get compensation for his losses, and had an emotional reunion with Perkins. He also collected information and allegations against the Peruvian Amazon Company. Although Hardenburg never met with Saldaña Rocca, who had left town and gone to Lima, he did meet with his son Miguel Gálvez, who gave Hardenburg some of his father's documents on the Putumayo. He also found copies of *La Sanción* and *La Felpa*, in which he read, despite his poor Spanish, the most lurid tales of barbarism he had seen to date.[46]

Several interests pushed Hardenburg to take up where Saldaña had left off in the campaign against the Casa Arana. The American claimed to be an honest, God-fearing man who had discovered a righteous cause to tell the world of the slaughter of innocent and peaceful Indian brothers in the jungle's green hell. He felt duty-bound to do this work in the spirit of the "white man's burden" so prevalent at the time. Hardenburg's biographer, Richard Collier, vouched for his character, calling him a "one-hundred carat idealist who could never resist a challenge," a man of "simple Christian standards" who took on the cruelty and oppression practiced in the Putumayo to "right the wrong," undeterred by mortal danger.[47] But Hardenburg was more than just an idealist. He was an adventurer, a man on the make, one who not only lost face but also a good business venture during his short tenure in the Putumayo. Revenge must also have stiffened his lip. Moreover, he had stumbled onto a great story, one sure to peak the interest of reformers, governments, progressives, and scandalmongers. After all, the Casa Arana was now a British company, one which allegedly practiced rape, torture, brutality, slavery, and assassination to dominate whites, Barbadians (British subjects), and Indians alike. In short, a British company was practicing slavery in South America during the twentieth century in order to amass great profits. Britain, after leading the antislavery cause in the nineteenth century, had an eighteenth-century skeleton in her closet. Hardenburg left Iquitos in June 1909, and after one month in Manaus, he boarded a steamer for England. The international connection to the Putumayo made his journey an easy one.

International demand for rubber had opened Amazonia to the economy, culture, and technology of the world. The boom brought many foreigners to the

Putumayo and introduced them to an alien yet alluring world of green. Capitalists, both native and foreign, tapped into the booming mercantile and financial sectors, creating transnational corporations in Amazonia. This complex international matrix helped place the Putumayo on the world stage. In 1907, while Arana was in London and Saldaña Rocca was using his press to attack him, the telegraph reached Iquitos and put it in direct communication with the world.[48] Nonetheless, the world was still a little slow and old-fashioned.

After completing his long journey to London — his bags full of notes, documents, and copies of Saldaña's newspapers — Hardenburg needed to find some individual or some organization interested in his revelations. As it turned out, London, the financial and political center of the world, would be crucial for the future of Hardenburg, the Putumayo, and for the scandal he carried in his bags.

SEVEN

THE PUTUMAYO AND THE SCANDAL, 1907–1910

Scandals excite, outrage, entertain, embarrass. They reveal corruption, a breach of virtue, the misuse of power. They make news, and they often make money. Most scandals follow a similar pattern: a transgressor creates a victim; a purifier or whistle-blower reveals this wrong; public outrage promotes social or legal action; the transgressor is punished; reforms follow; normality returns. Scandals help reinforce norms and values as they strengthen bonds of social morality and create scapegoats. In both liberal democracies and authoritarian regimes, scandals might encourage mass mobilization and faith in reform, or they might expose illegitimacy and cynicism. Frequently, the initial charges fade in importance to the subsequent investigation — unless the substantive charges offend values deeply and widely across cultures.[1] Scandals, however, do not always uncover truth. Allegations and half-truths can suffice almost as well as proven facts in providing the grist for scandal.

The Putumayo sustained a scandal of international proportions from 1909, when W. E. Hardenburg transplanted Benjamín Saldaña Rocca's campaign against the Casa Arana from Iquitos to London, until 1913. In response to Hardenburg's claims, investigations by British, North American, and Peruvian commissions attempted to document crimes and punish the guilty. The counterattack by the Casa Arana created scandals of its own. This remote region, changed by the rubber industry and the world economy, became the site of national and global infamy; however, the international politics and complex personalities of the scandal obscured much of the reality and history of the region. In short, critical analysis of the scandal must avoid political, moralistic, or nationalistic pitfalls, and must place it within the larger history of the region and of reform politics.

Hardenburg arrived in London in July 1909 and began his search for British organizations, newspapers, and publishers interested in the Putumayo allegations. Short of money and eventually of patience, Hardenburg finally contacted Rev. John H. Harris, the organizational secretary of the Anti-Slavery and Aborigines Protection Society. This society — the sum of two Quaker reform groups formed in the 1830s to oppose slavery and mistreatment of native peoples by Europeans — and its secretary, Harris, campaigned against atrocities in another rubber-rich region, the Belgian Congo, from 1897 to 1906.[2]

In Harris, Hardenburg found an influential and well-known reformer. Harris looked at some of Hardenburg's documentation and concluded from his knowledge of the Congo investigation — not that of the Putumayo — that the dossier was credible.[3] Harris then introduced Hardenburg to other important individuals in British reform circles. Hardenburg called on Sydney Paternoster, assistant editor of the muckraking weekly *Truth*, and Mr. T. Fisher Unwin, editor of an important English press. Paternoster perused Hardenburg's evidence, as had Harris, and within a fortnight gathered equivocal confirmation of Hardenburg's charges. In September 1909, *Truth* began running a series of sensational articles based on information supplied by Saldaña Rocca and Hardenburg. The columns alleged that the employees of the Casa Arana, motivated by greed and sadism, had raped, tortured, dismembered, and murdered Putumayan Indians. Of course, now that the Casa Arana was the British-registered Peruvian Amazon Company (PAC), the reading public discovered English complicity in the crimes. The story had great news value and stimulated public interest in *Truth*, the only London paper to print the articles and to risk the wrath and libel charges of the PAC. Subsequently, in 1912, publisher Unwin built on the fervor created by the *Truth* articles and released Hardenburg's account of the Putumayo in book form.[4]

The marketing of the Putumayo scandal exposed some of the sustaining influences that kept it alive for four years. In his introduction to Hardenburg's book, C. Reginald Enock, himself a South American explorer and reformer, revealed that the Putumayo scandal became a paying venture only after the publication of the *Truth* articles and the lobbying efforts of the Anti-Slavery and Aborigines Protection Society had raised public ire.[5] The scandal brought in money for *Truth*, the Anti-Slavery and Aborigines Protection Society, Unwin, and Hardenburg. Moreover, Enock and other writers used the "black legend" — that Spaniards had an unusually cruel and vicious character, especially in relations with Indians — to win British sympathy and focus it against the Casa Arana. Enock blamed some of the worst crimes of the Putumayo on "a sinister human element — the Spanish and Portuguese character. The remarkable trait of callousness to human suffering which the Iberian people of Portugal and Spain — themselves a mixture of Moor, Goth, Semite, Vandal, and other peoples — introduced into the Latin American race is here shown in its intensity." Enock avoided a condemnation of colonialism — for England was the world's leading colonial power of the day — and instead focused on race and the centuries-old British antipathy for Spain in his explanation of why Peruvians committed such crimes in the Putumayo. He recognized, however, that "other European races have abused the Indians of America, but none have that peculiar Spanish attitude towards them of frankly considering them as non-human."[6] Anti-Spanish, and by extension, anti-Latin American prejudices then, informed many English minds against the "criminals" of the Putumayo. This same focus kept the spotlight of the scandal off British responsibility for the crimes, while it reinforced British attitudes of racial and cultural superiority.

To highlight the suffering of the Putumayan Indians, Hardenburg described them as humble and hospitable victims of the PAC. In his eyes, the Huitotos were obvious victims; the company kept them in nakedness, presumably to limit costs, and forced the women to work in the fields. That these practices were normal in Huitoto society did not matter; to Hardenburg and English reformers, such abuses had to stop. In other parts of his book, Hardenburg dwelled on allegations made by Saldaña Rocca and the 1910 investigation by Casement, for he himself witnessed few crimes. Nonetheless, the lurid details of flogging, mass slaughter, decapitation, rape, dismemberment, and pleasure-killing reinforced the dynamic between the PAC transgressors and their native victims.[7]

Although the Putumayo allegations made their biggest impact in London after 1909, other individuals and governments knew of crimes in the region prior to the scandal. For decades, regional and national authorities in Colombia, Ecuador, and Peru had reported on the mistreatment, killing, and enslavement of Indians in northwestern Amazonia. Independent of Saldaña Rocca and Hardenburg, Colombian officials had begun to investigate Putumayo crimes in 1907. In February, the governor of Cauca reported to the minister of government in Bogotá the "horrible tortures" endured by Indians in the Caraparaná at the hands of both Colombian and Peruvian caucheros. The minister of foreign relations hurriedly ordered the governors of Huila, Cauca, and Nariño to send officials to their respective Amazonian jurisdictions to protect the Indians. But the governor of Nariño, Julián Bucheli, raised problems with this plan. For one, he wanted the federal government rather than his department to pay for the expenses incurred by commissions sent from Pasto. Second, it was unclear to Bucheli and to the other two governors how and where the Amazonian lowlands fell into their jurisdiction. Finally, it appears that Bucheli, or one of his relatives, worked for the Casa Arana and was implicated in crimes committed against both Indian and Barbadian workers.[8] After a few months of administrative clarification, Bucheli and Caicedo shared policing duties in the upper Putumayo, while a small seven-man squad commanded by a special inspector appointed from Bogotá headed for the Caraparaná.

Unfortunate incidents followed. In October, Bucheli reported that the special inspector decreed that all "uncivilized Indians" in the upper Putumayo be congregated into supervised villages. This abuse of authority inevitably caused more problems; congregation intensified disease and intertribal conflicts, while opening the way for theft of Indian lands. Moreover, the Caraparaná, not the upper Putumayo, should have been the focus of Colombian action. Efforts to "protect" Indians in this instance only prompted more abuses.

In late 1907, Colombians clashed with Peruvians at La Unión, near the confluence of the Igaraparaná and Putumayo Rivers. It remains unclear if this collision and subsequent ones—which rudely introduced Hardenburg to the Putumayo—involved just Colombian caucheros or members of the commission sent to the Caraparaná by the Colombian government. The pro-Arana newspapers of Iquitos reported the 1907 incident as a great Peruvian victory over the invading Colombian army. *El Oriente* packaged the battle at La Unión in a nationalistic wrapping, invoking the memories of War of the Pacific heroes Miguel Grau and Alfonso Ugarte as it praised the "cauchero militias" of the Casa Arana for protecting the national interests and territorial integrity of Peru. Predictably, Saldaña Rocca and *La Felpa* blamed the Casa Arana and its ruthlessness and expansionism for the conflict.[9] Although Colombian initiatives failed in the Middle Putumayo under the weight of Peruvian and Casa Arana power, the Colombian actions of 1907 and subsequent developments introduced another aspect to the scandal: nationalism. Over the next years, the Casa Arana and "patriotic Peruvians" blamed Colombian and Ecuadorian incursions into their territory for the violence in the Putumayo. Conversely, Colombians and Ecuadorians attacked the Casa Arana and Peru for their criminal actions, claiming moral and legal foundations to bolster their own respective territorial claims to the region.

The U.S. government had also received news in early 1908 from its consul in Iquitos, Charles C. Eberhardt, of mistreatment of Indian rubber collectors in the Putumayo. Eberhardt sent two long reports to Washington, dated November 30 and December 3, 1907.[10] In the first report, the American consul drew on information from Eugenio Robuchon's book, recently published by the Casa Arana, and from the ex-prefect of Loreto, Jorge M. Von Hassel. This report, subsequently published for its ethnographic value by the Smithsonian Institution, provided a rough enumeration of tribes in areas around Iquitos and a short description of a few noteworthy ones. But a section on slavery, highlighted six years later in the wake of the scandal, emerged as the key element of this work. As other observers had done before, Eberhardt equivocated on the state of Indian/white relations in northwestern Amazonia. He recalled the images provided by Francisco Pizarro, the conqueror of Peru in the 1530s, of humble and peaceful Indians "who seem to expect no better fate than to become the servants of some *padron,* whom they serve submissively, but with little complaint." In his next paragraph, however, he stated that most Indians who came into contact with whites became slaves. Yet he then stepped back again by writing "for the greater part, however, they are not treated harshly, and in their submissive way, with enough to eat and drink, seem to be contented and probably as well off as when roaming the woods. Their condition might be termed a system of peonage. The Indians enter the employ of some rubber-gatherer, often willingly, though not infrequently by force, and immediately become indebted to him for food, etc." Although Eberhardt remained vague on the difference between peonage and slavery, and on the degree of abuse suffered or independence displayed by Indians, he did predict that most Indian tribes would vanish within twenty years—through intermarriage, disease, and war—and would "meet the fate of their brothers in North America."[11]

If Eberhardt's first report sustained the hazy imagery of Indians as noble savages, simple people, and victims, his second contained some damning facts about Casa Arana operations in the Putumayo. Consul Eberhardt visited the Igaraparaná and Caraparaná districts for six weeks in late 1907 motivated by two *New York Times* articles of September 6 and 19, which reported on the activities of a U.S.-Colombian rubber company in the Upper Putumayo and Caquetá. He found the Casa Arana in control of most trade in the region, but he also heard some distressing tales of mayhem, brutality, and murder. As Roger Casement did later, Eberhardt collected complaints from English-speaking Barbadian employees of the Casa Arana. They spoke openly and, Eberhardt believed, honestly. One Barbadian man claimed that a section boss, angry at an Indian woman for bringing in little rubber, shot her through the foot and immediately sent her out to collect more rubber. Another woman, slowed in her work by her infant, watched in horror as a foreman smashed her child's skull against a tree to rid her of this impediment to rubber collection. Moreover, foremen told Eberhardt of their "severe and even brutal measures

which they considered necessary to adopt to keep the Indians under control."
But then they tried to persuade him, presumably under orders of the company,
that they had been exaggerating. Eberhardt concluded that "the Peruvians are
seeking to get the benefit of the Indian's labor before he disappears entirely and
to that end do not hesitate to reform the most outrageous acts of cruelty."[12]
This second report, along with Eberhardt's "use it before you lose it" analysis
of the mistreatment of Indian workers in the Putumayo, lay dormant for some
years, until a conducive political climate and the invigorating force of scandal
resurrected it. Here we have another example of the scandal's contradictory
influence on the history of the Putumayo. It distorted and obscured some
subjects — like the nature of Indian societies and the region's history before
and after the scandal — while it rescued other documents and testimonies —
like Eberhardt's reports — from the obscurity of dusty, forgotten tomes.

Another voice amplified by the scandal added resonance to the lesson that
one need not be Indian to suffer hardship in the Putumayo. Joseph Froude
Woodroffe spent seven and a half years in Amazonia, about half of them in the
Putumayo from 1908 to 1911, initially trying to get rich, but eventually just
trying to get home. In 1906, this Englishman opened a store in Nauta, a small
town fifty miles up the Marañón from Iquitos, and, in a rather shady deal with
the local governor, got control of seventy Indian peons. Woodroffe and his
workforce then headed up the Tigre River to collect rubber, but when they
returned to Nauta eight months later, they found that the price of rubber had
dropped, and that Woodroffe's manager had stolen all of the store's merchandise. Several hundred pounds in debt, Woodroffe became the charge of the
Casa Arana after his creditors transferred his debt to the company in exchange
for the cancellation of part of their debts to Arana. He became an accountant
at El Encanto and toiled three and a half years to regain his freedom.[13]

Woodroffe's subsequent book, published in 1914 with the support of
John H. Harris and the Anti-Slavery and Aborigines Protection Society, revealed that whites and even Englishmen suffered injustice and debt-peonage
along with Indians in the Putumayo. This account, tinged with a strong anti-
Catholic bias, included surprisingly few references to crimes or atrocities.
Woodroffe, however, expressed concern for the ill treatment of Indian women
kept as concubines, a practice which left them "morally and physically
ruined."[14] On the larger issue of Indian labor, Woodroffe asserted that Indians
were swindled rather than enslaved. He noted that Indians received trade
goods worth only one-eighth the value of the rubber they collected, yet he
made clear that they could choose any items they wanted.[15] Perhaps the Englishman emphasized the unfair terms of the aviamiento trade system to highlight his own experience rather than draw attention to slavery and atrocities,

as had Hardenburg. Nonetheless, as an eyewitness in the Putumayo from 1908 to 1911, Woodroffe's account does temper some of the more sensational emphases of the scandal literature.

English army captain Thomas Whiffen also joined the scandal players in 1908 and later published his tale of "some months spent among cannibal tribes." His book, published in 1915 after the scandal had faded from prominence, appealed more to the armchair traveler than to the reformer. Its author had a colorful past. Wounded in the Boer War and drawing half-pay from the army and a twelve-hundred-pound allowance from his father, the thirty-one-year-old captain spent some months in 1908 living among Huitoto, Bora, and Resigaro Indians. His guide and cultural broker, John Brown, a Barbadian familiar with indigenous languages, told Whiffen some of the horror stories circulating about the Casa Arana and its rubber business in the Putumayo. But Whiffen attracted the spotlight of the scandal not because of his book, but because he allegedly tried to extort money from Arana in exchange for a favorable report about the Putumayo.[16]

Back in London in October 1908, Whiffen contacted Arana, and the two men went to dinner. Arana must have felt uncomfortable. He was a cultured and proud gentleman, more at home with opera and Enrico Caruso than with the popular theater and loud bars preferred by Whiffen. After Arana had paid several tabs, and Whiffen had indulged his prodigious thirst for drink, the two men finally found time for business. Arana asked the now drunk Whiffen how much money he would need to write his report for the Peruvian and, presumably, English governments. Whiffen replied that his expenses for the trip reached fourteen hundred pounds, a sum Arana agreed to pay. Next, it seems that Arana tried to have him sign a contract, but Whiffen refused. Obviously, signing such a document would have undermined most of Whiffen's remaining credibility.[17] Whiffen's place in the scandal underlined three basic points: first, world attention provided opportunities for fame and profit; second, the character and motivations of all scandal players must be scrutinized; third, the Casa Arana used countercharges to discredit the men and allegations arrayed against it.

Arana and his supporters did, indeed, sustain an offensive strategy to counter the charges levied against them. Arana must have been annoyed with Saldaña Rocca, Hardenburg, and Whiffen, men seemingly bent on hurting his reputation and his business venture. While other companies and investors rode the English speculative wave for rubber in 1907 and 1908, Arana never sold all the stocks he offered. True, the prospectus for the PAC was padded, and the stocks overvalued, but Arana hoped to sell many more than the 10 percent offered.[18] To even the score, Arana struck back at Hardenburg, claiming that the American had committed fraud, forgery, and theft while in Brazil. Moreover, he asserted that Hardenburg had tried to blackmail him and was only interested in money. The PAC manager in Iquitos, Victor Macedo, levied charges at Saldaña Rocca and a disgruntled ex-PAC employee, Julio Murriedas. Macedo said that Saldaña Rocca favored Colombian interests in the Putumayo and that Colombians such as Benjamín Larraniaga committed most of the crimes in the Putumayo prior to 1904. He argued further that the Putumayans routinely killed and ate one another and were far from the tranquil, humble beings described by both Saldaña Rocca and Hardenburg.[19] Arana and his powerful friends weren't going to back down from a small-town socialist newspaper editor or a few foreign meddlers.

Yet the British foreign office and the Englishmen sitting on the board of directors of the PAC found it more difficult to deflect the public outcry marshalled by the scandalous articles in *Truth*. The Anti-Slavery and Aborigines Protection Society took the lead in lobbying the company and the foreign office, and in May 1910, the company named a five-man inspection committee to the Putumayo. Unhappy that this commission's charge involved more of a commercial than a criminal investigation, Secretary Harris contacted Roger Casement in June and shared with him part of Hardenburg's dossier. Harris and Casement had worked together on the 1903 Belgian Congo scandal, one alleging gross mistreatment of African rubber workers in that colony. Casement, an Irish nationalist assigned to the English foreign service, and a man seemingly destined for controversy, had made a good showing during the Belgian Congo investigation, and by July 1910, the foreign office ordered Casement, then British consul general in Rio de Janeiro, to investigate the charges that the PAC mistreated its Barbadian and native workers.[20]

During late 1910, Casement collected evidence and testimony in Iquitos and in the Putumayo. He interviewed a number of PAC middle managers and as many Barbadians as he could find; because the Barbadians were British subjects, he focused on them. His report to the foreign secretary, eventually published by the British government in 1912, contains a wealth of information about the rubber industry in the Putumayo. He described how the company operated and how it treated workers; and he gathered evidence supporting the veracity of claims made by Hardenburg and Saldaña Rocca. Casement's most damning evidence of mistreatment of Indians involved the liberal use of a tapir hide whip; he estimated that more than 90 percent of the natives had suffered severe whippings. He insisted that this practice, and that of locking Indians into stocks for long periods of time, could not be justified, for the Indians had committed no crimes. In short, Casement described a system of terror employed by the PAC to dominate Indians and to force them to collect rubber.[21]

Casement counted 101 well-armed men supported by a slightly higher number of Indian assistants who oversaw PAC operations from ten rubber-collection sites. The section bosses received commissions on the rubber output from their section, therefore providing the incentive to keep output high and expenses low, thus encouraging severe abuse of Indians. But as Casement revealed, rubber output fell in the Putumayo from a high of 644,897 kilos in 1906 to 489,016 in 1908, finally dropping to 316,913 kilos in 1910.[22] Perhaps some of the violence stemmed from the frustration felt by section bosses in light of falling production and profits.

The Indian overseers, the *muchachos de confianza,* Casement described as "orphaned" Indian boys raised around the rubber stations and then trained to track and trap Indians and runaways. Equipped with Winchester rifles and familiar with the rain forest, these assistants helped enforce discipline and oversaw rubber collection. Casement mentioned that the muchachos especially enjoyed attacking or abusing rival Indian tribes. In essence, the PAC tapped into the orphan pool of Putumayans — as did Indians and whites before it — and raised the boys and indoctrinated them. Instead of sharing cultural secrets, as would an adopting Indian headman, the section bosses shaped the muchachos into a colonial instrument of control. Women became conduits of white domination as well. In one case, Casement reported that a section boss ordered his Bora wife to take his rifle and shoot an Indian prisoner, an order she swiftly obeyed.[23]

Casement decried the immoral influence PAC employees had on Indians, and he roundly criticized the practice of keeping Indian women as concubines. Some section bosses even kept harems, reminiscent of an Indian captain who benefited socially and economically by doing so. He also criticized the company's sending muchachos to raid peaceful Indian villages for more captive labor, and in particular he focused on two long-distance forays across the Caquetá River involving muchachos in 1906 and 1910.[24]

The consul general committed much of his energy to interviewing thirty Barbadian employees of the Casa Arana. Some of these young men refused to talk to Casement, but some did so grudgingly, and others willingly. He learned from them some of the difficulties of working in the Putumayo: low pay, little food, debt, and pressure to hurt or kill recalcitrant or unproductive Indian collectors. Evelyn Batson testified that small boys received a whipping for bringing in too little caucho. Augustus Walcott revealed that his boss, the infamous Normand, told the Andokes that the Barbadians were cannibals in order to terrify them into working and obeying orders. Westerman Leavine, an unreliable but convenient witness for Casement, admitted that he personally killed and flogged Indians without direct orders. He corroborated the "worst charges" published in *Truth,* and even though these charges could not be proven, Casement gathered enough testimony to warrant additional investigation.[25]

These "worst charges" gave Casement's report the Dantean tenor familiar to readers of *Truth,* Hardenburg, or Saldaña Rocca. The practices described by Casement conjured images of a "black legend" highlight film, ones strikingly similar to the infamous charges penned by Bartolomé de Las Casas: little boys held under water until their bowels filled with water; workers strangled almost to death; people yanked off the floor and hung by a chain around the neck; deliberate starvations, savage beating, callous murder; burning at the stake, dashing children's brains against tree trunks, public quartering of victims left to a slow and horrible death; mayhem; genitalia mutilations; lurid images and sadistic cruelty, which even if just imagined turned the Putumayo into an infamous region, and Arana into a devil.[26]

Attributing such practices to a system gone bad, Casement reported that the combined economic impact of debt-peonage, monopoly control of markets, outrageously high prices for imported goods, and unprecedented world demand for rubber established the conditions for abusing Indians and Barbadians. Politically, he found that the lack of government regulation in the Putumayo as well as competition between Colombian and Peruvian caucheros encouraged wanton violence. Socially, he identified an attitude akin more to the Spanish conquistador than to the British colonizer that led the "civilized intruders" to subjugate natives. All of these influences came together to create a criminal environment and sustain sociopathic behavior. Casement did concede that it seemed illogical to slaughter Indian laborers, since they supplied the labor and profits for caucheros. Addressing this question of why a cauchero would "deliberately kill the goose that lays the golden eggs," Casement argued, "His first object was to get rubber, and the Indians would always last his time. He hunted, killed, and tortured to-day in order to terrify fresh victims for to-morrow. Just as the appetite comes in eating so each crime led on to fresh crimes, and many of the worst men on the Putumayo fell to comparing their battues and boasting of the numbers they had killed." In short, murder and terror became the means, or perhaps even an end, of rubber collection in the region.[27]

Casement fashioned what he saw and heard into his new cause. After weeks of cold coffee, hungry mosquitos, long games of bridge, and less than edifying conversation, Casement left the Putumayo. Back in Iquitos, he pressed the prefect to begin an investigation and to arrest the accused. He urged Juan Tizón, manager at La Chorrera, to reform PAC practices such as flogging. Although Casement adopted a young orphan boy as his personal servant, he hypocritically urged Peruvians to treat the docile and gentle Indians with respect. In the conclusion to his report, he argued that the evidence and allegations against the PAC warranted severe legal indictments. To pressure the foreign office to take swift action, Casement quietly filed independent reports with the Anti-Slavery and Aborigines Protection Society — much to the anger of the foreign office — to ensure that the British government would neither bury his report, as it had with his work on the Congo, nor scotch a future investigation.[28]

The images of death and destruction found in Casement's report also run through indigenous oral accounts of the Putumayo during the rubber boom. Drawn from oral tradition and anthropological research, this ethnographic information mixes myth with history and is chronologically vague; it is, nonetheless, no less reliable than the politically motivated scandal literature. For example, the Andokes labeled whites "*quemadores*" (burners) in the first decade of the twentieth century, when the Casa Arana was taking over the Putumayo. Perhaps "burners" reflected white assaults on malocas, or the unprecedented clearing of forest to make room for large agricultural plots.[29] Antonia Nomiya, a widowed Huitota, testified that in 1908 and 1909, PAC bosses and a rival Yabuyanos chief nailed several Indians to crosses, doused them in kerosene, and burned them alive. She stated that children were whipped to death, and that adults were strangled and mutilated.[30] The oral account of O'ioi tells the story of Isabel, his Bora grandmother. Isabel grew up at the PAC rubber station Abisinia during the boom years. She said that whites killed Indians who collected less than seven kilos of rubber a week. One day, her cousin dejectedly told her parents that this was his last meal because he had collected so little rubber the previous week. The following day, section boss Abelardo Agüero weighed her cousin's rubber, whipped him, shot him, and then burned his corpse.[31] Isabel's declarations, as told by her grandson, might be allegorical. And they might be true.

Casement reported that Indians did violently resist conquest and demands from caucheros, citing a 1903 incident involving Andokes who slaughtered the Colombian and Brazilian caucheros in their midst. They reportedly immersed some of the body parts in water and showed them to other Indians as proof of their effective resistance. The most famous and oft-repeated example of Indian resistance focused on the Bora chief Katenere. In 1907, Katenere and his people began to collect rubber for Normand at Abisinia but then fled the harsh treatment. The following year, Katenere was captured and placed in stocks. In rage, he witnessed a white man rape his wife. He escaped with the aid of an Indian girl, gathered some men and Winchester rifles, and began a two-year guerrilla war on caucheros and their Indian peons while seeking to kill the man who raped his wife. In August 1910, while trying to rescue his wife, Katenere was shot by an Indian sentry at Abisinia.[32] Although the scandal marginalized Indian responses to their condition by casting them as victims, these few cases suggest that Indians did openly resist demands from outsiders and attempt to shape their relationship with caucheros.

While the Putumayo scandal grabbed international headlines, Ecuador, Colombia, and Peru continued their respective campaigns to control northwestern Amazonia. The scandal may have highlighted a new era for the Putumayo on the international scene, but many of the national and regional realities for these three South American countries remained unchanged.

Ecuador, as usual, found it difficult to create a national government, one with the resources, resolve, and policies to protect the Oriente from challengers. Eloy Alfaro once again took the presidency following his sacking of a rival Liberal administration in January 1906, but now an old and sick warhorse, he faced repeated challenges from both Liberal and Conservative rebels as his political base slowly eroded from under him. He had one grand but largely symbolic victory, however. On July 25, 1908, the Guayaquíl-Quito railroad was finally inaugurated. Although his enemies tried to sabotage its completion, and the railroad put the country deeply into debt, Alfaro enjoyed a moment of joy, but his political problems and those of the country did not fade away. As he increasingly relied on the army for power, he alienated university students, once an important force favoring his reforms, and many former Alfaristas joined the opposition. In trouble, Alfaro revived the Bolivarian dream of federating Ecuador, Colombia, and Venezuela into a great republic, one capable of acting defensively and offensively against Peru — and one presumably under Alfaro's tutelage. This idealistic dream, one that could never come true given partisan and national divisions, illustrates the ethereal but decaying leadership at the very top of the Ecuadorian government.[33]

Given the drift and fragility of the central government, the Oriente passed through yet another period of malignant neglect by Quito. The Peruvian river town Iquitos controlled the economic lifeline of the Ecuadorian Oriente; Iquitos supplied ten times the imports by value as did Quito.[34] As in the past, Ecuadorian economic and administrative weaknesses at both the national and regional levels opened opportunities to foreign interests in the Oriente. By 1910, relations between Ecuador and Peru had reached the breaking point.

Peru and Ecuador had decided twenty years earlier to submit their border dispute in northwestern Amazonia to the King of Spain for arbitration. Finally, in 1910, the king's council of state reached a decision favoring Peru's claims (see map). Ecuadorians expressed anger at this decision, claiming that Spain favored Peru because of their intimate and profitable relationship during the colonial period. Ecuador refused to recognize the Spanish decision, supported diplomatically by Colombia and Chile. In the debris of failed negotiations, war fever erupted. Both Ecuador and Peru quickly mobilized armies of twenty thousand men each.[35] The Ecuadorian Senate revved into gear and authorized a series of extraordinary and expensive measures. To raise money, the Senate approved higher taxes on luxury items, rural and urban property, official documents, tobacco, and alcohol. Moreover, all public servants were to "donate" 10 percent of their salaries to the war effort, an exaction particularly unpopular with the poorly paid police force.[36]

Local "patriotic councils" (*juntas patrióticas*) stepped forward with proposals to help the government incorporate the Oriente into the national domain during this time of crisis. The patriotic council of Latacunga requested and received fifty thousand sucres from Quito to build a road down to the Napo. The junta patriótica of Tungurahua urged Quito to build an Ambato-Baños-Curaray rail line. Short of cash, however, the government pledged to raise the necessary money in Europe and the United States. Both councils hoped to link their respective Andean region with the Amazon, thus countering Peruvian challenges to the Oriente. Yet these proposals, and others depending on foreign companies to colonize the Oriente, only highlighted the past indifference of Quito to the development of the province. Luckily, Ecuador once again dodged the bullet of national humiliation. Argentina, Brazil, and the United States mediated an agreement between Ecuador and Peru, thereby averting a costly, and probably losing, war for Quito.[37]

In 1910, the tensions created by the scandal and border conflicts spilled into Colombia as well. From August to December, a series of reports described the situation in the Aguarico, Putumayo, and Caquetá. In Aguarico, Colombian and Ecuadorian competition for the region exacerbated the disorder created by Colombian criminals operating under Peruvian protection, presumably an indirect reference to PAC operations. In both the Caquetá and Putumayo, Colombian regional officials reported Peruvians on the move. The governor of Nariño, Eliseo Gómez Jurado, stated that Peruvians and some Colombians abused Indians as they tried to establish absolute domination over these regions, another oblique reference to the PAC. The governor reasoned that Colombia could protect her indigenous "sons and daughters" only by congregating them and turning them over to missionary direction.[38]

The rekindled interest in congregating and protecting Indians paralleled a similar concern to conserve the other essential factor of production for the rubber industry: trees. By 1907 and 1908, the destruction of wild *Castilloa* rubber trees worried both governmental and business interests. In September 1907, the governor of Nariño appointed a forest inspector to patrol the Upper Putumayo and Caquetá to halt the destruction of remaining *Castilloa* and

Hevea trees. A month earlier, a newspaper in Popayán had published an article describing the best methods to plant and care for plantation rubber trees. Some months later, Rafael Uribe Uribe, erstwhile "war Liberal" and now gentleman farmer, published a long paper on the history and future of the Amazonian rubber industry and on the advanced Asian rubber plantations just starting to make an impact on world markets. He suggested that Colombians intercrop cacao and *Hevea* trees in order to replenish diminished forests and to avoid fungal and parasitic invasions common when rubber trees were planted too close together.[39]

Land-tenure issues also percolated to the attention of the Colombian government during the scandal years. Common to other frontiers in the country, land conflicts in the Caquetá often pitted land speculators against colonists (*colonos*).[40] Businessmen who owned or controlled rubber-rich property usually attempted to preserve their privileged status while colonos petitioned the government to back their rights to settle and work on federal lands (*tierras baldías*). Colonos feared that legal maneuvers in distant Bogotá could strip them of their lands and homes in the Upper Caquetá.[41]

As the colonists petitioned for relief, however, the government of Rafael Reyes began to unravel. The 1907 financial crisis in the United States combined with low coffee prices adversely affected the Colombian economy. Politically, Reyes's dictatorship kindled opposition from both Conservatives and Liberals, while his highly unpopular courtship of the United States — which in 1903 helped wrest Panama and her strategic canal away from Colombia — rubbed nationalists the wrong way. Backed into a corner, Reyes agreed to hold congressional elections in early 1910, thereby reopening the political system and sealing his own demise as president. Amid public demonstrations against his government, Reyes abandoned the presidency and the country in June 1909.[42] Ironically, this "hero of the Amazon" left the country just as the Putumayo became an international cause célèbre.

With Reyes out of the way, state and national officials received a flood of telegrams and letters, some asking for public posts, others requesting governmental assistance, still others criticizing former President Reyes. Caraparaná residents Cornelio Josa and Sebastían González complained that in April 1911, one hundred heavily armed Peruvians supported by two launches sporting a machine gun and a cannon invaded and burned homes, killing at least forty Colombians, but that the Reyes government remained silent about such serious attacks.[43] A widow complained to the new president that Reyes had ignored her pleas for justice for four long years after an employee of the Casa Arana, José Allende, allegedly murdered her husband and son on the banks of the Caraparaná in 1905. Moreover, she asserted that the Reyes government did nothing to investigate the crime because the murderer Allende had had several meetings with a high-level partner of Reyes, presumably his nephew and secretary of foreign affairs, Carlos Calderón.[44] The Calderón/Reyes link dated back to the quina boom of the 1870s, and the Calderón family owned a rubber company in the Putumayo until 1906, when the Casa Arana bought them out. Some Colombians concluded that Arana enjoyed a close business and political relationship with the Reyes government.

Another voice in the emerging anti-Reyes chorus belonged to Santiago Rozo. Reyes had exiled Rozo to the Putumayo early in his administration. In 1910, Rozo wrote two long letters concerning the Putumayo. The first, addressed to the PAC commission investigating the region, contained a list of charges against the Casa Arana and the PAC for crimes committed against Colombians.[45] He tried to see Casement in Manaus, but the English consul ducked him. The second, addressed to the president of Colombia and his ministers, blasted the Casa Arana for its violent takeover of the Putumayo and its designs on the Caquetá. Yet Rozo levied his most serious charges against the Reyes government for allowing such aggression against Colombian territory and citizens. He claimed that Pedro Antonio Pizarro—who along with the Calderón brothers had received ample land grants from the Reyes government—had abandoned his post as customs agent in the Lower Putumayo and treasonously turned over the territory to the Casa Arana. In essence, he charged that Pizarro, Calderón, and Reyes had sold out the country and left Colombian caucheros to the dubious mercy of the Peruvians. Rozo urged the new government to bolster Colombian cauchero and military interests in the Caquetá (to avoid losing it, too), to expel PAC employee Normand from the region, and to recover what was left of national honor.[46] Although Rozo faced separate charges of exceeding his authority as Colombian consul in Manaus, his allegations and others like them hounded Reyes and tarnished his reputation over the next several years.

As Reyes's national political career wound down, so too did the local political career of Manuel Pinedo in Iquitos. In 1907, the sixty-four-year-old Pinedo faced yet again the vicissitudes of the international economy. The financial crisis of 1907 and unstable rubber prices had exacerbated monetary scarcity and inflation in Iquitos. Although Pinedo, now serving on the departmental council, boasted more than four decades of administrative experience in Loreto, neither he nor any other local person could control or even ameliorate the economic instability brought to Iquitos from abroad from 1907 to 1910. Economic insecurity and the developing Putumayo scandal dovetailed as the Amazonian rubber boom reached its zenith.[47]

Pinedo was not the only familiar face seen on the streets and in public offices of Iquitos during these unsettling years. Although the Casa Arana found itself embroiled in the scandal, it still maintained a strong direct connection to regional political power. Carlos Rey de Castro, an Arana business associate, continued to protect PAC business interests from his post as Peruvian consul in Manaus. PAC manager and Arana brother-in-law Pablo Zumaeta served on an ambitious commission to build a grand church in Iquitos in 1910. Although Zumaeta could not find the money, materials, or bishop for the proposed cathedral, he nonetheless kept a high profile during the scandal years. So, too, did Juan Tizón, ex-manager at La Chorrera, who served as Loreto's prefect beginning in 1909. During the same year, *Loreto Comercial* printed a large PAC advertisement offering free medical care and transportation to the Putumayo, good wages, and bonuses for men who agreed to work in the far-off district. The company did demand solid recommendations from all applicants, however.[48] In Iquitos, the scandal had little immediate impact.

Economic difficulties, rather than the scandal, stirred up great consternation in the city in 1908 and 1909. Inflation and popular anger at the high cost of essential goods touched off a series of riots and public disturbances, most of them aimed at foreigners. On the afternoon of August 10, 1908, one such action began. People peacefully gathered in the main plaza of Iquitos to protest the high cost of food. They assembled again the following afternoon to see what action the authorities had taken. Finding little accomplished, about two hundred protesters attended the Chamber of Commerce meeting that evening and traded hostile remarks with some of its members. Police began to patrol the streets following the meeting. During the afternoon of August 12, the protesters switched their tactics; they decided to march to the municipal store and to take the food they needed. Turned back by police, they next targeted an important mercantile firm operated by the British consul; police again drove them off and prevented the store's sacking. About an hour later, around 8 P.M., the protestors, now swelled in number to a mob of six hundred, focused their wrath on outlying stores away from the police patrols. Some members discharged firearms, others threw bricks and bottles, and still others crashed the doors of five small retail markets, three of them owned by Chinese merchants. In a subsequent legal action supported by the Chinese consul and numerous witnesses, Fermín Yong, Felipe Chong, and Julio Yong filed a complaint against Rubén Obando for inciting riot and theft, but the case was dropped in 1914 for lack of evidence.[49]

While retailers, particularly Chinese shopkeepers, had suffered popular discontent in August, rioters turned to wholesalers, particularly to Jewish merchants, by November. During the celebration of All Saints Day, alcohol, discontent, and rumor provoked a serious incident. After several hours of revelry, a few people within the Catholic crowd claimed that Jewish merchants were overcharging for goods and were insensitive to the people's suffering. About 8 P.M., five to six hundred armed and inebriated rioters stormed the homes and businesses of Moises Edery and José and Fortunato Levy. The mob managed to steal firearms and ammunition before some fellow merchants massed a force and drove the looters away. In an exchange of fire, three people were killed and two injured. Anti-Semitism and xenophobia were not new to Iquitos, but the economic crisis and attacks on businesses pushed the "men of property" to defend Edery and the Levy brothers.[50] Who, after all, might become the next target of popular frustration?

Unfortunately for Antonio Verite dos Santos, he was next. Dos Santos, a Portuguese citizen, was working in Iquitos when a Peruvian man began to insult him. Protecting his honor, and in hot temper, dos Santos hit the Peruvian in the head with a rod and broke his skull. The lieutenant governor who investigated the matter exonerated dos Santos, who still paid the Peruvian's wife seven gold pesos to cover medical expenses. However, a group of thirty-eight workers vowed to punish dos Santos and "recuperate the blood lost by the Peruvian." A few days later, they cornered dos Santos, beat him, and broke his skull.[51] This action, and the others involving Chinese and Jewish merchants, illustrates the strong antiforeign sentiment stirred up by the vagaries of the rubber industry, the international economy, and the scandal.

Things were getting out of hand in Iquitos. In March 1909, the city's police inspector requested permission from Lima to expel all known criminals from the city. The inspector claimed that most of the "flotsam and jetsam," primarily North American and European, preyed on the local people and then skipped town. Lima okayed this antiforeign measure in July 1909.[52]

Yet the following year, Iquitos faced more serious administrative, economic, and criminal difficulties. In January, an *El Oriente* editorial blasted the Loretano subprefects "who exploit the inhabitants they should help protect" and who consequently touched off popular demonstrations. In May, Booth and Company, the English firm in control of the dock works, pulled out of its contract with the city, citing the commercial and industrial crisis as justification.[53] Moreover, throughout 1910, the departmental council (junta departamental) found itself caught in a series of problems. First, unhappy with dwindling receipts from the provinces, Lima had formed a national tax company to collect receipts for the junta departamental. The arrival of the tax company representative, Benjamín Aviles, in Iquitos signalled the beginning of some embarrassing revelations about misuse of public funds. It became known, for example, that the junta departamental had overcharged businesses for annual taxes. When Aviles demanded the books for 1901 to 1907, none were found.

Back in November 1909, treasurer Guillermo N. Barreto had absconded with the council's books and cash, apparently with the approval of some other council members.[54] Subsequently, council members and Aviles clashed publicly over these matters, adding to the developing financial and administrative scandal. Once again, this local affair, and not the international Putumayo scandal, grabbed the attention of Iquiteños.

Indeed, the city's residents needed to look no farther than their own environs to find serious legal, criminal, and health problems. A series of *El Oriente* articles reported the dangerous and contentious conditions in and around Iquitos. In late January 1910, a group of twenty soldiers abducted a young woman and would have raped her in the street a scant six blocks from the main plaza had not residents of the neighborhood come to her aid. In March, the paper covered a story of the Indian community at Munichis—about six hours from Iquitos on the Itaya River—losing most of its lands through a legal maneuver carried out in Iquitos. In May, civil statistics for the previous month revealed disturbing patterns: deaths more than doubled births; of the 119 dead, 100 were infants; measles, malaria, and bronchial pneumonia raged in the city, and yet many of the ill received no medical attention.[55]

Foreign policy tensions also kept Loretano minds off the Putumayo scandal in 1910. As diplomatic and military tensions between Ecuador and Peru reached the breaking point in April, the new editor of *El Oriente*, Rómulo Paredes, struck a belligerent stance. In a year's time he would investigate the Putumayo charges for the Peruvian government, but first he shot off some strong words in his newspaper. He argued that war with Ecuador was imperative, for "it is more than patriotism, it is duty. The defense of the fatherland is the defense of our mothers, of our children, of our homes. A people that does not defend itself, falls, succumbs, agonizes, and dies."[56] Jumping on the patriotic bandwagon, the chamber of commerce increased export duties on rubber by 10 percent to pay for armament. The surtax raised an impressive amount of money, though the hardware was not tested in battle.[57]

New taxes and record prices for rubber in world markets supplied additional revenues for the department by 1910. Under instructions from President Augusto Leguía, Loreto and the national government financed commissions and spies to organize and reconnoiter the outlying border regions claimed by Peru. In Iquitos, the police force received a long-overdue raise. Merchants Kahn and Polack were reimbursed for outfitting and transporting a military unit to a frontier post the previous year. Hardenburg and Perkins received five thousand soles in compensation for the loss of their canoe and supplies two years earlier in the Putumayo. To pay for an ambitious electric lighting system for Iquitos, the city levied a new tax on a representative body of property and business owners. Those slated to pitch in for the necessary wire, generators, and bulbs included import/export houses and steamship lines; taverns, restaurants, and inns; banks, factories, and urban property owners; the proprietors of the carousel, of the urban Lilliputian railroad, and of the various opium dens scattered around town; and professionals and craftsmen, from doctors and lawyers to tailors and barbers.[58]

Iquiteños clearly had better things to do than focus on the fulminations of foreigners and the British press concerning the Putumayo scandal. Business rebounded nicely in 1910. Once again, mountains of imports filled store shelves. But the scandal was about to catch up with Loreto and Peru. In November 1910, the superior court in Iquitos slowly moved to investigate the numerous criminal allegations, but three of the four judges assigned to the court were absent and one was dead. Nonetheless, England, Colombia, and Ecuador increased their pressure on Lima to take action. In 1910, even a group in Brazil, not known for its enlightened policies in Amazonia, formed an Indian Protection Society in response to the developing Putumayo scandal.[59] At year's end, the substantive stage of the scandal gave ground to its more torturous procedural stage.

EIGHT

THE SCANDAL AND THE PUTUMAYO, 1911–1913

The years from 1911 to 1913 marked the second and most complicated stage of the Putumayo scandal. After the Peruvian, British, and U.S. governments ordered their respective representatives to investigate the Putumayo, each of these commissioners collected information on crimes committed in the past and on the conditions they themselves witnessed. During these ongoing criminal and commercial inquiries, familiar faces continued to shape the history and perceptions of the Putumayo. Sir Roger Casement, knighted in 1911 for his contributions in the Belgian Congo and Putumayo, urged the British government to take immediate action against Peruvian Amazon Company (PAC) employees and managers, be they Peruvian or English. In late 1911, he returned to the Putumayo for a second time and then stopped off in Washington, D.C., where he lobbied President William Howard Taft to press the Putumayo inquest.

During this time, Arana, Rey de Castro, and Zumaeta kept up their countercharges against any and all who attacked them or the PAC. In northwestern Amazonia, the political economy of rubber continued to shape, alter, and, at times, destroy life and indigenous society. In 1911, Colombia and Peru fought a famous battle at La Pedrera in the Caquetá, foreshadowing their war for Leticia twenty-two years later. Although the scandal, propelled and sustained by external forces, intruded on the region more than it had previously, life still responded mostly to local conditions and problems rather than to international pressure and politics. Yet, in all the hoopla of the scandal, the history of the region faded into the background as national and international lenses distorted the Putumayo merely by focusing upon it.

Nonetheless, international pressure jump-started the Peruvian judicial system into motion by 1911. Although Saldaña Rocca's criminal complaint was already four years old, the Casa Arana's clout with local and national officials blocked any serious pursuit of the charges. In the wake of his sensational articles in *La Sanción* and *La Felpa* — reprinted in some of Lima's dailies — the Peruvian government had in early 1908 ordered Loreto's prefect, Carlos Zapata, to investigate the company's treatment of Indians. Accompanied by his friends Arana and Rey de Castro, Zapata submitted a highly favorable report about what he saw and heard. Casement and the high-profile PAC commission of 1910, however, prompted Lima to take more concerted steps. In August 1910, Peru's attorney general ordered an investigation into the Putumayo after he read a horrifying article reprinted in Lima's prestigious *El Comercio*. In November 1910, the Peruvian Supreme Court directed Judge Carlos Valcárcel to pursue the matter. Valcárcel, however, did not receive the necessary funds from the prefect of Loreto to journey to the Putumayo until the following calendar year. He also took ill and went to New York for treatment in early January 1911. Thereafter, the slender and stern thirty-two-year-old Rómulo Paredes took over for Valcárcel and left for the Putumayo in March 1911.

Valcárcel and Paredes were outsiders in Iquitos: Valcárcel had become a judge in Iquitos in July 1910; Paredes had resided in Iquitos only since 1907. The latter worked awhile for the pro-Arana *Loreto Comercial* before buying *El Oriente* in 1910. In Iquiteño politics, non-Loretano professionals, politicians, and reformers were relegated to a political faction called "La Cueva de Inocentes," (The Den of Innocents). "La Liga Loretano" (The Loretano League) comprised the other major faction in the city's politics, one dominated by anticentralist, federalist, probusiness merchants from Loreto. Both Valcárcel and Paredes ran into stiff resistance from the powerful Loretano League, which included the Casa Arana, from 1911 to 1913.[1]

After a sumptuous send-off dinner at the Bellavista Restaurant, Paredes left behind the comforts of Iquitos at midnight, March 15, 1911, beginning his three-month sojourn in the Putumayo. Paredes carried confidential but somewhat ambiguous instructions from the prefect. He was to follow the letter of the law and fulfill his duties as a judge; to observe the behavior of the Indians and their exploiters and to report secretly the same to the government and to punish the guilty and prosecute the murderers with the utmost tenacity. However, he was "not to damage the Arana company or interfere with our garrisons which are performing a genuinely patriotic duty in defending those faraway frontiers of our territory." Accompanied by a scribe, a medical doctor, two interpreters, and a small guard, Paredes set out to gather hard criminal evidence.

Upon arrival in the Putumayo, Judge Paredes collected testimony from witnesses and, with Dr. Vicente Romero Fernández, looked for physical evidence to corroborate killings and massacres. Initially unaware of who he was and what status he held among whites, Indians refused to talk with Paredes. Paredes assured them that only President Leguía outranked him and that, as a powerful man, he could protect the Indians from reprisals by section bosses or overseers. Unfortunately, the PAC had sent Benjamín C. Dublé and Pablo Zumaeta, both high-ranking company officials, to the Putumayo two months before Paredes arrived, and had given some of the accused PAC employees the opportunity to flee or to destroy evidence.[2]

Paredes, Romero Fernández, and their small team of assistants collected an impressive amount of testimony and physical evidence pertaining to crimes committed in the Putumayo during the previous decade. They took statements from PAC employees, Barbadians, and Indians and then asked the witnesses to show them massacre sites. There, Doctor Romero Fernández indeed found human bones, some perforated or smashed by the bullets found next to them. After visiting thirteen rubber-collection posts, Paredes identified the most infamous section bosses and criminals: José Inocente Fonseca, Andrés O'Donnell, Miguel Flores, Armando Normand, Rafael Calderón, Aurelio and Aristides Rodríguez, Abelardo Agüero, Augusto Jiménez, and Miguel Flores.[3]

These section heads killed for various reasons, according to Paredes. "Disciplinary killing" comprised one major category of violence. They killed while capturing or controlling workers. Those who refused or avoided work met a violent and premature death. Indians who collected too little rubber or who acted "inappropriately" might find a boot in their side, a whip at their back, or a gun to their head. Fear of Indian ceremonies — in which Indians were said to transform themselves into powerful jaguars and to remember their primordial myths — propelled some section bosses to kill all participants. To maintain or enforce discipline, the bosses often ordered their Indian assistants, the muchachos, to do their dirty work for them.[4]

But some of the white supervisors made killing a sport, a diversion, a competition, a ritual. Consumption of alcohol usually preceded such bouts of "sport killing." For example, O'Donnell shot at Indians while reclined in a hammock, and Fonseca and Agüero allegedly practiced their target shooting on Indians. Other PAC employees, either drunk or frustrated, took life for no apparent reason. Paredes describes such crimes as "cruelties and atrocities that had been carried on with the refinement of an art."[5]

Terror underpinned the logic and illogic of violence reported by Paredes. "Demonstration violence" — involving public whipping, torture, or execution before assembled Indians — reinforced the dominant and brutal role of caucheros. White overseers terrorized their subordinates as well, especially Barbadians and muchachos, ordering them to punish, hurt, or dismember Indians or risk the same fate. However, terror also haunted the minds of the supposedly superordinate section bosses. Their imaginations placed then in the midst of innumerable "cannibalistic," ferocious, and mysterious Indians.[6] While overseers punctuated their position with terrorism, its application revealed their fear that they were not really in control of the region or of its peoples.

Anyone in the region could justifiably fear becoming the next victim of brutality. Indian captains attracted a great deal of unwanted attention from overseers intent on controlling Indian labor. Some overseers forced Indians to collect rubber by imprisoning their captains. Many headmen suffered whippings if the yield from the forest was small. Other captains suffered death. Fonseca killed Chorechema in order to take the captain's wife. Elías Martinengui assassinated three chiefs, claiming they had transformed themselves into predatory jaguars, and then he displayed their heads around his camp. Normand burned Indian captains as witches for participating in tobacco ceremonies.[7]

Women, children, and the elderly enjoyed little if any protection from harm. Paredes's investigation told of rapes of Indian girls, forced abortions among concubines, and the murder of female syphilitics. Both boys and girls reportedly suffered genital mutilation as a form of punishment. Children, like their mothers and fathers, were expected to serve the caucheros absolutely and endured the consequences if they did not or could not. Paredes noted that the elderly were targets, too. Casa Arana employees killed old men to erase a tribe's collective memory, its roots, its traditions; old women were murdered because they had little usefulness to the company (*"no sirven para nada"*) either as workers or concubines.[8]

Paredes returned to Iquitos on July 15, 1911, and brought with him evidence of torture, terror, and massacre. His subsequent report yielded a 1,242 page indictment and 215 arrest warrants issued by Valcárcel. Within a week, Paredes found himself under attack from the pro-Arana newspaper *El Heraldo*. An article criticized Paredes and his investigation as "unpatriotic." Paredes responded through the pages of *El Oriente* on July 21: "This deals with a delicate and grave question. It deals with hecatombs that have gained world attention. They aren't legends: they are tangible facts, they are real facts. The crime is not a single one, but a multiple one. . . . To apologize for the criminals, forgetting the prestige and renown of the country, is to wrap oneself in the same crime. . . . Justice has no country . . . for what is a crime here, is a crime in England and in all parts of the world."[9]

Contrary to his rhetoric, however, Paredes realized that justice and crime are relative concepts. As an outsider, an ascribed member of the Den of Innocents, and now in direct conflict with the most powerful organization in Iquitos, the Casa Arana, Paredes had to tread carefully. Foreshadowing some of the difficulties he experienced later, the Peruvian government replaced Paredes *while he was in the Putumayo* with a pro-Arana judge, Dr. Pinillos Rossell.[10] Clearly, local politics rather than universal justice assumed the more important role in responding to the scandal in Iquitos.

In subsequent publications, Pablo Zumaeta barraged Paredes with countercharges. Zumaeta, Arana's brother-in-law and PAC manager in Iquitos, questioned the judge's motives and actions and complained that he was especially irked that his own name appeared on the arrest list compiled by Paredes. This defender of the Casa Arana faulted Paredes on legal grounds, claiming that he took testimony from incompetent and savage Indians; that his assistant, Doctor Romero Fernández, was a dishonorable man who owed the PAC money; and that Paredes had tried his case publicly through the press rather than privately through the courts. Zumaeta also pointed to logical inconsistencies in the investigation, exposed vague or contradictory language in the indictment, and simply indulged in character assassination.[11] Zumaeta took special exception to admitting the testimony of Indians against whites. He invoked colonial memory and imagery to describe Indians as absolutely ignorant and incompetent beings, as savages in the process of transition to civilization, and as children who "have not the slightest notion of the law and of what constitutes right. . . . " Pointing to the colonial period as a model of Indian organization, Zumaeta wrote that in "the viceregal epoch, they ordered the establishment of Indian reductions, that they be taught Spanish and evangelical doctrine, and with this end dictating to them the necessary laws."[12] Indeed, according to this attitude, Indians could not bring legal charges because they were too incompetent, and their education in the lessons and morality of colonialism was too incomplete.

Not only was the weight of the colonial night with Zumaeta, so was the court in Iquitos. Days after ordering Zumaeta, Victor Macedo, and Martín Arana (Julio César's brother) into custody, Judge Valcárcel boarded a steamship for Europe. Although the judge claimed that he was merely taking his government-authorized leave, Valcárcel must have feared for his life after issuing these arrest orders. In his absence, the Iquitos court not only canceled the judge's orders, but ordered his arrest for abandoning his post. Fearful of returning to Iquitos, Valcárcel appeared before the Peruvian Superior Court in Lima to clear himself of all charges. Predictably, the Iquitos court ignored subsequent warrants issued by Valcárcel for the arrests of Zumaeta, Julio César Arana, and Victor Macedo.[13]

In a subsequent book summarizing the evidence and legal action concerning the Putumayo investigation, Valcárcel listed the various difficulties and problems that he and Paredes had encountered in arresting and trying the accused. He noted the legal, political, and economic roadblocks that kept him from touring the region. When Paredes returned with his evidence, Valcárcel contended with Casa Arana influence in the local courts, with Judge Pinillos Rossell, and even with the national government of President Leguía. During Leguía's first term in office, from 1908 to 1912, Arana promoted two of his friends and associates first to the Senate and then to Leguía's cabinet: Julio Egoaguirre, Arana's personal lawyer and a friend of Leguía's, became minister of public works in 1909, and Miguel A. Rojas, related to an Arana business partner, became minister of government in 1908. Valcárcel claimed that Egoaguirre, in particular, held up the Putumayo investigation, and that President Leguía sided with some of the men charged with crimes. Moreover, the volume of crimes overwhelmed the courts — more than 215 indictments — while local officials and the Casa Arana actively covered crimes and hindered the workings of the judicial system. Valcárcel finally became the target of countersuits from the Iquitos court between 1910 and 1912, and he was run out of town by a mob — allegedly raised by the PAC — in December 1912.[14]

National politics certainly clouded the Putumayo investigation. The Casa Arana consistently portrayed itself as a nationalistic and pioneering force in savage, frontier Putumayo, one promoting civilization and Peruvian national interests. Therefore, critical voices — like those of Saldaña Rocca, Valcárcel, and Paredes — were unpatriotic or even pro-Colombian. Building his defense, Arana warned Peruvians that an embarrassing anti-Peruvian scandal would weaken the country's moral and legal claim to the Putumayo. He even argued that the 1906 modus vivendi between Colombia and Peru, prohibiting the intrusion of officials from either country into the Putumayo, invalidated Paredes's 1911 investigation. In short, by matching PAC economic and territorial goals to Peruvian national interests, Arana and company helped deflect some of the sting of the scandal.

Nonetheless, the scandal embarrassed President Leguía (1908–12) once the Putumayo became an internationally infamous region. The British government placed intense pressure on Peru to capture and punish the guilty. Leguía, in explaining the slow progress in the Putumayo case, and aware of the politically disastrous diplomatic and political fallout if Peru lost control of the area, cited the great communication and logistical problems involved in imposing justice in the remote region. He and other Casa Arana defenders suggested that most of the crimes occurred prior to 1907, before the formation of the PAC and before Leguía took office. To placate the Pro-Indian Association, founded in Lima in 1909, Leguía revived legislation to regulate the enganche system in the Peruvian montaña and to prohibit the export of Peruvian Indians out of the country. The president met with Rómulo Paredes in May 1912, four months before leaving office, and reportedly the two men had an extensive conference. What the president heard must have upset him. After all, Paredes, like Casement, had found evidence of institutionalized murder and slavery practiced during Leguía's term as president.

Along with these diplomatic and political liabilities, Leguía appreciated the Putumayo's importance to the national economy. In 1910, for instance, Iquitos collected 10 percent of Peru's national income. Given these concerns, Leguía did little to press the national or departmental governments to clean up the Putumayo or to punish the guilty. Because of some of these same factors, Valcárcel waited until Leguía left office to publish his book on the investigation, in which he stated that most of the crimes occurred during Leguía's term and that ten thousand Indians were murdered between 1908 and 1910 alone.[15]

The scandal stirred up nationalism and charges of treason among high-level officials in Colombia as well. The focus of Colombian concerns and actions centered on the Caquetá, for the Casa Arana and Peru already controlled much of the Putumayo. In light of the scandal, however, Colombia revived its interest in administrating these districts by forming two new federal territories. The Colombian government created the Comisaría of Putumayo in 1910, followed two years later by the Comisaría of Caquetá. With Colombia rekindling its administrative initiatives in the region, it was no wonder that Colombians "discovered" worrisome events, particularly in a district near the confluence of the Caquetá and Apaporis Rivers. In 1906, 1909, and 1911, João Reis, a notary in Manaus, requested title to federal lands (tierras baldías) near these two rivers. The Colombian consul general in Manaus, Heliodoro Jaramillo, vouched for Reis's character and the validity of his claim to a large chunk of the Caquetá. That Reis and Jaramillo were close personal friends and business partners escaped official notice until colonists and caucheros on the requested lands challenged Reis's claims. Complicating matters further, Jaramillo allegedly planned to take over Reis's grant and then sell it to Julio César Arana.[16]

Santiago Rozo, who assumed the consulship in Manaus, pressed these allegations against Jaramillo and attempted to tie the cover of deceit and intrigue to the top of the Colombian government. Rozo was an ambitious and driven man. Early in his term, President Reyes threw Rozo in jail for eight months—where his jailers broke his arm—for opposition to his government, particularly to Reyes's conciliatory attitude toward the United States regarding the independence of Panama and the canal. Rozo personally knew Liberal champion Eloy Alfaro of Ecuador—a rival of Reyes's—and owed the Ecuadorian president a favor. Eventually, Reyes exiled Rozo to the Putumayo. From there, Rozo traveled downriver to Manaus and eventually into his post as consul. In 1910—as he blasted Rafael Reyes, Carlos Restrepo, and Carlos Calderón for their assistance to the Peruvians in taking over the Putumayo—Rozo initiated a campaign to save the Caquetá from Peru and from Colombian traitors. He suggested that Colombia enter into direct commercial and military conflict with Arana and thereby halt the foreign invasion into the Colombian Caquetá.[17]

In addition to these suggestions, Rozo hoped to expose the Colombians responsible for selling out Colombian interests in the Putumayo. Rozo questioned Pedro Antonio Pizarro, who had received land grants in the Caquetá and Putumayo in 1905 from the Reyes government, lands which then fell into Arana's domain. As he did with so many other Colombian caucheros, Arana supplied Pizarro with goods and markets, thereby controlling him through debt. But what Rozo purportedly discovered was that Reyes authorized Pizarro to sell his lands to Arana. Arana allegedly offered Reyes U.S. $100,000 for the lands in the Putumayo, with Florentino Calderón and Colombian minister to the United States Enrique Cortés brokering the deal. Rozo learned of this sell-out by Reyes from some of Pizarro's business partners in Manaus.[18]

Charges such as these against Reyes—the erstwhile "hero of the Amazon"—and against Leguía in Peru amplified the nationalistic and partisan passions stirred by the Putumayo. Rozo's charges, like all the others, must be appraised critically. Rozo hated Reyes and his top assistants and seemed to get along with few people. His ambition to work his way up the bureaucracy and to clear his name added fire to his campaign against Jaramillo, Pizarro, and Reyes. His nationalistic pleas for Colombia to turn back the Peruvians, however, did highlight the fact that Colombia had lost hold of the Putumayo and was about to lose the Caquetá during the Reyes dictatorship. Predictably, Julio César Arana labeled Rozo just another scoundrel among many others. Arana charged that Rozo had obtained some stolen PAC documents in Manaus and then tried to blackmail him. The kingpin of the Putumayo subsequently took legal action against Rozo and forced him to flee Manaus.[19]

Although these allegations stirred little more than emotion, the scandal and nationalism prompted real conflicts in the Putumayo and Caquetá in mid-1911. Early that year, the Colombian government ordered more than one hundred men to La Pedrera, a strategic point on the Caquetá. The three commanders of this unit carried orders to retake the Caquetá and, if possible, to reconnoiter and wrest the Putumayo from Peru and the Casa Arana.[20] However, the Peruvian navy and the Casa Arana responded quickly to these Colombian movements in the Caquetá. Working out of Iquitos, now a city of nineteen thousand inhabitants, and having access to numerous steamboats and far more men, material, and money, the Peruvians held a much stronger position. But they were not sure what the Colombians were up to. Would they risk an attack on the Casa Arana in the Putumayo? To discourage such an action, the formidable gunboat *América,* sporting 37mm cannons fore and aft and two machine guns, cruised the Putumayo in May and June. To attack in the Putumayo would have spelled doom for the Colombians. Not only did the *América* and her supporting boats dwarf the Colombian canoes, but Arana could mobilize a sizable private army on land. Moreover, thanks to a PAC construction project, a trail linked the Napo to the Putumayo, cutting traveling time from Iquitos to El Encanto to just five days. Therefore, Peru could rush reinforcements and supplies to the Putumayo if necessary and swamp the isolated Colombians. The Colombians wisely opted to stay at La Pedrera, but nonetheless, on June 28, 1911, Peruvian commander Lt. Col. Oscar R. Benavides left Iquitos leading four Peruvian ships en route to La Pedrera.[21]

The ensuing combat at La Pedrera, one included in both Colombian and Peruvian history books, initially favored the entrenched Colombians. Gen. Issac Gamboa had five trenches dug to protect his position and managed to draft several hundred Huitoto and Bora Indians as soldiers. The Peruvians tested these defenses on July 10 and 11 and finally flanked and routed Gamboa's men on the twelfth. This "great victory," which catapulted Commander Benavides to national fame and then to the Peruvian presidency in 1914, set off celebrations once news reached Iquitos in late July. However, victory soon became defeat. Ironically, the Peruvian and Colombian governments reached an agreement concerning the Caquetá on July 19, unaware of the battle's outcome. Soon thereafter, Peruvian forces withdrew from La Pedrera under orders from their government and returned their war booty and trophies to the Colombians. On August 3, two hundred Iquiteños rallied in the city's main plaza against what they perceived as Limeño treachery and the sell-out of the nation and its victorious army and navy.[22]

More misfortune awaited Benavides and his men. On July 29, a soldier fell ill and died that same day. Three or four others succumbed daily for the next month until Benavides evacuated La Pedrera. The scourges—beri-beri, malaria, cholera—took many more lives than had combat, a reality in most wars until recently. Even after their victorious welcome in Iquitos in early September, other soldiers and sailors took ill and died. *El Oriente* reported this bad news as the public seethed with the confusion wrought by disaster on the heels of victory.[23]

El Oriente editor Rómulo Paredes took a decidedly nationalistic stance during these confusing times, a position reflecting popular sentiment. Recently back from his Putumayo investigation, Paredes had to tread a fine line between his concern for justice and the political realities around him. For example, on July 19 an *El Oriente* article praised the "heroic, patriotic, and civilizing achievements" of the PAC as it spread Peruvian sovereignty to the Caquetá. As part of the defense against the invading Colombians, the paper reported, the PAC had organized a herculean task — reminiscent of a famous scene in Werner Herzog's film *Fitzcarraldo* — when the company had Indians drag its launch, the *Audaz,* overland from the Igaraparaná to the Caquetá — a distance of at least ten miles. The article criticized the Bora chiefs Julian Nebema and Tiracahuaco for "criminally counseling" the Indians near Abisinia not to work for the whites and their cause. But noting the final success of the operation, the paper congratulated the PAC for opening up the new and heavily populated Caquetá for the good of the country and the company.[24]

Once the La Pedrera fervor faded, however, the scandal and Paredes's conflict with Arana and the PAC resurfaced. Once again, pro-Arana papers blasted the antipatriotic campaign sustained by *El Oriente*. Paredes reminded his readers that he and other truly patriotic Peruvians wanted the country and its citizens not simply to conquer far-off districts but also to introduce them to justice. In a sentence, Paredes answered his critics in *El Heraldo*: "Patriotism without justice is not patriotic."[25]

Four days later, an erudite reader analyzed the *El Heraldo-El Oriente* feud. He wrote, "Crimes have been committed in the Putumayo; many necessary, others excusable, most uselessly ferocious. Even when committed under extenuating circumstances, crimes were committed — that no one can doubt — crimes for which the Arana company and its directors may or may not be responsible but which the company and its directors have no right to ignore." Yet in a strange twist, one reflecting the social Darwinism and positivism of the day, he added that "not all human lives are equal. Seen from the point of view of social utility, all are not equally precious to society. Not all crimes produce the same alteration in the life of society; an assassination in the Putumayo has less significance than one committed in Iquitos."[26] In this hard-headed manner, this author defined the realities of the scandal and reminded Iquiteños that the social and cultural context of crime and murder was, and still is, crucial in shaping public perceptions and actions toward these acts.

In 1912, however, the Colombian government again pursued an aggressive but poorly conceived policy to reassert its hold over both the Putumayo and

Caquetá, knowing that dislodging the Peruvians would be no easy task. Local, departmental, and national officials knew in January 1912, for example, that Peru had five gunboats and one thousand men on the Putumayo downriver from Güepi. Moreover, Peru had six well-fortified structures complete with machine guns, artillery, and five hundred soldiers at Puerto Pizarro on the Caquetá. Downriver from these strongholds, one found the heart of Casa Arana operations. Nonetheless, the Colombian minister of government sent secret instructions to the special commissioners of the Putumayo and the Caquetá outlining the country's strategy to push Arana and Peruvians out of the region. In essence, Bogotá ordered their commissioners to pose as caucheros and, once in the Putumayo, to evaluate Peruvian military and commercial strength, to establish a network of white and Indian spies, and, if possible, to raise a revolt among the natives of the Caraparaná and Igaraparaná. Both ventures failed in subsequent months for lack of men, weapons, supplies, and steamboats.[27]

Along with its northern neighbor, Ecuador faced severe challenges in its Amazonian territories. Many events and difficulties weakened Ecuadorian administration in the Oriente. First, the expulsion of the Jesuits and other religious orders in 1895 and 1896 had gutted the most effective administrative organization under Ecuadorian jurisdiction. Second, the political and economic proclivities of sierran and coastal Ecuador continued to work against an effective policy for the Oriente. Third, the power of Arana and Peru simply overwhelmed the small number of Ecuadorians living in the country's extensive Amazonian territories. While Ecuador maintained a small force in the Aguarico in 1911, there was no way it could resist the larger, better-equipped Peruvian forces. In fact, some Ecuadorians working in northwestern Amazonia adopted Peruvian citizenship. In May 1911, twenty-one young Ecuadorians, men from various parts of the country — Quito, Cuenca, Guayaquil, Loja, Daule — became naturalized Peruvians in a ceremony in Iquitos.[28]

Ecuador still lacked an effective national government, a fact symbolized in the decline and death of the country's leading Liberal caudillo, Eloy Alfaro. His political base had eroded dramatically during his second term in office (1906–11), when both Conservatives and Liberals deserted the sixty-nine-year-old warhorse. But the wily Alfaro tried to engineer yet another political coup. After his hand-picked successor predictably won the 1911 presidential election, Alfaro pressured him to resign and turn the presidency over to him. When the president-elect refused to step down, an angry coalition of Liberals and Conservatives forced Alfaro into exile. But the following year, the opportunist returned to Ecuador during yet another civil war, again hoping that chaos would elevate him to the top spot in Quito. However, after he and some followers were captured and imprisoned in Quito, an enraged mob — apparently containing disgruntled soldiers from the Oriente — attacked the jail and murdered Alfaro and his lieutenants. In a macabre ritual of popular justice, the mob then paraded the mutilated and dismembered bodies around the city before burning their remains at El Ejido, a park then on the outskirts of the city.[29]

Without a stable central government or much concern for the Oriente, the country's weak policy devolved to old schemes and patriotic initiatives from citizens. The Senate tried to support railroad and colonization projects in the province, but lacking money, these efforts failed to meet expectations. Rumors floated around Iquitos that the weak Ecuadorian government had ceded one million hectares of lands between the Pastaza and Santiago Rivers to a foreign company, reminiscent of past plans to rely on foreign resources to settle and administer lands claimed by Ecuador. The Congress, however, approved a law in 1914 to divide the province in half, to structure a rational bureaucracy, and to reduce Indians to civilization.[30] But this law came too late and failed to address the basic problem: Ecuadorian inattention to the province over decades when it promised so much.

At first glance, Peruvian Iquitos seemed secure in its place of preeminence in northwestern Amazonia. Workers from neighboring provinces like Amazonas, the Andean and montaña department southwest of Loreto, continued to seek work in the department. Loreto's junta departamental (administrative council) spent more than five thousand pounds for a new hospital in the first eight months of 1911. In 1912, the local public charity planned to augment the electric-light system functioning in public buildings with a gas-light system for the public streets. Prefect Francisco Alayza Paz-Soldán optimistically hoped to import iron buildings, like the famous Eiffel iron house in the main plaza of Iquitos, to improve the Peruvian customs post at Leticia. Paz-Soldán argued that these expensive iron buildings, imported in pieces from the United States, would last longer in the humid heat of the jungle and would improve the country's image along the Colombian and Brazilian borders. All of these projects and expenditures suggested that the future for Iquitos looked bright.[31]

The economic situation also appeared strong for Arana and the PAC. Although Saldaña Rocca, Hardenburg, Casement, Valcárcel, and Paredes all had levied serious attacks on his person and business, Arana had found a way to survive. He continued to advertise in *Loreto Comercial* and occasionally in Paredes's *El Oriente*, proudly announcing that the Peruvian Amazon Company, address 529–531 Salisbury House, London Wall, London, England, was the successor of the Casa Arana. Meanwhile, in the Putumayo, Arana's men oversaw the production of a cheap but plentiful amalgam of various latexes

Table 9. Export of Putumayo Tails from Iquitos, 1909–20

Year	Kilos Exported	Price-Peruvian Pounds per Kilo	% of Iquitos Rubber Exported by J.C. Arana
1909	404,699	—	16.2
1911	233,179	—	11.2
1912	145,202	.313	5.0
1913	346,117	.186	13.7
1914	285,260	.103	18.6
1915	476,285	.065	18.9
1917	369,329	.078	14.5
1918	230,934	.100	17.9
1919	762,568	.080	28.2
1920	108,676	.071	9.9

Source: De la Flor Fernández, "Economía de exportación," 149.

called "Putumayo tails." Although volume and price of Putumayo tails varied widely during the scandal years, they nonetheless remained an important export from the region years after the scandal faded from view (see table 9). Moreover, Arana continued his operations as an aviador and shipper in the Upper Amazon, handling rubber shipments from distant regions such as the Purús in Brazil.[32]

Nonetheless, Arana and Iquitos faced a rapidly changing and volatile world market after 1910. Although the price of "Fine Pará" rubber reached a record high U.S. $2.92 a pound in 1910, exports from Iquitos lagged at low levels. Both nature and the mobilization for war against Ecuador and Colombia inhibited rubber collection. Flooding during the first half of a wet 1910 cut down on rubber collection and shipments to Iquitos. Military drafts took some caucheros away from their work, while others fled to Brazil to avoid service. Further cutting into expected profits was an increase in rubber export duties by the Peruvian government after 1910, setting an 8 percent duty on the Liverpool retail price of rubber rather than on its lower wholesale price in Iquitos. Arana confronted even more difficulties with his Putumayo tails in 1911 because customs officials charged him the same tax on this cheaper export as they did on the more valuable "sernambí de caucho." A few quick letters from Pablo Zumaeta and Prefect Paz-Soldán got the tax rate on Putumayo tails reduced.[33]

A crisis in imports unsettled matters further. Fewer goods arrived in port, yet Lima simultaneously increased import duties. Fewer ships called at Iquitos, and at longer intervals. Prices for basic goods — rice, sugar, butter, milk, cooking oil, kerosene, soap, and candles — increased as store shelves emptied, lead-

Table 10. Wild and Plantation Rubber Production, 1906–20
(tons and % of output)

Year	Southern Asian Plantation Production	%	Amazonian and African Wild Production	%
1906	577	0.9	62,004	99.1
1908	1,796	2.7	64,770	97.3
1910	7,269	9.0	73,477	91.0
1912	30,113	29.0	73,834	71.0
1914	73,153	60.4	48,052	39.6
1916	159,993	75.7	51,086	24.3
1918	180,000	83.1	36,711	16.9
1920	304,671	89.3	36,404	10.7

Source: Figart, "Plantation Rubber in the Middle East," U.S. Department of Commerce (Washington, D.C.: GPO, 1925), 5, cited in Pennano, Economía del caucho, 121.

ing to hoarding, discontent, and popular protests. Local retail merchants, half of them Chinese, received instructions from the chamber of commerce to charge a maximum 20 percent above cost for all articles of primary necessity. The middle sector bore the brunt of this scarcity and inflation because the working class lived off native foods — bananas, manioc, and fish. Adding to the crunch in the import sector, lower rubber revenues in 1911 and 1912, along with a shortage of coin exacerbated by the growing trade imbalance, pushed prices up for Iquiteños willing to spend more for fewer goods. Some upper- and middle-class families insulated themselves from the crisis by selling their domestic servants downriver to labor brokers in Brazil.[34]

By 1912, changes in world rubber markets and Amazonian dependency on rubber extraction and foreign economies were signaling the beginning of the "great crisis" in Iquitos. Asian plantation rubber, planted in Dutch, English, and French colonies, had grown spectacularly after 1905 and totaled 29 percent of world production in 1912. A mere two years later, plantation rubber accounted for more than 60 percent of the world's output of rubber (see table 10).

The better quality and cheaper Asian plantation rubber undermined collection of wild rubber in both the Amazon and Africa in a few short years. Prefect Paz-Soldán noted some of the worrisome patterns of 1912: Loreto could not compete with the Asian rubber economy; the Booth Company still had a stranglehold on shipping from Iquitos to Europe; and European trading houses had cut back on credit to their customers in both Iquitos and Brazil. Worried merchants such as Emilio Strasberger expressed concern about the rising unemployment and bread riots in Iquitos and hoped that cotton production could replace rubber as the engine of the regional economy. In a cruel coinci-

dence, then, the Amazonian rubber boom collapsed at the height of the Putumayo scandal.[35]

Sir Roger Casement focused his discontent not on economic decline but on
the failures of both Peru and England to punish the men responsible for crimes
in the Putumayo. In London, Casement maintained his contacts with Secretary
Harris of the Anti-Slavery Society and thereby kept pressure on foreign secretary Sir Edward Grey to pursue the Putumayo issue. As for the Peruvian investigation, Casement initially applauded Paredes and Valcárcel for their combined efforts and for the 215 arrest warrants issued by Valcárcel in July 1911.
But in the following months, with the case stalled in its preliminary stage,
Casement's views dimmed concerning the Peruvian judicial system. He made
derogatory remarks about Peru, calling it "this Iberian cess pit," and by 1912,
he decided that "Paredes had joined the enemy." He even suggested that he
might lead a group of upstanding English and Irishmen into the Putumayo to
impose justice via rifle barrel, shooting the worst known offenders on sight.[36]

In October 1911, Casement returned to Iquitos to shake things up and to see
whether he could force Peruvian judges and courts to arrest the most infamous
criminals, the section bosses and middle managers of the Casa Arana. Most of
the accused had either fled or enjoyed protection from the Casa Arana and
local officials in Iquitos. Casement knew that José Inocente Fonseca and Alfredo Montt had taken their Indian peons downriver to Brazil. He tried, un-
successfully, to have them extradited by Brazilian officials. By December 1911,
Casement revealed only one section boss, Aurelio Rodríguez, was in custody,
along with eight lower-level PAC employees whom Casement described as
men "who had merely carried out the orders of their supervisors, and had
derived no direct profit from their crimes with which they were charged."[37]

On his way back to London, Casement spent a few days in Washington,
D.C., where he discussed the Putumayo situation with President Taft and his
advisers. Diplomatically, England wanted the United States to join a united
effort to press Peru into taking decisive action to clean up the Putumayo. But
the U.S. government wisely avoided entanglement in what its officials correctly perceived as a British and Peruvian problem. U.S. interests would have
suffered had it adopted an active role in the Putumayo scandal, or in the explosive trilateral border claims of Colombia, Ecuador, and Peru. While looking to
strengthen pan-Americanism and hemispheric solidarity, the United States, by
choosing any side in this mess, would have damaged its policies in Latin
America. Moreover, U.S. officials distrusted both Casement and the British
government, for both were lobbying Washington to support the publication of
Casement's report, called "the Blue Book." U.S. ambassador to Peru H. Clay
Howard argued, for example, that if Washington supported this action, then

"the consent of the United States could be assigned by England as the cause of the publication, casting upon the former the brunt of the indignation it would cause in wrongly blaming Lima officials, while England could pose as a torch-bearer of civilization into the darkest Andes."[38] Despite the special Anglo-American relationship, Washington declined to follow the British lead, and England unilaterally published the Casement Blue Book in July 1912.[39]

The Blue Book raised the expected fervor in London and Lima. Casement had written most of his report in early 1911, adding a few remarks to it over the subsequent eighteen months. He summed up the scale of destruction in the Putumayo in a single, long sentence:

> The number of Indians killed either by starvation—often purposely brought about by destruction of crops over whole districts or inflicted as a form of death penalty on individuals who failed to bring in their quota of rubber—or by deliberate murder by bullet, fire, beheading, or flogging to death, and accompanied by a variety of atrocious tortures, during the course of these twelve years in order to extort these 4,000 tons of rubber, cannot have been less than 30,000, and possibly came to many more.[40]

Casement's report, however, contained some embarrassing statements regarding British complicity in the horrors of the Putumayo. The diplomatic fallout of the scandal, heaviest in Peru and unwelcome in Washington, indeed damaged British prestige in various corners of the globe. Perhaps it was Casement's Irish nationalism, his distaste for the British foreign office, or his reformist fire that prompted him to write,

> In this instance the force of circumstance has brought to light what was being done under British auspices—that is to say, through an enterprize with head-quarters in London and employing both British capital and British labour—to ravage and depopulate the wilderness. The whole of the rubber output of the region, it should be borne in mind, is placed upon the English market, and is conveyed from Iquitos in British bottoms. Some few of the employés in its service are, or were when I left the Amazon, still British subjects, and the commercial future of the Putumayo (if any commercial future be possible in a region so wasted and mishandled) must largely depend on the amount of foreign, chiefly British, support those exploiting the remnant of the Indians may be able to secure.[41]

As members of Parliament called for an investigation into British complicity in the Putumayo crimes, London tried to elicit support from Brazil, much as it had with the United States, to influence Peru to reform operations in the Putumayo. In the Blue Book, Casement urged Brazil to help repress "the ruthless and destructive human exploitation which has been permitted to grow up on the Putumayo."[42] But Brazil, like the United States, declined to follow the British lead. The U.S. ambassador to Brazil, Edwin V. Morgan, succinctly explained in September 1912 why the Brazilian government avoided an embarrassing entanglement in the scandal,

> There are reasons to believe that the ill-treatment of Indians by the employees of rubber companies is not confined to the Putumayo Peruvian district but that atrocities somewhat similar to those described by Sir Roger Casement in his report . . . have occurred throughout the rubber zone of the Amazon and its tributary streams, irrespective of the nationality of the territory. The Brazilian Government cannot be unconscious that such is the case and it cannot safely throw stones at Peru while its own house is made of glass.[43]

As the diplomatic dust raised by the publication of Casement's report settled into various international corners, the U.S. and British governments in mid-1912 ordered their consuls in Iquitos, Stuart J. Fuller and George B. Michell, respectively, to tour the Putumayo, to inspect commercial conditions, and to ascertain the impact of reforms implemented since Casement's tours in 1910 and 1911. Michell, who had years earlier investigated conditions in the Belgian Congo, received instructions to focus on British responsibility for past atrocities and to count the number of British subjects still present in the region. Both consuls found it impossible, however, to travel to the Putumayo without the support of local officials in Iquitos and that of the Casa Arana. In fact, the Peruvian government had appointed Carlos Rey de Castro — Arana intimate, PAC employee, and Peruvian consul in Manaus — as its representative to this new international commission. Along with Rey de Castro, Arana and his entourage joined Fuller and Michell at the mouth of the Putumayo and traveled with them during most of their tour.[44] Both consuls complained that the PAC actively worked to limit the information and freedom of movement available to them. Fuller reported obstacles to Washington: "anyone traveling through here is of necessity entirely dependent on the company. None but their men know the roads, there is no food but what they have, there are no facilities for water transportation but what they own, carriers can only be obtained through them, and all the time one is traveling on their private property."[45]

Given the power of the PAC and the presence of Rey de Castro, Arana, and their informants, Fuller and Michell both resented the espionage and theatrics that surrounded them. Michell complained that "Señor Rey de Castro seemed bent on 'spreading whitewash' with a lavish hand, and Señor Arana everywhere wished to be called 'Papa Arana' by the women and children." Nonetheless, the consul reported that the PAC had ended the wholesale flogging of Indian workers. Only by sneaking away for three days under the cover of darkness could the consuls speak freely with Indian leaders. Those interviewed complained of little, but the captains hoped that rubber collection would end soon and that the whites and their goods would leave the region. In essence, these people wanted to be left alone.[46]

Michell and Fuller could see the decline of the Amazon rubber boom by September 1912. Both noted the drop in the number of Indian workers at the stations they called upon. They found some section bosses beginning an aggressive effort to cultivate rubber trees after the Asian model. They also reported the presence of cattle herds at some stations, suggesting a shift in economic focus. Fuller reported, however, that appreciable quantities of rubber still flowed out of the Putumayo; 225 tons in 1911 and an estimated 350 tons in 1912.[47]

Michell and Fuller reached similar conclusions following their tour of the Putumayo. In their opinion, conditions had improved appreciably since the infamous years prior to 1910. Michell went so far as to say that the Belgian Congo abuses eclipsed those of the Putumayo, and he stressed the uselessness of exaggerating the crimes of the latter region. Both consuls agreed that the persistence of PAC power and weak independent public oversight would slow reforms in the future.[48] American consul Fuller clearly perceived the problems confronting a well-intentioned Peruvian official: "A government officer, to become conversant with the local situation in the Putumayo, must be prepared to stay in the district a year or more, well and independently equipped, and having back of him ample authority from the Peruvian Government. Such a man would have to be absolutely honest and well paid (to remove the possibility of temptation). He must be prepared and unafraid to risk his life in many ways while he is there. Men of this kind are hard to find."[49]

While they agreed on most of their conclusions, the American Fuller placed more blame on the British for the Putumayo atrocities than did Michell:

As to the past, the truth is that the district was the ash barrel of both Peru and Colombia, and the concessionaires, though cognizant of this, were so anxious to make money that they took into their employ, without investigation any of the ashes who professed a willingness to work. This deplorable result is already known to the department. It was due to the criminal negligence of the Peruvian and British concerns, who, in turn controlled the district, and the total absence of Government supervision. The British directors who entrusted the conduct of their business here entirely to Peruvian hands can not rely on that as relieving them from responsibility in the matter.[50]

While in Iquitos, Fuller perceived little interest in the publication of the Casement report, but in the remaining months of 1912, the scandal prompted both private and public reassessments of the region in Lima and Iquitos. As might be expected from one of the most powerful syndicates in the Loretano town, the Casa Arana took an active role in these actions. Rey de Castro, for example, pressed criminal actions against three Peruvians in the Alto Purús on charges of murder, fraud, and extortion. Presumably the consul general hoped to pursue this prosecution, and not the one in the Putumayo, to demonstrate Peruvian resolve to end crimes in western Amazonia. Julio César Arana predictably pursued a more direct line and in April 1912 sought title to the lands of the Putumayo. Nervous and perhaps worried over the damaging ramifications of the scandal, this lord of the realm now wished to legitimize his claim to thousands of square miles of land and to the Indians upon them. It just so happened that his petition for title ended up on the desk of his friend, the associate minister of public works, Julio Egoaguirre. On the other hand, Arana distanced himself from the PAC and his position as a prominent rubber exporter. He liquidated the company and pulled his advertisements from *El Oriente,* and his name vanished from the list of the biggest rubber exporters in the region. It appears, however, that Arana used Cecilio Hernández, a friend and business partner, as a front man. In 1911, Hernández placed thirteenth on the list of exporters by value but leapt to first the very next year. Hernández was also related to the Arana clan by marriage and drew much of his rubber from the Putumayo.[51]

In Lima, the scandal and British pressure stirred some action in 1912. In April, the government named a high-level commission — one including attorney general Salvador Cavero, the notable sociologist Javier Prado, and ex-minister Julio Egoaguirre — to study the Putumayo and like regions and then propose legislation to Congress. By September, Congress had received the documentation collected by Paredes and discussed the scandal and the British role in it. Both congressmen and newspaper editors expressed concern about the unfolding parliamentary debate in London and the accompanying sensational articles in the English press. Some Limeños feared that England would use the scandal as justification for backing Colombia's territorial claims to the Putumayo, thus wresting it from Peru. When the minister of foreign affairs reported to Congress on some of the diplomatic implications of the scandal, he mentioned the 1910 conflict with Ecuador and that country's intransigent stance on a border treaty, the battle at La Pedrera in 1911 with the Colombians, and the persistent, unfortunate, and false accusations made against Peru in British publications. However, he did reassure the congressmen that the government had the situation under control and that crimes in the Putumayo had ceased.[52]

Rómulo Paredes kept his hand in the scandal politics throughout 1912 as well. In New York City in July, the former investigative judge told journalists for the city's *Herald*, *Sun*, and *Times* why the Peruvian government had had difficulties prosecuting the accused. Back in Iquitos in September, Paredes shared his appraisal of the scandal with the readers of his newspaper. Surprisingly, or perhaps out of nationalistic considerations, Paredes grew critical of the English position on the Putumayo. He criticized Casement and his investigation for relying almost solely on the statements of Barbadians, whom the judge labeled criminals rather than victims. He also argued that Casement had simply built on Saldaña Rocca's accusations published in 1907, and that the muckraking editor of *La Sanción* was "a man of questionable morality." Paredes even criticized an English plan to send missionaries to the Putumayo, for he and other nationalists resented the idea of "foreign missionaries" operating on Peruvian soil. Finally, he suggested that the level of violence had dropped, especially after his investigation, and that all was well in the Putumayo. He noted that government patrol boats now kept order and protected Indians from abuses. Paredes reported that Commander Antonio Castro, for example, had returned from an eight-month tour of the Putumayo, where he cleaned up the region while magnanimously allowing two hundred Colombians to continue working on Peruvian soil. However, Castro claimed that Colombian, not Peruvian, criminals still enslaved and massacred Bora Indians north of the Putumayo along the Cahuinari. Judging from his opinions and the news he printed, Paredes had dramatically altered his position on the Putumayo since the previous year.[53]

Like Paredes, Rey de Castro and Arana maintained a high profile in Iquitos. Just as Consul Fuller packed up to leave Iquitos, prominent merchants and public officials threw Arana a gala dinner party in "The Hall of Mirrors" of the Hotel Continental, complete with imported delicacies and champagnes. Luís F. Morey, a rich merchant, applauded his peer Arana for bringing civilization and employment to the Putumayo. Carlos Rey de Castro lauded his boss as well, while Arana thanked both men, saying that he had had to organize a strong and powerful company in order to dominate "the savage and cannibalistic tribes" of the Putumayo. A single dissonant voice broke the celebratory rhythm, when a speaker reminded Arana that world opinion still awaited his words and defense concerning the serious charges levied against his person and company.[54]

The year ended with a bang. On December 10, Judge Valcárcel ordered the arrest of Arana, charging him with knowledge of crimes in the Putumayo, hiding his role in them, obstruction of justice for trying to cover them up, and with attempting to frustrate a criminal investigation. Valcárcel, who in 1911 had ordered 215 others arrested, took a great risk by going after Arana. On December 13 — three days after the issuance of the warrant for Arana — an armed mob allegedly raised by the PAC took to the streets in search of Valcárcel. Paredes came to Valcárcel's defense, chastising Arana's friends for inciting rebellion and disrespect of officials. Paredes also criticized the prefect and subprefect for allowing these incidents to take place in the heart of Iquitos. On December 17, *El Oriente* reprinted a telegram from the new Peruvian president, Guillermo Billinghurst, in which he pledged his support for Valcárcel. Billinghurst called the judge "a credit to the nation," as he reminded Peruvians that their behavior during the Putumayo investigation affected the nation's reputation. Clearly Arana lacked the clout with Billinghurst that he had enjoyed with outgoing President Leguía.

On New Year's Eve 1912, Paredes summarized the Putumayo question this way: (1) the English and U.S. press had made the Putumayo an international scandal; (2) the Peruvian government was not an accomplice to the crimes, even if some officials in Leguía's government had cloaked the truth and held up the investigation; (3) the attorney general had studied the Putumayo for six months, and the nation awaited his just and measured decision; (4) President Billinghurst signaled a new beginning by bravely standing up for Judge Valcárcel. Yet even this positive assessment could not hide the fact that Valcárcel left Iquitos for Manaus for his own safety, and that Julio César Arana never saw the inside of a jail cell.[55]

That the new year began in controversy was almost expected given the past few years. Although Arana avoided the commercial spotlight, one could still track his power in Iquitos. In 1913, for example, the departmental and national governments began the complex process of revising annual business and property taxes. The man in charge of drafting the new tax roles ran into stiff opposition from Cecilio Hernández, Pablo Zumaeta, and Christian Alzamora, all powerful allies of Arana. Hernández, in particular, foiled attempts to increase taxes on the wealthiest and most influential families of Iquitos. In fact, as president of the town council, Hernández managed to lower his own taxes and those of his friends. Luís F. Morey, the merchant who toasted Arana the previous November, joined the campaign against higher taxes as well. Morey, who organized a tax-resistance league, argued that increasing taxation during a deep recession was both unjust and unwise.[56]

The accumulation of bad news from Iquitos by August 1913 — recession, tax problems, and especially the scandal—convinced Loreto's prefect, B. Puente, that his department needed to encourage a "good news" campaign. Accordingly, Puente courted reporters from various newspapers, especially those from Lima's *El Comercio* and *La Prensa*, befriended them, and then offered to pay all their telegraph charges when they dispatched their stories. The prefect claimed that this public relations project would "counter the malicious and defamatory charges against Peru." Puente paid about seventy soles for this service in its first month and hoped that in the future the federal government would reimburse him for all expenses. He stated boldly that he planned "to make skillful and extensive propaganda" (*hacer extensiva y práctica la propaganda*).[57]

While some Peruvians, notably Arana, wanted the Putumayo scandal to dissipate and disappear, it tenaciously held public interest. The continuing investigations, indictments, and diplomatic difficulties certainly helped keep the scandal hot. So, too, did a series of publications filled with lurid details and sensational charges of sex, violence, and torture, providing vicarious horrors and juicy entertainment for the public of the world. One of many works in this vein, penned by an anonymous Colombian Liberal in 1913 or 1914, reviewed the horrors imposed on the Putumayo by Arana and the Peruvians. This publication—part travelogue, political tract, and gossip sheet—recapped the findings of Robuchon, Valcárcel, Paredes, and Casement and added a few new damning reports from Peruvian intellectuals and army officers.[58]

Carlos Rey de Castro and Julio César Arana actually added fuel to the scandal. In a series of pamphlets during 1913 and 1914, they proclaimed their innocence while blaming unscrupulous scoundrels for creating such an international fuss. Whereas Pablo Zumaeta had pummeled Peruvians for their involvement in exposing or investigating crimes—primarily Saldaña Rocca, Paredes, and Valcárcel—Rey de Castro saved his best invective for Englishmen. He launched a preemptive strike against Joseph Froude Woodroffe, who planned a book on the Putumayo, for he assumed Woodroffe would criticize his former employers. Rey de Castro claimed that the company fired Woodroffe for "ineptitude, peevishness, and lewdness." He called Casement a vain, overstuffed "specimen of the British bourgeoisie . . . a slave of the powerful" and a man "who thirsted for rewards and facile honors." Furthermore, as British subjects, Rey de Castro described the Barbadians interviewed by Sir Roger as "barely superior to the Huitoto," simpletons who told their king's representative whatever he wanted to hear.[59]

Rey de Castro supported his anti-British case by quoting from Spanish and French newspaper articles critical of English politics, society, and diplomacy. Furthermore, he dug up some uncomplimentary telegrams lambasting Britain for colonization of Ireland, India, and South Africa. He reminded his readers of the massacres of "Red Skins"; of criminal policies in Australia, Jamaica, and Africa; and of the forced introduction of opium in China as evidence of English viciousness and hypocrisy. According to Rey de Castro, in its campaign against Arana and Peru, England adopted the high ground of morality and justice, but ground soiled by harsh reality, false Puritanism, and English colonial history. In fact, he argued that civilization had advanced most conspicuously in the Putumayo, not in Europe, thanks to the Casa Arana. In Europe, Rey de Castro noted, women wore feathers, painted their faces, and consulted fortune tellers and witches, and he chided these supposedly advanced societies for finding fascination in drugs, death, consumption, cannibalism, and pornography.[60]

Rey de Castro concluded that almost everyone except the top leadership of the Casa Arana held some responsibility for the crimes of the Putumayo. From his perspective, Colombians, Americans, and the British had ganged up on poor Peru for various crass or duplicitous reasons. He faulted the Barbadians, the Indians, and even a majority of the white PAC employees for selling out the company. Finally, he warned everyone that it was time for this "unjust calamity" to end and for British politicians and speculators to learn that "one cannot play with the honor of a people nor with the liberty and decorum of men with impunity."[61]

Arana likewise penned his version of the Putumayo and the scandal in 1913. He, too, questioned Anglo and American motivations for the Putumayo investigations. He portrayed himself a patriot, a Peruvian nationalist, a man who supported civilization and his country's interests. Because his critics accused him of complicity in a wide array of crimes, Arana took some effort to answer specific charges. In the case of Eugenio Robuchon, the French explorer contracted to reconnoiter the Putumayo, Arana denied that he or Rey de Castro edited out unwelcome sections from Robuchon's report. Arana claimed that Robuchon himself omitted some material because he discovered "the truth." Of course, he disclaimed any role in killing Robuchon, an act he attributed to cannibalistic Indians. As for Hardenburg, the American adventurer who took the scandal evidence to London, Arana said nothing complimentary. He called the American a criminal, a man who falsified evidence to blackmail the Casa Arana. According to Arana, Hardenburg developed strong anti-Peruvian attitudes because the Casa Arana foiled his business venture with the Colombian cauchero David Serrano. Arana also charged that Colombian gold fueled Hardenburg's campaign and that it, along with Anti-Slavery Society money, paid for the publication of his sensational, but erroneous, book.[62]

Arana denied that he witnessed or ordered any atrocities, though he personally visited the Putumayo five times between 1901 and 1912. He stated that during his first three trips (1901, 1903, 1905), he simply settled accounts with debtors and bought out most of his Colombian competitors. In 1908, accompanied by Prefect Carlos Zapata and Rey de Castro, Arana inspected Peruvian defenses in expectation of a Colombian attack. He had also looked into Saldaña Rocca's allegations and found no corroboration of them. Finally, in 1912, he returned to the Putumayo in the company of Consuls Michell and Fuller.[63]

Arana did, however, admit that some crimes, even some atrocities, had been committed in remote reaches of the Putumayo. Some of these he attributed to the "savage and cruel characters" of the Barbadians contracted to oversee Indian rubber collectors. But he insisted that he never ordered any crimes, never knew of any atrocities, never rewarded any criminals. Essentially, Arana blamed the section bosses and their subordinates for the killing and torture practiced at these remote posts. He denied that the commission system drove employees to abuse Indians. He noted that the Igaraparaná, the so-called "theatre of horrors," produced only one-half the quantity of rubber compared to the more peaceful Caraparaná sections. In short, Arana absolved himself of all responsibility for the Putumayo malignancies.[64]

While Arana's pamphlet and political clout enabled him to avoid prosecution by Peruvian officials in Iquitos and Lima, he found it impossible to control the international impact of the Putumayo scandal. By 1911, the combined effect of poor economic conditions and the scandal was threatening the future of the PAC. In response, Arana tried, but failed, to sell his PAC stock, thinking that by liquidating he could distance himself from the Putumayo mess. He did, however, have his wife, Eleonora, collect a sixty-thousand-pound sterling mortgage from the company, for she was listed as a prime creditor of the PAC. Also in 1911, with cash reserves down to a few pounds and debts high, Lloyd's Bank cut off all credit to the PAC. In 1912, German rubber dealers, troubled by the scandal, refused to purchase any Putumayo rubber. Finally, on November 5, 1912, Parliament ordered all PAC records in England seized, and the following day, the Parliamentary Committee on the Putumayo began six months of hearings into the scandal. Given Valcárcel's warrant for Arana's arrest and the parliamentary investigation, *Peru To-Day* of Lima described the once untouchable Arana as "now practically a fugitive from justice." Nevertheless, the indefatigable Arana pledged to travel to Europe, "to protect his interests and those of his country."[65]

The parliamentary inquiry of November 1912 through April 1913 reviewed the scandal documentation and probed the individual responsibility of the British directors of the PAC for the crimes committed in the Putumayo since 1907. The committee also discussed the necessity of changing English commercial law, particularly the Companies Acts, regulations on companies head-quartered in England but operating overseas. This inquiry afforded young, aggressive politicians—such as James Ramsay McDonald, a Labour Party M.P. since 1911 and the party's first prime minister in 1924, and John Gordon Swift MacNeil, a tough-minded Irishman—an ideal stage for professional advancement and political fame.[66]

The witnesses who appeared before the committee amounted to a "who's who" of the Putumayo scandal. W. E. Hardenburg testified, as did Anti-Slavery and Aborigines Protection Society secretary John H. Harris, publisher G. S. Paternoster, and author C. Reginald Enock, all men who assisted Hardenburg in publicizing his charges in London back in 1909. Sir Roger Casement re-counted his experiences and findings, as did Consul George B. Michell. Captain Thomas W. Whiffen summarized his conclusions and defended himself from the blackmail charges brought by Arana. David Cazes, the British consul in Iquitos, explained why he failed to denounce the crimes he knew were committed in the Putumayo prior to 1907. Julio César Arana endured three days of interrogation, most of the tough questions coming from Mr. Swift MacNeil. Finally, three prominent English members of the PAC board revealed what they knew and when.[67]

The backgrounds of these three board members illuminated aspects both of the political economy of British investments in Latin America and of Julio César Arana's shrewd business sense. John Russell Gubbins boasted thirty-eight years experience in Peru, working primarily with import and export houses. He knew Spanish, Peruvian society, and President Augusto B. Leguía. PAC board member Herbert M. Read, like Gubbins, knew Spanish and Peruvian society. Read had been born in Peru, educated in England, and then returned to the country of his birth to begin twenty years in business. He became manager of the London Bank of Mexico, director of the powerful Peruvian Corporation, and director of the Lima Light, Power, and Tramways Company. Conversely, Sir John Lister-Kaye knew little of Peru, Spanish, or the rubber business, but he did have excellent connections to the cream of British society. Sir John, in fact, held a court appointment from King Edward VII, son of Queen Victoria. In Gubbins and Read, Arana had two men who spoke with authority on Peru, his company, and the rubber business. In Lister-Kaye, he had the perfect front man to reassure prosperous English investors of the strength and solvency of the PAC.

Although the committee made clear that Arana controlled the majority of PAC stock and exercised "a hypnotic power" over the other board members, the Englishmen did not escape criticism. After all, these directors presumably knew something about the PAC, for they had enjoyed increasing annual salaries from the company during the scandal years. In a telling exchange, John Russell Gubbins accurately stated, "The subjection of Indians by commercial companies is the condition prevailing in the whole of the Amazon Valley." In response, Mr. Charles Roberts moralistically retorted, "That does not make it any better." None of these English gentlemen claimed to know much about the labor situation in the Putumayo, a void the committee termed "negligent ignorance." The Rev. Canon H. Hensley Henson made a similar charge in a sermon in Westminster Abbey in August 1912, a charge answered by a slander suit from Sir Lister-Kaye and company. Reverend Henson spiritedly responded to the slander charge: "Your clients maintain that they were ignorant of the facts. I reply that such ignorance was culpable. My concern is to press on the English mind that the plea of ignorance is not permissible in the case of men whose business it was to know. Do your clients contend that they were entitled to commend to the British public as a sound investment a business the character and methods of which they knew nothing about?"[68]

Apart from the individual responsibility of the English directors, C. Reginald Enock proposed that the committee and the British government develop a plan to protect both indigenes and British investors from a repetition of the Putumayo experience. Enock suggested that absentee capitalism would continue to exploit, and even destroy, native labor under tropical conditions unless Britain adopted a scientific, organized development of these regions both inside and outside the empire. This development plan included conservation of natural resources — including native labor — and the education of Indians. Enock ended his testimony by requesting that the government establish a bureau to censor companies promoting the exploitation of native labor, and to investigate the employment conditions of workers in the tropics.[69]

These hearings offered numerous opportunities for high drama and showmanship. During his testimony to the committee, Casement held up gruesome photographs, presenting them as did other progressive reformers as incontrovertible evidence of mistreatment, starvation, and torture of Indians by the Casa Arana. He also dumped a variety of trade goods on the polished marble table in front of him, demonstrating the junk for which Indians worked and died.[70] That Indians saw these goods as more than trifles seemed to escape Casement and the committee members. But perhaps the denouement of the hearings arrived when Julio César Arana addressed the committee and the charges filed against him, while Hardenburg sat behind him scrutinizing every word.

Arana encountered a hostile setting. The only Peruvian in a sea of Englishmen, he was compared to "black legend" stalwarts Hernando Cortés and Francisco Pizarro. He might have privately welcomed these comparisons, but to many Englishmen, they conjured images of bloodthirsty, ruthless conquerors. The hearings engendered a highly moralistic and ethnocentric atmosphere, one permeated with pro-British and anti-Spanish prejudices. Moreover, as Arana's lawyer, Mr. Douglass Hogg, stated, the extensive publicity and sensationalistic character of the scandal encouraged some committee members to lose their objectivity, to prejudge the facts, and to presume the guilt of his client. In addition, Hogg noted, the committee had admitted hearsay evidence, unlike a court of law, and that neither he nor his client had access to a number of documents held by the committee.[71]

Nonetheless, Arana addressed the charges made against him. He employed a mixed strategy of challenging the evidence, of denying knowledge of some crimes, and of attacking the character and reliability of witnesses testifying against him. For example, he reiterated his charges of bribery against Hardenburg, Saldaña Rocca, and Whiffen. However, he accepted the reports of Casement and Paredes as accurate, if somewhat exaggerated, while proclaiming his ignorance of crimes prior to their two investigations.[72]

On the issue of Indian labor, Arana and his interrogators talked past one another. They disagreed on vocabulary and translation. For example, the word *conquistar* conjured the English "conquer," the bloody military conquest of Indians. Arana defined this verb as winning over Indians to trade, more a cultural or economic, rather than a military, definition. In addition, Arana denied that he imposed slavery on Indians or even that he forced a debt-peonage system upon them. He simply inherited the latter labor form from his Colombian predecessors. Finally, the labor of "orphans" caused confusion. When questioned on the buying and trading of Indian women and children in northwestern Amazonia, Arana stated that these people were "orphans." Committee members could not understand how adult women could be orphans, a reflection of their cultural and linguistic definition of the word. That orphans meant in Amazonia quasi-persons cut off from culture and clan, low-status individuals traded like commodities, Arana failed to make clear, and committee members therefore failed to grasp.[73] The committee concluded that "the callous indifference and guilty knowledge" of Arana and the "negligent ignorance" of the English PAC board members resulted in the crimes of the Putumayo and their scandalous reverberations through the world. However, the committee reached a more far-reaching and disturbing conclusion:

> In the course of the Inquiry your Committee have been impressed with the fact that ill-treatment is not confined to the Putumayo. It appears rather, that the Putumayo case is but a shocking bad instance of conditions of treatment that are liable to be found over a wide area in South

America. . . . It may be hoped that these depths of brutality are un-
paralleled elsewhere. But your Committee regret that they are unable to
regard the ill-treatment of the Indians, of which the Putumayo case is an
abominable instance, as an isolated phenomenon.[74]

A summary of this parliamentary investigation found some very troubling
patterns. The Putumayo was not an isolated notorious region of murder, slavery, and terror, but more representative of conditions found elsewhere in Amazonia, South America, and tropical zones around the world. It found the
British board members of the PAC negligent, and found that absentee capitalism built upon legacies of colonial exploitation, be they British or Spanish, to
willingly exploit, and at times destroy, native labor around the globe.

It was not these findings or British diplomatic pressure which hurt Julio
César Arana, however, but a business decline that deepened after 1914. Falling rubber prices, caused by the introduction of huge quantities of Asian
plantation rubber, undercut Arana's profits. Nonetheless, Arana still owned
and extracted rubber from the Putumayo and transported it on his boats to
Iquitos. Although British foreign minster Sir Edward Grey lobbied Brazil to
help his government shut down Peruvian rubber exports in 1913, the plan
failed because of U.S. and Brazilian resistance to its implementation. The First
World War sustained great demand for rubber, so Arana kept his Peruvian
Amazon Company in operation until 1920.[75]

Violence and diplomatic difficulties persisted in northwestern Amazonia.
Caucheros of all nationalities still hunted, captured, traded, and transported
thousands of Indians. Although the Putumayo was now relatively quiet, less
disturbed regions such as the Napo, the Ucayali, and areas south of Pebas experienced the man hunts and violence made infamous by the Putumayo scandal. In 1913, a Peruvian army unit explored the Morona near its juncture with
the Cagimina, an area claimed by Ecuador, and was attacked and annihilated
by Jívaro Indians. Both the Ecuadorian and Peruvian governments registered
protests in wake of this battle, each claiming the Morona River as part of their
national domain.[76] Not much had changed in northwestern Amazonia. The
social, cultural, economic, and political underpinnings of violence remained
intact as the horrors of the Putumayo faded into those of the Great War.

NINE

THE FIRST WORLD WAR AND
THE BUST OF 1914-1918

The August 19, 1914, edition of *El Oriente* heaped kudos on Prefect Benjamín J. Puente. The good colonel had been busy that year dealing with revolts and crises in Iquitos brought on by the decline of imports and exports and the resulting economic displacement, inflation, and political turmoil. Nonetheless, outside the department capital, Puente followed the pattern of his predecessors by moving aggressively to conquer and administrate disputed or troublesome districts within his jurisdiction, including sending one hundred men on a punitive raid up the Morona to avenge the killing of Peruvians by Jívaro Indians. He also oversaw the completion of a wireless telegraph system in the Putumayo and a trail linking the Putumayo with the Napo, the latter region being of increasing interest to Julio César Arana. He had established military colonies, attended to foreign claims along the Napo, and studied yet another road project into the rebellious Chazuta region. In a way, Puente's achievements harkened back to the glory days of former prefect Samuel Palacios and of Peruvian expansion in the midst of the rubber boom. But by 1914, the rubber boom was over. From August to December, the remote war in Europe dominated the front page of *El Oriente,* now a skimpy two-page sheet largely devoid of advertisements.[1]

The Great War affected Iquitos immediately. Between August and December 1914, only one ship arrived in port, whereas six months earlier, transatlantic vessels had lined up for loading and unloading. Five hundred tons of caucho sat on docks in Iquitos, and another 120 tons awaited transportation in the Putumayo. Trade ceased abruptly with The Hague and

Hamburg, slowed with Britain, but began to increase with the United States. Basic commodities such as rice, sugar, butter, milk, and cooking oil became scarce, their prices skyrocketing and forcing consumers to hoard what they could find.[2] Self-sufficient residents shifted back to locally available foods — fish, game, yuca, fruits, nuts — but for middle- and upper-class residents, the wartime trade interruption meant scrounging for essential goods.

The other near fatal shock to the regional economy came via international market competition from Asian plantation rubber. British, French, and Dutch plantations in south and southeast Asia had managed in just a few years to revolutionize production and consumption patterns for premium rubber. Back in 1907, when Hardenburg began his fateful descent of the Putumayo, Asian plantations provided less than 2 percent of the world's rubber supply, but by 1914, it dominated the market with more than 60 percent. The seventy-three thousand tons shipped from Asia in 1914 — and triple that by 1917 — addressed the staggering industrial, military, and consumer demand for rubber, a demand that the limited wild rubber supply of Amazonia simply could not satisfy (see table 10). By 1910, the primary consumers of rubber, automobile tire and tube manufacturers, had already signaled a shift by agreeing to buy and process Asian plantation rubber, hitherto thought to be of inferior quality. In fact, the Asian rubber was of higher quality, and its lower cost and greater availability made it most attractive. Arana family member and Iquitos chamber of commerce president Pablo Zumaeta noted the ominous trend in 1915; output of Asian plantation rubber had more than doubled wild rubber production, and by July it was selling at a higher price because of its superior quality.[3]

The good news, though, for rubber exporters such as Arana was that the rubber market was so extensive that various niches opened up for consumption of wild rubber. For Arana and the Putumayo, the cheap but plentiful amalgam of latexes found in Putumayo tails continued to find markets throughout the war years (see table 9). Moreover, tough and durable *gutta percha* and *balata* latex were being used as insulation for submarine cable and telegraph and telephone lines, and for valve covers, airplane parts, and golf balls. Even though prices for these lower-quality niche latexes fluctuated during the war, local exporters found a way around the dominance of Asian plantation production of fine rubber.[4]

Other economic opportunities opened up as the boom slid toward bust. With less competition from imports, local producers of cotton, corn, coffee, peanuts, rice, yuca, spirits, butter, and meat found a hungry market in Iquitos and in adjoining towns. Many settlements lost residents who left to colonize and work lands along the main rivers, leading in some cases to a labor shortage and a better bargaining position for some workers. For example, one peon in Sarayaco accepted a rather sizeable advance from one patrón but was wooed away by another offer, leaving the first employer with a debt, no worker, and no support from the prefect in Iquitos.[5]

Inventories of the belongings of two dead men reveal the impact on material culture of the rubber boom, one ending with these two men's lives. Forty-eight-year-old Ramón E. Palacios died of malaria at El Encanto in late 1913, leaving behind a record of bourgeois style made possible by imports. Along with his Gillette razor, two pairs of eye glasses, and two silver watches, he had two pairs of suspenders, seven neckties, seven handkerchiefs, and seven pairs of socks. His fashion accessories — two sport coats, four pairs of trousers, and six dress shirts — ensured a fresh look each day of the week. His recipe book and a women's portrait suggest he had company, and the account book and cash left behind hint at a mercantile interest.

Before Sgt. Maj. Pedro J. Barreto shot a Winchester rifle bullet through his thorax, he, too, had acquired an impressive quantity of property. He owned a store, one well stocked with imported tins of sugar, chocolates, meats, fish, soup, and butter. He sold buttons, cloth, shirts, handkerchiefs, kerosene, castor oil, iodine, combs, matches, candles, liquor, and ammunition. Apparently, some of his customers bartered ivory nuts — totaling 672 kilos — in exchange for store goods. Barretto entertained friends and associates in a room graced by a sofa and six chairs from Vienna, and even his kitchen was adequate for a few guests.[6] Both Palacios and Barreto died badly but apparently lived well, albeit in debt, at the denouement of boom time.

Surviving Iquitos residents, meanwhile, faced taxes, fees, and high utility rates. In early 1914, a number of working-class petitioners, about half of them female, demanded that electricity rates be halved. The next month, the city's big merchants — Cecilio Hernández and Sons, Wesche and Company, Levy and Shuler, Israel and Company, the Iquitos Trading Company, and others — petitioned for the annulment of municipal taxes in Loreto, Ucayali, and Alto Amazonas, claiming that these flat taxes were unfair and too high given the war crisis. The following year, however, the city's small businesses, such as the Bar London and Café Roma, many owned by Chinese-Peruvians (San Lee owned one of two game rooms, Cang Juy an opium den, and Lee Nau Lao a restaurant) still paid monthly business fees.[7]

Along with the decline in imports and exports, currency shortages during the war worsened the business climate. Gold and bank checks issued in Lima disappeared almost overnight, spent on goods downriver or in foreign countries. To address this problem, the Commercial Bank of South America printed twelve thousand pounds worth of cheques good only in Loreto. By mid-1916, the prefect of Loreto suggested that a like sum be secured with gold and issued in Iquitos, with payment due at the end of the war.[8]

Shipping difficulties plagued the port as well. Just one month after the war began, prices for scarce European goods increased by one-third. Loreto's prefect suggested that Peru establish a maritime link between Lima and Iquitos via the Panama Canal, one carrying basic food stuffs to Iquitos, and rubber back to Callao. This plan collected dust for almost a decade. In the interim, E. Strassberger and Company planned to run a steamship up to Iquitos from Manaus. This competition irritated both the Booth Company, which had monopolized the carrying trade for decades, and the British government, which ordered Booth to blacklist Strassberger. Booth seemingly fended off this challenge, but its executives still complained about local taxes, higher insurance rates, and the decreased demand for imports such as coal. (Because of the high price and limited supply of coal, the electric company in Iquitos started burning wood.)[9]

As the war neared its end, conditions in Loreto worsened. After the entry of the United States into the war in mid-1917, even American goods, the last major lifeline for importers in the department, became scarce. With the rubber market almost dead, but with New York now setting rubber prices, companies and entrepreneurs scrambled for alternative moneymakers. Israel and Company remarked hopefully on the future of cotton cultivated in Loreto. Pedro Sosa had a tastier dream. He imported a steam-powered machine to make chocolates. Sosa envisioned meeting local demand and exporting the surplus abroad. All he needed was the cacao, which he hoped the Peruvian government would allow him to import duty free from Brazil.[10]

War's end also brought together physically — if not emotionally — two formerly hostile protagonists of the Putumayo scandal, investigator Rómulo Paredes and Casa Arana agent Pablo Zumaeta. By early 1918, Paredes was presiding over the board responsible for setting property taxes and professional fees for the next five-year period. This process brought with it the usual lobbying, complaining, and uproar. Zumaeta, head of the Iquitos Chamber of Commerce, rubbed shoulders with Paredes, while he urged the government in Lima to peg rubber export duty rates to international rubber prices. With prices low and dropping, and with duties fixed, Zumaeta warned Lima that the industry was dying.[11]

Paredes and Zumaeta also shared legal legacies from the scandal. Both surfaced in criminal complaints that were reopened in 1917 and 1918 by Attorney General Cavero. In one, Zumaeta, in May 1910, accused a Colombian of killing an Indian muchacho at El Encanto. Paredes subsequently questioned the notorious section boss Miguel Loayza about the crime, but Loayza contradicted much of his boss's denunciation. A justice of the peace in La Chorrera received the case in December 1915 but neglected it for nineteen months and was fined one pound. By 1920, Cavero closed the case because there were no witnesses, the victim's name was unknown, and there was no body.[12]

Attorney General Cavero closed two other cases pursued by Paredes back in 1911. One charged that various members of an army unit had whipped fifteen Huitoto Indians at Entre Ríos because they would not work. Paredes collected some testimony, but Cavero closed the case in 1917, lacking witnesses and facts about the victims.[13] The second case reflected the legal and logistical problems common to many investigations, but also the lesson that violence rather than justice often decided cases in northwest Amazonia. In 1911, Paredes collected testimony and eyewitnesses to the killing of Riveina, a Pirmesa Indian leader, by Peruvian Amazon Company (PAC) employee Enrique Zavala y Zavala. Zavala subsequently left the Putumayo for the Piedras River district, where he and a rival rubber trader, Carlos Scharff, were killed by Piros Indians. Cavero closed the case in September 1918.[14]

Familiar and notorious scenes of violence and abuse erupted through the war years as the culture and economics of exploiting opportunities remained unchallenged. In August 1914, *El Oriente* reported that labor-hungry patróns were kidnapping children off the streets of Iquitos and sending them to work elsewhere. Violence around the Putumayo took on characteristics of the notorious zone during the boom. In the Alto Purús, a new rubber-collection hot spot south of the Putumayo, the local commissar used his post and weapons to intimidate rival patrons and to steal their peons. North of the Putumayo in Vaupés, scandalous charges of rape, murder, enslavement, kidnapping, torture, and whipping of Indians were brought to the attention of Colombia's minister of foreign relations. In contrast to past crimes in the Putumayo, most of which the Colombian government could blame on the Peruvians, the legal and political problems this time were being raised by the actions of Colombians.[15]

The abuses of extractive economies and colonialism logically led to violent resistance from indigenous inhabitants. By mid-1915, Indians counterattacked caucheros in the Alto Ucayali near the Alto Purús. The local subprefect reported that the Indians had put the caucheros to flight for the following reasons: (1) race hatred; (2) cauchero attacks against Indian villages; (3) trafficking in women and children; (4) whites giving guns to Indians in exchange for children; and (5) economic recession and fewer goods for Indians, who saw the scarcity as bad faith by the caucheros.[16] The first three reasons amounted to self-defense, but the last two illustrate both the allure and danger of white trade. Trading children for guns did reveal the ongoing hierarchies and exploitation within indigenous societies themselves, but these divisions and injustices were made worse by trade. The final reason, scarcity of goods, suggests that some Indians had developed deep material and psychological dependencies on international trade and rubber collection, as had their distant neighbors in the plaza of Iquitos.[17]

Just how many Indians survived in the Putumayo and Caquetá following the boom? Census data, although often based on rough guesses, suggest that the scandal estimate of 30,000 dead in the first decade of the twentieth century overstates the case. Although it makes sense that the nadir of indigenous demography came at the end of the boom, census estimates in 1912, 1916, and 1918 reported the presence of tens of thousands of Indians. In 1912, the Putumayo district held an estimated 31,380 inhabitants, of whom 30,000 — the notorious figure of the scandal — were wild Indians (salvajes). In the Caquetá, a similar picture emerged: 22,500 salvajes in a total population of 24,543.[18] A 1916 census estimate reported a doubling of the white population in the Caquetá after four years, and it and another local census in 1918 dropped the estimated number of salvajes to 10,000.[19]

The 1918 national census provided data from more communities in both areas and substantially increased the estimated numbers of tribal Indians. An estimated 33,600 tribal Indians in the Putumayo reflected a 2 percent increase annually since 1912, but the census taker noted that their numbers might have actually decreased. The Caquetá yielded better data. The total number of tribal Indians in the comisaría of Caquetá in 1918 was 68,900, more than triple the 22,500 estimate for 1912. Jorge Villamil, who directed the census in both Huila and the Caquetá, knew the district firsthand and suggested that the 1912 estimate's low count stemmed from the fact that Indians then lived deep in inaccessible forests. Local officials also noted that Indians in both 1912 and 1918 fled approaching white men. Nonetheless, the estimates, rounded to thousands, are striking: 5,000 Carijona along the Caguán and Alto Yari Rivers; 28,000 Huitotos along the Caquetá and Igaraparaná; 2,000 Boras in the Lower Caquetá; and a startling 20,000 Andokes in the Middle Caquetá. Estimates for other tribal peoples — Coreguayes, Cabiyares, Yaúnas, Yucunas, Desanas — pushed the total to 68,900.[20] Some of the population increase in the Caquetá probably resulted from Indians migrating away from the Putumayo, but we must view these figures critically. The point, though, is that the rubber boom and its many crimes and atrocities did not obliterate indigenous culture nor the lives of tens of thousands of people still living in the Putumayo and Caquetá.

The multitude of Indians, national honor, the perceived economic future of northwest Amazonia, and the desire to colonize the tropical lowlands pushed Peru, Ecuador, and Colombia into pursuing their ongoing administrative and political initiatives in the region. Peru still held the advantage with its military, political, and economic operations headquartered in Iquitos. As usual, Ecuador and Colombia had to play catch-up after being left behind by their sister republic to the south during the rubber boom.

Ecuador's approach in the Oriente revealed unsuccessful programs inherited from the past. In 1916, Congress approved a plan introduced the previous year to allow electors in the Oriente to select two senators and one deputy. This initiative noted that residents of the province had the constitutional right to representation and that the lack thereof had led to the neglect of a region important to the nation.[21] During their first year in office, the Oriente's new representatives received a petition from colonists in the Napo and Curaray. They requested, and Congress approved in 1917, a plan to grant scholarships for twenty male and female students to attend school in Quito. The colonists noted that their region had few white inhabitants and that the closest school, in Tena, was hundreds of miles away. Their polite request and their anthem, that "we only live for the hope of tomorrow," garnered favor from both Congress and the ministry of public instruction.[22]

Although the twenty scholarships achieved something tangible for the students of the Napo and Curaray, they amounted to little compared to Ecuador's bigger problems in the Oriente. Political difficulties, partisan divisions and violence, and the fact that many Ecuadorians in government thought of the region as remote and foreign terrain blocked most plans to incorporate the province into the national domain. For example, in 1915, Congress rejected a plan to raise seventy-five thousand sucres for a colonization project and another fifty thousand for road construction and maintenance. Critics of inactivity warned that the nation would never blunt Peruvian aggression in the Oriente given the factiousness of partisan politics. By 1917, these critics pushed Congress to reopen colonization projects and administrative reorganization in the Oriente, but here, too, reality and penury imposed limits. For example, one plan proposed creating new cantons along the length of the province whose eastern limits would reach to the Marañon and Amazon Rivers, territory already dominated by Peru from Iquitos. Moreover, Congress postponed a railroad project to the Curaray region, scaling back the cost and scope of this risky investment by replacing it with a cheaper road and path project down the mountain to Puyo.[23] These infrastructure and colonization schemes highlighted Ecuador's problems in realizing its longtime national dream of playing an active role in northwestern Amazonia: lack of consensus, direction, resources, and will.

Colombia pursued a similar approach of road building and colonization in the Putumayo and Caquetá, albeit one better coordinated and funded than Ecuador's. But Colombia also had to contend with other national and regional problems once the war began. For one, Colombia depended on European shipping, German and British primarily, to carry its exports as well as letters of credit from London to complete international transactions. After August 1914, Colombian exports piled up on the docks as Europe imploded. Interestingly, the Colombian legation in Washington, D.C., took this opportunity to repair Colombian-U.S. relations, damaged primarily by the 1903 Panama imbroglio, by promoting better banking and shipping links between the two American republics. The Colombian delegation suggested to U.S. secretary of state Robert Lansing that United Fruit, now the major carrier of exports, augment its service to Colombian ports. Along with trade issues, a decade-long border dispute between the departments of Cauca and Nariño needed attention, as did the emergence of an indigenous organization in Cauca. Manuel Quintín Lamé, whose name a guerrilla group revived in the 1980s, used direct action to thwart land grabs by colonists and miners. Predictably, local authorities harassed and jailed Lamé for his attempts to protect indigenous property and culture.[24]

In the Putumayo and Caquetá, incursions into indigenous lands received enthusiastic support from both secular and religious authorities. Colombian expansion into the southeastern lowlands would depend on completing and maintaining the road from Pasto, in the Andean highlands, over the mountains to Mocoa, and then south to Rafael Reyes's former trading center at La Sofía, now called Puerto Asís. Along with the road came a colonization project, which its supporters promised would cement Colombian sovereignty as it reduced Indians to civilization. Migrants from the department of Antioquia, with its capital Medellín serving as the industrial and entrepreneurial heartland of the country, received credit for spearheading settlement in and around Mocoa and Sibundoy. However, the slowdown in exports by 1915 cut the budget for colonizing the Putumayo by ten thousand pesos, raising the patriotic ire of Colombians intent on conquering the emerald-green lowlands.[25]

Even with depleted federal funds, Colombians explored, claimed, and farmed lands in the Upper Putumayo and Caquetá throughout 1915 and 1916. Both colonists and the ministry of agriculture and commerce in Bogotá focused their colonization efforts on federal lands, efforts that led to violence and conflict. For example, at San Vicente in the Caquetá, soldiers took over the town and seized some property as a prelude to land occupations. In the Middle Putumayo, Peruvians still dominated, but a few Colombians started downriver anyway. And some North American businessmen came upriver looking for agricultural lands and mines, supposedly given the right to navigate up the Putumayo by the Peruvian government. Indeed, with so much land — for cattle, tobacco, cacao, bananas — the struggle to occupy and retain land entered a more intense phase.[26]

Peruvian presence and attacks from downriver continued in 1917 and 1918. In 1917, the special commissar for the Putumayo, José Diago, noted that Peruvians controlled all of the Putumayo from the Brazilian border up to Güeppi, two days below Puerto Asís by steamboat. The Peruvians were still trading for rubber and abusing Indians, but they were also allowing Colombians to trade in Iquitos and to smuggle goods up toward Puerto Asís. Acting practically, the minister of government ordered no action taken against the smugglers because colonists in the area needed the goods they carried.[27] However, regarding the Indians who lived in a deplorable state under the Peruvians, Diago revealed elements of a colonial consciousness by suggesting that the Colombian government do the following for Indians: "gather them, shelter them, and help them in order to guarantee their existence and their liberty." He did, however, mention that Indians fled from whites and "have formed an unfavorable concept of civilization," an attitude Diago could not readily understand.[28]

Diago's colleague in the Caquetá, Antonio Pastrana, recorded evidence of a Peruvian attack in the Caquetá in September 1918. He reported that four Peruvians and fifty well-armed Indian allies raided Las Delicias, killed three Indians, took four prisoners, and stole rubber and supplies. Reports indicated that the invaders worked for the Casa Arana and that they hoped to take over the entire right bank of the Caquetá.[29] Apparently, Arana and company retook the offensive just as the war in Europe was ending and trade opportunities were expanding.

While various secular programs were attempting to claim the Putumayo and Caquetá, missionary activity increased in both regions following the scandal. Franciscan missionaries arrived in the Putumayo in February 1913, the beneficiaries of a fifteen thousand pound sterling fund raised the previous year by Sir Roger Casement, Sir Arthur Conan Doyle, and Lord Rothschild. Mission planners assumed that Indians needed and wanted Western civilization and that through Christianity, not rapacious capitalism, the lessons from the West were best taught. The Franciscans reported upon arrival that the brutality of the past had ceased and that Indians lived and ate well. However, three years later, old patterns resurfaced. By September 1916, Indians had rebelled and killed thirteen white employees, retaliating against whippings and other abuses. The future looked so bleak for many women that they reportedly used "vegetable contraceptives to avoid bringing children into a hungry and bitter world." By August 1917, the Franciscans were claiming that they had no further mission in the Putumayo, and they left in November 1918.[30]

Capuchin missionaries proved much more persistent. In 1895, the bishop of Pasto invited the Catalonian-based order to the Putumayo and Caquetá. Four years later, one of the early arrivals, twenty-three-year-old Estanislao de les Corts, tackled the monumental task of planning and building a road from Pasto down to Mocoa. From 1900 to 1906, the order was sporadically represented in the Caraparaná, the heartland of Casa Arana operations. By 1905, the order had created an apostolic prefecture in the Putumayo and Caquetá, separating them from diocesan jurisdiction in Pasto. In 1912, the Colombian government established new special commissariats for both regions, ones working closely with Capuchin missionary goals.[31]

Both secular and missionary officials sought to fundamentally alter the Indian majority in their midst. Secular mandates ordered that Indians be reduced, civilized, and acculturated to Colombian norms and laws. The disciplined and focused head of the Capuchin mission, Fidel de Montclar, born Christmas Day 1867, cleverly played on Colombian nationalism. He championed the foreign-born missionaries as Colombian patriots, true Christians, and resolute conquerors of the last-known land on Earth. He likened the Capuchins to sappers, missionary servants who could bring light to the eternally savage while improving business opportunities, and perhaps even turning the Peruvian flank by pushing down the Putumayo and then taking the Napo.[32] Montclar's political and cultural rhetoric, combined with his persistent lobbying of state and church officials, made the Capuchins seem critical to the pursuit of progress, sovereignty, and justice.

Montclar and his Catalonian associates—Estanislao de les Corts, Benigno de Canet de Mar, and Gaspar de Pinell de Solsonès—had few, if any, qualms about bringing the superior news to the inferior Indians. They did, however, argue that the Capuchins must oversee this process and not allow greedy secular whites to abuse defenseless Indians. The missionaries jealously protected "their" childlike mission Indians from secular and private challengers, focusing immediate attention on the young. By 1912, their twenty-five schools in the Putumayo were attended by some 1,113 male and female students. In these boarding schools, students learned religion, prayers, Spanish, reading, and writing, with breaks for play and sports. The allure of white goods and the relative ease of children in learning white ways slowly undercut the cultural appeal and traditional authority of Indian caciques and shamans.[33]

While the lay and religious instructors focused their energies on shaping the minds and futures of youth, Montclar tackled equally important tasks. He

promoted steamship service on the Putumayo — used forty years earlier by
Rafael Reyes but subsequently monopolized by the Casa Arana and Peru — to
facilitate Colombian control and exploitation of the river and its surrounding
resources. He asked a British company to deliver a launch to the Pacific port,
Tumaco, where it would be hauled in pieces over the mountains and then
down to Puerto Asís. The launch did not materialize, and the Capuchins
continued to depend on canoes for riverine transportation. However, the Capuchin campaign for improved technology continued unabated. In 1918, Father Gaspar de Pinell went to Manaus hoping to purchase a steamboat in that
busy Brazilian port. Brazilian law, however, disallowed the sale and exportation of any launch during the war, driving Pinell to rent a forty-five-ton steamboat. He purchased trade goods and planned to exchange them for the agricultural products that Montclar was collecting in Puerto Asís. The plan, which
would have reaped a healthy profit for the order, ran into a major complica-
tion at Casa Arana headquarters in El Encanto. Peruvian naval authorities
searched the cargo, questioned the crew, and held the launch five days before
orderings its return to Manaus. The local commander stated that he had
orders to halt any craft that had not first called at Iquitos.[34] Clearly, neither the
Casa Arana nor Peruvian naval authorities were ready to allow Colombians or
Capuchins free and profitable navigation on the Putumayo.

Montclar and his associates achieved greater success in another transportation service in the Putumayo. The Capuchins argued that a road from Pasto
down to Mocoa and then south to Puerto Asís would serve as a vital conduit
for Colombian sovereignty, enterprise, and colonization. Building and maintaining the road proved to be a formidable undertaking. Father Estanislao and
twelve peons commenced work in 1899, but after just one week, he reported
that he was physically broken by the mountains and the pockets of solid rock.
The mountains of Pasto rise steeply before tumbling down to the valley of
Sibundoy. From Sibundoy, thickly forested ridges punctuated by hundreds of
streams and cascades dominate the route all the way to Mocoa, a distance of
about ninety miles. Over the next fourteen years, the Capuchins and thousands of Indian workers labored on the road amidst complaints from sub-
contractors and secular officials about slow and inefficient results.[35]

The Pasto-to-Mocoa link was completed in 1913. The Capuchins then battled both natural and political obstacles during the next five-year stage of the
project: the sixty miles over hills and swamps from Mocoa to Puerto Asís. A
victim of rival contractors and critical government officials, the order lost the
contract for this section in 1913. Montclar journeyed to Bogotá the following
year to lobby both the archbishop and the president of Colombia, Dr. José
Vicente Concha. Montclar claimed that the new contractor had accomplished

little over the previous eighteen months, lacking both expertise and sufficient workers even to maintain the existing road. Indeed, in the mountainous and wet region, washouts and landslides cut much of the road periodically. He argued that the Capuchins could finish the job with a 150,000 gold peso budget and the labor of a thousand peons.[36]

The new contractors, many of them military officers, encountered their own logistical, legal, and political difficulties. Allegations of malfeasance, incompetence, and breach of contract hounded them over the next three years. The Great War also held them up when their primary equipment supplier in New York could not fill its contracts. A Collins and Company advisory from 1917 noted that U.S. arms manufacturers were offering two to three times the customary wages for skilled workers, leaving Collins without the labor force to manufacture the machetes, picks, and shovels ordered for the Putumayo road project. In addition, the Capuchins — primarily Montclar, les Corts, and de Pinell — were acting as a fifth column, agreeing to subcontract for sections of the road, while harping about the chelonian pace of the project. By 1918, Capuchin complaints were paying dividends. A visiting treasury inspector suggested that the order retake primary responsibility for the road. He argued that Indians worked better for the missionaries and that the order could supply the food and supplies needed by the peons from their properties adjoining the road.[37]

By 1915, Montclar had assumed a pivotal political and administrative role in the Putumayo. He frequently found himself in the midst of land disputes involving the Capuchins, Indian villagers, colonists, and regional and national speculators. Moreover, the Colombian government had named Montclar "arbiter of 'public morality', and superintendent of police and of education."[38] In essence, Montclar and the Capuchins had the right to define proper behavior and could physically punish offenders with whips and stocks. The order also drew from Indians not one but two days of free labor per week — Monday for the church, Tuesday for the Blessed Virgin. This increased labor draft raised a storm of protest from competitors for Indian labor and from Liberal opponents to traditional church-state partnerships.[39]

Roads, schools, missions, trade, steamships — all supported the final component for transforming the Putumayo: colonization. Montclar and his order spearheaded efforts to westernize the region's society by drawing colonists ideally from Spain, possibly from Antioquia, and, if necessary, from Nariño. Montclar jabbed open the indigenous Sibundoy Valley to whites in 1911 by supporting the passage of law 51, which declared most of the lands in the valley vacant public lands, regardless of the presence and land titles of thousands of Indians.[40] Montclar actively supported colonization in and around

Mocoa and Puerto Asís as well. By 1914, both these towns had white majorities, and most of the region was opened to colonization, with the order securing various chunks for its operations.[41]

But the pride—and eventual nightmare-of the Capuchin dream to transform the Putumayo centered on Alvernia and its colonists from Antioquia. Two caravans of pilgrims founded the town; the second, made up of 147 colonists, arrived in 1917. Their journey led them up the Cauca Valley, then over the mountains to their new settlement north of Mocoa, a sojourn lasting forty-five days, one slowed by rain, floods, and smallpox. Montclar preferred these industrious, hardy souls over the more accessible, but reputedly slow-witted, Pastusos, but the colonists of Alvernia proved an aggressive and independent lot. Several members charged that the Capuchins withheld promised monies and supplies. By 1918, after several embarrassing allegations, the order decided to leave Alvernia.[42]

Power and money allegedly misused by the order provided the focal point for troubles at Alvernia and elsewhere. In both 1913 and 1914, Congress granted the missions some 100,000 gold pesos. By 1915, responding to the charges, Congress discussed cutting the annual mission subsidy to 30,000 pesos. The bishop of Pasto urged that lawmakers instead transfer some 20,000 pesos from the previous year's budget, citing the magnificent work of the Capuchins in the Putumayo. In 1917, as the discord grew in Alvernia, the order was still receiving five times the funds granted to the civil administration in the region, but, nonetheless, Capuchin supporters such as Nariño governor Francisco Albán, complained about the cuts made in Bogotá.[43] Funding for colonization peaked during the Putumayo scandal, then dwindled slowly as Congress dealt with war-related fiscal problems and heard charges leveled against Montclar and the Capuchins.

The declining subsidy and the end of the rubber boom had reshaped daily life by the end of the war. Although rubber and other forest products stood ready for collection, the lack of a market pushed the economic focus toward ranching and farming. Pasture for cattle, pigs, horses, and mules opened large swaths of forest to the searing sun, while farmers hoped that cotton, cacao, tobacco, and sugar would provide a growing, if not booming, economic future. Discouraged rubber traders came upriver to the new towns at Puerto Asís and Florencia, joined by other poor migrants moving down from Huila. Regional governments, both secular and religious, made money distilling and selling liquor. Land battles in the Sibundoy Valley remained intense. Indians sought protection from Capuchin and colonist invasions, claiming communal ownership of the entire valley, which they had purchased centuries earlier from the king of Spain himself.[44]

While the Indians of the Sibundoy Valley confronted colonists from the west, other Indians ascended the Putumayo and Caquetá from the east. These people migrated for various reasons. Some fled violence and labor demands from Peruvian caucheros still operating along the middle reaches of both rivers. Others, paradoxically, moved upriver because the bust of rubber left them without the goods they now desired and needed. Some apparently wanted to be rich, for which they needed goods and markets. Other clans of Huitoto, Bora, Carijona, and Piranga had been contacted by Capuchins and Colombian state officials, who offered goods, homes, and a settled future if they congregated in new villages upriver. For Montclar, the migration would save Indians from Peruvian excesses, while promising more labor and souls for the future. He insisted that the Capuchins could direct this "incipient society" away from savagery and toward civilization if Indians would extinguish their instinct, exchange superstition for faith, work and live in settlements, wear trousers and shirts, and speak Spanish. Both missionaries and state officials embraced the legally mandated "civilized conquest" of Indians during the war, be they upland residents of the Sibundoy Valley or former rain-forest dwellers of the Igaraparaná.[45]

While the Capuchins defined and directed civilization in the Putumayo, a final fascinating and bizarre episode connected the region to international intrigue and scandal: the political and sexual activities of Sir Roger Casement, and his execution for treason by the British government in 1916. Casement's politics, as well as his self, were often veiled, divided, and confused. He was an Ulster Protestant secretly baptized Catholic as an infant, and an Irish nationalist who frequently uttered anglophilic statements while serving in the British foreign office. Casement embodied the person living between worlds, one with complex motivations and identities.[46]

According to his diaries, Casement veiled his sexual orientation, not unusual given the formal restrictions on sexuality and the illegality of homosexuality within the guarded Victorian and Edwardian societies. Apparently, Casement focused most of his energies on his professional and political campaigns and then, given the opportunity, binged or fantasized to sate his personal sexual needs. The published, although highly controversial, diaries of Casement of 1910 reveal a careful, dedicated investigator, one both shocked and attracted by male sexuality in the Putumayo.[47] He observed several nude boys and young men masturbating and involved in sex play, fondling, and mock mounting, and the openness of such behavior gained Casement's attention and condemnation. Indeed, Casement had stumbled into another sexual world in northwest Amazonia, one of exposed bodies and physical intimacy, one where sexual activity was acceptable and even encouraged. Heterosexual unions usually occurred in the forest outside the village during daylight hours. Male homosexual activity, at least that witnessed by Casement, was even more public, often taking place during bathing. A recent anthropological study of Indians in the Vaupés suggests that men aged fifteen to forty accept fondling and group masturbation as a means of building social bonds, trust, and group acceptance. Arthur P. Sorenson, Jr., the author of the study, further suggests that open homosexual activity among men channels libidinous energy away from unavailable women, thereby limiting violence and enhancing group cohesion.[48]

According to the diaries, Casement checked most of his sexual activity while in the Putumayo, opening more to it in Iquitos and Pará, where he was under less scrutiny. His political passion for Irish independence flowered, ironically, after he was knighted by the Crown for his service in the Putumayo. In 1913, Sir Roger resigned from the consular service and immediately joined the cause for a free and united Ireland. The following year, he traveled to the United States to raise money for the cause, and then in August, when war broke out in Europe, he led a self-appointed mission to Germany to gain support for Irish independence. Although he was able to get an audience with under-secretary of state Count Arthur Von Zimmermann (soon famous for the Zimmermann telegram of 1917), he spent many agonizing months of disappointment and privation trying to rally German support for Irish volunteers to take on the English. By Easter 1916, Casement found himself deposited in a dingy off a deserted Irish beach by the U-boat captain who had sunk the *Lusitania*. Casement never managed to make contact with supporters of the rebellion in Ireland. The local constable arrested him, and he was soon shuttled off to London to stand trial for treason.[49]

Ironically, Casement returned to Ireland to halt the Easter Rebellion against the English, convinced that it was doomed to fail. Also bizarre was a telegram sent to the prisoner by Julio César Arana in June 1916. Arana urged Casement to confess his wrongdoing during the Putumayo scandal, a directive Casement ignored. Following his arrest, the prosecution exploited — some say manufactured — Casement's diaries, including his intimate observations and sexual activities while in the Putumayo in 1910. The prosecution strove to kill public sympathy, especially in the Irish American community in the United States, for their famous and noble prisoner and to deny the cause another martyr. Once Casement had been condemned, the Colombian government reconnected him to the Putumayo investigation and urged that his life be spared, but the English hung him anyway on August 3, 1916.[50]

Casement's life ended as it was lived, full of scandal, division, passion, and intrigue. For a man made internationally famous for his investigations in the

Congo and the Putumayo, his embrace of Irish freedom and of Britain's enemy Germany led him knowingly and tragically to infamous notoriety and to the hangman's noose. Casement's death, like the Putumayo scandal he nurtured, was, and still is, read alternately as the injustice of a brutal system or as the deserved end of an immoral animal. In this case, the colonial stage had made Casement the abused Indian, and the British government the sadistic master.

TEN

FROM A EUROPEAN TO AN AMAZONIAN WAR, 1918–1933

Northwest Amazonia's relationship with national and international systems underwent yet another major transformation between 1918 and 1930. War's end delivered a severe economic depression, one felt and fought by the restive working class of Iquitos. Slowly, French and German trade with northwestern Amazonia recovered; the British maintained their preeminent commercial position until 1925, then ceded that place to the Americans. Julio César Arana fought challenges to his economic and political domination by entering Peruvian national politics and by backing two major revolts against the Lima government. Ecuador continued a period of stasis, plagued by unsteady finances and its ingrained neglect of the Oriente. Colombia pursued earlier patterns built on roads, colonization, and Capuchin missionization in the Putumayo and Caquetá. In short, political and administrative trends persisted through the 1920s, while the economic downturn of rubber reoriented production toward farming, ranching, and timber cutting.[1]

Peru maintained its formula of military garrisons, naval power, and partnership with private companies to defend its Amazonian borders from challengers. Peruvian army units from the Thirteenth Infantry Regiment guarded frontier posts along the Ecuadorian border, on the Lower Putumayo at Tarapacá, and at Leticia and Nazareth, west of the Brazilian border. By mid-1918, acting prefect of Loreto W. Pinillos Rossell suggested that the small garrisons along the Ecuadorian and Colombian borders be reinforced to counter Capuchin and Colombian programs of colonization and road building. The Peruvians still had access to six now old and worn steam-powered warships, but they increasingly relied on private launches to transport government officials and supplies.[2]

The bust of rubber, war-time scarcity, and the resulting depression in the import and export trade sent waves of misery throughout the market economy of northwest Amazonia. In 1910, Iquitos handled 15.82 percent of Peru's total exports and 17.65 percent of her imports. By 1920, those numbers had shrunk to 1.08 percent for exports and 1.57 percent for imports.[3] Added to this commercial depression were lower prices for exports and higher ones for imports. In 1918, Loreto's government abolished import duties on flour, sugar, and rice, only to reinstate them the following year because of lost revenue. To avoid the obligatory customs stop in Iquitos, some enterprising planters tried to export sugar from Leticia to Europe.[4]

By 1921, both the political and economic crises had reached the flash point. Large stocks of rubber and cotton in world markets had depressed prices below their production costs in Loreto, and banks in Iquitos refused to loan money secured by either commodity. The department faced bankruptcy and a crushing debt of one million soles. Local officials discussed the viability of securing a loan to cover the debt, or of declaring a two-month moratorium on its obligations, including salaries and other routine expenditures. Merchants and public officials sought desperately for a remedy for their collective penury. Some promoted the free production and export of tobacco. Others hoped that logging cedar, then shipping or floating it downriver to Manaus en route to New York, would revive trade and the economy.[5]

Other proposals reflected pressures from an increasingly restive and militant working class in Iquitos. Proletarian protesters demanded that the departmental government and local businessmen create work, primarily public works projects, to relieve unemployment and hunger. Militants threatened direct action, strikes, and attacks if nothing was done. The Booth Company attracted particular ire because of the high rates it charged for carrying passengers and goods to Manaus.[6]

Discontent among the elite and the proletariat merged in an anticentralist revolt centered in Iquitos in the six months following August 1921. The titular leader of the revolt, Capt. Guillermo Cervantes Vásquez, opposed the Leguía dictatorship and harbored burning memories of past antipatriotic transgressions. A combatant at La Pedrera in 1911, he witnessed the overshadowing of Peru's victory by disease and diplomacy. This anticentralist revolt led by a man with a Quixotic name gained popular support throughout the department. But the opportunistic, cunning Arana took advantage of it as well. His primary concern, as it had been a decade earlier, was to thwart the transfer of his territory and its Indian assets to Colombian domain. Indeed, preliminary negotiations in 1921 favored the Colombian side, surprising given Arana's friendship and favor with President Leguía. Nonetheless, the negotiations continued, and Arana and many other Loretanos faced an uncertain future.[7]

In early 1922,the entrenched Cervantine rebel government in Iquitos issued its own currency to deal with the depression, and rebel leaders encouraged the people to sack any store or bank that refused the new tender. Forces loyal to President Leguía then counterattacked and won victories in Pucallpa and Yurimaguas before pushing north to Iquitos. Cervantes and other rebel leaders abandoned the capital and fled up the Napo into Ecuadorian territory. Although rebel support persisted in some areas, including the Casa Arana heartland along the Caraparaná, it had fizzled by March. Over the next several months, the government sorted out claims from loyal bureaucrats for back pay and for future positions in the departmental administration.[8]

President Leguía named a trusted military officer, Gen. Gerardo Alvarez, to assume responsibility for directing Loreto out of decay and discontent. Alvarez's reports for 1922 and 1923 revealed the historical weight of the past. The collection and export of forest products — now primarily balata latex and ivory nuts — persisted, but Alvarez insisted that collectors not destroy the trees in the process to avoid the fate of caucho. Alvarez also noted a vagrancy problem in Iquitos and suggested that the vagrants be rounded up and put to collecting balata. In addition, he cracked down on workers who took advances and then reneged on their obligations to patróns. As for Indians, the new prefect revealed both colonial and liberal tendencies. Looking backward, he suggested that Indians be congregated into towns where they would receive religious and secular instruction. In a more liberal view, he hoped that Indian men in the department would receive five hectares of land, and an extra hectare for a wife and each child, in order to guarantee them protection from feudal exploitation. Indeed, Alvarez oversaw the department at a time of complexity and contradiction. Even as ancient killers such as leprosy, malaria, and hookworm disease debilitated thousands of residents and took many to their graves, Elmer J. Faucett's new airplane service to Iquitos brought twentieth-century technology and a glimpse of a modern future for eyes turned toward the sky.[9]

While Alvarez directed affairs in Iquitos, Julio César Arana moved to Lima, where from 1921 to 1925 he represented Loreto in the Senate. Arana could nonetheless still count on Pablo Zumaeta, mayor of Iquitos in 1923, and allies such as Victor Israel and Cecilio Hernández to keep an eye on his businesses in the Putumayo. In Lima, Arana profited by his proximity to Leguía, often lobbying the president for favorable decisions on commercial, territorial, and administrative matters in Loreto, particularly in the Putumayo. During his tenure as senator and up to about 1928, Arana continued to export Putumayo tails and balata in quantities sometimes matching output during the boom years.[10]

Prices for both balata and Putumayo tails tended to increase until about 1927, when saturated markets warned of the Great Depression. However, rubber production in the 1920s eerily resembled practices of earlier decades. Both latexes involved killing the tree to collect its milk, effectively destroying the resource in the drive for profit. Indian labor held in place through force and debt-peonage was also still a reality in the Putumayo.[11]

As Arana and the Peruvians grappled with the legacies and permutations of the Great War, Colombian officials confronted the promise of the future and the weight of the past. By 1919, German, British, and American oil companies were scrambling for exploration and drilling concessions in Colombia, and a proposal for a radio network offered hope of better communications. Meanwhile, some bureaucrats in Bogotá worried about the Bolshevik threat to the country. The worldwide flu epidemic reached the Putumayo and Caquetá early that year, weakening the health of thousands of residents who already lived with epidemic levels of syphilis, malaria, tropical anaemia, hookworm disease, and alcoholism. One health worker worried that wretched health would keep the population mired in poverty and ignorance, thwarting any chance of social and economic progress.[12]

Worrisome reports of Peruvian threats to the Putumayo also surfaced in 1919. Reinforced Peruvian units at Pantoja and Yuvineto threatened to cut Güeppi off from its riverine link to Puerto Asís, where Peruvian steamboats called at will. They smuggled in trade goods and exported forest products, underlining the lack of a Colombian steamship service on the Putumayo. Saber rattling and psychological warfare prevailed throughout the next year. One local official promised to send eight hundred black Colombian machete warriors ("negros macheteros") to clear the area of Peruvians, which he said would "fill them with terror." By 1924, the Putumayo commissar had drafted a detailed strategic plan to expel the Peruvians, primarily the Casa Arana, from both the Caquetá and Putumayo.[13]

Capuchin missionaries tried to repel Peruvian inroads as well. In October and November 1919, Fidel de Montclar resumed his campaign for transportation improvements on the Putumayo, this time suggesting that gasoline-and alcohol-burning outboard motors would facilitate communication downriver from Puerto Asís. He highlighted that the Peruvian commercial houses of Arana, Israel, and Marius were intensifying their operations in both the Putumayo and Caquetá, contracting for tons of quina and dried meat in return for delivering trade goods. Montclar and Gaspar de Pinell warned that the Peruvians would surely take over what the Colombians treated with indifference.[14]

Colombian efforts to construct or reinforce their position at La Tagua, Caucaya, Güeppi, and Puerto Asís raised the ire of Peruvians. Peruvians promised to match any Colombian moves and claimed that such a buildup violated a modus vivendi signed by both countries. Peruvian protests did push the ministry of foreign relations to order the colony built at Puerto Asís instead of Caucaya, for Colombia and Peru were then engaged in delicate negotiations for the entire Putumayo and the Leticia trapezoid. Nonetheless, Commissar Chaves and Father Montclar pushed ahead at Caucaya, using an Evinrude motor attached to a canoe to ferry arms and ammunition down from Puerto Asís. Even a reported Peruvian attack at La Tagua failed to slow these two stalwarts.[15]

The proposed colony at Caucaya remained tiny and did not flourish as hoped. Chaves requested a police force for Caucaya in 1921 and opposed moving the penal colony upriver to Puerto Asís. He also indirectly criticized the Capuchins for not increasing their activities in Güeppi and Caucaya. By 1926, Chaves's successor, Enrique Puertas, lobbied again for opening the penal colony at Caucaya, which he suggested would become a center of morality and progress, with men cutting the road through to the Caquetá, and women weaving cloth and collecting rubber and ivory nuts. Nonetheless, by the next year, reality defied this ideal, for Caucaya had only ten police agents, a handful of colonists, and plenty of biting snakes and dangerous waters to make life unpleasant.[16]

Throughout the 1920s, Colombian ambitions in northwestern Amazonia were undermined by an ongoing difficulty: the lack of national steamship service on either the Putumayo or the Caquetá. In 1921, the Colombian government finally approved a steamship for the Putumayo, but when it arrived the following year, its motor lacked the horsepower to move upriver against the current. On the Putumayo, Peru still enjoyed market links to Iquitos, upon which Colombians and Ecuadorians depended. Peruvian launches, flying the Colombian flag, called at Caucaya, Güeppi, and Puerto Asís throughout the decade. On the Caquetá, the rapids and waterfalls around Angosturas and Araracuara complicated all schemes to link Huila and Caquetá to the Amazon River.[17]

More talk, this time at a high-level cabinet meeting in Bogotá, addressed the stunted progress of Colombian initiatives in the Putumayo and Caquetá. Recommendations made at that meeting echoed some of those made by Montclar a decade earlier: two steamboats on the Putumayo, one on the Caquetá; a larger, more heavily armed military presence, one drafting recruits from all men in the Putumayo; an agricultural colony at La Tagua, with a road linking it to Caucaya; and a penal colony at Puerto Asís, a place where one local official stated that Colombians could serve the country and "pay for their crime in a place able to inspire terror in even the most criminal."[18] Again, fine ideas, great rhetoric, no action.

Presumably one reason for this inaction was that the informal, non-national steamships on the Putumayo functioned adequately and met the needs of merchants and consumers alike. With the Casa Arana, Casa Israel, and even the Ecuadorian captain Cornelio Terán Puyana delivering tons of goods on a regular basis and exporting tons of balata and other forest products to Iquitos duty free, national honor and sovereignty took a back seat to economic reality. Moreover, the shipping charge from Manaus to Puerto Asís was only U.S. $30 per ton, so Colombians along the river had little incentive to back a Colombian line that would raise fees and duties. Powerful merchants in Pasto probably profited from the non-national status quo as well. The freight rate from Europe or New York, through the Panama Canal, down to Tumaco, overland to Barbacoas, and then over the mountains to Pasto amounted to $205 a ton. Conversely, the Europe or New York link to Manaus, Puerto Asís, then up to Pasto totaled $115, a savings of $90 a ton over the Pacific route.[19] Why then challenge a cheap, functional, albeit informal, steamship service on the Putumayo?

Although Montclar recognized the possible advantages of Colombian steamships on the Putumayo and Caquetá, he knew for a fact that roads were indeed vital to the transformation of both regions. After Montclar and the Capuchin order regained the contract for the maintenance and continuing construction of the Pasto–Puerto Asís road in August 1919, Montclar again found himself central to the bureaucratic, partisan, and resource politics inherent in the order's involvement with the road. Land battles in the Sibundoy Valley flared again from 1918 through 1921, with both colonists and Indians bringing charges against the Capuchins. Complaints intensified from the Caquetá as the road from Guadalupe, Huila, to Florencia, Caquetá, down to Mocoa, Putumayo, attracted more colonists, cattle, and horses to lands now hurriedly claimed and cleared of forest. Miners intent on exploiting the gold, coal, petroleum, and radium of the Caquetá and Putumayo added to the anticipated recovery of the region following the decline of rubber, but also to the battles for control of land and labor.[20]

The Pasto–Puerto Asís road became a burden to the order in the early 1920s. Damage from rain, floods, and landslides kept missionaries and workers occupied, while critics harped about the morass encountered on the muddy and blocked road. Montclar still depended on hand tools imported from New York, shipped via Tumaco and Pasto, a telling statement on Colombian dependency on imported manufactured goods. Liberals in Puerto Asís raised disturbing charges of Capuchin contempt for their human and religious rights, stating that priests withheld medicines and last rites and tried to expel all Liberals from town. Indians held on criminal charges in the white town of Sucre, established by the Capuchins in the Sibundoy Valley, found that pride and assertiveness often led to their incarceration, and that they could face criminal charges for petty theft, minor damage to property, disrespect, insults, and arguing with officials.[21]

By 1924, the ministry of public works cancelled its contract with the Capuchins, citing lack of progress in the technical planning to complete the last leg of the road from Umbría to Puerto Asís, a distance of forty-eight kilometers. Nonetheless, the seesaw battle for the road tilted back to the order the following year, and it focused on this last section of what was now a quarter-century-long campaign. Montclar turned over temporary supervision to Father Benigno de Canet de Mar, twenty-three years his junior. Over the next four years, Canet de Mar lobbied for government attention and funds for the Umbría–Puerto Asís link. He argued that the road would stimulate colonization, break the isolation of the Putumayo from Colombian administration, and save lives; indeed, hundreds had drowned in the swift, dangerous waters descending from Umbría in canoes. He argued that the order needed two thousand pesos monthly for the entire road system, but Bogotá authorized only half that much. The daily workers received a paltry seven cents an hour for a nine-hour day. By 1929, Canet de Mar sounded much like Montclar in earlier decades, pleading for more money and warning of the physical and political damage done by funding cuts.[22]

A number of important changes occurred in 1930. The Great Depression constricted financial and commercial markets, dropping the value of Colombian exports and increasing the cost of imports. The Conservative Party split that year, yielding the presidency to the Liberals for the first time in forty-four years. Pope Pius XI elevated the Caquetá prefecture to an apostolic vicariate, overseeing all of the Caquetá, Putumayo, and Amazonas territories. And, even given the Depression, Colombia finally managed to restore its own steamship service on the Putumayo.[23]

That same year, the Colombian military threw its support behind the completion and improvement of roads in both the Putumayo and Caquetá. In particular, Col. Luis Acevedo lobbied for the widening and termination of the Pasto–Puerto Asís, Mocoa–Florencia, and La Tagua–Caucaya roads. Acevedo wrote that these routes should be wide enough for horses and improved further for vehicles where possible. Gaspar de Pinell, now apostolic vicar, echoed Acevedo's recommendations. He noted that the last twenty kilometers of road from Puerto Asís to San Pedro would complete the international transportation link available with two steamships plying the waters of the Putumayo, Caquetá, and Amazon. He also recommended that both the departments of Nariño and Huila receive a public subsidy until river traffic increased to lower operating costs, and he heralded the arrival of yet more technology connecting the Putumayo to the rest of the world. A telegraph service in Puerto Asís, along with a proposed hydroplane service on the rivers and lakes of the region, promised to overcome the ancient necessity of walking or canoeing over great distances. Finally, the vicar suggested that seven new schools — with qualified teachers earning a whopping seventy pesos a month — be established in what had been Arana territory. Indeed, by 1930, Colombia rallied in the Putumayo, while many other Latin American countries struggled with the economic and political chaos brought by the Depression.[24]

Ironically, Fidel de Montclar missed the achievements of 1930. After returning to his beloved homeland, Catalonia, in 1928 to attend to his failing health, he resigned his Putumayo post the following year. He died in a small town near Barcelona in 1934.[25] Montclar, like Rafael Reyes and Julio César Arana before him, left a lasting and controversial impression on the history and peoples of the Putumayo.

Montclar's campaign likely left a bitter legacy for the native Indians in the Putumayo. The roads meant labor: some of it compulsory, some of it paid. The roads also brought colonists, markets, machines, land battles, and diseases into the natives' daily lives. In addition, the Capuchin drive to convert and acculturate Indians to Western civilization, although often resisted, inevitably undermined established traditions and customs. Some clan elders in the 1920s and 1930s underwent a crisis of confidence, while, paradoxically, some Indian orphans reconstructed societies and ethnicities that both responded to changing circumstances and questioned the old order.[26]

Throughout the 1920s, whites sought to contact and congregate Indians who lived independent of recognized authority. Indians such as the Tetetes of the Napo, the Caimitos of the Caraparaná, or the "nomadic and savage" Indians of the Yari found themselves the most recent targets of the Columbian exchange. Some fought, some fled, and others accepted the new authority. At Güeppi, congregated Indians built new outposts and schools. The new corregidor put them to collecting balata, enslaving them when he deemed it necessary.[27]

Migration emerged as another strong theme of the 1920s. Thousands of Indians moved either voluntarily or involuntarily out of lands claimed by the Casa Arana. Some moved northwest up the Putumayo, but many settled on the northern tributaries of the Caquetá, along the Orteguaza, Caguán, and

Yari Rivers. Casa Arana employees tracked fleeing Indians into the Yari River district, but nonetheless tens of thousands of Huitoto, Andoke, and Carijona Indians made the Yari their new home.[28]

Some 6,719 Indians—2,351 of whom were children—did not escape the Casa Arana. From 1924 through 1930, Arana employee Carlos Loayza oversaw the removal of these Indians from the company's sections in the Igaraparaná, Caraparaná, and Caquetá. Loayza directed this systematic removal to the south bank of the Putumayo, first ordering men to clear and prepare fields, and subsequently women to plant, so that the migrating tribes had food and shelter when they arrived.[29]

Arana moved these Indians south because he feared that Peru might turn over much of his domain to Colombian jurisdiction. Arana kept abreast of all discussions about the Putumayo between the two countries and managed to wrest an incredible sweetheart deal from the Peruvian government in 1921. The Leguía government granted Arana title to the lands contested by Colombia along the length of the Putumayo and Caquetá Rivers. This grant totaled 5,774,000 hectares, some 35,798 square miles, roughly the size of Portugal. In addition, Arana, as senator for Loreto and as an interested party, made sure that the 1922 Salomón-Lozano treaty stipulated payment if he lost lands granted to Colombia.[30]

The Salomón-Lozano treaty promised a new and defined territorial and diplomatic future for the Putumayo. The treaty, approved by Colombia in 1925 and by Peru in 1927, made the Putumayo the border between Peru and Colombia, and it also stipulated Colombian access to the Amazon River and to Leticia via a trapezoid-shaped territory south of the Putumayo. Of the 1921 land grant to Arana, more than 60 percent now fell under Colombian jurisdiction, real estate the title holder would part with for two million pounds sterling.[31]

From 1924 to 1930, this treaty set the context for Carlos Loayza's draining of the Putumayo and Caquetá of its most valuable resource: Indian labor. Living along the Putumayo, Algodón, and Ampiyacu Rivers, these Indians raised crops and coffee, built villages, and collected balata. But in 1932 and 1933, Arana and these resettled Indians found themselves in the middle of yet another violent international conflict.[32]

In August 1932, a "patriotic junta" in Iquitos, whose members included Arana's son and daughter, pledged to return Leticia to Peruvian sovereignty, with Arana supplying the Winchester rifles to do it. By September, supporters of the junta took Leticia, garnering civil and military support from many areas of Peru, although Lima reassured Bogotá that the Peruvian government had nothing to do with the action. Nonetheless, both countries were headed for war and frantically scrambled to secure ships, submarines, and warplanes.

From February to May 1933, almost the entire length of the Putumayo, from Güeppi in the west to Tarapacá in the east, became the scene of bombing and strafing, artillery barrages, and infantry raids. During the fighting, another strange twist brought the region's past to the present; Oscar R. Benavides, hero of the Peruvian victory over Colombia at La Pedrera in 1911, regained the presidency following the assassination of his predecessor. But Benavides, pressured by the United States and Brazil, cut the war short, and the two belligerents signed a cease-fire agreement on May 25, 1933. Colombia regained the left bank of the Putumayo and the Leticia corridor, while Arana and his children lost their historic gamble.[33]

The war brought more suffering to the Indians. Both sides impressed Indians as porters, oarsmen, scouts, and warriors. Colombian forces attacked some of the Casa Arana's reconstituted villages along the Putumayo, including the one at Pucaurco, carrying away food, cattle, and people. Survivors were moved farther south to the Ampiyacu, yet another geographic and psychic displacement. A measles epidemic killed half of the Casa Arana's Indian personnel in some areas, annihilating entire clans in the process.[34]

Arana's glory days passed with the Leticia episode. In 1939, after some forty years of prominence, he sold his Colombian claim to partner and associate Victor Israel for 300,000 soles. Israel then reportedly sold the Casa Arana documentation to the Colombian government for 200,000 soles. Bogotá made a final payment of U.S. $160,000 to Israel in 1964 for Arana's old lands in the Colombian Putumayo.[35]

Arana lived out his final days in a dark, rather small home in Magdalena, a neighborhood in Lima. He, the most famous and infamous member of the Moyobamba Social Center, still snapped orders and demanded attention, but he was old, his heavy head hanging down near his chest, with the weight of time, the tropics, scandal, intrigue, and prodigious amounts of work having taken their toll. He died in Lima in 1952, almost unnoticed by the capital's busy populace. He had lived eighty-eight years, time enough to bury the ghosts of Rafael Reyes, Sir Roger Casement, Fidel de Montclar, and the thousands who had worked and died for his profit.[36]

CONCLUSIONS

A combination of local, regional, national, and international elements provoked great social, cultural, economic, and political changes in northwestern Amazonia from 1850 to 1933. Only with a broad and inclusive perspective can one begin to fathom what happened. An exclusive focus on the Putumayo scandal assumes a viewpoint foreign to the realities and the history of the region. A clearer picture places the scandal into historical perspective and approaches the study of northwestern Amazonia from a kaleidoscope of angles.

The physical and cultural environment set the stage for much of what happened during the rubber boom. Indigenous definitions of culture, of the land, and of their place in the world grounded the region and its peoples in an Amazonian and non-Western milieu. Early commercial pioneers brought with them a different set of agendas, hopes, and visions, but the successful ones adapted to local ecological and social realities. From the resulting interactions between Indians and whites emerged examples of cultural confusion, ethnocentrism, cooperation, and, inevitably, conflict. Although he was not the first white explorer to enter the area, Rafael Reyes became emblematic of these interactions. As a quinero pioneer, Reyes initially demonstrated a degree of sensitivity and respect for Indians, needing their labor to ensure the success of his business. By trading labor for goods, Indian leaders acquired desirable and powerful products, such as metal tools, from Reyes. However, his alliances with the warring Huitoto and Bora and the spread of tuberculosis to the Cosacuntí revealed that any external contact and exchange, no matter how benevolent, would change Indian societies, often for the worse.

The rubber economy, of course, became the engine of more profound change in the region, particularly after the 1880s. The great expansion of world rubber demand created by the scientific, transportation, industrial, and consumer breakthroughs of the nineteenth century directly changed life in northwestern Amazonia. Technological advances such as the steamboat, the telegraph, and the repeating rifle brought the wider world, its people, and products into this frontier region. The changing material, demographic, and economic situations changed life for Indians and non-Indians alike, some groups adapting better than others.

Access to and control of labor were primary concerns for caucheros set on making it rich. The aviamiento system sustained debt-peonage throughout Amazonia; however, certain conditions in northwestern Amazonia worsened conditions for workers. First, being so far upriver and distant from the major trade centers in Manaus and Pará meant that goods were expensive and rubber worth very little because of high transport costs. Second, because of the international competition for the region, caucheros tended to claim lands and the Indians upon them and then use violence to protect or intimidate their labor pool. Third, eventually one company controlled most of the Putumayo, so workers could not play one patrón off another and thereby negotiate better terms or conditions of employment. Finally, Indians, rather than acculturated caboclos or mestizos, formed the most plentiful and potentially profitable labor force, and caucheros tended to exploit them ruthlessly.

Nonetheless, the attraction of trade, in addition to labor demands, acted as a strong force pulling Indians into social and economic relations with caucheros. From this perspective, the benefits and opportunities afforded by trade and even by debt-peonage mitigated some of the obnoxious baggage of labor exploitation. Some captains clearly increased their material and spiritual powers through trade, as did some muchachos and women working for the Casa Arana.

Along with debt-peonage, slavery formed another active institution in the region during the rubber boom. In a colonial society of "discovery," conquest, and patriarchy, it was not unusual for slavery to persist. Concepts of "just war," ransoming, and the use of slavery to civilize Indians lasted through the nineteenth and into the twentieth century. The charge of cannibalism — although seemingly groundless — granted caucheros the moral and legal basis to enslave Indians defined as savages. In part, then, institutions and practices introduced by European colonialism sustained forced labor systems. The history of northwestern Amazonia and that of other areas of Latin America suggests that colonialism often reflects a set of social and cultural characteristics impervious to traditional administrative or chronological definitions.

But indigenous traditions also helped sustain these exploitative practices. Northwest Amazonians had traded human beings for goods prior to the rubber boom and continued to do so thereafter. The technological and spiritual allure of European products provided the stimulus for the Carijona to specialize in slave raiding, and the Huitoto created the mythology of the "Axe of the East" as the provider of life, a product/spirit of vital importance for the survival of the people. This mythology built consensus in support of white trade and quieted some of the discontent from those slated for barter and slavery. Inevitably, however, existing hierarchy and exploitation, coupled with the disease and labor demands brought by caucheros, had myriad and frequently fatal consequences for individuals and entire cultures.

The orphan caste within indigenous communities supplied the most important source of potential slaves. These individuals, separated from their clans and their claim to humanity, were traded by Indians for imported goods. Women and children filled this orphan pool and became important to the developing economy of the caucheros. Men, too, were traded as slaves, the victims of war and kidnapping by either rival Indians or caucheros.

On the other end of the social scale from these low-status individuals, Indian captains often brokered labor relations between whites and Indians. At times willingly, and at other times compelled to do so, these captains played a crucial role in the region's labor history. Either as brokers, cultural translators, or pawns, captains often filled an intermediate role between caucheros and Indian workers. In short, along with European colonial culture, indigenous hierarchy and exploitation provided the other crucial cultural and institutional basis supporting forced labor in the Putumayo.

Conflicting territorial claims and the increased political and economic value of the Putumayo during the rubber boom prompted attempts by regional and national governments in Peru, Colombia, Brazil, and Ecuador to include the region in their administrative orbits. Since 1850, a combination of factors favored the development of the Peruvian administration in Loreto. First, the national government in Lima adopted an aggressive policy in Loreto as early as the 1850s of sending army and navy units to Iquitos, followed in the 1860s with the purchase of technologically advanced steamboats, craft that gave Peruvians great advantages over the Colombians and Ecuadorians in later decades. Moreover, Lima, more so than Bogotá or Quito, consistently supported its departmental officials based in Moyobamba and Iquitos. In part, Peru had a distinct advantage in controlling Iquitos, a vital port and commercial hub for all of northwestern Amazonia. The second factor favoring the Peruvians centered on the economic growth of the rubber industry in Loreto. While much of the rest of the country floundered during the upset caused by the War of the Pacific (1879–83), Loreto, connected to world trade through the Amazonian trade system, experienced unprecedented economic growth and opportunity. Political leadership at the regional level displayed dynamism as well. The two to three prefects ruling simultaneously during the confused but profitable 1880s gave way to the stable and focused direction of Prefect Samuel Palacios. Palacios pursued aggressive policies, followed up by his successors in subsequent decades, to encourage Peruvian commerce and to bolster the nation's control over disputed border regions. By 1895, Peru enjoyed a strong economic, political, and military position in northwestern Amazonia.

After 1895, Peru and the departmental government in Loreto built on the strategic and economic importance of Iquitos to expand its hold over border regions such as the Putumayo. Lima maintained the necessary men, money, and equipment for civil and military officials in Loreto. Once Julio César Arana set his sights on the Putumayo, he counted on assistance not only from his national and departmental political allies but also from that of the Peruvian army and navy. Contrary to the accepted wisdom, government activism, not inattention, provoked violence in the Putumayo. Peru, in short, fashioned a coherent and effective strategy to expand its hold over much of northwestern Amazonia. Arana deserves some credit for this success, for he organized a strong alliance between international, national, and regional actors to emerge as the most powerful commercial and political actor in the Putumayo.

To the north, Colombia started well when the Reyes brothers penetrated the Putumayo in the 1870s, capitalizing on Amazonian commercial routes and the steamboats that carried their products. Colombians organized a small but effective bureaucracy in the Caquetá and collected customs duties on forest-product exports. After the bust of the quina boom, however, Colombians lost some momentum in the region. At the national level, frequent civil wars interrupted Colombian administration of both the Caquetá and the Putumayo. At the regional level, the Peruvian port of Iquitos emerged as the center of lowland trade and the hub of maritime activity in the 1880s and 1890s, so Colombian caucheros became more dependent on their Peruvian neighbors. The War of a Thousand Days (1899–1902) interrupted Colombian administration and severed trade and communication routes down to its southeastern territories. Economic dependency on Iquitos and Peruvians such as Arana intensified during these years and left Colombia and her caucheros at a distinct disadvantage. Subsequent efforts by President Rafael Reyes to regain control of the Putumayo failed for lack of resources and resolve. Moreover, disturbing allegations pinned on Reyes much of the blame for Arana's expansion upriver.

One can trace Ecuador's problems in the region to Quito and to the province's capital, Archidona. Although national politicians in Quito and Guayaquil pointed with pride to Ecuador's huge Amazonian claim, they did little to attend to the problems of Oriente province. Quito furnished a minimum amount of material, personnel, and money because economically the country faced west, toward the cacao plantations of the Pacific lowlands, not east toward the rubber-rich Amazon basin. Concerned with regional partisan divisions and civil wars, Ecuadorians ignored their eastern frontier. In the Oriente, the provincial capital at Archidona also faced west and up the mountain to Quito rather than downriver toward the Amazon basin. Governors depended on appropriations from Quito and failed at the regional level to establish a network of customs houses to collect revenues from the rubber trade. Lacking the necessary men and supplies, Ecuadorians neglected the Oriente's far-flung borders. When the governor sent out a patrol, his few men traveled in canoes, not in steamboats. And no Ecuadorian merchant managed to patch together an alliance of international investors and national political support as had Reyes in Colombia and Arana in Peru. As a result, caucheros in the Oriente lacked the technology, capital, markets, and military necessary to compete with Colombian and Peruvian challenges to their territory. Ecuadorian dependence on Iquitos — like that of Colombia's — for trade and transportation links into the Amazon basin reinforced the Peruvian position, while it further undermined that of Ecuador in northwestern Amazonia.

A point sealing the Ecuadorian loss of the Oriente arrived in 1896 when the Liberal government of Eloy Alfaro expelled the Jesuits from their missions in the province. Ecuador subsequently lost its most organized and best financed administration in the region, again opening the way for the expansionist Peruvians. Thus Ecuadorian inattention and lack of policy combined with Peruvian opportunism left much of the Oriente in Peruvian hands by 1910.

Along with these issues of national administration, the international political economy of rubber became the catalyst for profound demographic, political, economic, social, and cultural change in the Putumayo. At times, negative consequences haunted these alterations at the local level; it appears that extractive industry drained, rather than filled, local economies and societies, as Stephen Bunker and others have suggested. Yet the political economy of the world-system, whether labeled capitalist or imperialist, enabled local elites — including Rafael Reyes in Colombia and Julio César Arana of Peru — to form international relationships that promoted the expansion of Colombian and Peruvian territorial claims to the Putumayo. Ecuador, although it tried, failed to fashion such an alliance and lost ground at international, national, and regional levels.

Local society, both indigenous and white, shaped the changes introduced from outside. Particularly in the realm of labor, one must consider both native and European perspectives on labor and trade to comprehend how things worked in the Putumayo. Although their motivations in pursuing trade often differed because of culture, both Indian and white elites employed leverage in a hierarchical and exploitative society to justify the practices of forced labor, debt-peonage, and slavery. In addition, the local environment — defined in social, cultural, economic, political, and biological terms — placed constraints on the depth, if not the breadth, of changes associated with external forces. In short, international systems, local realities, and national policies collectively shaped life and change in the Putumayo during and after the rubber boom.

The Putumayo scandal brought a peculiar and horrible image of the region to world attention. Here, too, regional, national, and international elements coalesced into a complex and distorted collage. Local politics played a major role in creating the scandal. In Iquitos, Saldaña Rocca lambasted the Casa Arana and its exploitation of labor in the Putumayo as part of a larger critique of capitalism. In part, this crusading newspaper editor built support for socialism by exposing the evils of slavery and murder. Yet much of the evidence for the sensational stories printed in the pages of *La Sanción* and *La Felpa* came second- and thirdhand and could not be corroborated. Nonetheless, the nature of the allegations themselves and the public's appetite for gossip created a stir in Iquitos. To reach a larger audience, Saldaña Rocca needed an international courier, a role filled by the American adventurer W. E. Hardenburg.

Following his eventful sojourn through the Putumayo, Hardenburg gathered the stories and evidence marshalled by Saldaña Rocca and subsequently broke the story in London. Hardenburg's own tales of Peruvian brutality, mixed with Saldaña Rocca's exposé, became the meat of the scandal printed in the London newspaper *Truth*. As with Saldaña Rocca, one must analyze Hardenburg's motivations in pursuing the scandal. First, he did suffer property loss and personal discomfort at the hands of Peruvians in the Putumayo. Second, his partnership with the Colombian *cauchero* David Serrano ended in failure as a result of Casa Arana actions. Third, the timing to pursue the allegations raised by Saldaña Rocca could not have been better. The registration of Arana's company in England in 1907 linked charges of brutality and slavery to England just as Arana was trying to attract investors to his new concern. Finally, whether rewarded through fame or silver, Hardenburg made a name for himself as a resolute Yankee bringing reform and the light of justice to the jungle.

Roger Casement's subsequent investigations in the Putumayo, spurred by the publication of the sensational articles in *Truth* and the lobbying of the foreign office, brought the region even more infamy. Casement focused on the liberal use of the whip and the mistreatment of Barbadian workers and only indirectly corroborated the "worst charges" originally raised by Saldaña Rocca and relayed by Hardenburg. Nonetheless, Casement's active schedule from 1910 to 1913 and his activities in Iquitos, London, and Washington, D.C., helped sustain international concern for the region.

An analysis of the motivations prompting people to take part in the scandal debate reveals some of the complexity of this affair. Clearly, politics pushed many to take a particular stand; the national interests of Peru, Colombia, Ecuador, England, Brazil, and the United States, for example, often informed the perspectives adopted by government officials or citizens of these various countries. But regardless of any coherent patriotism or nationalism, individuals and factions within countries found room for disagreement. In Peru, Saldaña Rocca, Valcárcel, Paredes, and others criticized their compatriot Arana and decried the violence and crime of the Putumayo. Some Peruvians criticized President Leguía for backing Arana in the Putumayo, especially after Guillermo Billinghurst assumed the presidency in 1912. In Colombia, partisan political differences focused on the role of President Reyes in allowing the Peruvian seizure of the Putumayo and Caquetá. In Ecuador, fingers pointed at the government in Quito, blaming it, along with the aggressive Peruvians, for the loss of the Oriente and, indirectly, for the crimes of the Putumayo. In England, the Irish nationalist Casement allied himself with the Anti-Slavery and Aborigines Protection Society while working for the British government to press the foreign office to take more effective action. In Parliament, some members questioned the culpability not only of the British directors of the Peruvian Amazon Company but also that of British absentee capitalism and its operations in the tropics. When the Putumayo became an international cause célèbre after the registry of the Casa Arana in London—suggesting that not only the company, but also the fate of the region was now a global concern—the scandal opened the way for political dialogue and conflict at regional, national, and international levels.

Did the scandal reflect or distort the realities of the Putumayo? Were thirty thousand Indians systematically slaughtered by sadistic and greedy caucheros during these years? Probably not. However, did thousands of Indians suffer the bite of the whip, endure the effects of slavery, disease, warfare, and displacement because of the demands of caucheros and government officials? The historical record reveals that the answer to this question is yes. The more sensational charges—torture, mass murder, sexual assault, and sport killings—did occur, but these heinous crimes, highlighted by the popular press and the scandal, fit into the larger context of the effects of international trade, nationalism, and colonialism. The scandal actually distorted more than it revealed about the region. Indians were cast as victims, Peruvian and Colombian caucheros as latter-day "black legend" conquistadores, and the British as reforming saviors. Although these roles fit into a particular view of culture and experience, they were construed in an ahistorical, ethnocentric, politicized, and non-Amazonian environment.

The First World War relegated the Putumayo to the scrap heap of past atrocities, replacing it with ever larger and uglier catastrophes. Plantation rubber from European colonies in Asia gutted the Amazonian rubber industry at the same time, yet caucheros stubbornly sought niches in what was still a booming and huge world market for latex. Caucheros continued to rely on debt-peonage and coercion to direct Indian labor for their benefit. Julio César Arana tenaciously defended his domain in the Putumayo and Caquetá from all challengers, yet lost it following the 1922 Salomón-Lozano treaty and the failed 1932 takeover of Leticia. However, after the era of Arana and the rubber boom, the Capuchins and their roads, schools, missions, and colonists introduced a formidable replacement for the intense changes lived in previous decades.

What does all of this suggest about northwestern Amazonia in the larger context of Latin America's deeper incorporation into the world economic system during the last half of the nineteenth century? First, given the richness of history, interdisciplinary, cross-cultural, and multinational studies focused on regional, national, and international levels can yield surprising and even unorthodox conclusions. True, international currents changed life in northwestern Amazonia — as they did in much of the world during this era — but not in a uniform or rational fashion. The peoples of the region used their culture and social systems to filter arriving international currents and thus responded to and shaped change around local conditions. Yet along with this regional-international interaction, national policies also affected economic, social, and political realities in the Putumayo. Peru, for example, found Arana's regional, national, and international resources good not only for business and revenues but also for its territorial ambitions in northwestern Amazonia. In short, this alliance between a local elite, his government, and "imperialism" promoted, rather than undermined, Peruvian national interests, at least in the short term. However, the scandal and the bust of the rubber boom revealed that these complex alliances were fragile, temporary, and often destructive at the regional level.

ABBREVIATIONS USED IN
NOTES AND BIBLIOGRAPHY

ABFL(Q)	Archivo/Biblioteca de la Función Legislativa, Quito, Ecuador
AC(B)	Archivo del Congreso, Bogotá, Colombia
AGN(L)	Archivo General de la Nación, Lima, Peru
AH(P)	Archivo Histórico, Pasto, Colombia
ANC(B)	Archivo Nacional de Colombia, Bogotá, Colombia
ANH(Q)	Archivo Nacional de Historia, Quito, Ecuador
APJ(I)	Archivo del Palacio de Justicia, Iquitos, Peru
BE(C)	Biblioteca Ecuatoriana "José María Espinosa Polit," Cotocollao, Ecuador
BGMRE(Q)	Biblioteca General del Ministerio de Relaciones Exteriores, Quito, Ecuador
BN(B)	Biblioteca Nacional, Bogotá, Colombia
BN(L)	Biblioteca Nacional, Lima, Peru
BR(B)	Banco de la República, Hemeroteca "Luis López de Mesa," Bogotá, Colombia
CETA(I)	Centro de Estudios Teológicos de la Amazonía, Iquitos, Peru
GBFO	Great Britain, Foreign Office
GBHC	Great Britain, House of Commons
HAHR	Hispanic American Historical Review
LARR	Latin American Research Review
LC	Library of Congress, Washington, D.C.
NA	National Archives, Washington, D.C.
UC-CIH(P)	Universidad del Cauca, Centro de Investigación Histórica, "José María Arboleda Llorente," Popayán, Colombia
USDC	United States, Department of Commerce
USDS	United States, Department of State

NOTES

All translations done by the author unless otherwise noted.

INTRODUCTION

1. The term "rubber industry" refers to the network of collecting, trading, and transporting rubber in exchange for imported goods.
2. Domínguez, *Amazonía Colombiana*; Domínguez and Gómez, *Economía extractiva*; Gómez, "Amazonía Colombiana, 130–54; Pineda Camacho, "El sendero," 29–58; Pineda Camacho, *Historia oral*.
3. Chirif, "Ocupación territorial," 265–95, and "El colonialismo interno," 47–80.
4. San Román, *Perfiles históricos*; Flores Marín, *La explotación*.
5. Pennano, *Economía del caucho*.
6. L. García, *Historia de las misiones*; Jouanen, *Los jesuitas*; Costales and Costales, *Amazonía*.
7. For the earliest extensive anthropological study, see Preuss, *Religion und mythologie*.
8. Gasché, "Comunidades nativas," 11–31; Gasché, "Ocupación territorial," 2–19; Gasché and Guyot, "Recherches ethnographiques," 267–83; Guyot, "El relato de O'ioi," 3–10; Garzón and Macuritope, "El chontaduro," 295–316.
9. Taussig, *Shamanism*, 3–36.
10. Hardenburg, *The Putumayo*, 184–85. For an English translation of Las Casas's famous charges, see Las Casas, *A Short Account of the Destruction of the Indies*.
11. Great Britain, Foreign Office (GBFO), *Correspondence Respecting the Treatment of British Colonial Subjects*.
12. I will use the word "white" as it was understood by contemporary inhabitants and observers of the Putumayo to mean a non-Indian, be they white, black, mestizo, or mulatto.

CHAPTER 1

1. For a classic introduction to the cultural and physical geography of Amazonia, see Meggers, *Amazonia*.
2. For a description of the "notorious region" during the Putumayo scandal, see Enock's introduction to Hardenburg, *The Putumayo*, 15.
3. For an excellent source on the physical geography of the Colombian Amazon, see República de Colombia, *Amazonía Colombiana*, vol. 1.
4. De Friedemann and Arocha, *Herederos*, 125–35.
5. Denevan, "Aboriginal Population," 63–72.
6. Rumrrill, *Amazonía Peruana*, 68.
7. Domínguez, *Amazonía Colombiana*, 29–30.
8. This spherical frontier attracted adventurers, rubber traders, and colonists from all points of the compass.
9. Chaumeil and Chaumeil, "De un espacio mítico," 16–18.
10. Most of the tribal names for Putumayans were coined by whites or Indian enemies. For example, the Carijona used their word for enemy or slave, *itoto,* to refer to the Huitoto. Individuals identified themselves by clan name rather than by the given tribal names. See Llanos V. and Pineda C., *Etnohistoria,* 90–92.
11. GBFO, *Report by His Majesty's Consul at Iquitos,* 7.
12. Correa, "Amazonía Colombiana," 187–92; and Gasché, "Comunidades nativas," 21.
13. Domínguez, *Amazonía Colombiana,* 123; Lathrap, *Upper Amazon,* 38–44; Robuchon, *En el Putumayo,* 28.
14. For more information on Huitoto and Bora society, see Gasché and Guyot, "Recherches ethnographiques," 267–77; on marriage customs, see Shapiro, "Marriage Rules," 14, 26–27.
15. *Censos de población* (1870), vol. 2, *Estado Soberano del Cauca,* fols. 378–504, ANC(B).
16. Bierhorst, *Mythology of South America,* 27; and Guzmán G., "Los andokes," 60.
17. Rojas Paredes, "Mitos, leyendas, y creencias," 105–6.
18. San Román, "Mitos de los Huitoto," 113–18.
19. Garzón and Macuritope, "El chontaduro," 301.
20. Pineda Camacho, *Historia oral,* 61–63.
21. For a somewhat idealized vision of pre–Columbian life in the Amazon, see Hemming, *Amazon Frontier,* 7–9.
22. For a discussion of indigenous strategies of adaptation to fragile Amazonian ecologies and the use of violence and other practices to limit population density, see Meggers, *Amazonia*.
23. Author interview with cacique Touera Buinama (Victor Martínez), La Chorrera, Amazonas, Colombia, 9 July 1994.
24. For the Bora account of traditional tribal relations, see Guyot, "El relato de O'ioi," 10 n. 37; see also Chaumeil and Chaumeil, "De un espacio mítico," 17–18.
25. For background information on early Spanish exploration of northwestern Amazonia, see Costales and Costales, *Amazonía,* 9–14, 22; and Domínguez, *Amazonía Colombiana,* 143–44.

26. Llanos V. and Pineda C., *Etnohistoria*, 25, 39–41.
27. Hemming, *Red Gold*, 430–31.
28. Domínguez, *Amazonía Colombiana*, 135–38.
29. Llanos V. and Pineda C., *Etnohistoria*, 83.
30. Hemming, *Amazon Frontier*, 29, 38.
31. Unfortunately for the Carijonas, prosperity turned to decline in the early twentieth century after four waves of epidemics carried off most of their population. See Llanos V. and Pineda C., *Etnohistoria*, 77–80; and Pineda Camacho, *Historia oral*, 17–18.
32. Hemming, *Amazon Frontier*, 220–21; and Llanos V. and Pineda C., *Etnohistoria*, 90–92.
33. On the impact of political independence in Colombia, see Dix, *Politics of Colombia*, 17; for the renaissance interpretation of the early nineteenth century, see Stocks, "Indian Policy," 42–43; for more background on this period, see Domínguez, *Amazonía Colombiana*, 150; and San Román, *Perfiles históricos*, 99–103.
34. San Román, *Perfiles históricos*, 118–19.
35. Hemming, *Amazon Frontier*, 175–77.
36. Colombia continued to send exiles and prisoners to the Putumayo into the twentieth century. See Gasché, "Ocupación territorial," 15.
37. Hispano [pseud.] *De París al Amazonas*, 248–50.
38. LeGrand, *Frontier Expansion*, 6, 152.
39. For information on chincona bark and efforts since the seventeenth century to use it as a cure for malaria, see Caufield, *In the Rainforest*, 209–17.
40. Reyes, *Memorias*, 70–71, 194.
41. Domínguez and Gómez, *Economía extractiva*, 25, 90–91.
42. Bergquist, *Coffee and Conflict*, 220–21.
43. Reyes, *Memorias*, 88–89.
44. Ibid., 90–97.
45. M. Edward Andree, *América Equinoccial: Colección América pintoresca* (Cali: Carvajal, 1982), 3:771–73, quoted in Domínguez and Gómez, *Economía extractiva*, 61–62.
46. The Orejones enlarged their earlobes with wooden disks, thus the name "Big Ears." See Reyes, *Memorias*, 123–25.
47. Reyes's memoirs must be read critically. He wrote his account of his Putumayo explorations forty years after the fact when he was in exile from Colombia. He naturally embellished, altered, or edited his account to protect his place in history.
48. Reyes, *Memorias*, 131–32.
49. Ibid., 134.
50. W. Ruiz Salgar, Pref. del Caquetá, to Sec. de Gobierno, Cauca, 13 July 1874, UC-CIH(P), 1874/127/29.
51. Ibid., 31 Aug. 1874, 1 Oct. 1874.
52. Pedro F. Urrutia, Pref. del Caquetá, to Sec. del Estado en el Despacho de Gobierno, 14 Nov. 1874, UC-CIH(P), 1874/127/29.
53. Reyes, *Memorias*, 150–58.
54. Simson, *Travels*, 221–49; "Certificación del Prefecto del Caquetá, Simón Restrepo," 29 Feb. 1876, UC-CIH(P), 1876/134/39.

55. Restrepo to Sec. de Gobierno, Cauca, 22 Feb. 1876, UC-CIH(P), 1876/134/39.

56. The following documents all refer to Peruvian and Brazilian activities on the Putu-mayo: 1 Feb. 1874, 19 Feb. 1874, 21 Mar. 1874, UC-CIH(P), 1874/127/29.

57. Peru, Min. de Guerra i Marina, "Se ordena al comandante general del Departa-mento de Loreto proceda a constituir autoridades fluviales i militares en el Río Putumayo, 18 dic. 1875," in Larrabure i Correa, Colección de Leyes, 7:376–77.

58. J. N. Montero to Pref. del Caquetá, 10 Mar. 1876, ANC(B), Gobernaciones Varias, vol. 24, fols. 274–75.

59. Costales and Costales, Amazonia, 246.

60. "Ordinario: Vicente Lloreda con Elias Reyes por intereses procedentes de daños y perjucios causados por la falta de cumplimiento en su contrato," UC-CIH(P), 1876/1597/256.

61. Reyes, Memorias, 184; Domínguez and Gómez, Economía extractiva, 79.

62. Reyes, Memorias, 209.

63. Corregidor de Cantinera to Sec. de Gobierno, 29 July 1878, UC-CIH(P), 1878/141/2; F. Mantilla, Sec. de Hacienda, Cauca, to Sec. de Estado en el Despacho de Hacienda de la Unión, 17 Aug. 1881, ANC(B), Correspondencia Consular de Cauca, Panamá, y Magdalena, fols. 497–97v.

64. Reyes, Memorias, 115–16.

65. Dean, Brazil and the Struggle for Rubber, 11–12.

66. Ibid., 239.

67. Domínguez and Gómez, Economía extractiva, 76.

CHAPTER 2

1. Santos, História econômica da Amazônia, 42–43; Woodruff, Rise of the British Rubber Industry, 1.

2. Santos, História econômica da Amazônia, 45–47; Woodruff, Rise of the British Rubber Industry, 8–9.

3. For a more complete list of the many uses of rubber, see Dean, Brazil and the Struggle for Rubber, 4–9; and Pennano, Economía del caucho, 74–76.

4. Pennano, Economía del caucho, 75.

5. Weinstein, Amazon Rubber Boom, 143.

6. Scharff, Taking the Wheel, 8–13.

7. Dean, Brazil and the Struggle for Rubber, 4.

8. The five rubber companies were: B. F. Goodrich, 1870; United States Rubber Com-pany, 1892; Goodyear Tyre and Rubber Company, 1898; Pneumatic Tyre Com-pany (Dunlop), 1899; Firestone Tyre and Rubber Company, 1900. See Pennano, Economía del caucho, 76.

9. Woodruff, Rise of the British Rubber Industry, 145–46.

10. For a comment on the Eurocentric "discovery" of plants, peoples, and continents, see Domínguez and Gómez, Economía extractiva, 114.

11. Dean, Brazil and the Struggle for Rubber, 364.

12. Hemming, Amazon Frontier, 273; Weinstein, Amazon Rubber Boom, 165.

13. Burns, History of Brazil, 332.

14. Barbara Weinstein noted some of the great transformations introduced into Ama-

zonia by the rubber industry, but she discounted them because they did not converge to lead Amazonia to a capitalist mode of production (*Amazon Rubber Boom,* 258–61).

15. Agassiz and Agassiz, *Journey in Brazil,* 190–91.

16. Burns, *History of Brazil,* 333–35.

17. Weinstein, *Amazon Rubber Boom,* 62.

18. Hemming, *Amazon Frontier,* 284–85.

19. Weinstein, *Amazon Rubber Boom,* 62.

20. Hemming, *Amazon Frontier,* 284–86.

21. Emory, U.S. Commercial Agent in Manaus, to Second Assistant Secretary of State, 20 Jan. 1882, U.S. Department of State (USDS), NA, T478 r. 5.

22. For a more in-depth description of the numerous genuses and species of rubber in the Putumayo, see Domínguez and Gómez, *Economía extractiva,* 79–112.

23. "La industria gomera en el Departamento de Loreto por el ingeniero Jorge M. Von Hassel," in Larrabure i Correa, *Colección de leyes,* 5:438–41.

24. For a contemporary description of cauchero and seringuero work habits and lives, see "La goma de Loreto por el ex-prefecto de ese departamento, Doctor Hildebrando Fuentes," in Larrabure y Correa, *Colección de leyes,* 14:85–90.

25. For more information on rubber collecting and curing, see Domínguez and Gómez, *Economía extractiva,* 79–102.

26. Ibid., 87–92.

27. Domínguez, *Amazonía Colombiana,* 151.

28. A. N. Hueriques, Consul in Buenaventura, to Asst. Secretary of State, 1 Nov. 1874, USDS, NA, M140 r. 23.

29. Felipe Meléndez, Sec. de Hacienda, Cauca, to Min. de Estado, 1 Dec. 1886, ANC(B), Min. de Industrias, Baldíos, 7:93; Pedro F. Urrutia, Pref. del Distrito del Caquetá, to Sec. de Hacienda, Cauca, 7 Jan. 1887, 8:36–39.

30. "Comisión de Hacienda to Excmo. Señor," 18 June 1884, ABFL(Q), 1894 Senado, legajo 8, doc. 3.

31. Pedro F. Urrutia, Pref. del Caquetá, to Sec. de Estado, Cauca, 16 Apr., 16 July 1868, UC-CIH(P), 1868/99/22.

32. Ibid., 1 Sept. 1869, UC-CIH(P), 1869/103/38.

33. Orton, *Andes and the Amazon,* 222.

34. "Ordenado que las lanzas importadas por Don Juan Howxuell para distribuirlas entre las salvajes del Rio Napo sean nuevamente reexportadas," in Larrabure i Correa, *Colección de leyes,* 5:150.

35. Reyes, *Memorias,* 211.

36. Author interview with cacique Touera Buinama (Victor Martínez), La Chorrera, Amazonas, Colombia, 9 July 1994.

37. GBFO, *Correspondence Respecting the Treatment of British Colonial Subjects,* 27.

38. Tobar shared his account with a Colombian anthropologist in the 1970s, nearly ninety years after Crisóstomo's exploits. Although Aquileo's oral history is fascinating, it, as well as most Putumayo documents, must be read critically or allegorically. For a transcript of his tale, see "La conquista de la huitocia," in Domínguez and Gómez, *Economía extractiva,* 201–26.

39. Oral tradition offers rich cultural and social history but also great hazards. Myth and history blend together, and the tale is open to interpretation from both the

speaker and the listener. Memories become clouded, and chronology and consistency are often irrelevant. For a few caveats on reading and interpreting oral tradition, see Guzmán G., "Los andokes," 64.

40. Domínguez and Gómez, *Economía extractiva*, 206–7.

41. Ibid., 207–11.

42. "... en éste caso tu eres nuestro jefe, háganos el bien de abrir para ver su contenido y tu serás el que mandas en el trabajo y yo mandaré mi gente en lo que ordenes"; cited in Domínguez and Gómez, *Economía extractiva*, 214.

43. John Hemming noted a trend in colonial Brazil for Indians to follow a strong man, one who had either defeated them militarily or who had introduced new and desirable materials. See, "Indians and the Frontier," 172.

44. Domínguez and Gomez, *Economía extractiva*, 220–26.

45. Pineda Camacho, *Historia oral*, 97

46. Guyot, "Cantos del Hacha de los Bora y Miraña de las selvas colombiana y peruana," *Amazonía Indígena* 4 (8) (1984): 21, cited in Pineda Camacho, *Historia oral*, 82.

47. Pineda Camacho, *Historia oral*, 78–83.

48. "Como ninguna de las dos personas se comprendía sus idiomas, la solución era la muerte." Relato de Aurelio Muiname, cited in Pineda Camacho, *Historia oral*, 125.

49. Pineda Camacho, *Historia oral*, 73–74, 123–28.

50. García, *Historia de las misiones*, 190, 220–21; Romero, *Iquitos y la fuerza naval*, 25.

51. Orton, *Andes and the Amazon*, 380.

52. Romero, *Iquitos y la fuerza naval*, 23–29; Rumrrill, Dávila H., Barcia G., *Yurimaguas*, 191.

53. Smith, "Patterns of Urban and Regional Development," 86.

54. Orton, *Andes and the Amazon*, 389–93.

55. For more information on Loreto's exports of hats, sarsaparilla, and rubber, see "Estado commercial de la región peruana," in Larrabure i Correa, *Colección de leyes* 16:120–30.

56. Romero, *Iquitos y la fuerza naval*, 60–62.

57. Rumrrill, Dávila H., Barcia G., *Yurimaguas*, 191; Guillaume, *Amazon Provinces of Peru*, 46.

58. Davies, *Indian Integration in Peru*, 33–34.

59. Guerra to Sargento Mayor, 17 May 1879, AGN(L) 1879, 539/4(1); "Buenas Cuentas y socorros suministrados a la columna 'Voluntarios de Loreto,'" 31 July 1879, 539/4(26).

60. The eminent Peruvian historian Jorge Basadre noted that rubber receipts more than matched Lima's normal annual subsidy by 1882 (*Historia de la república del Perú*, 7:3205).

61. Stefano Varese, *La sal de los cerros* (Lima: Universidad Peruana de Ciencia y Tecnología, 1968), 97, cited in Pennano, *Economía del caucho*, 155.

62. "Decreto 117 del prefecto y comandante general del departamento, David Arévalo Villacis," 2 May 1881 (Moyobamba); "Decreto de Tadeo Terry, colonel prefecto y comandante general del departamento de Loreto," 5 Aug. 1882 (Yquitos); AGN(L) 1885 O.L. 561/174; Terry to Marcelino del Castillo, 22 May 1883 (Moyobamba), O.L. 539/4.

63. "Documentos oficiales relativos a la destrucción de la aduana de Iquitos, 1 Sept. 1883," AGN(L) 1885 O.L. 561/174; Pinedo to Oficial Mayor del Min. de Hacienda, 17 Jan. 1884, 1884 O.L. 556/228.

64. "Decreto de los vecinos de Yquitos," 23 Dec. 1883, AGN(L) O.L. 561/174.

65. Smith to Señor de Estado, 23 Mar. 1886, AGN(L) 1886 O.L. 567/2139; Smith to Señor de Estado, 1886 O.L. 565/699, 3 Apr. 1886; Ex-pref. Tadeo Terry to Dir. Gen. de Aduanas, 28 Oct. 1887, 1887 O.L. 571/1001.

66. Estrella to Pref. de Loreto, 30 Dec. 1887, AGN(L) 1888 O.L. 577/1445.

67. Mamique to Benavides, 10 Oct. 1890, AGN(L) O.L. 589/963.

68. Guillaume, *Amazon Provinces of Peru*, 46.

69. Medina to Oficial Mayor del Min. de Hacienda y Comercio, 12 May 1885 (Yquitos), AGN(L) 1886 O.L. 565/699; Silva to Pref. de Loreto, 16 July 1888, 1888 O.L. 577/1460.

70. Rivera to Dir. Gen. de Gobierno, 30 June 1893, AGN(L) 1893 O.L. 607/429.

71. Quirós to Dir. de Gobierno, 23 Mar. 1898. AGN(L) Min. de Industrias 1898 no. 54; Rumrrill set 1906 as the year that Iquitos became the capital (see *Amazonía Peruana*, 28–30).

72. De la Flor Fernández, "Economía de exportación," 41.

73. Collier, *River That God Forgot*, 38–42.

74. Domínguez and Gómez, *Economía extractiva*, 178–79; a map insert in Guillaume's *Amazon Provinces of Peru* locates the "Aranas Indians" near the Juruá River, suggesting that Arana had a great impact on the people in that Brazilian region.

75. Collier, *River That God Forgot*, 41–43.

76. Ibid., 45–46; Domínguez and Gómez, *Economía extractiva*, 179; Arana, *Cuestiones del Putumayo*, 3:7.

77. Hispano, *De París al Amazonas*, 254.

78. De la Flor Fernández, "Economía de exportación," 42; Collier, *River That God Forgot*, 49–50; Pennano, *Economía del caucho*, 162.

CHAPTER 3

1. Furneaux, *The Amazon*, 151; for a brief but solid overview of the bandeirantes, see Hemming, *Red Gold*, 238–82; on Lope de Aguirre, see Hemming, *Red Gold*, 195–97; Rumrrill, Dávila H., Barcia G., *Yurimaguas*, 36–40; also see Werner Herzog's cinematic extravaganza, *Aguirre, Wrath of God*.

2. Hennessy, *Frontier in Latin American History*, 32–34.

3. Ibid., 29, 40; Chirif, "Ocupación territorial," 268.

4. Hemming, "Indians and the Frontier," 177: Gómez, "Amazonía Colombiana," 137.

5. Alistair Hennessy raised this question in *Frontier in Latin American History*, 16.

6. Hispano, *De París al Amazonas*, 251; Orton, *Andes and the Amazon*, 195.

7. Hemming, *Amazon Frontier*, 144.

8. Domínguez and Gómez, *Economía extractiva*, 123.

9. San Román, *Perfiles históricos*, 138.

10. Bunker, *Underdeveloping the Amazon*, 12.

11. Ibid., 21.

12. Ribeiro, *Os índios,* 22.

13. Susan M. Deeds has suggested that scholars of the U.S./Mexican borderlands address such questions by using an ethnohistorical approach ("New Spain's Far North," 226–35).

14. GBFO, *Correspondence Respecting the Treatment of British Colonial Subjects,* 11.

15. Hemming, *Amazon Frontier,* 301.

16. Pineda Camacho, *Historia oral,* 17–18, 40.

17. Ibid., 62–63, 101–2; Guzmán G., "Los andokes," 69.

18. Guyot, "La maison des Indians Bora et Miraña," *Journal de la Société des Americanistes* 66 (1972): 157–58, cited by Pineda Camacho, *Historia oral,* 63–64.

19. Hemming, *Amazon Frontier,* 301; Domínguez, *Amazonía Colombiana,* 125–29; Taussig, *Shamanism,* 61.

20. Pineda Camacho, *Historia oral,* 40, 67.

21. Ibid., 41, 69–70.

22. Ibid., 78–82; in his fascinating book *The Highest Altar: Unveiling the Mystery of Human Sacrifice,* Patrick Tierney presents evidence that the practice of physically sacrificing "orphans" to ensure the survival and prosperity of a people continues to the present day in Chile, Bolivia, and Peru(see 108–9, 133–34, 173).

23. Pineda Camacho, *Historia oral,* 77, 103.

24. Agassiz and Agassiz, *Journey in Brazil,* 226.

25. Ibid., 193.

26. Hemming, *Amazon Frontier,* 264.

27. San Román, *Perfiles históricos,* 104–5.

28. Santos, *História econômica,* 97–110; Hennessy, *Frontier in Latin American History,* 111; Loureiro, *Amazônia,* 167.

29. Santos, *História econômica,* 156–60; Weinstein, *Amazon Rubber Boom,* 11–12; Bunker, *Underdeveloping the Amazon,* 67–70.

30. Dean, *Brazil and the Struggle for Rubber,* 40; Bunker, *Underdeveloping the Amazon,* 66–68.

31. San Román, *Perfiles históricos,* 149.

32. Taussig, *Shamanism,* 69; Orlando Patterson argues that debt servitude approximated the control masters wielded over slaves, except that debt status was usually not carried on to the next generation. But in Amazonia and other areas of Latin America, debt could be passed down through the family. See Patterson, *Slavery and Social Death,* 9, 124–26.

33. Furneaux, *The Amazon,* 150, 158.

34. Manuel Lerda, Gobernación de la Provincia Oriental, to Min. de Estado, 16 Aug. 1854, ANH(Q), Min. del Int., caja 7.

35. Various, AGN(L), 1870 O.L. 503/1569.

36. "Decreto de trabajo personal por el prefecto del territorio del Caquetá, Maximiliano Díaz Erazo," 25 Apr. 1872, UC-CIH(P), 1872/116/26.

37. Andrade Marín, Gobernación de la Provincia de Oriente, to Min. de Estado, 18 Jan. 1885, ANH(Q), Min. del Int., Oriente (1885–98).

38. Ibid., 27 June 1885.

39. "Informe del Gobernador de Oriente, Andrade Marín," 27 June 1885, ANH(Q), Min. del Int., Oriente (1885–98).

40. Juan Mosquera, Gobernación de la Provincia de Oriente, to Min. de Estado, 16 July

1891; Vidal Falconí Robalino, Gobernación Accidente de la Provincia Oriental, to Min. de Estado, 19 Dec. 1892; ANH(Q), Min. del Int., Oriente (1885–98).

41. *Registro Oficial del Departamento de Loreto,* vol. 1, no. 18, 31 Aug. 1888, AGN(L), O.L. 577/1468.

42. "Artículo 56: Ningún operario podrá abandonar su establecimiento sin haber pagado antes con trabajo ó en dinero, el saldo que resulte en su contra." For a transcript of this law see Peru, Min. de Fomento, *Leyes,* 136–47.

43. For a contemporary opinion of debt-peonage, see the testimony of C. Reginald Enock in Great Britain, House of Commons (GBHC), Select Committee on Putumayo, *Report and Special Report,* 447; for the enganche system in Peru and how it related to the Putumayo, see Davies, *Indian Integration in Peru,* 54–58.

44. Martín Restrepo Luján, Sec. de Instrucción Pública, to Min. de Gobierno, 31 Dec. 1895, ANC(B), Gobernaciones, Cauca, vol. 13, fols. 539–40.

45. GBHC, Select Committee on Putumayo, *Report and Special Report,* xxxi.

46. Collier, *River That God Forgot,* 62.

47. Rey de Castro, *Pobladores del Putumayo,* 6, 33, 38.

48. Reyes, *Memorias,* 126.

49. Up de Graff, *Head Hunters,* 43, 46, 92–94.

50. Lange, *In the Amazon Jungle,* xiii.

51. Ibid., 344, 371–88.

52. Ibid., 346–49.

53. Métraux, "Warfare," 404.

54. Steward, "The Witotoan Tribes," 756.

55. Pineda Camacho, *Historia oral,* 69–71.

56. Whiffen, *North-West Amazons,* vii.

57. Ibid., 120–23.

58. Robuchon, *En el Putumayo,* v, 39.

59. Ibid., 44–45, 57–65.

60. Rey de Castro wrote the introduction to Robuchon's book and highlighted the achievements of the Casa Arana in the Putumayo and its service to the nation (see v–viii).

61. It seems reasonable when approaching emotional and controversial topics that historians insist that hearsay, politically inspired allegations, and fear not suffice as a burden of proof.

62. Grubb, *Lowland Indians of Amazonia,* 136; "Decreto de la República del Ecuador" (n.d.), ABFL(Q), Senado 1892, legajo 3, doc. 59.

63. Kaplan, "Images of Cannibalism."

64. Ribeiro, *Os índios,* 23–25; San Román, *Perfiles históricos,* 147; Domínguez, *Amazonía Colombiana,* 150.

65. "Declaración de José Antonio Ordoñez to el Prefecto del Caquetá, Lope Restrepo," 24 Sept. 1870, UC-CIH(P), 1870/108/42.

66. Morrison, Brown, and Rose, *Lizzie,* 71–72.

67. Presbítero Santiago Santacruz to W. Ruiz Salgar, Pref. del Caquetá, Aug. 1874, UC-CIH(P), 1874/127/29.

68. Guyot, "El relato de O'ioi," 5.

69. Hemming, *Amazon Frontier,* 246–53; Ribeiro, *Os índios,* 27–28.

70. Malasén to Palacios, 3 Jan. 1890 (Leticia); Palacios to Dir. Gen. de Gobierno,

18 Jan. 1890 (Yquitos); Note from Enrique Benites, 2 Apr. 1890 (Lima); AGN(L), Min. del Int. 1890/15.

71. Becerra to Pref. de la Provincia, Caro Jordán, 14 July 1896, UC-CIH(P), 1896/233/56.

72. Antonio Llori to Min. de Estado, 8 Mar. 1887, ANH(Q), Min. del Int., Oriente (1885–98).

73. Juan Elías Albán, Jefatura Política de la Provincia de Oriente, to Min. de Estado, 28 Aug. 1893, ANH(Q), Min. del Int., Oriente (1885–98).

74. Emilio Sandoval, Gobernación del Districto de Chazuta, to Gobernador del Districto del Cercado, 15 July 1893; Alejandro Rivera, Pref. de Loreto, to Dir. Gen. de Gobierno, 2 Aug. 1893; AGN(L), Min. del Int., 1893/33 (Loreto).

75. "Instrucciones del prefecto Alej. Rivera to Sargento Mayor Pedro Ygnacio Rossell," 10 Aug. 1893; Rivera to Dir. Gen. de Gobierno, 20 Aug. 1893; AGN(L), Min. del Int., 1893/33 (Loreto).

76. Alej. Rivera to Dir. Gen. de Gobierno, 17 Aug. 1893, AGN(L), Min. del Int., 1893/33 (Loreto).

77. Rapoport, *Fights, Games, and Debates* (Ann Arbor: University of Michigan Press, 1960), 62–71, cited by Patterson, *Slavery and Social Death*, 334–36.

78. Patterson, *Slavery and Social Death*, 1–11, 79.

79. Ibid., quote appears on 44; for more information on social death and natal alienation, see 38–39, 46, 337.

80. Ibid., 105, 132.

81. Although Patterson does qualify in-situ slavery as "unsuccessful," he notes that its long-term consequences were usually disastrous (see 111–13).

82. Patterson, *Slavery and Social Death*, 190–193; Hennessy, *Frontier in Latin American History*, 71.

83. Hemming, *Amazon Frontier*, 305.

CHAPTER 4

1. William Sherman has referred to the "colonial hangover" and Charles Gibson to the "living museum" upon reflection on the colonial legacy in Latin America.

2. Bákula, "Relaciones del Perú," 13–14.

3. Pennano, *Economía del caucho*, 215.

4. Loureiro, *Amazônia*, 157–59.

5. Rumrrill, *Yurimaguas*, 191.

6. Aguila to Dir. de Contabilidad, 25 Feb. 1867, AGN(L), 1867 O.L. 481/372.

7. "Instrucciones para el Coronel d. Lino Olario," 4 Nov. 1868, AGN(L), 1869 O.L. 496/1129.

8. Aguila to Dir. de Contabilidad, 19 Jan. 1868, AGN(L), 1868 O.L. 489/733; J. Alzamora to Pref. de Loreto, 21 Mar. 1868, O.L. 489/737.

9. "Comerciantes de la plaza de Yquitos al prefecto del departamento," 27 Sept. 1869, AGN(L), 1869 O.L. 496/1128.

10. Lino Olario to Min. de Estado, 8 Feb. 1870, AGN(L), 1870 O.L. 501/1759.

11. Allende to Min. de Hacienda, 30 Sept. 1871, AGN(L), 1871 O.L. 505/1324.

12. For transcripts of these treaties and the replies to Colombian and Ecuadorian protests to these agreements, see Larrabure i Correa, *Colección de leyes,* 1:80–94.

13. AGN(L), 1872 O.L. 509/579, passim.

14. Vargas to Cajero Fiscal del Dept., 23 May 1873, AGN(L), 1873 O.L. 516/1480.

15. Alvarado to Min. de Estado, 7 Apr. 1872, AGN(L), 1872 O.L. 509/983.

16. Ríos to Min. de Gobierno, 26 July 1874, AGN(L), 1874 O.L. 518/1500; Ríos to Dirección de Policía, 16 Jan. 1875, 1875 O.L. 522/805; Ríos to Gen. Min. de Guerra y Marina, 24 Mar. 1875, 1875 O.L. 522/814.

17. Pike, *Modern History of Peru,* 150.

18. Stanfield, "Rubber Collection," 35.

19. See the final sections of chapter 2 to review the situation in Loreto during the 1880s.

20. J. Laura to Dir. de Adminstración, 17 May 1876, AGN(L), 1876 O.L. 526/404.

21. Pinedo to Oficial Mayor del Min. de Hacienda, 17 Jan., 11 Mar. 1884, AGN(L), 1884 O.L. 556/228.

22. Smith to Min. de Estado, 3 Apr. 1886, AGN(L), 1886 O.L. 565/699.

23. Reyes Guerra to Dir. Gen., 7 Feb., 6 Oct., 10 Nov. 1891, AGN(L), 1891 O.L. 595/1108; Reyes to Dir. Gen., 28 Jan. 1892, 1892 O.L. 601/514; 1892 O.L. 601/602a, passim.

24. Jose Bgo. Samañez Ocampo to Dir. de Hacienda, 14 May 1887, AGN(L), 1887 O.L. 571/990.

25. "Copia de la ley de 4 de noviembre de 1887," AGN(L), O.L. 609/1070; O.L. 628/783, passim.

26. "Pagos hechos con cargo de reintegro por la adminstración de Yquitos," 23 Oct. 1891, AGN(L), 1891 O.L. 595/1137; *Registro oficial del departamento fluvial de Loreto,* vol. 1, no. 18, 31 Aug. 1888, O.L. 577/1468. For more information on Basagoitia's labor decree, see chapter 3.

27. Silva to Pref., 16 July 1888, AGN(L), 1888 O.L. 577/1460; Basagoitia to Dir. Gen. de Gobierno, 31 May 1889, 1889 O.L. 583/1062.

28. Fajardo to Dir. Gen. de Gobierno, 31 May 1889, AGN(L), 1889 O.L. 583/1046.

29. Basagoitia to Dir. Gen. de Gobierno, 31 Dec. 1889; Palacios to same, 30 Apr. 1890; AGN(L), Min. del Int., 1889/9.

30. Palacios to Dir. de Policía, 15 Oct. 1889, AGN(L), Min. del Int., 1889/9; Palacios to Dir. Gen. de Gobierno, 26 Oct. 1889, 1889 O.L. 583/1068; Larrabure i Correa, *Colección de leyes,* 2:104–5.

31. Palacios to Administrador de la Aduana Departamental, 15 Nov. 1889, AGN(L), 1890 O.L. 589/860.

32. Palacios to Dir. Gen. de Gobierno, 28 Nov. 1889, AGN(L), Min. del Int., 1889/9.

33. Ibid., 17 Dec. 1889; Palacios to Dir. de Hacienda, 26 Mar. 1890, 1890 O.L. 589/851.

34. Palacios to Dir. Gen. de Gobierno, 3 Mar., 6 Nov. 1890, AGN(L), Min. del Int., 1890/15.

35. Rivera to Gobierno, 20 Feb. 1893, AGN(L), Min. del Int., 1893/33; Rivera to Dir. de Policía, 5 Sept. 1893, 1893/33.

36. Ydiaguez to Dir. Gen. de Hacienda, 15 Nov. 1893, AGN(L), 1893 O.L. 609/1794.

37. Rivera to Dir. Gen. de Hacienda, 24 Nov. 1894, AGN(L), 1894 O.L. 613/303.

38. Jane Rausch has suggested that the Colombian llanos shared more similarities with

the Ecuadorian, Peruvian, and Bolivian Amazonian frontiers than it did with the Venezuelan llanos. The Venezuelan plains were more geographically and administratively accessible than the Colombian llanos or Amazonian regions like the Putumayo(see *Tropical Plains Frontier,* 245).

39. Gasché, "Ocupación territorial," 15; Hispano, *De París al Amazonas,* 250.
40. "Declaración de José Antonio Ordoñez to Pref. del Caquetá, Lope Restrepo," 24 Sept. 1870, UC-CIH(P), 1870/108/42.
41. "Decreto del Prefecto Pedro F. Urrutia," 31 Jan. 1868, UC-CIH(P), 1868/99/22.
42. Urrutia to Sec. de Estado, 20 Mar. 1869, UC-CIH(P), 1869/103/38.
43. Ibid., 21 Sept. 1869.
44. Díaz Erazo to Sec. de Estado, 30 Jan. 1872, UC-CIH(P), 1872/116/26.
45. W. Ruiz Salgar to Sec. de Gobierno, 30 July 1874, UC-CIH(P), 1874/127/29.
46. Santacruz to Pref. del Caquetá, Aug. 1874, UC-CIH(P), 1874/127/29.
47. Montero to Pref., 10 Mar. 1876, ANC(B), Gobernaciones-Várias, vol. 24, fols. 274–75.
48. Barreiro to Sec. de Gobierno, 11 May 1878, UC-CIH(P), 1878/141/2.
49. Ibid., 29 July 1878; "Relación de los pagos definitivos hechos por la administración municipal de hacienda de Pasto en el mes de enero de 1880," 1880/154/70.
50. "Relación de pagos hechos por la administración municipal de Hacienda de Pasto durante el mes de noviembre del año de 1881"; Correspondencia consular de Cauca, Panamá, y Magdalena, fols. 548–48v, ANC(B); Aduana — Aduana de Buenaventura y Mocoa, fol. 672, ANC(B).
51. Aduana — Aduana de Buenaventura y Mocoa, fols. 801, 805a–8a, ANC(B).
52. Quijano to Sec. de Gobierno, 27 Sept., 4 Oct. 1882, UC-CIH(P), 1882/160/16.
53. Urrutia to Sec. del Tribunal Superior, 22 Oct. 1888, ANC(B), Min. de Gob. 1a, vol. 15, fols. 212–13; "Decreto 121," Gobernaciones, Cauca, 27 Jan. 1888, vol. 13, fol. 82; "Decreto de Pedro F. Urrutia," 20 Jan. 1889, Gobernaciones, Cauca, vol. 12, fols. 43–44.
54. Sanclemente to Min. de Gobierno, 20 May 1891, ANC(B), Gobernaciones, Cauca, vol. 12, fol. 647.
55. Gaitán to Antonio Roldán, 12 Sept. 1891, ANC(B), Min. de Industrias, Baldíos, vol. 12, fol. 186.
56. Suárez to Gov. de Cauca, 22 June 1891, UC-CIH(P), 1891/196/32.
57. Mosquera to Min. de Estado, 26 June, 21 Aug. 1891, ANH(Q), Min. del Int., Oriente (1885–98); Mosquera to Min. de Estado, 2 May, 1 June 1892 (1854–1905).
58. UC-CIH(P), 1892/199/35, passim.
59. Caro Jordán to Sec. de Gobierno, 12 Oct. 1893, ANC(B), Min. de Industrias, Baldíos, vol. 14, fols. 82–83; Angulo to Min. de Hacienda, 20 Apr. 1894, vol. 15, fol. 143; Jordán to Sec. de Gobierno, 9 June 1894, UC-CIH(P), 1894/215/80.
60. Bákula, *Política internacional,* 61 n. 52.
61. Ibid., 40; San Román, *Perfiles históricos,* 181.
62. Rodríguez, *Search for Public Policy,* 34–37; San Román, *Perfiles históricos,* 181–82.
63. Rodríguez to Min. de Estado, 25 June, 16 Aug. 1857, ANH(Q), Min. del Int., Oriente (1854–1905).
64. Rodríguez to Min. de Estado, 16 Aug. 1857, ANH(Q), Min. del Int., Oriente (1854–1905).

65. Before the interruption of the archival record in late 1862, one can discern this reality in Cárdenas to Trujillo, 2 Nov. 1861; and Cárdenas to Min. de Estado, 8 Aug. 1862; ANH(Q), Min. del Int., Oriente (1854–1905).

66. Chiriboga, "Auge y crisis," 73.

67. Biddle to Fish, 18 Mar. 1875, USDS, NA, T-50 r. 3.

68. Orton, *Andes and the Amazon,* 191–92.

69. Cosme Quesada to Min. General, 28 Dec. 1877, ANH(Q), Min. del Int., Oriente (1854–1905).

70. Ibid., 28 Jan. 1878.

71. De la Guerra to Min. en el Despacho del Interior, 11 Feb., 9 May 1878, ANH(Q), Min. del Int., Oriente (1854–1905).

72. One could presume that de la Guerra had some successful business dealing in the Oriente and that he might have paid for his title. See de la Guerra to Min. en el Despacho del Interior, 3 Sept. 1878, 10 Feb. 1879, ANH(Q), Min. del Int., Oriente (1854–1905).

73. Ibid., 11 Apr., 22 Apr., and 29 May 1879.

74. Ayala Mora, *Lucha política,* 185–90.

75. Ecuador, *Informe del Ministrio de lo Interior, 1886,* 22, BGMRE(Q).

76. Vickers, "Indian Policy," 9–19; on the contemporary politics of savages and *aucas,* see Kane, *Savages.*

77. Ecuador, *Informe del gobernador de la provincia de Oriente,* BE(C); Ecuador, *Informe del Min. de lo Interior, 1885,* 10, BGMRE(Q).

78. Andrade Marín to Min. de Estado, 11 Oct., 8 Dec. 1884, 27 June 1885, ANH(Q), Min. del Int., Oriente (1885–98).

79. Juan Rodas to Antonio Llori, 16 Oct. 1886; B. Orellana to Muy Señor Mio, 14 Aug. 1887; ANH(Q), Min. del Int., Oriente (1885–98).

80. AGN(L), O.L. 599/1, passim; Villavicencio to Min. del Estado, Jan.–Aug. 1889, passim, ANH(Q), Min. del Int., Oriente (1885–98).

81. "Varios artesanos desean establecer una colonia en el Oriente . . . ," [1890?], ABFL(Q), Senado 1890/8/48; Mosquera to Min. de Estado, 24 June 1890, ANH(Q), Min. del Int., Oriente (1885–98).

82. Mosquera to Min. de Estado, 15 Oct., 15 Nov. 1890, ANH(Q), Min. del Int., Oriente (1854–1905).

83. Min. de Gobierno 1a, vol. 42, fols. 882–84; Min. de Gobierno 1a, vol. 46, fols. 980–82; ANC(B).

84. Estupiñán to Min. de Estado, 28 Feb. 1890; Mosquera to Min. de Estado, 9 June, 24 June 1890; ANH(Q), Min. del Int., Oriente (1854–1905).

85. Mosquera to Min. de Estado, 23 May, 21 July, 29 July, 18 Aug., 15 Sept. 1890, ANH(Q), Min. del Int., Oriente (1854–1905).

86. Albán to Min. de Estado, 15 Jan. 1891; Mosquera to same, 3 July 1891; ANH(Q), Min. del Int., Oriente (1885–98); Mosquera to same, 1 Apr. 1892, (1854–1905).

87. Mosquera to Min. de Estado, 10 Mar., 17 May, 21 Aug. 1891, ANH(Q), Min. del Int., Oriente (1885–98); Mosquera to same, 21 Aug. 1891, 19 Feb., 30 June 1892, (1854–1905).

88. Alban to Min. de Estado, 15 Feb. 1891; Mosquera to Min. de Estado, 1 Mar. 1892; Pío Terán to Min. de Estado, 1 Aug. 1894; ANH(Q), Min. del Int., Oriente, (1854–1905); Mosquera to Min. de Estado, 29 Oct. 1891, (1885–98).

89. García, *Historia de las misiones,* 269–71; Mosquera to Min. de Estado, 1 Aug., 2 Sept., 5 Sept., 6 Sept. 1892; Borja to Min. de Estado, 14 Sept., 18 Sept., 4 Oct., 6 Oct., 17 Oct., 15 Nov. 1892; ANH(Q), Min. del Int., Oriente (1854–1905).

90. Llori to Min. de Estado, 16 Apr., 19 May, 28 Aug. 1893, ANH(Q), Min. de Estado, Oriente (1885–98).

91. Ibid., 19 May, 6 Sept., 12 Dec. 1893; Albán to Min. de Estado, 11 July 1893; ANH(Q), Min. de Estado, Oriente (1885–98).

92. Pío Terán to Min. de Estado, 18, 27 Mar. 1894, ANH(Q), Min. del Int., Oriente (1854–1905).

93. Among other pro-church measures in the 1869 Constitution, article 10 required all Ecuadorians to be Catholic. See Ayala Mora, *Lucha política,* 122–51; and García, *Historia de las misiones,* 257–64.

94. Zapata to Sec. de Gobierno, 10 Aug. 1870; Lope Restrepo to Sec. de Gobierno, 4 Nov. 1870; UC-CIH(P), 1870/108/42; García, *Historia de las misiones,* 257–60.

95. Santacruz to Pref. del Caquetá, 24 July 1872; Díaz Erazo to Sec. de Estado, 14 Aug. 1872; UC-CIH(P), 1872/116/26.

96. Barreiro to Sec. de Gobierno, 9 Feb. 1878, UC-CIH(P), 1878/141/2.

97. "Naturales i vecinos de los pueblos . . . al jefe municipal," 8 June 1878; "Cabildos de indígenas de Sibundoy, Santiago, San Andres de Putumayo to Señor prefecto de Caquetá," 22 July 1878; UC-CIH(P), 1878/141/2.

98. Ayala Mora, *Lucha política,* 166; García, *Historia de las misiones,* 264–65; Costales and Costales, *Amazonía,* 245; Wullweber to Secretary of State Fish, 18 Dec. 1875, USDS, NA, T-50 r. 14.

99. García, *Historia de las misiones,* 265; Ecuador, *Informe del Min. de lo Interior, 1885,* 9.

100. José Ignacio to Presidente del Senado, 10 July 1885, ABFL(Q), Senado (1885), Oficios de organizaciones varias; "Decreto apropado de la República del Ecuador, s.f.," Senado 1885/2/16.

101. Pierre, *Viaje de exploración,* 68, 74; "Decreto del Congreso de la República del Ecuador," 26 July 1888, ABFL(Q), Senado 1888/1/13.

102. Páez to Presidente del Senado, 5 July 1888, ABFL(Q), Senado 1888/4/42.

103. "Decreto del Congreso," 7 Aug. 1888, ABFL(Q), Senado 1888/1/50; "Decreto del Congreso," 8 Aug. 1890, 1890/1/19; "Comisiones unidas de negocios eclesiasticos to excmo. sr.," 22 July 1890, 1890/6b/57.

104. Estupiñán to Min. de Estado, 16 Apr. 1890, ANH(Q), Min. del Int., Oriente (1885–98); Tovía to Min. de Estado, 16 Apr. 1890; Mosquera to Señor Ministro, 23 May 1890; (1854–1905).

105. Mosquera to Min. de Estado, 15 Sept., 15 Oct., 15 Nov. 1890; Tovía to Min. de Estado, 27 July 1891; ANH(Q), Min. del Int., Oriente, (1854–1905).

106. Albán to Min. de Estado, 15 Jan. 1891, ANH(Q), Min. del Int., Oriente (1885–98); Tovía to Min. de Estado, 28 Mar., 1 Sept. 1892, (1854–1905).

107. Falconí Robalino to Min. del Interior, 29 Nov. 1892; Tovía to Min. de Estado, 12 July, 9 Sept. 1893; ANH(Q), Min. del Int., Oriente, (1854–1905).

108. Tovía to Presidente del Senado, 1 July 1892, ABFL(Q), Legislativa 1892/26/7b/57.

109. Tovía to Min. de Estado, 25 Nov. 1891, ANH(Q), Min. del Int., Oriente (1854–1905); "Informe de la comisión eclesiastica to excmo. señor, s.f.," ABFL(Q),

Senado 1892/5/26; Rivera to Dir. Gen. de Gobierno, 6 Mar., 13 Mar. 1893, AGN(L), Min. del Int., 1893/33 (Loreto).

110. Tovía to Min. de Estado, 1 Sept. 1893, 15 Mar., 21 Mar. 1894; Pío Terán to Min. de Estado, 22 Jan. 1894; ANH(Q), Min. del Int., Oriente (1854–1905); García, *Historia de las misiones,* 272.

CHAPTER 5

1. Pío Terán to Min.de Estado, 4 Mar., 28 Mar. 1895; Rojas to Min. de Estado, 28 Mar. 1895; ANH(Q), Min. del Int., Oriente (1854–1905).
2. Pío Terán to Min. de Estado, 23 May 1895; Luís Anda to Min. de Estado, 24, 25 May 1895; ANH(Q), Min. del Int., Oriente (1854–1905).
3. Martz, *Ecuador,* 63–67.
4. Pedro Rafael González y Calisto, "Novena carta pastoral, con motivo del radicalismo" (Quito: Imprenta del Clero, 1895), cited by Ayala Mora, *Lucha política,* 198.
5. Rodríguez, *Search for Public Policy,* 46–47.
6. García, *Historia de las misiones,* 272–74.
7. Sandoval to Min. de Estado, 10 May, 26 Aug. 1896, ANH(Q), Min. del Int., Oriente (1885–98).
8. Hurtado to Min. del Interior, 12 Mar., 29 Apr., 12 May, 30 May, 1 Sept., 21 Dec. 1898, ANH(Q), Min. del Int., Oriente (1885–98).
9. Ibid., 22 Dec. 1896; Ecuador, *Informe que el gobernador,* 1–13.
10. Hurtado to Min. del Interior, 3 Feb., 23 June, 10 Nov. 1898, ANH(Q), Min. del Int., Oriente (1885–98).
11. Ibid., 5 Sept. 1898.
12. Ibid., 16 July, 6 Aug., 1 Sept., 18 Nov. 1898; Ecuador, *Informe del Ministerio de Relaciones Exteriores,* 155–68.
13. Thorp and Bertram, *Peru, 1809–1977,* 40.
14. Alejandro Rivera to Dir. Gen. de Hacienda, 3 Mar. 1895, AGN(L), 1895 O.L. 619/501; Wesche and Cia. to Señor Especial Quirós, 27 Dec. 1897, 1897 O.L. 635/640; Quirós to Min. de Estado, 8 Feb. 1898, 1897 O.L. 635/640.
15. Emilio Viscarra to Min. de Hacienda, 8 Oct. 1896, AGN(L), 1896 O.L. 626/641.
16. Benigno Jimenes Pimental, Sec. Accidental, 10 Apr. 1901, AGN(L), Min. del Int. 1901/76.
17. García Rosell, *Conquista de la montaña,* 48–49; "Expedición a Loreto. . . . ," 4 Dec. 1896, AGN(L), 1896 O.L. 627/18; Romero, *Iquitos y la fuerza naval,* 79.
18. Juan Ibarra to Administrador de la Aduana, 1 Dec. 1896, AGN(L), 1896 O.L. 627/17; Pennano, *Economía del caucho,* 160–62.
19. Otoniel Melena to Pref. de Loreto, 17 May 1895, AGN(L), 1895 O.L. 619/504; Pinedo to Quirós, 18 Sept. 1897; Quirós to Min. de Estado, 19 Sept. 1897; 1897 O.L. 635/525; "Decreto del comisionado especial," 26 Oct. 1897, 1897 O.L. 635/529; Quirós to Min. de Hacienda, 8 Jan. 1898, 1898 O.L. 642/199.
20. Quirós to Min. de Estado, 9 Feb. 1898, AGN(L), 1898 O.L. 642/205.
21. "Decreto del comisionado especial," 6 Nov. 1987, AGN(L), 1897 O.L. 635/532;

Quirós to Dir. de Gobierno, 23 Mar. 1898, Min. del Int. 1898/54; "Decreto de Eloy G. Caballero," 5 Apr. 1898, 1898 O.L. 642/208; Quirós to Dir. de Admin., 4 May 1898, 1898 O.L. 640/252; "Expediente de la junta departamental," Apr. 1898, 1898 O.L. 642/422.

22. Quirós to Min. de Hacienda, 22 Jan. 1898, AGN(L), 1898 O.L. 642/204; Francisco Almenara Butler to Min. de Estado, 29 Nov. 1898, 1898 O.L. 649/164; Quirós to Min. de Estado, 1 Dec. 1898, 1898 O.L. 642/231.

23. Larrabure i Correa, *Colección de leyes,* 7:512–20.

24. Quintero to Sec. de Gobierno, 4 June 1895, UC-CIH(P), 1895/220/11; "Acuerdo 9 del concejo municipal de Mocoa," 29 Nov. 1895, 1895/221/58; "Acuerdo 14 del concejo municipal de Mocoa," 15 Feb. 1896, 1896/231/116.

25. Min. de Gobierno, vol. 13, fols. 260–60v, 305–7v, 943–954v; Díaz to Gobernación del Cauca, 25 Apr. 1899, Min. de Hacienda, vol. 436, fols. 824–26; ANC(B). Rogerio María Becerra to Pref. de la Provincia, 14 July 1896; Jordán to Sec. de Gobierno, 6 July 1896; UC-CIH(P), 1896/233/56.

26. Bergquist, *Coffee and Conflict,* 80–110; Domínguez and Gómez, *Economía extractiva,* 142, 177–83; LeGrand, *Frontier Expansion,* 20–22; S. Ortíz, "Colonization," 207–8; on the situation around Mocoa, see AH(P), PC (12), 5–8.

27. "Sesión extraordinaria del día 23 de mayo de 1899, Junta departamental de Loreto," AGN(L), 1899 O.L. 657/718; Teob González to Dir. de Hacienda, 4 Aug. 1900, 1900 O.L. 655/785; Sargento Mayor Fausto Narvarte, Consul General del Perú en el Pará, 12 Aug. 1899; Quirós to Min. de Estado, 22 Sept. 1899, Min. del Int., 1899/65.

28. J. Capelo to Min. de Hacienda, 14 Dec. 1899, AGN(L), 1899 O.L. 649/761.

29. "Decreto de J. Capelo," 30 Apr. 1900, AGN(L), 1900 O.L. 655/761; "Expediente relativo á presupuesto de la junta departamental para el año 1900," 23 Feb. 1900, 1900 O.L. 657/717.

30. Teob González to Dir. de Gobierno, 31 Aug. 1900; Enrique Benites to Dir. de Gobierno, 20 Nov. 1900; AGN(L), Min. del Int., 1900/68.

31. González to Dir. de Hacienda, 7 Nov. 1900, AGN(L), 1900 O.L. 655/774–75; Larrabure i Correa, *Colección de leyes,* 1:304, 358, 496; 14:352, 410.

32. Capelo to Min. de Hacienda, 27 Jan. 1900, AGN(L), 1900 O.L. 657/397; Bueno to Min. de Hacienda, 15 Mar. 1900, 1900 O.L. 649/179; Portillo to Dir. de Admin., 3 Sept. 1901, 1901 O.L. 662/658; González to Dir. de Gobierno, 28 Dec. 1900, Min. del Int., 1901/76.

33. Obviously, such an equal currency exchange would also benefit the economy of Iquitos; see "Informe del prefecto Pedro Portillo," 21 June 1901, AGN(L), 1901 O.L. 664/799; Portillo to Dir. de Gobierno, 17 Aug. 1901, 1901 O.L. 662/654; "Representación de los vecinos de Iquitos al señor prefecto departamental," 26 Sept. 1901; "Resolución de Portillo," 30 Sept. 1901; 1901 O.L. 662/664.

34. Ramírez del Villar to Dir. de Admin., 1 Nov. 1901, AGN(L), 1901 O.L. 662/672; see Portillo's version of his adventures in *Acontecimientos,* 5–27.

35. Portillo, *Acontecimientos,* 27.

36. For a few examples of foreign ministry orders for Portillo to cool it, see *Acontecimientos,* 9–20.

37. Portillo to Oficial Mayor de Relaciones Exteriores, 22 Sept. 1902, AGN(L), 1902

O.L. 669/291; Portillo to same, 18 Dec. 1902, 1902 O.L. 669/303; Muñoz to Min. de Estado, 14 Sept. 1903, Min. del Int., 1903/91; "Gastos de la prefectura de Loreto," 10 Aug. 1903, Min. del Int., 1904/97.

38. Portillo to Dir. de Gobierno, 10 July 1903, AGN(L), Min. del Int., 1903/91; Portillo to Dir. de Gobierno, 13 Aug. 1904, 1904/97; for information on the Peruvian push into the Juruá and Purús, see Portillo to Dir. de Admin., 26 Nov. 1903, 1903 O.L. 676/219; Talledo to Subpref., 22 Dec. 1902, Min. del Int., 1903/91; Portillo to Dir. de Gobierno, 5 Feb. 1904, 1904/97.

39. Ayala Mora, *Nueva historia,* 129–31.

40. Ecuador, *Informe del Ministerio de Relaciones Exteriores,* 5:155–56; "Convenio al servicio," 23 Jan. 1900, AGN(L), 1900 O.L. 657/395.

41. "Criminal contra le sr. Enrique Trajano Hurtado," 1900, ANH(Q), Criminales 354.

42. Ecuador, "Provincia de Oriente," *Informe del Min. de Relaciones Exteriores.*

43. Larrabure i Correa, *Colección de leyes,* 17:502–33; 7:596–601.

44. Ibid., 9:215–28, 259–65; Rumrrill, *Yurimaguas,* 101.

45. Portillo, *Acontecimientos,* 7–20; Villanueva to Portillo, 3 Aug. 1903, AGN(L), Min. del Int., 1904/97; Portillo to Dir. de Gobierno, 22 May 1903; Portillo to Detrano, 22 July 1904; 1904 O.L. 683/234.

46. Ecuador, *Proyecto de ley,* 7–45.

47. "Decreto 18," 6 Oct. 1899; Oveido to Sec. de Gobierno, 15 June, 21 July 1902; UC-CIH(P), 1902/311/57.

48. Calderón et al. to Pref. del Caquetá, 22 May 1902; Oveido to Sec. de Gobierno, 3 Oct. 1902; UC-CIH(P), 1902/311/57. Navarrete et al. to Gen. Reyes, 22 Aug. 1904, AC(B), Fondos básicos, Informes de comisiones, Senado 1904, vol. 3, fols. 131–33.

49. Oveido to Sec. de Gobierno, 19 July 1902, UC-CIH(P), 1902/311/57.

50. Larrabure i Correa, *Colección de leyes,* 17:514–25; Portillo, *Acontecimientos,* 26.

51. Valcárcel, *Proceso del Putumayo,* 30–31, 205–14; Portillo, *Acontecimientos,* 26–27.

52. Sampson to Hay, 10 Mar. 1904, USDS, NA, T-50 r. 19.

53. De la Flor Fernández, "Economía de exportación," 43–44.

54. Arana, *Cuestiones del Putumayo,* 8.

55. Portillo to Dir. de Admin., 15 July 1902, AGN(L), 1902 O.L. 669/286; Arana to Subprefecto, 10 Nov. 1902, Min. del Int., 1903/91; Arana, *Cuestiones del Putumayo,* 7.

56. Arana, *Cuestiones del Putumayo,* 9, 14, 37; see also Pennano, *Economía del caucho,* 163; De la Flor Fernández, "Economía de exportación," 46–48.

57. De la Flor Fernández, "Economía de exportación," 71, 83, 137–38, 141.

58. Haring, "Burguesia regional," 70; García Rosell, *Conquista de la montaña,* 52–53; De la Flor Fernández, "Economía de exportación," 73–75, 81; "Aduana fluvial de Yquitos," AGN(L), H-4.

59. Pike, *Modern History of Peru,* 183–85; Karno, "Julio Cesar Arana," 90–92; De la Flor Fernández, "Economía de exportación," 44–45.

60. Chirif, "Colonialismo interno," 57; Stocks, "Indian Policy," 44–45.

61. Haring, "Burguesia regional," 71.

62. De la Flor Fernández, "Economía de exportación," 5, 111.

63. Collier, *River That God Forgot,* 53–61; Domínguez and Gómez, *Economía extractiva,* 185–92.

64. Morrison, Brown, and Rose, *Lizzie,* 95–96.

65. De la Flor Fernández, "Economía de exportación," 78–80; Weinstein, *Amazon Rubber Boom,* 185–89.

66. For a short discussion of the introduction of new moral codes in a different setting, see Montejano, "Is Texas Bigger," 622.

67. Robuchon, *En el Putumayo,* 18, 53.

68. Guyot, "El relato de O'ioi," 6.

69. Hemming, *Red Gold,* 142–47; *Amazon Frontier,* 281–91.

70. Hemming, *Amazon Frontier,* 361; Pineda Camacho, *Historia oral,* 90–94.

71. Bonilla, *Gran Bretaña y el Perú,* 198.

72. Raygado to Dir. de Admin., 13 Oct. 1904, AGN(L), 1904 O.L. 683/240; "Proyecto de presupuesto," 26 June 1905, 1905 O.L. 690/232; Fuentes to Dir. de Admin., 6 July 1905, 1905 O.L. 690/233; Raygado to Pref., 4 May 1905, Min. del Int., 1905/103.

73. Larrabure i Correa, *Colección de leyes,* 14:29–32; Costales and Costales, *Amazonía,* 248.

74. Larrabure i Correa, *Colección de leyes,* 7:637–77.

75. In 1905, the Putumayo shipped rubber worth 62,678 Peruvian pounds to Iquitos but only imported supplies and food worth 9,709 Peruvian pounds. Profits must indeed have been high for J. C. Arana; see Larrabure i Correa, *Colección de leyes,* 16:62a–62b.

76. Woodroffe, *Upper Reaches,* 29–35; San Román, *Perfiles históricos,* 138–39.

77. "Memorándum para el Min. de Gobierno," 21 Jan. 1905, ANC(B), Min. de Gob., vol. 11, fols. 670–71; "Decreto 457," vol. 59, fol. 900; Gálvez to Min. de Gobierno, 12 Oct. 1905, vol. 604, fols. 512–13v; "Documentos comprobantes del presupuesto . . . de 1905," vol. 604, fols. 557–67v; "Decreto 42," 25 Nov. 1905, vol. 604, fols. 608–12; Becerra to Min. de Gobierno, 24 Jan. 1906, vol. 502, fols. 11–25.

78. Caicedo to Min. de Gobierno, 11 Mar. 1906, ANC(B), Min. de Gob., vol. 499, fol. 162; Caicedo to Min. de Gobierno, 27 June 1905, vol. 604, fol. 446; Rafael Puyo to Min. de Gobierno, 13 July 1905, vol. 604, fol. 443.

79. Uribe Uribe to Min. de Relaciones Exteriores, 12 June 1905, ANC(B), Min. de Hacienda, vol. 459, fol. 583–94; Uribe Uribe to Vásquez Cobo, 3 Dec. 1906, AC(B), Fondos básicos, Informes de comisiones, Cámara 1911, vol. 8, fols. 262–65.

80. Julian Bucheli to Min. de Guerra, 25 May 1906, ANC(B), Min. de Gob., 1a, vol. 518, fols. 376–79; "Sueldos, alimentación, gastos de la colonia penal de Mocoa en mayo á julio de 1906," vol. 537, fols. 564–76.

81. Becerra to Min. de Gobierno, 16 Sept. 1905, ANC(B), Min. de Gob., vol. 68, fols. 619–19v; for the Mocoa office inventory, see AH(P), G-C (13), 1–9, 1–13.

82. Becerra to Reyes, 24 Aug. 1905, ANC(B), Min. de Gob., vol. 11, fols. 578–80v; "Memorándum presidencial para el señor ministro de gobierno," 1 June 1905, fols. 682–83v.

83. Lezana B. to Presidente, 27 June 1906, ANC(B), Min. de Industrias, Baldíos, vol. 25, fols. 454–54v; Mejía to Reyes, 5 Mar. 1906, fols. 512–13.

84. Camacho to Min. de Gobierno, 20 Aug. 1905, ANC(B), Min. de Gob., vol. 59, fols.

903–5,; Velasco to Min. de Gobierno, 15 Nov. 1905, vol. 604, fols. 472–76; Jordán to Min. de Gobierno, 7 Dec. 1905, fols. 517–18v.

85. Becerra to Min. de Gobierno, 8 Aug. 1905, ANC(B), Min. de Gob., vol. 68, fols. 610–11; Gálvez to Min. de Gobierno, 2 Sept. 1905, fols. 613–15v; "Decreto 26," 12 Sept. 1905, vol. 604, fols. 543–61; "Decreto 6," 29 July 1905, fols. 578–82; Reyes to Mins. de Gobierno, Relaciones Exteriores, Guerra, Hacienda, Tesoro, 17 Oct. 1905, vol. 11, fols. 620–21.

86. Velasco to Min. de Gobierno, 18 Oct. 1905, ANC(B), Min. de Gob., vol. 59; "Reglamento interno," 20 Nov. 1905, vol. 604, fols. 487–89; Jordán to Min. de Gobierno, 7 Dec., 31 Dec. 1905, fols. 507–11.

87. Caicedo to Min. de Gobierno, 11 May 1906, ANC(B), Min. de Gob., vol. 502, fols. 6–7.

88. Becerra to Min. de Gobierno, 21 Dec. 1905, 17 Jan. 1906, ANC(B), Min. de Gob., vol. 68.

89. Becerra to Min. de Gobierno, 24 Jan. 1906, ANC(B), Min. de Gob., vol. 502, fols. 11–25.

90. Velasco to Reyes, n.d., ANC(B), Min. de Gob., vol. 604, fols. 490–93v.

91. Rey de Castro, *Pobladores del Putumayo,* 66a.

92. The literature on the 1905 modus vivendi is extensive. For starters, see Arana, *Cuestiones del Putumayo,* fols. 3, 33; Colombia, *Soberanía de Colombia,* 44–46; Hispano, *De París al Amazonas,* 234–35; Larrabure i Correa, *Colección de leyes,* 7:224–26; San Román, *Perfiles históricos,* 183–84.

93. Vásquez Cobo to Min. de Gobierno, 25 Feb. 1907, ANC(B), Min. de Gob., 1a, vol. 592, fol. 501; "Memorándum reservado, n.d.," AC(B), Leyes autografas de 1907, fols. 135–40.

94. Uribe Uribe to Vásquez Cobo, 3 Dec. 1906, AC(B), Fondos básicos, Informes de comisiones, Cámara 1911, vol. 8, fols. 262–65.

95. Arana, *Cuestiones del Putumayo,* 21–22; Hispano, *De París al Amazonas,* 237; San Román, *Perfiles históricos,* 183–84.

96. For more specific information on these border conflicts, see Ireland, *Boundaries,* 180–90; Wood, *Aggression and History,* 41–50; Bákula, *Política internacional,* 41–63, 87–106; San Román, *Perfiles históricos,* 181–84.

CHAPTER 6

1. For a spirited debate on this question, see Stern, "Feudalism," 829–72; and Wallerstein, "AHR Forum," 873–85.

2. Pennano, *Economía del caucho,* 92–95.

3. Ibid., 113.

4. "Informe del consul de Iquitos Sr. Adamson, correspondiente al año 1898," in Bonilla, *Gran Bretaña y el Perú,* 3:194.

5. Lange, *In the Amazon Jungle,* 59–60, 110.

6. "Informe sobre el intercambio comercial de Iquitos para el año 1904, por el vicecónsul Sr. Cazes," in Bonilla, *Gran Bretaña y el Perú,* 3:205.

7. Rodríguez, *Search for Public Policy,* 17–19.

8. Mahany to Greshaw, 29 Apr. 1893, USDS, NA, T-50 r. 4; Sampson to Hay, 26 Apr.

1901, r. 17; Sampson to Hay, 1 May 1900, r. 17; Sampson to Hay, 15 Dec. 1903, r. 18; Sampson to Hay, 30 Apr. 1904, r. 19; Lee to Root, 23 Feb., 28 Feb. 1906, r. 19; 1905 telegrams, passim, ANH(Q), Min. del Int., Oriente (1854–1905).

9. Chavarría, *José Carlos Mariátegui,* 13–15; for an intimate and entertaining business history of the Grace Company, see Clayton, *Grace.*

10. Agassiz and Agassiz, *Journey in Brazil,* 247.

11. For an intriguing analysis of civilization and nature in both U.S. and Latin American societies, see Pike, *United States and Latin America.*

12. LeGrand, *Frontier Expansion,* 12.

13. Larrabure i Correa, *Colección de leyes,* 6:200–68.

14. Lerda to Min. del Interior, 2 Mar., 3 July 1854, 26 Jan. 1856, ANH(Q), Min. del Int., Oriente (1854–1905); "Decreto del Congreso," 2 Oct. 1903, ABFL(Q), Diputados 1903, caja 35, Proyectos aprobados en ambas cámaras; Lee to Root, 20 June 1906, USDS, NA, T-50 r. 19; Sáenz, "Establecimiento de colonias."

15. Lange, *In the Amazon Jungle,* 338–89.

16. Up de Graff, *Head Hunters,* 43–148, 225–315, passim.

17. Morrison, Brown, and Rose, *Lizzie,* 46.

18. Ibid., 75, 52.

19. Ibid., 137–41.

20. Greenfield, "Barbadians," 46–53.

21. GBFO, *Correspondence Respecting the Treatment of British Colonial Subjects,* 21, 55–139 passim.

22. Ibid., 7–8, 17, 84, 106.

23. Ibid., 104–27.

24. Weinstein, *Amazon Rubber Boom,* 145–79; U.S. Department of Commerce, *Rubber Statistics,* 5.

25. Larrabure i Correa, *Colección de leyes,* 5:381–84.

26. Morrison, Brown, Rose, *Lizzie,* 141–42.

27. Flores Marín, *La Explotación,* 75–76.

28. Karno, "Julio César Arana," 90–91.

29. Robuchon, *En el Putumayo,* vi–vii, 93–96.

30. Karno, "Julio César Arana," 91; De la Flor Fernández, "Economía de exportación," 54.

31. Collier, *River That God Forgot,* 60–63; De la Flor Fernández, "Economía de exportación," 73.

32. Karno, "Julio César Arana," 91.

33. De la Flor Fernandez, "Economía de exportación," 53–54; Collier, *River That God Forgot,* 61–62.

34. Bákula, *Política internacional,* 61 n. 54.

35. For various interpretations of how international systems shaped Amazonia and the developing world, see San Román, *Perfiles históricos,* 124; Chirif, "Colonialismo interno," 53: Domínguez and Gómez, *Economía extractiva,* 10–11, 227–29; Pennano, *Economía del caucho,* 23–43; De la Flor Fernández, "Economía de exportación," 70, 96–99; Bunker, *Underdeveloping the Amazon,* 12–16, 22; Wallerstein, *Capitalist Agriculture,* 27, 38; Gasché," Comunidades nativas," 28–29; Weinstein, *Amazon Rubber Boom,* 2, 267–68; Montejano, "Is Texas Bigger," 600–625; Hall, "Incorporation in the World-System," 390–402; Stern, "Feudalism," 846–71, 877–82; also see Wallerstein's "Comments" to Stern, 877–82.

36. Olarte Camacho, *Crueldades*, 86–93.
37. Unfortunately, copies of *La Sanción* and *La Felpa,* both edited by Saldaña Rocca, are not available in either Iquitos or Lima. For a copy of the first edition of *La Sanción,* see Rey De Castro, *Pobladores del Putumayo,* 50a–52a.
38. Rey de Castro, *Pobladores del Putumayo,* 50a–52a.
39. Olarte Camacho, *Crueldades,* 30–31.
40. Ibid., 161–73; for English translations of *La Sanción* and *La Felpa* articles, see Hardenburg, *Putumayo,* 225–38.
41. Hardenburg, *Putumayo,* 71, 81; Collier, *River That God Forgot,* 81.
42. Hardenburg, *Putumayo,* 117–39.
43. Ibid., 146–95; Collier, *River That God Forgot,* 100–112.
44. He also saw twenty-two Peruvian soldiers at Arica, near the confluence of the Igaraparaná and Putumayo, who looked "ill and emaciated," probably from malaria. See Hardenburg, *Putumayo,* 192.
45. Ibid., 175–80.
46. Collier, *River That God Forgot,* 112–34.
47. Hardenburg, *Putumayo,* 196–99; Collier, *River That God Forgot,* 81, 125.
48. Collier, *River That God Forgot,* 162; Rumrrill, *Amazonía Peruana,* 66.

CHAPTER 7

1. Markovits and Silverstein, *Politics of Scandal,* vii–7.
2. Temperly, *British Antislavery,* 267.
3. The Congo and Putumayo scandals attracted the attention of some of the same powerful actors: the Anti-Slavery and Aborigines Protection Society and Secretary Harris, Foreign Office investigator Roger Casement, and Sir Edward Grey, British foreign minister. See Ure, *Trespassers of the Amazon,* 80–85.
4. GBHC, *Report and Special Report,* 65, 94–95, 155–56; Collier, *River That God Forgot,* 162–71; Hardenburg, *Putumayo.*
5. See Enock's introduction to Hardenburg, *Putumayo,* 31; for one of C. Reginald Enock's books, see *Andes and the Amazon.*
6. Hardenburg, *Putumayo,* 37.
7. Ibid., 153–208 passim.
8. Singleton-Gates and Girodias, *Black Diaries,* 242.
9. Caicedo to Min. de Gobierno, 19 Feb. 1907, ANC(B), Min. de Gob. 1a, vol. 592, fol. 497; Memorandum, 26 Feb. 1907, fols. 504–5; Bucheli to Min. de Gobierno, 21 July 1907, vol. 592, fols. 498–99; Bucheli to Presidente, 5 Sept. 1907, fol. 229; Bucheli to Min. de Gobierno, 24 Oct. 1907, fol. 203; Bucheli to Min. de Gobierno, 23 May 1907, vol. 597, fols. 195–96; Bucheli to Min. de Gobierno, 19 July 1907, fols. 222–23; *El Oriente* (Iquitos), 21 Jan. 1908; Olarte Camacho, *Crueldades,* 187–92.
10. For the 30 Nov. 1907 report, see Eberhardt, "Indians of Peru," 181–94; for excerpts of both reports, see USDS, *Papers Relating to Foreign Relations,* 1246–49.
11. Eberhardt, "Indians of Peru," 193–94.
12. USDS, *Papers Relating to Foreign Relations,* 1247–49.
13. Woodroffe, *Upper Reaches,* vii, 89–108, 136–41.

14. Ibid., 133.

15. Ibid., 160–61.

16. Whiffen's book is only notable because of its focus on cannibalism, evidence of which the author cited from Robuchon (*En el Putumayo*) and Casa Arana editor Carlos Rey de Castro (*Escándolas del Putumayo*); see Whiffen, *North-West Amazons*, 119–20.

17. For various accounts of the Whiffen/Arana deal, see Arana, *Cuestiones del Putumayo*, 38; Collier, *River That God Forgot*, 177–82; Hardenburg, *Putumayo*, 31–32; GBHC, *Report and Special Report*, 519–20.

18. Furneaux, *The Amazon*, 169; De la Flor Fernández, "Economía de exportación," 56.

19. Arana, *Cuestiones del Putumayo*, 9–12; Collier, *River That God Forgot*, 171; Valcárcel, *Proceso del Putumayo*, 381–89.

20. Basadre, *Historia de la República*, 8:3656; for a transcript of his report and more on Casement's extraordinary life, see Singleton-Gates and Girodias, *Black Diaries*, 211–15; Collier, *River That God Forgot*, 210.

21. GBFO, *Correspondence Respecting the Treatment of British Colonial Subjects*, 34–38.

22. Ibid., 33, 140–41, 158.

23. Singleton-Gates and Girodias, *Black Diaries*, 238, 242, 298.

24. GBFO, *Correspondence Respecting the Treatment of British Colonial Subjects*, 47, 88, 94, 127.

25. Ibid., 96–127; Singleton-Gates and Girodias, *Black Diaries*, 266–68, 290.

26. GBFO, *Correspondence Respecting the Treatment of British Colonial Subjects*, 34–77.

27. Ibid., 9–20, quote on 44; for more on the culture of torture, terror, and death, see Taussig, *Shamanism*.

28. GBFO, *Correspondence Respecting the Treatment of British Colonial Subjects*, 2, 157; Singleton-Gates and Girodias, *Black Diaries*, 249, 306; Furneaux, *The Amazon*, 175.

29. Guzmán G., "Los andokes," 64, 74.

30. "Declaración de Antonia Nonuya, viuda Huitota," 4 June 1923, ANC(B), Min. de Gob., 1a, vol. 937, fol. 19.

31. Guyot, "El relato de O'ioi," 3–10.

32. Singleton-Gates and Girodias, *Black Diaries*, 234, 236, 294, 296; Furneaux, *The Amazon*, 183–84; De la Flor Fernández, "Economía de exportación," 82.

33. USDS, NA, M862 r. 116, 819/3; r. 287 3010/8, 3010/25, 3010/36, 3010/40–49; Ayala Mora, "De la revolución alfarista," 132–34.

34. Ecuador, "Informe del jefe político del Napo," in *El Oriente Ecuatoriano* 11:29–31.

35. Wood, *Aggression and History*, 3–4.

36. ABFL(Q), Senado 1910, caja 25, Proyectos aprobados (extraordinario), 6 June, 14 June, 24 June 1910.

37. ABFL(Q), Senado 1910, caja 25, Proyectos aprobados (extraordinario), 21 June 1910; Sancionados, 29 Aug. 1910; Cámara de diputados, 1910, Sancionados, 14 Sept., 3 Oct. 1910; Informes Varios, 24 Sept. 1910; Wood, *Aggression and History*, 4.

38. ANC(B), Min. de Gob., 1a, vol. 638, fols. 456, 463, 465, 486–87.
39. Bucheli to Min. de Obras Públicas, 13 Sept. 1907, ANC(B), Min. de Industrias — Baldíos, vol. 27, fol. 258; UC-CIH(P), *La Paz* (Popayán), 13 Aug. 1907; Uribe Uribe, "Cultivo de caucho hevea."
40. For an excellent study on frontier violence in Colombia, see LeGrand, *Frontier Expansion.*
41. ANC(B), Min. de Industrias, Baldíos, vol. 31, fols. 171–72v; vol. 32, fol. 624: vol. 33, fol. 24; vol. 34, fols. 295–96v.
42. Lemaitre, *Rafael Reyes,* 336–60; Bucheli to Min. de Gobierno, June, July 1909, passim, ANC(B), Min. de Gob., 1a. vol. 625, fols. 385–95.
43. "Informe que rinde el señor Sebastían González al sr. Gob. de Pasto," 29 Apr. 1911, AH(P), G-C (14), 1–7; Cornelio Josa M. to Gob. de Nariño, 20 Dec. 1911, G-C (14), 1–12.
44. Olarte Camacho, *Crueldades,* 32–34.
45. Ibid., 195–97.
46. Rozo to Presidente, 25 Oct. 1910, ANC(B), Min. de Gob. 1a, vol. 665, fols. 293–94.
47. AGN(L), O.L. 704/204; O.L. 707/51; O.L. 713/329a; O.L. 720/311; O.L. 722/32; O.L. 725/312.
48. Rey de Castro to Dir. de Admin. de Hacienda, 19 Feb. 1907, AGN(L), O.L. 708/5; O.L. 727/245b, Nov.–Dec. 1907, passim; Tizón to Dir. de Gobierno, 3 Jan., 6 Jan. 1909, Min. del Int., 1909/126.
49. Tizón to Pref., 13 Aug. 1908, AGN(L), Min. del Int., 1908/118; Cazes to Presidente de la Junta Departamental, 16 Nov. 1910, O.L. 727/245a; "Criminal contra Rubén Obando, Asonada y robo," 19 Aug. 1908, APJ(I).
50. Tizón to Dir. de Gobierno, 30 Nov. 1908; Torres to Tizón, 23 Dec. 1908; AGN(L), Min. del Int., 1909/26.
51. "Criminal contra los autores ó cómplices de los deltios de homicidio frustrado en la persona de don Antonio B. Dos Santos," 19 Feb. 1909, APJ(I).
52. R. J. Solis C. to Pref., 23 Mar. 1909, AGN(L), Min. del Int., 1909/126.
53. The contract would have expired in 1926; see *El Oriente,* 11 Jan. 1910; Espinoza to Dir. de Hacienda, 4 May 1910, AGN(L), O.L. 725/317.
54. Gómez to Presidente de la Junta Departamental, 24 Jan. 1910, AGN(L), O.L. 727/237; Aviles to Dir. de Compañía Nacional de Recaudación, 28 Feb. 1910, O.L. 727/238; Alvarado to Presidente de la Junta Departamental, 14 May 1910, O.L. 727/243.
55. *El Oriente,* 24 Jan., 26 Mar., 2 May 1910.
56. Ibid., 8 Apr. 1910.
57. Alayza Paz-Soldán to Presidente Leguía, 1 May 1910, AGN(L), O.L. 725/316.
58. Porras to Min. de Estado, 24 May 1910, AGN(L), O.L. 730/48; Urrutia to Alayza Paz-Soldán, 22 Feb. 1910, Min. del Int., 1910/133 (Loreto); Alayza Paz-Soldán to Dir. de Policía, 30 Sept. 1910, 1910/133 (Loreto); Kahn and Polack to Alayza Paz-Soldán, 12 Oct. 1910, 1911/141 (Paquete Min. de Hacienda); Porras to Min. de Estado, 26 Oct. 1910, O.L. 730/66; "Tarifa de los impuestos municipales," 30 June 1910, O.L. 720/311.
59. Althaus to Dir. de Gobierno, 27 Oct. 1910, AGN(L), Min. del Int., 1910/133 (Relaciones); Sanareno to Min. de Estado, 28 Nov. 1910, 1910/133 (Min. de Justicia); *El Oriente,* 16 May 1910; Ribeiro, *Os índios,* 128.

CHAPTER 8

1. Valcárcel, *Proceso del Putumayo*, 12–18; Rumrrill, *Amazonía Peruana*, 84–85; Zumaeta, *Cuestiones del Putumayo* 1:20.

2. *Peru To-Day* (Lima) 4 (5) (Aug. 1912): 245, 248, BN(L); Valcárcel, *Proceso del Putumayo*, 17, 52–54; *El Oriente*, 18 Feb., 9 Mar. 1911.

3. Valcárcel, *Proceso del Putumayo*, 49, 51, 64, 75–109, 142–52, 172–200.

4. Ibid., 44–45, 68, 81, 114–15, 135, 157, 178, 188, 226.

5. Ibid., 51, 64, 179, 208, 221; *Peru To-Day* 4 (5) (Aug. 1912): 245, BN(L).

6. Valcárcel, *Proceso del Putumayo*, 52, 62–63, 85, 143, 152, 193.

7. Ibid., 45, 52, 80, 151.

8. Ibid., 49, 59, 63–64, 69, 85, 96, 100–102, 124, 128, 143, 146, 149, 155, 159, 176–78, 180, 193.

9. *El Oriente*, 21 July 1911.

10. Valcárcel, *Proceso del Putumayo*, 18.

11. Zumaeta, *Cuestiones del Putumayo*, 1:11–18; 2:10–42.

12. Ibid., 1:13.

13. Valcárcel, *Proceso del Putumayo*, 19–24.

14. Ibid., 18, 22, 259–61, 270–71, 288–91, 304: Zumaeta, *Cuestiones del Putumayo*, 1:20.

15. Karno, "Julio César Arana," 92; Davies, *Indian Integration in Peru*, 52–58; Stanfield, "Rubber Collection," 68–69; *El Oriente*, 24 May 1912; Leguía y Martínez to Min. de Gobierno, 3 Aug. 1911, AGN(L), Min. del Int., 1911/141 (Paq. Min de R. E.).

16. ANC(B), Min. de Industrias, Baldíos, vol. 32, fols. 234–38v, 464–66: vol. 35, fols. 55–60; Junta Arquidiocesana Nacional, *Las misiones en Colombia, 1912*, 51–61.

17. Rozo to Pres. de la República, 25 July 1910, AC(B), Fondos básicos, Informe de comisiones, Cámara 1911, vol. 8, fols. 213–39.

18. AC(B), Fondos básicos, Informe de Comisiones, Cámara 1911, vol. 8, fols. 188–204, 246–54.

19. Arana, *Cuestiones del Putumayo*, 3:36; Restrepo to Min. de Gobierno, 29 Dec. 1911, ANC(B), Min. del Gobierno, 1a, vol. 665, fol. 485.

20. *El Oriente* 14 Feb., 16 Feb. 1911; Romero, *Iquitos y la fuerza naval*, 110.

21. Romero, *Iquitos y la fuerza naval*, 116–17; Paz-Soldán to Presidente, 12 Apr. 1911, AGN(L), O.L. 733/21.

22. Romero, *Iquitos y la fuerza naval*, 110–11; *El Oriente*, 4 Aug. 1911.

23. *El Oriente*, 4 Sept. 1911; ANC(B), Min. de Gob., 1a, vol. 665, fols. 433, 482.

24. *El Oriente*, 19 July 1911.

25. Ibid., 16 Sept. 1911.

26. Ibid., 20 Sept. 1911.

27. ANC(B), Min. de Gob., 1a, vol. 684, fols. 18–20; vol. 698, fols. 356–60.

28. ANC(B), Min. de Gob., 1a, vol. 660, fols. 102, 111; *El Oriente*, 7 July 1911.

29. Ayala Mora, "De la revolución alfarista," 134–37.

30. *El Oriente*, 20 Feb. 1911; "El poder ejecutivo de acuerdo con la junta promotora del FF.CC. construirá la via ferrea de Ambato al Curaray," Sept./Oct. 1912, ABFL(Q), Senado 1912, caja 33, Proyectos aprobados en ambas cámaras; "Pro-

yecto por el cual se construirá una carretera de la provincia de Chimborazo a la región oriental," Sept./Oct. 1913, Senado 1913, caja 40, Documentos varios; Ley reformatoria de Oriente, Cámara de diputados 1913, caja 35, Proyectos.

31. "Ley del Congreso," 12 Aug. 1911, AGN(L), Min. del Int., 1911/141 (Paquete, Cámara diputados); Paz-Soldán to Dir. de Gobierno, 20 Oct. 1911, (Paquete-Loreto); García Zorrilla to Min. de Hacienda, 9 Aug. 1911, O.L. 735/269; Dublé to Dir. Gen. de Justicia y Beneficencia, 20 Apr. 1912, O.L. 743/15.

32. *Loreto Comercial,* 11 May 1912, AGN(L), Min. del Int., 1912/148; Paz-Soldán to Dir. de Admin., 18 Sept. 1911, O.L. 733/222.

33. "Informe sobre el comercio de Iquitos correspondiente al año 1911, por el cónsul G.B. Michell," in Bonilla, *Gran Bretaña y el Perú,* 3:228; Alayza Paz-Soldán to Dir. de Admin., 15 July 1911, AGN(L), O.L. 733/220; Zumaeta to Pref., 5 Aug. 1911, O.L. 733/221; Alayza Paz-Soldán to Superintendente Aduanas, Callao, 9 Oct. 1911, O.L. 733/223.

34. Althaus to Pref., 7 Mar. 1912, AGN(L), O.L. 740/351; E. Strasberger to Pref., 13 Jan. 1912, O.L. 740/359; Alayza Paz-Soldán to Dir. de Admin. de Hacienda, 14 Mar. 1912, O.L. 740/349; "Informe sobre el comercio de Iquitos al año 1911, por el consul G. B. Michell," in Bonilla, *Gran Bretaña y el Peru,* 3:231; *El Oriente,* 11 Apr. 1912.

35. E. Strasberger to Pref., 10 Jan., 13 Jan. 1912; Paz-Soldán to Dir. de Admin., 12 Mar. 1912; AGN(L), O.L. 740/359.

36. Furneaux, *The Amazon,* 187–93; Stanfield, "Rubber Collection," 62.

37. GBFO, *Correspondence Respecting the Treatment of British Colonial Subjects,* 154; Collier, *River That God Forgot,* 218.

38. H. Clay Howard to Secretary of State, 3 Apr. 1912, USDS, *Papers Relating to the Internal Affairs of Peru,* M746 R.14, 823.5048/14.

39. For a sample of diplomatic correspondence between the foreign ministries of England, the United States, and Peru, see GBFO, *Correspondence Respecting the Treatment of British Colonial Subjects,* 142–65; Coletta, "William Jennings Bryan," 486–501.

40. GBFO, *Correspondence Respecting the Treatment of British Colonial Subjects,* 158.

41. Ibid., 158.

42. Ibid., 159.

43. Morgan to Acting Secretary of State Huntington Wilson, 9 Sept. 1912, USDS 823.5048/96.

44. USDS, *Papers Relating to the Foreign Relations of the U.S.,* 1241, 1263, 1279; GBFO, *Report by His Majesty's Consul at Iquitos,* 3; Collier, *River That God Forgot,* 221.

45. USDS, *Papers Relating to the Foreign Relations of the U.S.,* 1267.

46. GBFO, *Report by His Majesty's Consul at Iquitos,* 10; USDS, *Papers Relating to the Foreign Relations of the U.S.,* 1268–69.

47. GBFO, *Report by His Majesty's Consul at Iquitos,* 4–5; USDS, *Papers Relating to the Foreign Relations of the U.S.,* 1277.

48. GBFO, *Report by His Majesty's Consul at Iquitos,* 2, 14.

49. USDS, *Papers Relating to the Foreign Relations of the U.S.,* 1269.

50. Ibid., 1278.

51. Paz-Soldán to Dir. de Gobierno, 29 May 1912, AGN(L), Min. del Int., 1912/148; "Estadistica de los productos nacionales exportados," 1911, 1912, O.L. 742/86; *El Oriente,* 12 June 1912.

52. *El Oriente,* 11 June, 14 Sept., 17 Sept. 1912; *Memoria que presenta al Congreso ordinario de 1912 el Min. de Relaciones Exteriores* [Dr. Germán Leguía y Martínez] (Lima: Tide "El Lucero," 1912), xix–xxxiv, AGN(L), H-6 (1776).

53. *El Oriente,* 18 Sept., 19 Sept., 21 Sept., 10 Oct., 17 Oct., 19 Nov. 1912.

54. *El Oriente,* 4 Nov. 1912; USDS, *Papers Relating to the Foreign Relations of the U.S.,* 1284.

55. *El Oriente,* 14 Dec., 16 Dec., 17 Dec., 31 Dec. 1912; Valcárcel, *Proceso del Putumayo,* 272–78.

56. Tola to Pref., 5 Jan., 14 Feb. 1913, AGN(L), O.L. 742/86; "Relación de los señores sustanciales . . . para el cobro de las contribuciones en 1912," AGN(L), O.L. 742/86; Morey to Presidente de la Junta Dept., 26 Nov. 1913, O.L. 749/485; Pindeo to Dir. de Admin., 17 June 1914, O.L. 754/283; "Queja del Luis F. Morey," Dec. 1914, O.L. 756/492.

57. Puente to Dir. de Gobierno, 2 Aug. 1913, AGN(L), Min. del Int., 1913/157.

58. Hispano, *De París al Amazonas,* 245–99.

59. Rey de Castro, *Escándolos del Putumayo,* 25n, 56n, 57–60.

60. Ibid., 10, 39–52, 55–62.

61. Ibid., 65–68; Rey de Castro, *Pobladores del Putumayo,* 50–56.

62. Arana, *Cuestiones del Putumayo,* 41–67.

63. Ibid., 9–12.

64. Ibid., 14, 21, 27, 44–45.

65. Collier, *River That God Forgot,* 215–22; Pennano, *Economía del caucho,* 167–68; De la Flor Fernández, "Economía de exportación," 57–58; *Peru To-Day* 4 (10) (Jan. 1913): 530, BN(L).

66. Collier, *River That God Forgot,* 224–26.

67. GBHC, *Report and Special Report,* xlix–l.

68. Ibid., xix, 185, 252, 304–5: Collier, *River That God Forgot,* 235–66; Henson quote in *Times* (London), 24 Aug. 1912, 3.

69. GBHC, *Report and Special Report,* 449.

70. Collier, *River That God Forgot,* 228–29.

71. Ibid., 270–71; GBHC, *Report and Special Report,* 528–29.

72. *Peru To-Day* 5 (1) (Apr. 1913): 694, BN(L); GBHC, *Report and Special Report,* 459, 480.

73. GBHC, *Report and Special Report,* 485; for an English transcript of Arana's statement to the committee, see 612–17; Collier, *River That God Forgot,* 254.

74. GBHC, *Report and Special Report,* xix–xx.

75. Pennano, *Economía del caucho,* 168; Domínguez and Gómez, *Economía extractiva,* 199; De la Flor Fernández, "Economía de exportación," 60; "Statement of Sir Edward Grey to House of Commons, 1 Aug. 1913," in Thomson, *Putumayo Red Book,* 144–45.

76. USDS, *Papers Relating to the Foreign Relations of the United States,* 524–25, 1147–50; *Peru To-Day* 5 (5) (Aug. 1913): 904–7; 5 (7) (Oct. 1913): 1006–7; BN(L).

CHAPTER 9

1. *El Oriente,* 19 Aug. 1914; Aug.–Dec. 1914, passim.
2. On the trade slowdown, see Bonilla, *Gran bretaña y el Perú,* 3:283; De la Flor Fernández, "Economía de exportación," 61–62.
3. On plantation rubber, see Dean, *Brazil and the Struggle for Rubber,* 4–9, 22–35, 43–46; for Zumaeta's observations, see Zumaeta to Pref., 18 Oct. 1916, AGN(L), O.L. 770/232.
4. Dominguez and Gómez, *Economía extractiva,* 104; De la Flor Fernández, "Economía de exportación," 65–66, 149; AGN(L), O.L. 770/230 (varios).
5. Rumrrill, *Yurimaguas,* 148; San Román, *Perfiles históricos,* 118; "Contrato entre el señor Eduardo Arévalo y (peón) Pedro Castro," 15 Jan. 1915, AGN(L), Min. del Int., 1917/193 (Loreto).
6. "Inventario de las especias dejadas," AGN(L), Min. del Int., 1914/164.
7. "Vecinos de Iquitos...," 20 Feb. 1914, AGN(L), O.L. 756/566; "Los armadores i comerciantes...," 18 Mar. 1914, O.L. 756/161; "Licencias y multas...," 31 Mar. 1915, O.L. 761/303.
8. Caballero y Lastres to Min. de Hacienda, 22 Aug. 1916, AGN(L), O.L. 770/276.
9. Cateriano to Dir. Admin., 5 Sept. 1914, AGN(L), O.L. 754/286; Bentijle to Dir. Gen. de Hacienda, 27 May 1916, O.L. 768/467; Caballero to Dir. de Admin., 9 June 1916, O.L. 770/839; Harrison to Pres. de Junta Dept., 30 June 1916, O.L. 770/743.
10. Pinillos Rossell to Dir. de Fomento, 7 Apr. 1918, AGN(L), O.L. 782/468; Israel y Cia. Revista Mensual, 15 Oct. 1917, O.L. 777/815; Sosa to Pref., 25 June 1918, O.L. 782/471.
11. "Borda pide la nulidad," 4 Jan. 1918, AGN(L), O.L. 784/563; Zumaeta to Senadores por Loreto, 11 Jan. 1918, O.L. 777/678.
12. "Denuncia criminal de Pablo Zumaeta contra el colombiano Sebastían González por homicidio en la persona de un muchacho al servicio de la Peruvian Amazon Company," 15 May 1910, APJ(I).
13. "Criminal por denuncia contra el tenente Risco y la guarnación de su mando, por el delito de flagelación en las personas de quince indios witotos de la nación 'Aymenes,' Entre Ríos, R. Igaraparaná," 20 Apr. 1911, APJ(I).
14. "Criminal de oficio contra Enrique Zavala y Zavala por homicidio en la persona del indio 'Riveina,' Provincia de Bajo Amazonas," 26 Apr. 1911, APJ(I).
15. *El Oriente,* 7 Aug. 1914; Velasco to Zegarra, 4 May 1915, AGN(L), Min. del Int., 1915/174 (Loreto); Riascos Plata to Min. de R. E., 12 Nov. 1914, ANC(B), Min. de Gob., 1a, vol. 731, fols. 78–85.
16. Castañeda to García, 20 Sept. 1915, AGN(L), Min. del Int., 1915/174 (Loreto).
17. On the cultural impact of white trade on indigenous societies, see Friedemann and Arocha, *Herederos,* 136–37.
18. *Censo general de la república, 1912,* 52, ANC(B).
19. Montoya to Min. de Agricultura, 22 Mar. 1916, ANC(B), Min. de Industrias, Baldíos, vol. 40, fols. 400–401; "Visita practicado en el corregimiento de Niña María," 25 Jan. 1918, Min. de Gob., 1a, vol. 796, fols. 438–40.
20. Censo 1918, *Censo de población,* 432–33, ANC(B); on Indians fleeing white cen-

sus takers, see Bucheli to Min. de Gobierno, 2 Oct. 1918, ANC(B), Min. de Gob., 1a, vol. 795, fol. 407.

21. "Proyectos de decreto sobre elección de representates por la provincia del Oriente," 4 Sept. 1915, ABFL(Q), Diputados 1915, caja 45, Proyectos.

22. Cabezas Borja to Presidente, 1 Oct. 1917; Guerrero to Honorables Legisladores; ABFL(Q), Diputados 1917, caja 54, Solicitud con informe.

23. "Se arbitran medios para fomentar la colonización," 19 Aug. 1915, ABFL(Q), Diputados 1915, caja 46, Proyectos negados; "El congreso considerando," 17 Sept. 1917; Syura to Sec., 17 Sept. 1917; "El congreso decreta," 2 Oct. 1917; Diputados 1917, caja 53, Proyectos aprobados en ambas cámaras; Astudillo, *El Oriente Ecuatoriano*, 10:16–22.

24. Ancízar to Min de R. E., 27 Oct. 1914, ANC(B), Min. de Industrias, Baldíos, vol. 37, fols. 253–55; Gobierno del Cauca to Sec. de la Cámara, 9 Sept. 1914, AC(B), Fondos básicos, Informes de comisiones, Senado 1914, vol. 10, fol. 299; "Memoria de Quintín Lamé," 17 Oct. 1914, UC-CIH(P), Rep.-Judicial (JV-4 cv), 1914–20, sig. 8043.

25. Sicard Briceño to Min. de Obras Públicas, 15 Jan. 1914, ANC(B), Obras públicas, vol. 1409, fols. 291–92; Pérez, Montclar, Zarama to Min. de Gobierno, 2 Apr. 1914, Min. de Gob., 1a, vol. 730, fols. 471–72; Zarama to Presidente, 20 Oct. 1915, AC(B), Fondos básicos, Informes de comisiones, Senado 1915, vol. 8, fol. 131.

26. ANC(B), Min. de Industrias, Baldíos, vol. 39, fols. 110–100v, 132–34v, 203–5v; Vélez to Min. de Gobierno, 6 Sept., 21 Sept. 1915, Min. de Gob., 1a, vol. 755, fols. 102, 104, 105.

27. Diago to Min. de Gobierno, 30 Apr. 1917, ANC(B), Min. de Industrias, Baldíos, vol. 41, fols. 31–32, 40–41.

28. Diago to Min. de Gobierno, 30 Apr. 1917, ANC(B), Min. de Gob., 1a, vol. 779, fols. 369–84.

29. Pastrana to Min. de Gobierno, 21 Oct., 25 Oct. 1918, ANC(B), Min. de Gob., 1a, vol. 796, fols. 465–66.

30. Collier, *River That God Forgot*, 220; Furneaux, *The Amazon*, 195, quote on 199.

31. Martí, *Estadística*, 41; *Las misiones en Colombia, 1912*, 61–64, 66–74, 80.

32. *Las misiones en Colombia, 1912*, 61–64, 66–74, 115–18, 131–33; Colombia, *Misiones católicas del Putumayo, 1913*, 36, 57, 67–68.

33. Colombia, *Informes sobre las misiones, 1917*, 14–15; "Estadistica gral. de las escuelas," AH(P), G-C (14), 1–7, fol. 57; Guyot, "El relato de O'ioi," 9.

34. Montclar to Min. de Gobierno, 18 Oct. 1912, ANC(B), Min. de Gob., 1a, vol. 694, fols. 283–86; Montclar to Min. de Gobierno, 19 Oct. 1912, fols. 291–93; Ramírez to Min. de Gobierno, 18 Dec. 1912, vol. 694, fol. 310; Ramírez to Min. de Gobierno, 31 Dec. 1912, vol. 719, fols. 79–79v; Montclar to Min. de O. P., 1 Aug. 1918, Obras Públicas, vol. 1412, fols. 83–84; Colombia, *Informes sobre las misiones, 1917*, 53–59; *Las misiones católicas en Colombia, 1919*, 40–48.

35. Fray Estanislao to Gobierno de Pasto, 5 Jan. 1900, AH(P), G-C (13), 1–2; Escandón to Min. de Gobierno, 12 Dec. 1912, ANC(B), Min. de Gob., 1a, fols. 365–68; Escandón to Min. de Gobierno, 15 May 1913, fols. 280–314; *El Cometa* (Popayán), 2 Mar. 1912.

For the modern traveler, the bus ride from Pasto to Mocoa provides gorgeous scenery, wide-eyed gasps of fright, an elevated pulse count, and an appreciation for the work invested in the road.

36. ANC(B), Obras Públicas, vol. 1409, fols. 71–71v, 291–92; Montclar to Arzobispo de Bogotá, 23 Sept. 1914, Min. de Gob., 1a, vol. 755, fols. 440–44.

37. ANC(B), Obras Públicas, vol. 1410, fols. 195–96, 255–55v, 400–402, 546–46v, 558–58v; vol. 1411, fols. 337–38, 422–24, 489–90, 497–500, 599.

38. Bonilla, *Servants of God,* 141.

39. Ibid., 140–41; Díaz to Pref. Apostólico, 2 Mar. 1915, ANC(B), Min. de Industrias, Baldíos, vol. 37, fols. 337–38.

40. For a critical review of this land grab, see Bonilla, *Servants of God,* 107–9.

41. Montclar to Presidente, 27 Nov. 1912, ANC(B), Min. de Gob., 1a, vol. 694, fol. 229; González to Min. de Gobierno, 1 May 1914, vol. 731, fols. 135–67.

42. Colombia, *Informes sobre las misiones, 1917,* 60–64; *Las misiones católicas en Colombia, 1919,* 31–35; Bonilla, *Servants of God,* 142–45; Diago to Min. de Gobierno, 9 Mar. 1917, ANC(B), Min. de Gob., 1a, vol. 779, fol. 364.

43. Colombia, *Las misiones católicas en Colombia, 1919,* 82–100; Bonilla, *Servants of God,* 159; Obispo de Pasto to Presidente, 20 Oct. 1915, AC(B), Fondos básicos, Informes de comisiones, Senado 1915, vol. 8, fol. 129; Vélez to Min. de Gobierno, 16 July 1915, ANC(B), Min. de Gob., 1a, vol. 755, fols. 98–98v; Albán to Min. de Gobierno, 27 Sept. 1917, vol. 778, fols. 171–72.

44. "Visita del commissar especial del Caquetá," 8 May 1917, ANC(B), Min. de Gob., 1a, vol. 779, fols. 491–508; "Informe del commissar especial del Caquetá," 31 Mar. 1914, vol. 730, fols. 270–300v; Montoya to Min. de Ag., 12 Apr. 1918, Min. de Industrias, Baldíos, vol. 43, fols. 47–52; Tisoy y Jansasoy to Min. de Gobierno, 10 Sept. 1918, fols. 470–71.

45. "Visita del commissar especial del Caquetá," Jan. 1913, ANC(B), Min. de Gob., 1a, vol. 719, fols. 2–12v; Calvo to Min. de Gobierno, 18 Sept. 1913, vol. 719, fols. 61–63; Vélez to Min. de Gobierno, 4, 30 Jan. 1915, vol. 755, fols. 1–2, 8; Montclar to Min. de Ag., 20 Feb. 1917, Min. de Industrias, Baldíos, vol. 41, fols. 363–67.

46. For biographies of Casement, see Inglis, *Roger Casement;* and Reid, *Lives of Roger Casement.*

47. On Casement's diaries, see Reid, *Lives of Roger Casement;* Inglis, *Roger Casement;* Singleton-Gates and Girodias, *Black Diaries;* and Maloney, *Forged Casement Diaries.*

48. For the sex play witnessed by Casement, see Singleton-Gates and Girodias, *Black Diaries,* 261, 271: Reid, *Lives of Roger Casement,* 109, 115–16. For the Vaupés study, see Arthur Sorenson, Jr., "Linguistic Exogamy and Personal Choice in the Northwest Amazon," in Kensinger, *Marriage Practices,* 180–91.

49. Reid, *Lives of Roger Casement,* 296–409, passim.

50. Reid, *Lives of Roger Casement,* 381–83, 418–19, 440–42.

CHAPTER 10

1. For trends in import and export trade, see De la Flor Fernández, "Economía de exportación," 123; for Ecuador's situation, see Martz, *Ecuador,* 67.

2. "Memoria del prefecto accidental," 17 June 1918, AGN(L), Min. del Int., 1918/ 201; Alvaro to Pref., 1 Aug. 1919, Min. del Int., 1920/212 (Loreto).

3. De la Flor Fernández, "Economía de exportación," 11.

4. Soyer to Dir. de Hacienda, 22 Mar. 1919, AGN(L), O.L. 789/494; Vigil to Senador Miguel Grau, 13 Nov. 1919, O.L. 789/540.

5. Hernández to Min. de Hacienda, 12 Mar. 1921, AGN(L), O.L. 803/702; Ruiz Pastor to Min. de Hacienda, 11 Mar. 1921, O.L. 803/702; Ruiz Pastor to Min. de Hacienda, 15 Mar. 1921, O.L. 803/702.

6. Pérez to Min. de Hacienda, 5 Mar. 1921, AGN(L), O.L. 803/702; Badani to Min. de Fomento, 22 Feb. 1921, O.L. 803/699; Ruiz Pastor to Senador Egoaguirre, 25 Feb. 1921, O.L. 803/699; Morey to Min. de Hacienda, 9 Mar. 1921, O.L. 803/702.

7. Rumrrill, *Amazonía Peruana*, 85; *Yurimaguas*, 229–34.

8. Rumrrill, *Yurimaguas*, 229–34; Chaves to Min. de R. E., 31 Jan. 1922, 18 Mar. 1922, ANC(B), Min. de Gob., 1a, vol. 860, fols. 67, 76; Agüero to Pref., 8 Aug. 1922, AGN(L), Min. del Int., 1922/228 (Loreto); Delgado to Pref., 7 July 1922, Min. del Int. 1922/228 (Loreto).

9. Alvarez to Supremo Gobierno, 1923, AGN(L), Min. del Int., 1923/238 (Loreto).

10. AGN(L), Min. del Int., 1923/238 (Loreto), Varios 1922–23, ; De la Flor Fernández, "Economía de exportación," 66–68, 149.

11. De la Flor Fernández, "Economía de exportación," 66–68; Dominguez and Gómez, *Economía extractiva*, 106–7.

12. ANC(B), Min. de Gob., 1a, vol. 808, fols. 120–28 passim; Montoya to Min. de Gobierno, 24 Mar. 1919, vol. 812, fol. 328; "Informe del médico de sanidad de Florencia to sr. comisario especial," 1919, vol. 842, fols. 148–52.

13. Muñoz to Min. de Gobierno, 8 Oct. 1919, ANC(B), Min. de Gob., 1a, vol. 813, fols. 1–2; Bucheli to Min. de Gobierno, 4 Dec. 1919, vol. 811, fol. 87; Chaves to Min. de Gobierno, 2 May 1920, vol. 842, fol. 198; Mora to Escobar, 12 Mar. 1924, Obras Publicas, vol. 1413, fols. 223–36.

14. Montclar to Min. de Gobierno, 10 Oct. 1919, 25 Nov. 1919, ANC(B), Min. de Gob., 1a, vol. 808, fols. 1–2, 24.

15. ANC(B), Min. de Gob., 1a, vol. 842, fols. 181–82, 212–13, 219–24v; Chaves to Min. de Gobierno, 26 May 1920, vol. 837, fols. 54–58.

16. Chaves to Min. de Gobierno, 13 Oct. 1921, ANC(B), Min. de Gob., 1a, vol. 846, fol. 489; Puertas to Min. de Gobierno, 21 May 1926, vol. 937, fols. 198–202; Puertas to Min. de Gobierno, 1 June 1927, vol. 955.

17. Bonilla, *Servants of God,* 178–79; Chaves to Min. de Gobierno, 31 Jan. 1922, ANC(B), Min. de Gob., 1a, vol. 860, fol. 67; Calderón to Commissar del Caquetá, 1921, vol. 859, fols. 509–15.

18. "Memo de comisíon de relaciones exteriores," June 1923, ANC(B), Min. de Obras Públicas, vol. 1414, fol. 518; Mora to Min. de Gobierno, 12 July 1923, Min. de Gob., 1a, vol. 937, fols. 2–5.

19. Puertas to Min. de Gobierno, 21 May 1926, ANC(B), Min. de Gob., 1a, vol. 937, fols. 198–202; Puertas to Min. de Gobierno, 21 Jan. 1927, 27 Mar. 1927, 1 June 1927, vol. 955, fols. 450, 455, 458–59.

20. Montclar to Min. de O. P., 14 May 1919, 17 Aug. 1920, 15 Aug. 1920, ANC(B), Obras Públicas, vol. 1412, fols. 169–73, 380–82, 451–61; Min. de Industrias,

Baldíos, vol. 44, fols. 277–81v; vol. 46, fols. 178–83; vol. 47, fols, 225–25v; vol. 48, fol. 45.

21. Montclar to Min. de O.P., 15 Aug. 1920, ANC(B), Obras Públicas, vol. 1412, fols. 451–61; Luna to Commissar Especial, 13 Nov. 1922, Min. de Gob., 1a, vol. 860, fols. 102–5; "Acta visita," 5 Dec. 1922, vol. 860, fols. 107–9.

22. Montclar to Min. de O. P., 14 Feb., 16 Feb. 1925, ANC(B), Min. de O. P., vol. 1414, fols. 42, 43; Colonos compatriotas to Min. de O. P., 21 Jan., 22 Jan. 1926, vol. 1414, fols. 347–50; Canet de Mar to Min. de O. P., 6 May 1928; Canet de Mar to Min. de O. P., 12 Apr. 1929, vol. 1415, fols. 442–45.

23. Bushnell, *Making of Modern Colombia,* 180–82; Martí, *Estadistica,* 42; Bonilla, *Servants of God,* 178–79.

24. "Memorándum sobre los distinctos negocios," 21 June 1930, ANC(B), Obras Públicas, vol. 1140, fols. 114–15; "Memorándum para el sr. ministro de obras públicas," vol. 1140, fols. 126–28.

25. Bonilla, *Servants of God,* 186–87; Martí, *Estadistica,* 92.

26. Rumrrill, *Yurimaguas,* 153; Gasché, "Comunidades nativas," 11–31; Pineda Camacho, *Historia oral,* 102–3.

27. Chaves to Min. de Gobierno, 16 Aug. 1919, ANC(B), Min. de Gob., 1a, vol. 813, fols. 54–63; "Informe del superior de la misión," 1920, vol. 842, fols. 139–47; Chaves to Min. de Gobierno, 22 May 1920, vol. 842, fols. 154–70v; Herrán to Min. de Gobierno, 4 Dec. 1925, vol. 937, fols. 183–84.

28. "Acta de la visita en Yari," 6 June 1926, ANC(B), Min. de Gob., 1a, vol. 937, fols. 103–8; "Primera y única visita de Curiplaya," 29 Nov. 1926, vol. 937; Gasché, "Ocupación territorial," 12.

29. San Román, *Perfiles históricos,* 185–86.

30. Bákula, *Política internacional,* 42–43, 249–53.

31. Ibid., 43, 251, 253.

32. De la Flor Fernández, "Economía de exportación," 67–68; Gasché, "Ocupación territorial," 2–19.

33. Bákula, *Política internacional,* 313–27.

34. San Román, *Perfiles históricos,* 186–87.

35. Bákula, *Política internacional,* 44, 47.

36. De la Flor Fernández, "Economía de exportación," 153.

SELECT
BIBLIOGRAPHY

ARCHIVES AND LIBRARIES
Colombia

Archivo del Congreso (Bogotá) AC(B)
Archivo Histórico (Pasto) AH(P)
Archivo Nacional de Colombia (Bogotá) ANC(B)
Biblioteca Nacional (Bogotá) BN(B)
Banco de la República, Hemeroteca "Luis López de Mesa" (Bogotá) BR(B)
Universidad del Cauca, Centro de Investigación Histórica, "José María Arboleda Llorente" (Popayán) UC-CIH(P)

Ecuador

Archivo/Biblioteca de la Función Legislativa (Quito) ABFL(Q)
Archivo Nacional de Historia (Quito) ANH(Q)
Biblioteca Ecuatoriana "José María Espinosa Polit" (Cotocollao) BE(C)
Biblioteca General del Ministerio de Relaciones Exteriores (Quito) BGMRE(Q)

Peru

Archivo General de la Nación (Lima) AGN(L)
Archivo del Palacio de Justicia (Iquitos) APJ(I)
Biblioteca Nacional (Lima) BN(L)
Centro de Estudios Teológicos de la Amazonía (Iquitos) CETA(I)

United States

National Archives (Washington, D.C.) NA
Library of Congress (Washington, D.C.) LC

GOVERNMENT REPORTS

Brazil. Congreso. *Política econômica: Defensa da borracha, 1906–1914.* Rio de Janeiro: Journal do Comercio de Rodrigues, 1915.

Colombia. *La Amazonía Colombiana y sus recursos: Proyecto radargramétrico del Amazonas.* Bogotá: Italgraf, 1979.

———. *Informes sobre las misiones del Caquetá, Putumayo, Goajira, Casanare, Meta, Vichada, Vaupés, y Arauca.* Bogotá: Imprenta Nacional, 1917; in *El Oriente Ecuatoriano* 8, BGMRE(Q).

———. [Norman Thomson]. *El libro rojo del Putumayo: Precedido de una introdución sobre el verdadero escándolo de las atrocidades del Putumayo.* Bogotá: Arboleda and Valencia, 1913.

———. *Misiones católicas del Putumayo: Documentos oficiales relativos a esta comisaría.* Bogotá: Imprenta Nacional, 1913; in *El Oriente Ecuatoriano* 9, BGMRE(Q).

———. *Las misiones católicas en Colombia: Labor de los misioneros en el Caquetá y Putumayo, Magdalena, y Arauca.* Bogotá: Imprenta Nacional, 1919; in *El Oriente Ecuatoriano* 8, BGMRE(Q).

———. Congreso. Senado. *La soberanía de Colombia en el Putumayo: Documentos que se publican de orden del Senado de la República.* Bogotá: Imprenta Nacional, 1912.

———. Ministerio de Relaciones Exteriores. *Los crímenes del Putumayo.* La Paz: Tipografía La Verdad, 1912.

Ecuador. *Documentos de la sección consular: Anexos a la memoria del Ministerio de Relaciones Exteriores presentada a la asamblea nacional de 1906.* Quito: Imprenta de "El Comercio," n.d.

———. *Informe del gobernador de la provincia de Oriente.* Quito: Imprenta del Gobierno, 1885, BE(C).

———. "Informe del jefe político del Napo Carlos A. Rivadeneyra." *El Oriente Ecuatoriano* 11: 29–31. BGMRE(Q).

———. *Informe del Ministerio de lo Interior y Relaciones Exteriores al Congreso Constitucional.* Quito: Imprenta del Gobierno, 1885, 1886.

———. *Informe del Ministerio de Relaciones Exteriores al Congreso ordinario.* Quito: Imprenta de la Escuela de Artes y Oficios, 1898; Imprenta del Clero, 1901; n.p., 1903.

———. *Informe que el gobernador de la provincia de Oriente, Sr. d. Enrique T. Hurtado, dirige al Ministerio de lo Interior.* Quito: Imprenta de Espejo, 1897.

———. *Memoria de Relaciones Exteriores presentada al Congreso nacional de 1904, 1905, 1906.* Vols. 10, 11, 12. Quito: Imprenta Nacional, n.d.; Tipografía Salesiana, n.d.; Jaramillo y Cia., 1906.

———. *Proyecto de ley especial de régimen administrativo interior para la región oriental.* Quito: Imprenta del Clero, 1905.

Great Britain. Foreign Office [Roger Casement]. *Correspondence Respecting the Treatment of British Colonial Subjects and Native Indians Employed in the Collection of Rubber in the Putumayo District.* Miscellaneous no. 8. 1912.

———. Foreign Office [George Michell]. *Report by His Majesty's Consul at Iquitos on His Tour in the Putumayo District.* London: His Majesty's Stationery Office, 1913.

———. Parliament. House of Commons. *Parliamentary Debates, 1907–1914.*

———. Parliament. House of Commons. Select Committee on Putumayo. *Report and*

Special Report from the Select Committee on Putumayo, Together with the Proceedings of the Committee, Minutes of Evidence, and Appendices. London: His Majesty's Stationery Office, 1913.

Peru. Ministerio de Fomento. *Leyes, decretos, y resoluciones relativas a la región oriental.* Lima: Imprenta del Estado, 1902.

———. Ministerio de Fomento. *Ley y reglamentos de terrenos de montaña.* Lima: Oficina Tipográfica de "La Opinión Nacional," 1910.

———. Ministerio de Relaciones Exteriores. *The Gum Industry in Peru: Official Publication for Capitalists, Tradesmen, and Settlers.* Lima: Imprenta del Estado, 1903.

United States. Department of Commerce [William L. Schurz et al.]. *Rubber Production in the Amazon Valley.* Trade Promotion Series, no. 23. Washington, D.C.: GPO, 1925.

———. Department of Commerce [P. W. Barker]. *Rubber Statistics, 1900–1937.* Trade Promotion Series, no. 181. Washington, D.C.: GPO, 1938.

———. Department of State. *Papers Relating to the Foreign Relations of the United States, 1913.* Washington, D.C.: GPO, 1920.

———. Department of State. *Papers Relating to the Internal Affairs of Peru, 1910–1929.* National Archives Microfilm, M746.

———. Department of State. *Slavery in Peru: Message from the President of the United States, Transmitting Reports of the Secretary of State, with Accompanying Papers Concerning the Alleged Existence of Slavery in Peru.* Washington, D.C.: GPO, 1913.

OTHER REFERENCES

Agassiz, Louis, and Elizabeth Cabot Cary Agassiz. *A Journey in Brazil.* Boston: Ticknor and Fields, 1868.

Akers, Charles Edmond. *The Rubber Industry in Brazil and the Orient.* London: Methuen and Co., 1914.

Alayza y Paz Soldan, Luis. "Algo de la Amazonía Peruana." *Mi País.* 8a series. Lima: Imprenta Gil, 1960.

Albán, Juan Elias. *Proyecto de ley especial de régimen administrativo interior para la región oriental elevado.* Quito: Imprenta del Clero, 1905.

Alzate Angel, Beatriz. *Viajeros y cronistas en la Amazonía Colombiana: Catálogo colectivo.* Bogotá: Corporación Araracuara, 1987.

Andrade Marín, Francisco. *Cuadro de las minas hasta hoy descubiertas en el territorio de la República del Ecuador.* Quito: Imprenta del Gobierno, 1893.

———. *Informe del gobernador de la provincia de Oriente.* Quito: Imprenta del Gobierno, 1884.

Angulo Puente, Juan Arnao. *Nuestras negociaciones diplomáticas de límites con las repúblicas vecinas durante los cien años de vida independiente (1821–1921) y la irredencia en Sud-america.* Lima: Imprenta Artística, 1921.

Arana, Julio César. *Las cuestiones del Putumayo: Declaraciones prestadas ante el comité de investigación de la Cámara de los Comunes y debidamente anotadas.* Vol. 3. Barcelona: Imprenta Viuda de L. Tasso, 1913.

———. *Exposición que hace a los electores del departamento de Loreto el genuino senador loretano Julio C. Arana. . . .* Lima: Tipografía de la Penitenciaría, 1924.

Arcila Robledo, Gregorio. *Las misiones franciscanas en Colombia: Estudio documental.* Bogotá: Imprenta Nacional, 1950.

Arnaud, Expedito. *Os índios mirânia e a expansào Luso-Brasileira: Medio Solimões-Japurá, Amazonas.* Belém, Brazil: Conselho Nacional de Desenvolvimento Científico e Tecnológico, Instituto Nacional de Pesquisas da Amazônia, 1981.

Asamblea Orientalista Nacional. *Proyecto de ley de Oriente que la "Asamblea Orientalista Nacional" somete a la consideración de la Legislatura de 1917.* Quito: Imprenta y Encuadernación Nacionales, 1917.

Astudillo, Dario R. "El Oriente Ecuatoriano: Conferencia dada en la sala de sesiones del Concejo Municipal de Riobamba, el 27 de abril de 1916." Guayaquil: Librería e Imprenta Gutenberg, 1916; in *El Oriente Ecuatoriano* 10.

Ayala Mora, Enrique. *Lucha política y origen de los partidos en Ecuador.* Quito: Corporación Editora Nacional, 1985.

———, ed. *Nueva historia del Ecuador.* Vol. 9. Quito: Corporación Editora Nacional, 1988.

Bákula, Juan Miguel. *La política internacional entre el Perú y Colombia.* Bogotá: Editorial Temis, 1988.

———. "Relaciones del Perú con Colombia: Antecedentes, situación, y perspectivas." In *Relaciones del Perú con los paises vecinos,* ed. Eduardo Ferrero Costa, 3–34. Lima: CEPEI, 1988.

Ballón Landa, Alberto. *Los hombres de la selva: Apuntes para un ensayo de sociológica aplicada.* Lima: Oficina Tipográfica de "la Opinion Nacional," 1917.

Basadre, Jorge. *Historia de la república del Perú, 1822–1933.* 5th ed. Lima: Ediciones "Historia," 1963.

Bates, Henry Walter. *The Naturalist on the River Amazons.* . . . London: J. Murray, 1892.

Baum, Vicki. *The Weeping Wood.* Garden City, N.Y.: Doubleday, Doran and Co., 1943.

Bergquist, Charles W. *Coffee and Conflict in Colombia, 1886–1910.* Durham, N.C.: Duke University Press, 1978.

———. "Los trabajadores del sector cafetero y la suerte del movimiento obrero en Colombia, 1920–1940." In *Pasado y presente de la violencia en Colombia,* comp. Gonzalo Sánchez and Ricardo Peñaranda, 111–66. Bogotá: Fondo Editorial CEREC, 1986.

Bierhorst, John. *The Mythology of South America.* New York: William Morrow and Co., 1988.

Bonilla, Heraclio. "El caucho y la economía del Oriente Peruano." *Historia y Cultura (Peru)* 8 (1974): 69–80.

———. "La emergencia del control norteamericano sobre la economía peruana, 1850–1930." *Estudios Sociales Centroamericanos* 5 (13) (Jan.–Apr. 1976): 97–122.

———, ed. and comp. *Gran Bretaña y el Perú (1826–1919): Informes de los consules britanicos.* Vols. 3, 5. Lima: Instituto de Estudios Peruanos, 1975, 1977.

Bonilla, Victor Daniel. *Servants of God or Masters of Men? The Story of a Capuchin Mission in Amazonía.* Harmondsworth, England: Penguin, 1972.

Buchwald, Otto Von. "Caminos al Oriente." *Boletín de la Sociedad Geográfica de Quito* 1 (1) (Oct. 1911): 78–88.

Bunker, Stephen G. *Underdeveloping the Amazon: Extraction, Unequal Exchange, and the Failure of the Modern State.* Urbana: University of Illinois Press, 1985.

Burns, E. Bradford. *A History of Brazil*. 2d ed. New York: Columbia University Press, 1986.

Bushnell, David. *The Making of Modern Colombia: A Nation in Spite of Itself*. Berkeley: University of California Press, 1993.

Canet de Mar, Benigno de. *Relaciones interesantes y datos históricos sobre las misiones católicas del Caquetá y Putumayo desde el año 1632 hasta el presente*. Bogotá: Imprenta Nacional, 1924.

Carmagnani, Marcelo. *Estado y sociedad en América Latina, 1850–1930*. Barcelona: Editorial Crítica, 1984.

Casement, Roger. "The Putumayo Indians." *Contemporary Review* 102 (1912): 317–28.

Castaño Uribe, Carlos. "Configuración cultural de los karib en Colombia: Algunos comentarios e hipótesis." *Revista Española de Antropología Americana* 14 (1984): 205–26.

Caufield, Catherine. *In the Rainforest*. New York: Alfred A. Knopf, 1985.

Centro de Investigación y Promoción Amazónica. *Crónica indígena de la Amazonía*. Lima: CIPA, 1984.

Chang-Rodríguez, Eugenio. "El indigenismo peruano y Mariátegui." *Revista Iberoamericana* 50 (127) (Apr.–June 1984): 367–93.

Chaumiel, Jean Pierre, and Chaumiel, Josette. "De un espacio mítico a un territorio legal o la evolución de la noción de frontera en le noreste Peruano." *Amazonía Indígena* 3 (6) (Mar. 1983): 15–22.

Chavarría, Jesús. *José Carlos Mariátegui and the Rise of Modern Peru, 1890–1930*. Albuquerque: University of New Mexico Press, 1979.

Chiriboga, Manuel. "Auge y crisis de una economía agroexportadora: El periódio cacaotero." In *Nueva Historia del Ecuador*, vol. 9, ed. Enrique Ayala Mora, 55–115. Quito: Corporación Editora Nacional/Editorial Grijalbo Ecuatoriana, 1988.

Chirif, Alberto. "El colonialismo interno en un país colonizado: El caso de la Amazonía Peruana." In *Saqueo Amazónico*, comp. Alberto Chirif, 47–80. Iquitos: Ediciones CETA, 1983.

———. "Ocupación territorial de la Amazonía y marginalización de la población nativa." *América Indígena* 35 (2) (Apr.–June 1975): 265–95.

Clastres, Pierre. *Society against the State: The Leader as Servant and the Humane Uses of Power among the Indians of the Americas*. Trans. Robert Hurley in collaboration with Abe Stein. New York: Urizen Books, 1977.

Clayton, Lawrence A. *Grace: W. R. Grace and Company, The Formative Years, 1850–1930*. Ottawa, Ill.: Jameson Books, 1985.

Coletta, Paolo E. "William Jennings Bryan and the United States-Colombia Impasse, 1903–1921." *HAHR* 47 (Nov. 1967): 486–501.

Collier, Richard. *The River That God Forgot: The Story of the Amazon Rubber Boom*. New York: E. P. Dutton and Co., 1968.

Cook, William Azel. *Through the Wilderness of Brazil by Horse, Canoe and Float*. New York: American Tract Society, 1909.

Correa, François. "Amazonía Colombiana: Organización social en el noroeste del Amazonas." *Revista Colombiana de Antropología* 25 (1984–85): 183–208.

Corts, Estanislao de las. "Datos etnográficos de los índios huitotos, boras, noanuyas, muinames, y ocainas de la región de La Chorrera, Amazonas." *Revista de Misiones* (Bogotá) 11 (1935): 107–12, 170–72, 566–69.

Costales, Piedad, and Costales, Alfredo. *Amazonía: Ecuador, Peru, Bolivia.* Quito: Mundo Shuar, 1983.

Crévaux, Jules Nicolas. *América pintoresca: Descripción de viajes al nuevo continente por los mas modernos exploradores Carlos Wiener, Dr. Crevaux, Dr. Charnay. . . .* Barcelona: Montaner y Simón, 1884.

Davies, Thomas M., Jr. *Indian Integration in Peru: A Half Century of Experience, 1900–1948.* Lincoln: University of Nebraska Press, 1974.

Davis, Harold Eugene, John J. Finan, and F. Taylor Peck. *Latin American Diplomatic History: An Introduction.* Baton Rouge: Louisiana State University Press, 1977.

Dean, Warren. *Brazil and the Struggle for Rubber: A Study in Environmental History.* Cambridge: Cambridge University Press, 1987.

Deeds, Susan M. "New Spain's Far North: A Changing Historiographical Frontier?" *Latin American Research Review* 25, no. 2 (1990): 226–35.

De la Flor Fernández, Alejandro Juan. "La economía de exportación en la Amazonía Peruana (1898–1930): El caso de las gomas." Thesis, Pontificia Universidad Católica del Perú, Lima, 1989.

Delboy, Emilio. *Memorandum sobre la selva del Perú.* Lima: Sanmarti y Cia., 1942.

Delpar, Helen. *Red Against Blue: The Liberal Party in Colombian Politics, 1863–1899.* Tuscaloosa: University of Alabama Press, 1981.

Del Valle, Carlos. *El tratado de comercio de 1905 entre Colombia y el Ecuador.* Bogotá: Tipografía Augusta, 1928.

Denevan, William M. "The Aboriginal Population of Western Amazonia in Relation to Habitat and Subsistence." *Revista Geográfica* (Instituto Panamericano do Geografía e História, Comissão de Geografía, Rio de Janeiro) 72 (1970): 61–86.

De Pinell, Gaspar. *Un viaje por el Putumayo y el Amazonas: Ensayo de navegación.* Bogotá: Imprenta Nacional, 1924.

Dix, Robert H. *The Politics of Colombia.* New York: Pareger Publishers, 1987.

Domar, Eusey D. "The Causes of Slavery or Serfdom: A Hypothesis." *Journal of Economic History* 30 (1970): 18–32.

Domínguez, Camilo A. *Amazonía Colombiana: Visión general.* Bogotá: Banco Popular, 1985.

Domínguez, Camilo, and Gómez, Augusto. *La economía extractiva en la Amazonía Colombiana, 1850–1930.* Bogotá: Corporación Colombiana para la Amazonía-Araracuara, 1990.

Drabble, J. H. *Rubber in Malaya, 1876–1922: The Genesis of the Industry.* New York: Oxford University Press, 1973.

Eberhardt, Charles C. "Indians of Peru." *Smithsonian Miscellaneous Collections* 52. Washington, D.C.: GPO, 1910: 181–94.

Eder, Phanor James. *Colombia.* London: T. Fisher Unwin, 1913.

Enock, C. Reginald. *The Andes and the Amazon: Life and Travel in Peru.* London: T. Fisher Unwin, 1910.

———. *Ecuador: Its Ancient and Modern History, Topography and Natural Resources, Industries and Social Development.* New York: Charles Scribner's Sons, 1914.

———. Introduction to *The Putumayo, the Devil's Paradise: Travels in the Peruvian Amazon Region and an Account of the Atrocities Committed upon the Indians Therein,* by C. Reginald Enock. London: T. Fisher Unwin, 1912.

Farabee, William Curtis. *Indian Tribes of Eastern Peru*. Cambridge, Mass.: Peabody Museum, 1922.

Felizardo, Joaquim José. *Historia nova da República Velha: Do Manifesto de 1870 a revolução de 1930*. Petropolis, Brazil: Vozes, 1980.

Ferrero Costa, Eduardo, ed. *Relaciones del Perú con los paises vecinos*. Lima: CEPEI, 1988.

Fisher, John. "Imperialism, Centralism, and Regionalism in Peru, 1776–1845." In *Region and Class in Modern Peruvian History*, ed. Rory Miller, 21–34. Institute of Latin American Studies Monograph Series no. 14. Liverpool: University of Liverpool, 1987.

Flores Marín, José A. *La explotación del caucho en el Perú*. Lima: Universidad Nacional Mayor de San Marcos, 1977.

Freitas, Décio. *Escravidão de índios e negros no Brasil*. Porto Alegre, Brazil: EST/ICP, 1980.

Friedemann, Nina S., and Jaime Arocha. *Herederos del jaguar y la anaconda*. Bogotá: Carlos Valencia Editores, 1985.

Fuentes, Hildebrando. *Loreto: Apuntes geográficos, históricos, estadísticos, políticos y sociales*. 2 vols. Lima: Imprenta de la Revista, 1908.

Furneaux, Robin. *The Amazon: The Story of a Great River*. New York: G. P. Putnam's Sons, 1970.

García, Genaro F. *Informe del gobernador de la provincia de Oriente al Ministerio de Instrucción Publica . . . 1909*. Quito: Tipografía de la Escuela de Artes y Oficios, 1909; in *El Oriente Ecuatoriano* 11. BGMRE(Q).

García, P. Lorenzo. *Historia de las misiones en la Amazonía Ecuatoriana*. Quito: Ediciones Abya-Yala, 1985.

García Rosell, Ricardo. *Conquista de la montaña: Sinopsis de los descubrimientos, expediciones, estudios, y trabajos llevados a cabo en el Perú para el aprovechamiento y cultura de sus montañas*. Lima: Tipografía "La Prensa," 1905.

Garzón, Nivia Cristina, and Vicente Macuritope. "El chontaduro: Una planta en el contexto cultural huitoto, Amazonía Colombiana." *América Indígena* 47, no. 2 (1987): 295–316.

Gasché, Jürg. "Las comunidades nativas entre la aparencia y la realidad: El ejemplo de las comunidades huitoto y ocaina del Río Ampiyacu." *Amazonía Indígena* 3, no. 5 (Sept. 1982): 11–31.

———. "La ocupación territorial de los nativos huitoto en el Perú y Colombia en los siglos 19 y 20: Apuntes para un debate sobre la nacionalidad de los huitoto." *Amazonía Indígena* 4, no. 7 (Oct. 1983): 2–19.

Gasché, Jürg, and Guyot, Mireille. "Recherches ethnographiques dans les bassins des Rios Caquetá et Putumayo, Amazonie Colombienne: Les witoto, les bora." *Journal de la Société des Americanistes* 58 (1969): 267–83.

Gómez, Augusto J. "Amazonía Colombiana: Formas de acceso y de control de fuerza de trabajo indígena, 1870–1930." *Revista Colombiana de Antropología* 26 (1986–88): 131–54.

———. "La selva oriental colombiana: Indígenas, herramientos, economía extractiva, y colonización." N.p., n.d.

Gorman, Stephen M. "Geopolitics and Peruvian Foreign Policy." *Inter-American Economic Affairs* 36, no. 2 (fall 1982): 65–88.

———. "The State, Elite, and Export in Nineteenth Century Peru: Toward an Alternative Reinterpretation of Political Change." *Journal of Inter-American Studies and World Affairs* 21, no. 3 (Aug. 1979): 395–417.

Greenfield, Sidney M. "Barbadians in the Brazilian Amazon." *Luso-Brazilian Review* (University of Wisconsin Press) 20, no. 1 (summer 1983): 44–64a.

Gridilla, Alberto. *Un año en el Putumayo.* Lima: Colección Descalzos, 1943.

Grubb, K. G. *Amazon and Andes.* London: Methuen and Co., 1930.

———. *The Lowland Indians of Amazonia: A Survey of the Location and Religious Condition of the Indians of Colombia, Venezuela, the Guianas, Ecuador, Peru, Brazil and Bolivia.* London: World Dominion Press, 1927.

Guillaume, H. A. *The Amazon Provinces of Peru as a Field for European Emigration....* London: Wyaman and Sons, 1888.

Guyot, Mireille. " El relato de O'ioi." *Amazonía Indígena* 3, no. 6 (Mar. 1983): 3–10.

Guzmán G., Manuel José. "Los andokes: Historia, conciencia étnica, y explotación del caucho." *Universitas Humanística* (Pontificia Universidad Javeriana, Facultad de Filosofía y Letras) 2 (Dec. 1971): 53–97.

Hall, Thomas D. "Incorporation in the World-System: Toward a Critique." *American Sociological Review* 51 (June 1986): 390–402.

Hardenburg, W. E. *The Putumayo, the Devil's Paradise: Travels in the Peruvian Amazon Region and an Account of the Atrocities Committed upon the Indians Therein.* London: T. Fisher Unwin, 1912.

———. "Story of the Putumayo Atrocities." *New Review* (New York) (July 1913): 629–34.

Haring, Rita. "Burguesia regional de la Amazonía Peruana, 1880–1980." Trans. Mariela Dreyfus. *Amazonía Peruana* 7, no. 13 (Sept. 1986): 67–84.

Helmsing, A. H. J. *Firms, Farms, and the State in Colombia.* Boston: Allen and Unwin, 1986.

Hemming, John. *Amazon Frontier: The Defeat of the Brazilian Indians.* London: Macmillan, 1987.

———. "Indians and the Frontier." In *Colonial Brazil,* ed. Leslie Bethell, 145–89. Cambridge: Cambridge University Press, 1987.

———. *Red Gold: The Conquest of the Brazilian Indians.* Cambridge, Mass.: Harvard University Press, 1978.

Hennessy, Alistair. *The Frontier in Latin American History.* Albuquerque: University of New Mexico Press, 1978.

Herndon, William Lewis, and Gibbon, Lardner. *Exploration of the Valley of the Amazon, Made under the Direction of the Navy Department.* Washington, D.C.: R. Armstrong, 1853–54.

Hispano, Cornelio [pseud.]. *De París al Amazonas: Las fieras del Putumayo.* Paris: Librería Paul Ollendorff, [1913?].

Horna, Hernán. "Transportation, Modernization and Entreprenurship in Nineteenth Century Colombia." *Journal of Latin American Studies* 14 (May 1982): 33–53.

Huamán Ramírez, Oscar. *Los misterios de la selva: Mitos, cuentos, leyendas, y narraciones folklorísticas de la Amazonía.* Lima: Imprenta Editores Tipo-Offset, 1985.

Hudelson, John E. "Indian Groups of the Northern Montaña: The Problem of Appellation." *El Dorado* (University of Northern Colorado) 4, no. 2 (Oct. 1979): 1–19.

Hurtado, Enrique T. *Informe que el gobernador de la provincia de Oriente dirige al Ministerio de lo Interior.* Quito: Imprenta de Espejo, 1897.

Inglis, Brian. *Roger Casement.* London: Hodder Paperbacks, 1974.

Ireland, Gordon. *Boundaries, Possessions, and Conflicts in South America.* Cambridge, Mass.: Harvard University Press, 1938.

Jouanen, José. *Los jesuitas y el Oriente Ecuatoriano, 1868–1898: Monografía histórica.* Guayaquil: Editorial Arquidiocesana Justicia y Paz, 1977.

Kane, Joe. *Savages.* New York: Alfred A. Knopf, 1996.

Kaplan, Joanna Overing. "Images of Cannibalism, Death, and Domination in a 'Non-Violent' Society." *Journal de la Société des Americanistes* 72 (1986): 133–56.

Karno, Howard Laurence. "Augusto B. Leguía: The Oligarchy and the Modernization of Peru, 1870–1930." Ph.D. dissertation, University of California, Los Angeles, 1970.

———. "Julio Cesar Arana: Frontier Cacique in Peru." In *The Caciques: Oligarchical Politics and the System of Caciquismo in the Luso-Hispanic World*, ed. Robert Kern, 89–98. Albuquerque: University of New Mexico Press, 1973.

Katzman, Martin T. "The Brazilian Frontier in Comparative Perspective." *Comparative Studies of History and Society* 17 (3) (July 1975): 266–85.

Kelly, Hank, and Dot Kelly. *Dancing Diplomats.* Albuquerque: University of New Mexico, 1950.

Kensinger, Kenneth M., ed. *Marriage Practices in Lowland South America.* Urbana: University of Illinois Press, 1984.

Klein, Harriet Esther Manelis, and Louisa R. Stark. "Lenguas indígenas del norte y oeste de la cuenca del Amazonas: Introducción." *América Indígena* 43, no. 4 (Oct.–Dec. 1983): 697–701.

Landaburu, Jon, and Roberto Pineda Camacho. *Tradiciones de la gente del hacha: Mitología de los indios andoques del Amazonas.* Yerbabuena, Colombia: Instituto Caro y Cuervo/UNESCO, 1984.

Lange, Algot. *In the Amazon Jungle: Adventures in Remote Parts of the Upper Amazon River, Including a Sojourn Among Cannibal Indians.* New York: G. P. Putnam's Sons, 1912.

Larrabure i Correa, Carlos. *Colección de leyes, decretos, resoluciones, y otros documentos oficiales referentes al Departamento de Loreto.* 18 vols. Lima: Imprenta de "La Nación," 1905–9.

———. *Perú y Colombia en el Putumayo.* Barcelona: Imprenta Viuda de L. Tasso, 1913.

Las Casas, Bartolomé de. [1542]. *A Short Account of the Destruction of the Indies.* Reprint, London: Penguin, 1992.

Lathrap, Donald W. *The Upper Amazon.* New York: Praeger Publishers, 1970.

LeGrand, Catherine. "Los antecedentes agrarios de la violencia: El conflicto social en la frontera colombiana, 1850–1940." In *Pasado y presente de la violencia de Colombia*, comp. Gonzalo Sánchez and Ricardo Peñaranda, 87–110. Bogotá: Fondo Editorial CEREC, 1986.

———. *Frontier Expansion and Peasant Protest in Colombia, 1850–1936.* Albuquerque: University of New Mexico Press, 1986.

Lemaitre, Eduardo. *Rafael Reyes: Biografía de un gran Colombiano.* 4th ed. Bogotá: Banco de la República, 1981.

Llanos Vargas, Hector, and Roberto Pineda Camacho. *Etnohistoria del Gran Caquetá (Siglos 16–19)*. Bogotá: Banco de la República, 1982.

Londoño Paredes, Julio. "El combate de la Pedrera." *Boletín de Historia y Antiguidades* 64, no. 718 (July–Sept. 1977): 393–406.

Loureiro, Antonio. *Amazônia: 10,000 anos*. Manaos: Editora Metro Cúbico, 1982.

Lowie, Robert H. "The Tropical Forests: An Introduction." In *Handbook of South American Indians*, vol. 3, ed. Julian H. Steward, 1–56. Washington, D.C.: GPO, 1948.

Luna Vegas, Emilio. *Perú y Ecuador en cinco siglos*. Lima: Okura Editores, 1986.

Maloney, William J. *The Forged Casement Diaries*. Dublin and Cork: Talbot Press Limited, 1936.

El Mariscal Benavides: Su vida y su obra. Vol. 1. Lima: Editorial Atlántida, 1976.

Markham, Clements R. *Peruvian Bark: A Popular Account of the Introduction of Chincona Cultivation into British India*. London: J. Murray, 1880.

Markovits, Andrei S., and Mark Silverstein, eds. *The Politics of Scandal: Power and Process in Liberal Democracies*. New York: Holmes and Meier, 1988.

Martí, Conrad J. *Estadística de la província de frares menors caputxins de Catalunya, 1900–1975*. Barcelona: Cúria Provincial, 1975.

Martz, John D. *Ecuador: Conflicting Political Culture and the Quest for Progress*. Boston: Allyn and Bacon, 1972.

Maybury-Lewis, David. "Demystifying the Second Conquest." In *Frontier Expansion in Amazonía*, ed. Marianne Schmink and Charles H. Wood, 127–34. Gainesville: University of Florida Press, 1984.

McGreevey, William P. *An Economic History of Colombia, 1845–1930*. Cambridge: Cambridge University Press, 1971.

Meggers, Betty J. *Amazonia: Man and Culture in a Counterfeit Paradise*. Chicago: Aldine-Atherton, 1971.

Métraux, Alfred. "Warfare, Cannibalism, and Human Trophies." In *Handbook of South American Indians*, vol. 5, ed. Julian H. Steward, 383–410. Washington, D.C.: GPO, 1949.

Michelena y Rojas, Francisco. *Exploración oficial por la primera vez desde el norte de la América del Sur siempre por rios*. . . . Brussells: A. Locroix, Verboeckhoven, 1867.

Miers, Suzanne. *Britain and the Slave Trade*. New York: Africana Publishing Company, 1975.

Miller, Rory M., ed. *Region and Class in Modern Peruvian History*. Liverpool: University of Liverpool, Institute of Latin American Studies, 1987.

Las misiones en Colombia: Obra de los misioneros capuchinos de la delegación apostólica, del gobierno, y de la junta arquidiocesana nacional, Caquetá y Putumayo. Bogotá: Imprenta de la Cruzada, 1912.

Monteiro de Castro, Raymundo C. *Cultura e exploração da borracha no valle do Amazonas*. Manaos: Mandado publicar pela Associação Commercial do Amazonas, 1913.

Montejano, David. "Is Texas Bigger than the World-System? A Critique from a Provincial Point of View." *Review* 4, no. 3 (winter 1981): 597–628.

Mora Sierra, Silvia. "Bases antropológicas para un estudio integral del corregimiento de La Pedrera en el Bajo Caquetá." *Revista Colombiana de Antropología* 18 (1975): 29–126.

Morrison, Tony, Ann Brown, and Ann Rose, comps. *Lizzie: A Victorian Lady's Amazon Adventure.* London: British Broadcasting Corporation, 1985.

Muratorio, Blanca. *Rucuyaya, Alonso, y la historia social y económica del Alto Napo, 1850–1950.* Quito: Ediciones Abya-Yala, 1987.

Ocampo, Jose Antonio. *Colombia y la economía mundial, 1830–1910.* México: Siglo Veinteuno Editores, 1984.

Olarte Camacho, Vicente. *Las crueldades de los peruanos en el Putumayo y en el Caquetá.* 3d ed. Bogotá: Imprenta Nacional, 1932.

Orellana, J. Gonzalo. *Las agresiones peruanas al Ecuador.* Quito: Imprenta y Papelería Colón, 1982.

———. *Resumen histórico del Ecuador, 1839–1930.* Vol. 1. Quito: Editorial "Fray Jodolo Ricke," 1948.

El Oriente (Iquitos, Peru) 1908, 1910–12, 1914. *El Oriente* office, Iquitos.

Ortíz, P. Dionisio. *Monografía del Purus.* Lima: Gráfica 30, 1980.

Ortíz, Sutti. "Colonization in the Colombian Amazon." In *Frontier Expansion in Amazonía,* ed. Marianne Schmink and Charles H. Wood, 204–30. Gainesville: University of Florida Press, 1984.

Ortíz Crespo, Gonzalo. *La incorporación del Ecuador al mercado mundial: La coyuntura socio-económica, 1875–1895.* Quito: Ediciones del Banco Central del Ecuador, 1981.

Orton, James. *The Andes and the Amazon, or Across the Continent of South America.* 3d ed. New York: Harper and Bros., 1876.

Paredes, Rómulo. *Report from the Select Committee on Putumayo Atrocities.* London: His Majesty's Stationery Office, 1913.

Park, James William. *Rafael Núñez and the Politics of Colombian Regionalism, 1863–1886.* Baton Rouge: Louisiana State University Press, 1985.

Paternoster, George Sidney. *The Lords of the Devil's Paradise.* London: S. Paul and Co., [1913].

Patterson, Orlando. *Slavery and Social Death: A Comparative Study.* Cambridge, Mass.: Harvard University Press, 1982.

Pearson, Henry C. *The Rubber Country of the Amazon.* . . . New York: India Rubber World, 1911.

Pennano, Guido. *La economía del caucho.* Iquitos: Centro de Estudios Teológicos de la Amazonía, 1988.

Perico Ramírez, Mario H. *Reyes: De cauchero a dictador.* Tunja: Universidad Pedagógica y Ayudas Educativas, 1974.

"Peruvian Rubber and International Politics." *American Review of Reviews* (Sept. 1912): 325–28.

Pierrre, François. *Viaje de exploración al Oriente Ecuatoriano, 1887–1888.* Quito: Abya-Yala, 1983.

Pike, Fredrick B. *The Modern History of Peru.* New York: Frederick A. Praeger Publishers, 1967.

———. *The United States and Latin America: Myths and Stereotypes of Civilization and Nature.* Austin: University of Texas, 1992.

———. *The United States and the Andean Republics: Peru, Bolivia, Ecuador.* Cambridge, Mass.: Harvard University Press, 1977.

Pineda Camacho, Roberto. *Historia oral y proceso esclavista en el Caquetá.* Bogotá: Banco de la República, 1985.

———. "El sendero del arco iris: Notas sobre el simbolismo de los negocios en una comunidad Amazónica." *Revista Colombiana de Antropología* 22 (1979): 29–58.

Pinzón Sánchez, Alberto. *Monopolios, misioneros, y destrucción de indígenas.* Bogotá: Ediciones Armadillo, 1979.

Place, Susan E., ed. *Tropical Rainforests: Latin American Nature and Society in Transition.* Jaguar Books on Latin America, no. 2. Wilmington, Del.: Scholarly Resources, 1993.

Platt, D. C. M. *Latin America and British Trade, 1806–1914.* London: A. and C. Black, 1972.

Ponce, N. Clemente. *Límites entre el Ecuador y el Perú.* Washington, D.C.: Gibson Bros., 1921.

Portillo, Pedro. *Acontecimientos realizados con los Ecuatorianos, Colombianos, y Brasileros en los Ríos Napo, Putumayo, Yuruá, y Purús durante los años de 1901 a 1904.* Lima: Tipografía del Panóptico, 1909.

Preuss, Konrad Theodor. *Religion und mythologie der Uitoto.* 2 vols. Gottingen: Vandenhoeck und Ruprecht, 1921.

Quito, Jacinto María de. *Relación de viaje en los Rios Putumayo, Caraparaná, y Caquetá y entre las tribus huitotas.* Bogotá: Imprenta de la Luz, 1908.

Rausch, Jane M. *A Tropical Plains Frontier: The Llanos of Colombia, 1531–1831.* Albuquerque: University of New Mexico Press, 1984.

Reid, B. L. *The Lives of Roger Casement.* New Haven, Conn.: Yale University Press, 1976.

Rey de Castro, Carlos. *Los escándolos del Putumayo.* . . . Barcelona: Imprenta Viuda de L. Tasso, 1913.

———. *Los pobladores del Putumayo: Origen—nacionalidad.* Barcelona: Imprenta Viuda de L. Tasso, 1914.

Reyes, Rafael. *Las dos Américas: Excursión por varios paises de las dos Américas, su estado actual, su futuro.* New York: Frederick A. Stokes Co., 1914.

———. *Memorias, 1850–1885.* Bogotá: Fondo Cultural Cafetero, 1986.

Ribeiro, Darcy. *Os índios e a civilização: A integração das populações indígenas no Brasil moderno.* Rio de Janeiro: Editora Civilização Brasilera, 1970.

Rippy, J. Fred. *The Capitalists and Colombia.* New York: Vanguard Press, 1931.

———. *Latin America and the Industrial Age.* New York: 1944.

Rivera, José Eustasio. *La vorágine.* Buenos Aires: Editorial Losada, 1985.

Robuchon, Eugenio. *En el Putumayo y sus afluentes: Edición oficial.* Lima: Imprenta la Industria, 1907.

Rodríguez, Linda Alexander. *The Search for Public Policy: Regional Politics and Government Finances in Ecuador, 1830–1940.* Berkeley: University of California Press, 1985.

Rojas Paredes, Aurelio. "Mitos, leyendas, y creencias de los huitoto." *Amazonía Peruana* 7, no. 13 (Sept. 1986): 103–18.

Romero, Fernando. *Iquitos y la fuerza naval de la Amazonía (1830–1933).* Lima: Dirección General de Intereses Maritimos, Ministerio de Marina, 1983.

Rumrrill, Roger, ed. *Amazonía Peruana, guía general: Loreto, Madre de Dios, San Martín, Ucayali: Economía, historia, cultura, turismo.* Lima: R. Rumrrill, 1984.

Rumrrill, Roger, Carlos Dávila H., and Fernando Barcia García. *Yurimaguas: Capital histórica de la Amazonía Peruana.* Yurimaguas: Concejo Provincial de Alto Amazonas, 1986.

Saeger, James Schofield. "Another View of the Mission as a Frontier Institution." *Hispanic American Historical Review* 65, no. 3 (Aug. 1985): 493–517.

Sáenz, Antonio. "Establecimiento de colonias en el Oriente Ecuatoriano." *Anales de la Universidad Central* (Quito) 1, no. 1 (July 1912): 25–46.

Safford, Frank. *Aspectos del siglo 19 en Colombia.* Medellín: Impresos Super, 1977.

Salamanca, Demetrio. *La Amazonía Colombiana.* Vol. 1. Bogotá: Imprenta Nacional, 1916.

Salvador Lara, Jorge. *Breve historia contemporánea del Ecuador.* México: Fondo de Cultura Económica, 1994.

Sánchez, Gonzalo, and Ricardo Peñaranda, comps. *Pasado y presente de la violencia en Colombia.* Bogotá: Fondo Editorial CEREC, 1986.

San Román, Jesús Víctor. "Mitos de los huitoto." *Amazonía Peruana* 7, no. 13 (Sept. 1986): 113–18.

———. *Perfiles históricos de la Amazonía Peruana.* Lima: Ediciones Paulinas — Pulicaciones CETA, 1975.

Santos, Roberto. *História econômica da Amazônia (1800–1920).* São Paulo: T. A. Queiroz, 1980.

Sañudo, José Rafael. *Otro panamismo: El tratado Colombo-Ecuatoriano.* Pasto, Colombia: n.p., 1917.

Sawyer, Roger. *Casement: The Flawed Hero.* London: Routledge and K. Paul, 1984.

Scharff, Virginia A. *Taking the Wheel: Women and the Coming of the Motor Age.* New York: Free Press, 1991.

Shapiro, Judith R. "Marriage Rules, Marriage Exchange, and the Definition of Marriage in Lowland South American Societies." In *Marriage Practices in Lowland South America,* ed. Kenneth M. Kensinger. Urbana: University of Illinois Press, 1984.

Simson, Alfred. *Travels in the Wilds of Ecuador and the Exploration of the Putumayo River.* London: Sampson Low, Marston, Searle, and Rivington, 1886.

Singleton-Gates, Peter, and Maurice Girodias. *The Black Diaries: An Account of Roger Casement's Life and Times with a Collection of His Diaries and Public Writings.* New York: Grove Press, 1959.

Smith, Clifford T. "Patterns of Urban and Regional Development in Peru on the Eve of the Pacific War." In *Region and Class in Modern Peruvian History,* ed. Rory Miller, 77–102. Institute of Latin American Studies Monograph Series no. 14. Liverpool: University of Liverpool, 1987.

Souza Carneiro, Antonio Joaquim. *A industria da borracha no Brasil, artigo popular.* Rio de Janeiro: Oficinas Gráphicas da Sociedade Anonyma Progresso, 1913.

Spires, Roberta Lee. "As linguas faladas no Brasil." *América Indígena* 47, no. 3 (July–Sept. 1987): 455–79.

Stanfield, Michael Edward. "Red Rubber, Bleeding Trees: Colombia, Ecuador, and Peru in the Putumayo, 1850–1914." Ph.D. dissertation, University of New Mexico, 1992.

———. "Rubber collection and the scandal of the Putumayo." Master's thesis, San Diego State University, 1984.

Stern, Steve J. "Feudalism, Capitalism, and the World-System in the Perspective of Latin America and the Caribbean." *American Historical Review* 93 (Oct. 1988): 829–72; Reply: "Ever More Solitary." *AHR* 93 (Oct. 1988): 886–97.

Steward, Julian H.. "The Witotoan Tribes." In *Handbook of South American Indians,* vol. 3, ed. Steward, 749–62. Washington, D.C.: GPO, 1948.

St. John, Ronald Bruce. "The End of Innocence: Peruvian Foreign Policy and the United States, 1919–1942." *Journal of Latin American Studies* 8, no. 2 (Nov. 1976): 325–44.

Stocks, Anthony. "Indian Policy in Eastern Peru." In *Frontier Expansion in Amazonía,* ed. Marianne Schmink and Charles H. Wood, 33–61. Gainesville: University of Florida Press, 1984.

Tambs, Lewis A. "Geopolitics of the Amazon." In *Man in the Amazon,* ed. Charles Wagley, 45–87. Gainesville: University Presses of Florida, 1974.

Taussig, Michael T. *Shamanism, Colonialism, and the Wild Man: A Study in Terror and Healing.* Chicago: University of Chicago Press, 1987.

Temperly, Howard. *British Antislavery, 1853–1970.* London: Longman Group, 1972.

Thomson, Norman. *Colombia and Peru in the Putumayo Territory; A Reply to the Defense of the Peruvian Government.* London: N. Thomson and Co., 1914.

———. *The Putumayo Red Book.* 2d ed. London: N. Thomson and Company, 1914.

Thorp, Rosemary, and Geoffrey Bertram. *Peru, 1890–1977: Growth and Policy in an Open Economy.* New York: Columbia University Press, 1978.

Tierney, Patrick. *The Highest Altar: Unveiling the Mystery of Human Sacrifice.* New York: Penguin Books, 1989.

Tobar, Aquileo. "Descubrimiento de los guitotos del Putumayo." N.p., n.d.

Tobar García, Julio. *Historia de límites del Ecuador.* 2d ed. Quito: Imprenta Alarcon, 1972.

Up de Graff, F. W. *Head Hunters of the Amazon: Seven Years of Exploration and Adventure.* Garden City, N.Y.: Garden City Publishing, 1923.

Ure, John. *Trespassers of the Amazon.* London: Constable, 1986.

Uribe Piedrahita, César. *Toa: Narraciones de caucheriás.* Ed. Arturo Zapata. Manizales: Arturo Zapata, 1933.

Uribe Uribe, Rafael. "Cultivo de caucho hevea." *Revista Nacional de Agricultura* (Bogotá) nos. 10–11, series 3 (Feb. 1908): 281–337.

Urrutia, Francisco José. *El protocolo Mosquera — Pedemonte.* Quito: Imprenta de Julio Sáenz R., 1910.

Valcárcel, Carlos A. *El proceso del Putumayo: Sus secretos inauditos.* Lima: Imprenta "Comercial" de Horacio La Rosa and Co., 1915.

Varese, Stefano. *La Sal de Los Cerros.* Lima: Universidad Peruana de Ciencia y Tecnología, 1968.

Vickers, William T. "Indian Policy in Amazonian Ecuador." In *Frontier Expansion in Amazonía,* ed. Marianne Schmink and Charles H. Wood, 8–32. Gainesville: University of Florida Press, 1984.

Villacres Moscoso, Jorge W. *Historia diplomática de la República del Ecuador.* Guayaquil: Imprenta de la Universidad de Guayaquil, 1972.

Wagley, Charles. *Amazon Town: A Study of Man in the Tropics.* New York: Alfred A. Knopf, 1964.

Wagner de Reyna, Alberto. *Historia diplomática del Perú, 1900–1945.* 2 vols. Lima: Ediciones Peruanas, 1964.

Wallace, Alfred Russel. *A Narrative of Travels on the Amazon and Rio Negro.* . . . London: Reeve and Co., 1853.

Wallerstein, Immanuel. "AHR Forum: Comments on Stern's Critical Tests." *American Historical Review* 93 (Oct. 1988): 873–85.

———. *Capitalist Agriculture and the Origins of the European World-Economy in the Sixteenth Century.* Vol. 1 of *The Modern World-System.* New York: Academic Press, 1974.

———. *Mercantilism and Consolidation of the European World-Economy, 1600–1750.* Vol. 2 of *The Modern World System.* New York: Academic Press, 1980.

Weber, David J. *The Mexican Frontier, 1821–1846: The American Southwest Under Mexico.* Albuquerque: University of New Mexico Press, 1982.

Weber, David J., and Jane M. Rausch, eds. *Where Cultures Meet: Frontiers in Latin American History.* Jaguar Books on Latin America, no. 6. Wilmington, Del.: Scholarly Resources, 1994.

Weinstein, Barbara. *The Amazon Rubber Boom, 1850–1920.* Stanford, Calif.: Stanford University Press, 1983.

Werlich, David P. "The Conquest and Settlement of the Peruvian Montaña." Ph.D. dissertation, University of Minnesota, 1968.

———. *Peru: A Short History.* Carbondale: Southern Illinois University Press, 1978.

Whiffen, Thomas. *The North-West Amazons; Notes of Some Months Spent among the Cannibal Tribes.* London: Constable and Co., 1915.

Whitehead, Neil L. "Carib Cannibalism: The Historical Evidence." *Journal de la Société des Americanistes* 70 (1984): 69–87.

Whitten, Normand E., Jr. "Etnocidio ecuatoriano y etnogénesis indígena: La resurgencía Amazónica ante el colonialism andino." *América Indígena* 39, no. 3 (July–Sept. 1979): 529–62.

———. *Sicuanga Runa: The Other Side of Amazonian Ecuador.* Urbana: University of Illinois Press, 1985.

Wilbert, Johannes. *Tobacco and Shamanism in South America.* New Haven, Conn.: Yale University Press, 1987.

Wise, Mary Ruth. "Lenguas indígenas de la Amazonía Peruana: Historia y estado presente." *América Indígena* 43, no. 4 (Oct.–Dec. 1983): 823–48.

Wolf, Howard, and Ralph Wolf. *Rubber: A Story of Glory and Greed.* New York: Covici, Friede, 1936.

Wolf, Teodoro. *Geografía y geología del Ecuador: Publicada por orden del supremo gobierno de la Repúblic.* Leipzig: Tipografía de F. A. Brockhus, 1892.

Wood, Bryce. *Aggression and History: The Case of Ecuador and Peru.* Ann Arbor, Mich.: University Microfilms International, 1978.

Woodroffe, Joseph Froude. *The Upper Reaches of the Amazon.* New York: Macmillan, 1914.

Woodroffe, Joseph F., and Harold Hamel Smith. *The Rubber Industry of the Amazon and How Its Supremacy Can Be Maintained.* London: John Bale, Sons and Danielsson, 1915.

Woodruff, William. *The Rise of the British Rubber Industry in the Nineteenth Century.* Liverpool: Liverpool University Press, 1958.

Yépez Chamorro, Benjamín. *La estatuaria murui-muniname: Simbolismo de la gente "Huitoto" de la Amazonía Colombiana.* Bogotá: Banco de la República, 1982.

Zumaeta, Pablo. *Las cuestiones del Putumayo: Memorial de Pablo Zumaeta.* Vol. 1. Barcelona: Imprenta Viuda de L. Tasso, 1913.

———. *Las cuestiones del Putumayo: Segundo memorial de Pablo Zumaeta.* Vol. 2. Barcelona: Imprenta Viuda de L. Tasso, 1913.

INDEX